# Study Guide for

# Kalat's
# Introduction to Psychology
## Fourth Edition

## Ruth H. Maki
North Dakota State University

with a Language Enhancement Guide by
## Jack Kirschenbaum
Fullerton College

**Brooks/Cole Publishing Company**

I(T)P™    An International Thomson Publishing Company

Pacific Grove • Albany • Bonn • Boston • Cincinnati • Detroit • London • Madrid • Melbourne
Mexico City • New York • Paris • San Francisco • Singapore • Tokyo • Toronto • Washington

## Acknowledgment

My sincere thanks to Amy Eliott and Michelle Marek who supplied the page references to the text and cross-referenced the objectives and the various types of test questions in the Study Guide.

Assistant Editor: Faith B. Stoddard
Cover Design: Roy R. Neuhaus
Cover Photograph: Londie G. Padelsky/Stock Imagery, Inc.
Editorial Assistant: Terry Thomas
Marketing Team: Gay Meixel, Jean Thompson
Permissions Editor: May Clark
Production Coordinator: Mary Vezilich
Printing and Binding: Patterson Printing

*For more information, contact:*

BROOKS/COLE PUBLISHING COMPANY
511 Forest Lodge Road
Pacific Grove, CA 93950
USA

International Thomson Editores
Campos Eliseos 385, Piso 7
Col. Polanco
11560 México D. F. México

International Thomson Publishing—Europe
Berkshire House 168-173
High Holborn
London WC1V 7AA
England

International Thomson Publishing GmbH
Königwinterer Strasse 418
53227 Bonn
Germany

Thomas Nelson Australia
102 Dodds Street
South Melbourne, 3205
Victoria, Australia

International Thomson Publishing—Asia
221 Henderson Road #05-10
Henderson Building
Singapore 0315

Nelson Canada
1120 Birchmount Road
Scarborough, Ontario
Canada M1K 5G4

International Thomson Publishing—Japan
Hirakawacho-cho Kyowa Building, 3F
2-2-1 Hirakawacho-cho
Chiyoda-ku, Tokyo 102
Japan

Printed in the United States of America.

10 9 8 7 6 5 4 3 2

ISBN 0-534-25020-3

# CONTENTS

**GETTING THE MOST OUT OF YOUR PSYCHOLOGY COURSE**   **VI**

Before the course begins *vi* / What to do during class *viii* / Sample notes *ix* / Get the most out of your study time *x* / Preparing for tests *xvi* / Taking tests *xvii* / If you have problems *xx* / Final note *xxi* / References *xxi*

**INTRODUCTION TO THE LANGUAGE ENHANCEMENT GUIDE**   **XXIII**

How to use this language enhancement guide *xxiii* / Vocabulary and three levels of verbal precision *xxiv*

**CHAPTER 1  WHAT IS PSYCHOLOGY?**   **1**

Objectives 1 / Comprehension check 2 / Answers and explanations for comprehension check 5 / Short-answer questions 7 / Answers to short-answer questions 9 / Posttest 10 / Answers to posttest 13 / Language enhancement guide 14 / I. Vocabulary, idioms and cultural concepts 14 / II. Vocabulary building 17

**CHAPTER 2  SCIENTIFIC METHODS IN PSYCHOLOGY**   **20**

Objectives 20 / Comprehension check 21 / Answers and explanations for comprehension check 25 / Short-answer questions 28 / Answers to short-answer questions 30 / Posttest 31 / Answers to posttest 35 / Language enhancement guide 36 / I. Vocabulary, idioms and cultural concepts 36 / II. Vocabulary building 40

**CHAPTER 3  THE BIOLOGICAL APPROACH TO BEHAVIOR**   **43**

Objectives 43 / Comprehension check 44 / Answers and explanations for comprehension check 48 / Short-answer questions 51 / Answers to short-answer questions 53 / Posttest 54 / Answers to posttest 59 / Language enhancement guide 60 / I. Vocabulary, idioms and cultural concepts 60 / II. Vocabulary building 63

**CHAPTER 4  SENSATION AND PERCEPTION**   **67**

Objectives 67 / Comprehension check 69 / Answers and explanations for comprehension check 73 / Short-answer questions 75 / Answers to short-answer questions 77 / Posttest 79 / Answers to posttest 83 / Language enhancement guide 84 / I. Vocabulary, idioms and cultural concepts 84 / II. Vocabulary building 88

**CHAPTER 5  ALTERED STATES**   **90**

Objectives 90 / Comprehension check 92 / Answers and explanations for comprehension check 95 / Short-answer questions 97 / Answers to short-answer questions 99 / Posttest 101 / Answers to posttest 105 / Language enhancement guide 106 / I. Vocabulary, idioms and cultural concepts 106 / II. Vocabulary building 109

**CHAPTER 6  LEARNING**   **111**

Objectives 111 / Comprehension check 113 / Answers and explanations for comprehension check 116 / Short-answer questions 119 / Answers to short-answer questions 121 / Posttest 123 / Answers to posttest 126 / Language enhancement guide 127 / I. Vocabulary, idioms and cultural concepts 127 / II. Vocabulary building 130

## CHAPTER 7 MEMORY 132

Objectives 132 / Comprehension check 134 / Answers and explanations for comprehension check 139 / Short-answer questions 141 / Answers to short-answer questions 143 / Posttest 146 / Answers to posttest 150 / Language enhancement guide 150 / I. Vocabulary, idioms and cultural concepts 150 / II. Vocabulary building 153

## CHAPTER 8 COGNITION AND LANGUAGE 155

Objectives 155 / Comprehension check 157 / Answers and explanations for comprehension check 161 / Short-answer questions 163 / Answers to short-answer questions 166 / Posttest 168 / Answers to posttest 172 / Language enhancement guide 173 / I. Vocabulary, idioms and cultural concepts 173 / II. Vocabulary building 175 / III. Structural Clues / 177

## CHAPTER 9 INTELLIGENCE AND ITS MEASUREMENT 178

Objectives 178 / Comprehension check 179 / Answers and explanations for comprehension check 182 / Short-answer questions 184 / Answers to short-answer questions 186 / Posttest 188 / Answers to posttest 191 / Language enhancement guide 192 / I. Vocabulary, idioms and cultural concepts 192 / II. Vocabulary building 194 / III. Structural Clues 195

## CHAPTER 10 DEVELOPMENT 196

Objectives 196 / Comprehension check 198 / Answers and explanations for comprehension check 203 / Short-answer questions 206 / Answers to short-answer questions 208 / Posttest 210 / Answers to posttest 214 / Language enhancement guide 215 / I. Vocabulary, idioms and cultural concepts 215 / II. Vocabulary building 218 / III. Structural Clues 219

## CHAPTER 11 MOTIVATION 221

Objectives 221 / Comprehension check 222 / Answers and explanations for comprehension check 226 / Short-answer questions 228 / Answers to short-answer questions 230 / Posttest 232 / Answers to posttest 236 / Language enhancement guide 237 / I. Vocabulary, idioms and cultural concepts 237 / II. Vocabulary building 239

## CHAPTER 12 EMOTIONS, HEALTH PSYCHOLOGY, COPING WITH STRESS 241

Objectives 241 / Comprehension check 242 / Answers and explanations for comprehension check 246 / Short-answer questions 248 / Answers to short-answer questions 250 / Posttest 252 / Answers to posttest 256 / Language enhancement guide 257 / I. Vocabulary, idioms and cultural concepts 257 / II. Vocabulary building 259 / III. Structural Clues 260

## CHAPTER 13 PERSONALITY 262

Objectives 262 / Comprehension check 264 / Answers and explanations for comprehension check 268 / Short-answer questions 270 / Answers to short-answer questions 272 / Posttest 274 / Answers to posttest 277 / Language enhancement guide 278 / I. Vocabulary, idioms and cultural concepts 278 / II. Vocabulary building 280

## CHAPTER 14 ABNORMAL BEHAVIOR 282

Objectives 282 / Comprehension check 284 / Answers and explanations for comprehension check 288 / Short-answer questions 291 / Answers to short-answer questions 293 / Posttest 296 / Answers to posttest 300 / Language enhancement guide 301 / I. Vocabulary, idioms and cultural concepts 301 / II. Vocabulary building 304

**CHAPTER 15  TREATMENT OF PSYCHOLOGICALLY TROUBLED PEOPLE**     **305**

Objectives 305 / Comprehension check 307 / Answers and explanations for comprehension check 310 / Short-answer questions 313 / Answers to short-answer questions 314 / Posttest 316 / Answers to posttest 320 / Language enhancement guide 320 / I. Vocabulary, idioms and cultural concepts 320 / II. Vocabulary building 322

**CHAPTER 16  SOCIAL PSYCHOLOGY**     **323**

Objectives 323 / Comprehension check 325 / Answers and explanations for comprehension check 330 / Short-answer questions 333 / Answers to short-answer questions 335 / Posttest 337 / Answers to posttest 341 / Language enhancement guide 342 / I. Vocabulary, idioms and cultural concepts 342 / II. Vocabulary building 343

**APPLIED PSYCHOLOGY**     **345**

Objectives 345 / Comprehension check 346 / Answers and explanations for comprehension check 348 / Short-answer questions 349 / Answers to short-answer questions 350 / Posttest 352 / Answers to posttest 354

**APPENDIX A  Textbook Dictionary**     **355**

**APPENDIX B  Prefix and Suffix Dictionary**     **370**

# GETTING THE MOST OUT OF YOUR PSYCHOLOGY COURSE (AND COLLEGE)

You are about to begin to study a fascinating subject--psychology. In some ways, you have been studying psychology for years. You have always been observing, predicting, and trying to control human behavior. Now, however, you are going to learn about how psychologists study behavior using scientific methods. Psychology is inherently an interesting topic, so you should be motivated to learn more about it. This introduction is designed to help you get the most out of your psychology course and out of your college experience.

## BEFORE THE COURSE BEGINS

### Start with a Positive Attitude

What you believe can influence how well you do. In your text, you will read about an experiment by Greenwald, Spangenberg, Pratkanis, and Eskanazi (1991) in which students listened to tapes that were supposed to have subliminal (below threshold for perception) messages. The messages were about losing weight or about increasing self-esteem. The subliminal messages themselves had no effect, but students' expectancies did produce changes. Those students who thought that the tape should increase self-esteem did increase in self-esteem (even when the tapes contained no messages). So, thinking that they would be more self-confident made the students feel more self-confident.

### Set Difficult, but Realistic, Goals

Expecting that you will do well in a course is the first step to doing well. But, thinking about doing well isn't enough. You need to produce a good study plan and stick to it to actually do well. Make a pronouncement at the beginning of the term that you will work as hard as possible to succeed in your courses. But, that's not enough. Set specific, difficult, but realistic, goals for each of your courses (getting all A's, a B average, or a C average--whatever is reasonable for you). In addition, set up a specific short-term goal for each test and assignment that you do for each course. Such goals will both help to increase your self-confidence and your performance (Locke and Latham, 1990). College instructors tend to give lower grades than high-school instructors, and the competition is much tougher. And yes, college instructors give Fs to students, even those who take all the tests (if, of course, they fail most of them). So, don't take success for granted. On the other hand, don't become discouraged. Set up realistic goals and work to meet them. Plan to reward yourself at the end of the term if you achieve your goal. The reward could be something like going on a camping trip to a favorite place, buying new clothes, or whatever might work to motivate you. Then, stick to your contingency plan. That is, give yourself the reward only if you meet your goal. Setting up smaller rewards for your short-term goals, such as getting a B on a test, is also a good idea.

### Look Through Your Textbook.

You have already purchased your book, so you have accomplished the first step to succeeding in your introductory psychology course. Take a look at your text. Although you may think that you already know what psychology is, you probably don't have a good idea of what this course will be about (even if you took a course in high school). In college, psychology is generally taught as a scientific discipline. So, you will observe as you look through your text that there is a chapter on research methodology early in the book. That chapter is critical for you to understand how psychological research is done and why it is important to do research in psychology. Start with an open mind; you are about to study behavior in a way that you never have before. Look at the various chapters in your book so that you can see the range of topics that it covers. Yes, there is biology in psychology; understanding the biological underpinnings of behavior is an important component of the area of psychology known as psychobiology. Other psychologists study learning, memory, development, and language. As you look at your text, you will discover that personality and mental disorders are covered toward the end of the book. You can understand those topics much better after you understand the biology of behavior, the principles of learning, and the development of behavior. So, read through the chapter objectives in your book to prepare yourself for the topics that you will study in the course. Knowing what is coming will make you better able to integrate and understand the topics.

## Find Some Friends (or Make Some) Who Are Taking the Course

One of the best ways to study is with a study group. Learning in a small group is a very effective way to learn. (Druckman & Bjork, 1994, Chapter 7). Such a group can force you to read the material and to understand it well enough to be able to present it to others. Four people is about the right number for your study group. Contact three other students and find a time once a week when you can meet for about 2 hours. Put this time into your schedule for the term and stick to it; plan to meet with your study group every week at the prearranged time. Make sure that you have serious students who are willing to spend the time both in and out of the study group to prepare for the course. Don't let anyone have a free ride. Everyone in the study group must be committed to learning as much as possible in the course.

## Make a Practical Schedule

At most universities, you are expected to spend about 2-3 hours a week studying for every 1 hour a week that you are in class. This means that you should study about 6-9 hours a week for a course that meets 3 hours a week. If you are taking five such courses, this translates into a "workweek" of 35-45 hours. Think of studying as your job. (If you have another job, think of studying as a second job.) Be sure that you are able to schedule enough hours to do the "job" that you are actually paying to do. Yes, college is different from other types of jobs in that you are paying to do it (or someone else is, if you are fortunate enough to have financial assistance). The fact that you are paying to be in college makes it doubly important that you take it seriously and do your studying "job" competently.

So before classes begin, set up a schedule that you are likely to be able to follow. Put in all the things that you must do at specific times--classes, the times when your study groups for various classes have agreed to meet, your other job for which you are paid (if you have one), meetings that you must attend, time for family obligations, social activities, and so on. Then, see where you can schedule blocks of time for study. Unlike high school, you will probably have lots of free time between classes during the day. USE IT! Don't look at those 2 hours between classes and assume that it is time to waste, or time to sit around and talk with friends. Assume that your psychology class meets 2 hours after another class 3 days a week. Schedule those 2 hours to go to the library and study for psychology on those 3 days. If you use those 2 hours to study for psychology 3 times a week, you have arranged for almost all the time that you need to study for the course. Add 2 hours for a study group for psychology, plus an hour to review one night a week, and you have provided enough study time for one of your courses, psychology. Set up a similar schedule for your other courses. It is important that you set up a studying schedule **that will work for you**. If you always get hungry and eat lunch, don't put study time in the library from 11 to 1. You simply won't stick to it. Also, if you cannot sit still very long, don't schedule a block of 4 hours straight for study. Put a study place in your schedule and stick to it. For most students, going to your Union's dining center and planning to study will not work. Friends will join you, and soon you will be talking and not studying. So, before classes even begin, work up a schedule that fits your life-style, including both specific times for study and also places where you will study. Try your schedule for a while; if some part of it is not working, rearrange it and try the new schedule for a while. The important aspect of setting up such a schedule is that you end up studying at a constant rate. You will be "up" on the readings and you will not need to cram for tests.

If you've tried to set up a schedule based on 3 hours of studying per course and you simply could not fit in enough hours because of your other commitments, you should think about changing your course schedule. Don't take more courses than you have time for. It is better to take longer to get through college with good grades than either to fail your courses or to squeak through with a minimal GPA. Too easy a schedule can be a mistake also. So, before the term begins, you need to assess your situation accurately and decide whether you will have the time to handle the course schedule that you have set for yourself.

## WHAT TO DO DURING CLASS

### Go to Class

In most college courses, your instructor won't take attendance, and he or she may not even know whether you're there or not. Still, it is important to attend every class. One reason is that many instructors present material in class that is not in the textbook, and that material is often included on tests. If you miss classes, you miss important material, and you will miss more test questions. (And no, don't tell your instructor that you missed the last class, and ask her whether she "covered anything important." Of course she did; instructors always cover topics that they, at least, deem important.) Even if your instructor does not ask test questions that are directly related to lecture, but not covered in the book, he or she still probably uses the lecture to emphasize certain topics. There is a huge amount of material covered in your introductory psychology textbook. No one could possibly learn it all in one, or even two, academic terms. Thus, students can use the lecture to determine which topics the instructor finds most important (and probably most interesting). Those topics are likely to be overrepresented on tests relative to topics that your instructor did not discuss in class. You cannot know which specific topics will be emphasized on the test unless you attend every class and listen to what is being covered.

### What to Do (and Not to Do) in the Classroom

You should attend class in order to learn. Hearing material, as well as reading it, will help you to understand and remember it better. If this is why you are attending class, why sit in the back of the room where both hearing and seeing will be more difficult? The backs of large classrooms are often noisy with students talking and otherwise disrupting the class. So, avoid the back. You have taken the time to come to class (and you have paid for it!), so sit in the front and make the most of it. Most of the best students sit in the front and they interact with the instructor. Sitting in front and being an active learner will both help you to learn better and help make the class more interesting to you. Even in very large classes, instructors usually get to know a few students who sit near the front and who interact with them.

Don't sit with your friends if you will end up talking with them during class. You should have "talk with friends" time in your schedule, and the middle of class isn't the time. Talking in class distracts the instructor, distracts your fellow students (who have also paid to attend the course), and means that you get less out of the course. If sitting with your friends means talking with them, sit somewhere else. And don't go to class either to read the newspaper or to study for tests in other classes. If those are your goals, go somewhere else where the lecturer won't distract you, and you won't distract the lecturer.

So, you are in class, and you have chosen a seat near the front where you can both see and hear well. You are all ready to pay attention and learn all you can. What do you do in class?

### Listen, and *Understand* What Is Being Said

Listen carefully and ask questions if you do not understand what is being presented. If you are embarrassed to raise your hand in class, ask your instructor before or after class or during office hours. Or if you have a teaching assistant, find him or her during office hours. Another alternative is to write out your question and hand it to the instructor or leave it on the podium before the next class. Most instructors will make every effort to answer students' questions. Don't let material that is unclear go by-- make every effort to understand it.

**Take Notes**

Taking notes improves class performance, and taking notes and reviewing those notes helps even more. Students take better notes with more experience in college. Notes become more organized, more selective, and more accurate (Van Meter, Yokoi, & Pressley, 1994). Your notes should differ depending upon what you will need to know for tests. If your instructor will want you to know definitions on a multiple-choice or a matching test, then you need to take down more verbatim facts. If, however, concepts will be stressed either on multiple-choice or essay tests, then you will need to write more general concepts in your notes (Van Meter et al., 1994). Whatever the final purpose of your notes, never try to write down everything verbatim without thinking about it. Try to pick out important points. After you understand a point, write it in your own words (unless it's a definition and you will need to know it verbatim for the test). Go back over your notes soon after class and put comments on them. While the lecture is still fresh in your mind, fill in gaps that you missed and clarify points that are fuzzy in your notes. Try to add some other examples or apply the concepts to other situations, and jot those down in your comments. Later, your notes, plus comments written very soon after the lecture, will make a great source to review for your tests.

An example of a good set of notes with comments written on them is shown on p. x. The student put the line down the left side before class. The class notes were written on the right side. The purpose of the left column is to add comments after class. The printed comments in the left column were added after the lecture to clarify the notes.

**Make Up Missed Classes**

If you have to miss class, get the notes from someone who takes good notes. (But do not miss class unless missing it is really necessary.) Don't assume that the material you missed won't be on the test; it surely will! Make an agreement in your study group that you will share notes with each other (but only when one member has a good reason for missing class). Even getting notes from someone won't be as good as being there yourself. Notes are personalized with material that the notetaker thought was important and material that the notetaker did not know before (Van Meter et al., 1994). Therefore, looking at two sets of notes would be a good idea. Go through one set of notes and write out your own notes in your own words. Then look at the other set of notes and fill in things that were missing from the first set and write in clarifications for the first set. Put in question marks where you don't understand something and be sure to have that clarified either in your study group or by your instructor or your teaching assistant.

**GET THE MOST OUT OF YOUR STUDY TIME**

The goal of studying is to understand and remember information so that it can be used at some later time: first, for tests in your course; later, as knowledge to help you better understand your experiences and solve real-world problems. If this broader goal is to be met, you need to understand material; simply memorizing terms and definitions is not enough. Most instructors will try to tap your understanding of material on tests. Understanding and applying material takes time, but the methods described below will make your studying more efficient and more effective than simply reading the textbook several times. As a student, your main job is to learn and apply information, so you should have already planned your time so that this can be accomplished on a regular basis, several times a week. Learning the material presented in your courses is a matter of getting information into memory and later getting it out. Chapter 7 of your textbook contains an entire chapter on memory processes, but those aspects that are specifically relevant to studying will be described below.

**Sample Notes for Improving Memory Lecture**

| | |
|---|---|
| Date: Wednesday, Oct. 17 | *Improving Memory by Using Mnemonic Devices*  Text: Chap. 7 |

|  |  |
|---|---|
| Mnemonic means memory in Greek | 1. Useful mnemonics |
| Also called peg system | A. Pegword |
| |    How does it work? |
| Need to be able to imagine thing you want to remember |      Uses words that rhyme with numbers (1 is a bun, 2 is a shoe) |
| Imagery plus verbal code puts it into memory twice |      Make interacting image of rhyme and thing to be remembered |
| |      Go through rhyme at retrieval, pulling out images |
| |    Useful for remembering imageable things in order (up to 10) |
| Originated by Greek speech-givers | B. Method of loci (locations) |
| |    How does it work? |
| Can use rooms in home |      Uses well-learned locations along a route |
| So, imagine what you want to buy in each place |      Make interacting image of location and thing to be remembered |
| This is the retrieval plan |      Imagine walking though locations at retrieval, pulling out images |
| |    Useful for remembering imageable things in order (many) |
| | C. First-letter mnemonic |
| |    How does it work? |
| Like "Every good boy does fine" |      Take first letter of words to form a sentence or story |
| |      Use the sentence or story to retrieve the first letters |
| |    Useful for memorizing in order (many things) |
| Need to watch that you don't remember rhyme, but not real items |    May be difficult to get from first letter to term |
| | D. Keyword mnemonic |
| |    How does it work? |
| Need to be able to imagine keyword |      Turn unfamiliar term into English keyword that sounds similar |
| |      Make an image of keyword and meaning of term |
| |      Unfamiliar term should result in retrieval of keyword plus image |
| |    When can it be used? |
| Think of Russian word delo as jello |      Foreign language vocabulary |
| Imagine a "cap race" with the leader changing often, for capricious |      English vocabulary |
| Use for plant species in hierarchy- imagine angel for angiosperm |      Biological taxonomies |
| | 2. Why do mnemonics work? |
| A. and B. are the two main points about memory | A. They promote a deep level of processing |
| To remember well, you need to |    1. Many use visual images which forces one to think of meaning |
| 1) get it in (encode) well | |
| 2) get it out (retrieve) |    2. Most tie new material to already known material |
| | B. They give a good retrieval scheme to pull memory out |

**Memory is Dependent Upon a High Level of Learning and Good Retrieval Cues**

Research on memory has shown that the amount of time that information can be retained in memory is directly related to the level of learning. *Information that is overlearned* (learned perfectly and then studied beyond that point) *is remembered longer* than information that is just barely learned (Krueger, 1929). One way to ensure that material is learned well is to *process the information to a deep or meaningful level* (Craik & Tulving, 1975). Material that you thought of only in terms of surface structure (e.g., what do the words sound like?) is not as well remembered as information that you thought of in terms of its meaning (how is this concept similar to one that I already know?). Students often repeat a definition over and over to themselves with the idea that this will strengthen the concept in memory. Memorizing a definition word for word is unimportant; being able to use the word is much more important. Furthermore, experimental studies have shown that mere repetition does not increase the likelihood that the material will be recalled later. Craik and Watkins (1973) showed that words that had been repeated over and over for 12 seconds or more were not remembered any better than words that had been repeated for only 1 second. On the other hand, *repetition that involves thinking about the meaning of material and connecting it with information that is already known is effective in increasing memory.*

Effective Ways of Producing High Levels of Learning

*Material that is understood is remembered better* than material that is not understood (Bransford & Johnson, 1973). Understanding material means that you have tied it into concepts that you already know, and this is one of the ways to produce a meaningful memory. If you do not understand material, don't simply try to memorize it by repetition. This is not effective. It is almost certain that the material you do not understand will appear on the test, so spend the time to ask someone to help you understand it. A good test of understanding is to try to apply the material to real-life situations or to come up with some examples of your own.

*Making images of concepts can help memory.* Images may help because they result in both a visual and a verbal memory code (Paivio, Walsh, & Bons, 1994). Making bizarre images can also help. Use bizarreness sparingly, however, because bizarre images are only remembered better when they are mixed in with common images (McDaniel, Einstein, DeLosh, May, & Brady, 1995). Things that you can imagine are also more related to other things, and relatedness helps memory (Paivio et al., 1994). Thus, try to visualize concepts whenever possible!

*Generating information can increase memory.* Jacoby (1978) showed that generating answers, even if they were simple, led to better memory for the answers than simply reading them. Foos, Mora, and Tkacz (1994) found that generating outlines, questions, and answers led to better test performance than reading instructor-prepared materials. However, make sure your questions and outlines hit most of the main points because generating helps only on test questions directly related to what you generate. Anything that you can do to produce material rather than being a passive reader should help (Linden & Wittrock, 1981).

*Repetitions of material should be distributed, not massed.* Many experiments, using many different types of materials, have shown that repeating material immediately after the first presentation (massed presentation) does little to help memory. *Repeating material after other material has been presented* (distributed presentation) *does help memory* (e.g., Melton, 1970). Studying once a day for a week will lead to better memory later than studying the same material seven times during a single day (Bahrick Bahrick, Bahrick, & Bahrick, 1994). For example, reading your text twice with 24 hours between the first reading and the rereading will produce better memory than reading it twice with no time between the readings (Krug, Davis, & Glover, 1990). So, a good plan would be to read a chapter before your instructor is going to lecture on it and then to reread it 2-3 days later, after hearing the lecture. Plan your study time so that you can take advantage of the effects of distributed study. Don't put off studying until the last minute so that all you can do is massed study (otherwise known as cramming). It won't be very effective in the long run.

## Retrieval Cues are Important to Get Information Out of Memory

*Retrieval is best when the conditions of testing match the conditions of learning* (Tulving & Thomson, 1973). No matter how well you know material, you must ultimately show your knowledge by pulling the material out of memory. Simply getting it into memory is not enough; retrieval is also necessary. Many experiments have shown that if you think of a concept in one way while learning it, you will need to think of it in the same way when your memory is tested. Otherwise, you may not be able to remember it. If you are going to have essay tests, plan how you would answer a question. Learn a series of key words that will help you to recall each point. You might find that a mnemonic system, such as the method of loci described in Chapter 7, could be helpful. If you are going to take a multiple-choice test, try to think of the concept in as many different ways as possible. *The more ways that you store a concept in memory, the more likely that your understanding will match one of the alternatives on the test.* Nitsch (1977/1979) has shown that people can better recognize a concept that is tested in a new way if they have learned with varied examples. So, try to think of as many different examples and ways of understanding a concept as you can.

*Similar physical conditions at encoding and retrieval help.* The match between study and test is also true for environmental conditions. There is some evidence that studying and being tested in the same room might help (Smith, Glenberg, & Bjork, 1978). However, don't worry if your tests are in a different place from your lectures. Saufley, Otaka, and Bavaresco (1985) found that students who took tests in rooms that were different from their classrooms did not do any worse than students who took tests in their classrooms. If you learn material well and in several different environments, you will probably be able to remember the material in any setting. However, there is some interesting recent evidence that suggests that the music you listen to may affect your ability to learn and remember on tests. Balch, Bowman, and Mohler (1992) found that students who read text material while listening to music that had words remembered less of what they read than students who either listened to no music or who listened to music without words. They also found that students who listened to either classical music or jazz while studying did better on tests when listening to that same music during the tests. Your instructor probably won't want you to listen to tape recorded music during your tests (he or she may become suspicious about what you're listening to if you have an ear phone in your ear). So, your best bet is to study without music. Instead of listening to music while studying, use music as a reward. After you have studied for an hour with no music, take a 15- minute music and refreshment break and listen to your favorite music, undisturbed by studying. External conditions and internal conditions, including drug states and mood, should be as similar as possible during learning and during testing.

## Using Your Study Group

Each week your study group should meet for about 2 hours; that time should be used for studying, not visiting. (You may plan to all go out afterward for an hour to visit, but visiting should be avoided during the study-group time itself.) Groups will need to work out their own study procedures, but here is a schedule that will make the group efficient in studying.

## Last Week's Material

1. Each member should have written questions over a part of the material as assigned at the last meeting. During the week, group members should write answers to all question. The study session should begin by trading the written answers to questions and having everyone "grade" someone else's questions. The textbook and notes should be used to ensure accurate grading.

2. A discussion about any difficult concepts or frequently missed questions should follow until everyone understands each answer.

## This Week's Material

3. Each group member will have been assigned a topic to "teach" (perhaps a section from the chapter, or from a recent lecture). How you break up the material may depend upon how much the instructor takes out of the book on tests and how much he or she takes out of lecture.

4. Each group member should "teach" the other members his or her assigned material. All group members should feel free both to ask questions and to clarify concepts as each person teaches.

## Next Week's Assignments

5. Everyone should have looked at what is coming next week and have an idea about what topic he or she would like to teach next. Part of the assignment will be to write about five questions on the topic; the other part of the assignment will be to prepare to teach it. Study groups may find other procedures that work for them. However, using the group to provide tests for each other is an essential aspect of the study plan. Use of the study group is incorporated into the SPAR system described below

## SPAR: A Method of Studying

The SPAR method is a study method that should help you to incorporate the guidelines described above. It was developed by Rusche (1984) and is similar to the SQ3R method (presented in Chapter 7), but it is easier to remember the key words that go with SPAR than with SQ3R (people forget the three Rs). **SPAR** stands for **S**urvey, **P**rocess meaningfully, **A**sk questions, and **R**eview and self-test. Application of this method, with your textbook and study guide, lecture material, and study group, will be described.

## Survey

The main goal here is to ask "What am I to learn?" Having a general idea of the topics will help you to tie the material in with concepts that you already know.

## Textbook and Study Guide

First, look at the Outline of the chapter in your book. This gives you an overview of the contents of the chapter. Next, read through the introductory material in the chapter to give you some idea about how the ideas presented in the chapter are relevant in everyday life. At the beginning of each section is a question that will be answered in the section. Think about how you would answer it before reading the chapter. There is a Summary at the end of each section. Read each point in the summary and think about what type of information would be needed to understand that point. Finally, read the Objectives in the study guide for a more detailed idea about the specific concepts to be learned.

## Lecture

Look at your course outline or syllabus so you know what your instructor will cover each day. Read the relevant material in your textbook before going to class so that you will have the background for the topic.

## Study Group

At the end of each weekly meeting, assignments of topics should be made for the next week. Looking over the upcoming material in order to agree on topic assignments will also serve the Survey function in SPAR. Each member should be assigned a specific topic to teach the next week and also to emphasize in writing questions.

## Process Meaningfully

The main goal here is to understand the material in a meaningful way, that is, to process it deeply and produce a high level of learning.

## Textbook and Study Guide

Read the chapter carefully. Do your first reading of the chapter before your instructor lectures on the topic. Stop and think about what you have read at the end of each section. Don't just try to recite what is in each section-- understanding is critical. Try to relate material to what you already know. Think of other examples of the concepts. If you can form visual images of the concepts, do so. Answer the questions that are asked in the Concept Check sections of each chapter. Try to answer the questions in the Something to Think About sections. Remember, it is better to generate answers than simply to read. If your instructor has assigned more than one section, it would probably be better to work with only one section at a time.

## Lecture

Go back over your notes soon after class and put comments in the left column. While the lecture is still fresh in your mind, fill in gaps that you missed and clarify points that are fuzzy in your notes. Try to add some other examples or apply the concepts to other situations, and jot those down in your comments. See the sample notes given earlier.

## Study Group

One of the best ways to learn is to teach others. Presenting material to other individuals forces one to process it meaningfully. Each member of the study group will need to process some of the material very meaningfully in order to "teach" the other members. "Knowing" something requires far less processing than "teaching" something. However, everyone should read all of the material and process it meaningfully as described above.

## Ask Questions

The goal here is to anticipate the types of questions that you will be asked later, so you will have practice in picking out the main concepts.

## Textbook and Study Guide

The study guide will make this portion of SPAR easy because the questions are provided. Complete the Comprehension Check portion of the study guide soon after reading the relevant section. The questions are similar to those that are likely to appear on a multiple-choice test. The questions, alternatives, and explanations include the terms that are described at the back of each textbook chapter in the Terms to Remember section. Circle the answer to each question without looking at your text. Check your answer. If your answer is wrong, write the correct answer in the blank beneath the question. Look up the concept on the page in your text indicated beside the correct answer. Write why your answer was wrong. Check your reason against that given in the study guide. If you want to remember the concept better, it is important that you generate the reason rather than simply reading it in the study guide. Also, look at why the other alternatives are wrong to be sure that you understand the concepts tested in the question. If you still do not understand, reread the section of text that is associated with the objective tested in the question. If that does not help, ask your instructor or teaching assistant to explain the concept to you.

## Lecture

Go back over your lecture notes. Write questions of the type given under the Short-Answer Essay section of your study guide. Try to write one question for each main point discussed in lecture. It is important that you write the questions, so you can use them later. Be sure that your questions are relevant to the material and that they are not too general, but also not too specific. Examples of good questions over the notes on memory are given below.

**Sample Questions from Memory Improvement Lecture**

1. How does the pegword system work? How is it similar to and different from the Method of Loci?

2. Describe how the keyword system can be used to remember definitions for abstract words?

3. How do all mnemonic systems encourage a deep level of processing?

4. In what ways do mnemonic systems work as effective retrieval schemes?

## Study Group

Here's where the study group really comes in. You can answer not only your own questions, but those written by the other members of your group. Each member of the group should be responsible for a specific topic. Part of the responsibility should be to write at least five questions on that topic that could be answered by the other group members. Short-answer questions are probably best. Because you have the study guide with questions covering text material, you should mostly write questions that focus on lecture material. After each group member has "taught" his or her topic, the questions prepared by group members should be passed out. Actually, simply preparing the written questions is a great way to learn.

### Review and Self-Test

The main goal here is to test your memory and understanding of the material by answering questions of the type that will appear on a test.

## Textbook and Study Guide

Presumably you have already read all of the assigned sections in a chapter and completed the comprehension check in the study guide. Wait at least 24 hours before going on. This will allow you to forget material that was not processed meaningfully enough. It is important that you find out which material was not well learned before the actual test in your course. Now, return to the study guide. Write out answers to the short-answer essay questions for the chapter. The questions require retrieval from memory with few cues, so that your level of learning can be tested. If you can write answers under these conditions, you know the material well enough to do well on any kind of test. The study guide provides answers to these questions so you can check yourself. It also provides the page in the textbook where the answer appears. Don't simply read the answers. You know by now that generating answers is important for later memory. Once you have checked your answer, keep trying to answer the questions yourself until you can produce a correct answer from memory without the textbook or your notes.

## Lecture

Write answers to the questions that you wrote over lecture material. Check your answers against your notes. If you cannot produce a good answer to a question, get some help. Once you have a good answer to each question, keep trying to produce that answer from memory without using your notes or text.

## Study Group

During the week, each group member should write answers to the questions prepared by other group members, as well as those he or she wrote, without looking at the book or notes. This should be done during the week between your meetings. At the beginning of the next meeting, you can exchange your answers, and everyone can "grade" someone else's. The group should discuss errors and make sure that everyone understands the concepts, especially those that were missed on the "test."

## PREPARING FOR TESTS

If you have followed all of the above advice, you will be almost ready for the test when it comes. There should be no need to do massive cramming on the night before the test. However, you should add an extra hour or two to review the material. Use the materials produced in your study group. Take out those short-answer questions that the members of your group wrote and write answers again. Write the answers to the short-answer questions in the study guide again. Spend some time scoring your answers and also look back at your original answers. What have you forgotten this time that you knew before? Have you corrected earlier mistakes, as judged by the answers that were "graded" by your study group? Look over your notes, paying specific attention to your comments. Did you get the answers to issues that you had questions about? Look at the chapter outlines in the study guide and in the textbook. Can you give a sentence or two explaining each topic? When you know all of the answers well, take the posttest without using your book or notes. Score the test. If you made an error, look up the correct answer on the page given. The study guide also provides numbers of questions that test the same concept in the Comprehension Check and the Short-Answer Essay sections. Look back and see if you understood those questions and why the alternatives on the Comprehension Check were wrong. If would be a good idea to review the posttest questions, the objectives in the study guide, and the summary in the text just before you take the test in your course.

### Watch Out for Overconfidence

There are many studies in psychology (e.g., Fischhoff, Slovic, & Lichtenstein, 1977) that show that college students tend to be overconfident. This is particularly true when tests are difficult (Schraw & Roedel, 1994). This means that you may go into a test thinking that you know more than you do. One of the best ways to combat overconfidence is to take a practice test that is as similar as possible to the actual test (Glover, 1989). However, make sure that the practice test is very similar; just answering a few questions may not predict how well you will do on an actual test (Maki & Serra, 1992). Probably, the best way to ensure against overconfidence is to take a test that is more demanding than the actual test. For example, if your test will be multiple-choice and you practice with short-answer essays, you probably won't be overconfident because essay tests demand more knowledge than multiple-choice tests. If your actual test will be short-answer essay, then using multiple-choice practice tests to gauge your level of knowledge would not be a good idea. Multiple-choice tests would be fine to use as part of your study, but do not assume that if you get everything correct on a multiple-choice practice test that you will be able to do well on a short-answer essay test. Write some essay questions for yourself or use essay questions produced by your study group, and use your performance on those to judge how well you will do on the actual test. Try to make your practice-test experience as similar as you can to the actual test, and better yet, make your practice-test experience more demanding than the actual test is likely to be.

## TAKING TESTS

### General Advice for All Types of Tests

<u>Be Prepared and Arrive Early at the Test Site</u>

Have everything that you need for the test. If you are to use a special ID number, make sure that you have found that before the test. If you need to use a special pencil or test booklet, make sure to have those with you. Arrive a few minutes early for the test. If you are allowed to select a seat, find a seat where distractions will be minimal. If students turn in their tests when they are finished, sit in a place where they will not be walking around you. In an auditorium, the best seats are in the middle of a row where students will not step over you. Don't sit near the place where the tests are to be turned in and don't sit near the door. If other students do begin to leave and you are not finished yet, don't panic. You will be allowed the full test time and if you do the test carefully and check your answers, you will probably need most of the time. Assume that those "early birds" did not know the material and guessed at most of the answers.

<u>Begin the Test By Surveying It</u>

You will probably have a time limit on your test. Still, begin by reading the test instructions and listening to any instructions or corrections given in class. Knowing what you are doing will save time in the end. Get an idea of how long the test is. Make sure that you have all the pages by checking that the question numbers are sequential.

<u>Ask Questions</u>

If you really don't understand a question, either put up your hand or walk up and ask the instructor or teaching assistant. Don't just answer the question based on one interpretation when there is another reasonable interpretation. Ask for clarification. If you don't know a word in a question, ask for a definition. If it is a word that you should know, your instructor probably won't give you the definition, but it doesn't hurt to ask.

<u>Pace Yourself</u>

If the room does not have a clock, wear a watch. Allow yourself enough time to finish the test. For example, if you are supposed to answer 50 questions in 50 minutes, you should average no more than 1 minute per question. Periodically, check yourself to be sure that your pace is right.

<u>Don't Cheat</u>

Learning the material in your courses will have lifelong benefits to you. The knowledge that you gain from your college courses will allow you to better understand and solve a lifetime's worth of problems. Doing well on tests by looking at your "brilliant" friend's answers or by using cheat sheets will gyp you of useful knowledge. Cheating also degrades the value of an education for everyone. If college graduates have not learned the knowledge expected of them because they cheated, the value of a college education is lessened. Furthermore, most universities have severe penalties for cheating. You could fail the test, fail the course, or even be suspended from school. So, don't be tempted to cheat. Instead, learn the material, and there is no need to consider being dishonest.

## Taking Multiple-Choice Tests

### Watch the Wording of Questions

Words like always and never mean there are no exceptions. Something always occurs or it never occurs. Such alternatives are usually (although not always) wrong. Few facts in psychology are that absolute.

### Pick the Best Answer

One answer may be correct under most circumstances and another answer may be correct under a more general set of circumstances. Select the answer that is most generally correct and that has the fewest exceptions. Don't immediately choose a, if a seems correct. Answer b may be correct also and perhaps even better. You are supposed to choose the best answer, not just one that is partly or possibly correct. Also, some instructors use double-answer questions. Both **a** and **b** may be correct and the correct answer is e, both a and b. Always read all of the alternatives before selecting the best one.

### Watch for Negative Questions

Read the question carefully and note if it contains a negative, such as "not" or "isn't." Many students miss that little word and select an alternative that is true. What they don't notice is that the question asked the student to select the alternative that is <u>not</u> true. Allow yourself some extra time to answer "not" questions and be sure to double-check your answer carefully.

### Mark out Incorrect Alternatives

Read each question and mark off the alternatives that you know are wrong. Don't be hasty about this. Read each alternative carefully, filling it in as the answer. If you're sure the answer is wrong, mark it out. Then, select the best choice among the items you did not eliminate.

### Skip the Difficult Questions

If you are not certain about your answer, skip the question and go back to it later when you will know how much time you can afford to spend on it. (But don't forget to come back to the ones you omitted!)

### Avoid Interference from Incorrect Alternatives

Research on memory has shown that it is sometimes harder to recognize (select) an answer that is embedded in other similar answers than to simply recall it from memory (Tulving & Thomson, 1973). Thus, for those difficult questions that you skipped, you might do better to turn the multiple-choice test into a short-answer test. When you go back to those questions, cover the alternatives and try to write what you think should be the correct answer. Then, look at the alternatives that you haven't eliminated as being wrong, and see which one best matches what you wrote. Choose that answer.

### Make your Best Guess

After you have gone through the test twice and eliminated wrong alternatives, make your best guess among the remaining choices. Because you have already marked out alternatives that you know are wrong, your chance of getting the question correct has improved. It's 50% if there are only two remaining alternatives.

### Don't Pay Attention to Patterns

Instructors usually don't look at the pattern of correct answers until after the test is printed. Some intentionally use a random-number sequence to determine the order of answers, so it's possible that the correct answer might be the same alternative on many consecutive questions, or that the correct answers might accidentally form some pattern. Select the best answer for each item and don't worry if there seems to be too many of one alternative or if the alternatives form a pattern.

## Put your Answers on the Answer Sheet Carefully

If your answers need to go on a special answer sheet, it is probably a good idea to wait until you have circled the answers to all questions before transferring them to the answer sheet. Make sure that you are on the right question as you mark the answer sheet. After you have transferred your answers, take an extra minute to check to ensure that the circled answer for each question is what you placed on the answer sheet.

## Check your Answers

When you finish, if you have time available, check your answers to each question. You may catch some mistakes.

## Taking Essay Tests

### Take a Few Minutes to Read all the Questions

This is particularly important if your instructor allows you to choose which of several questions you can answer. Look over all the questions and make a decision about which item you know the best. Start by answering your best questions. They will go quickly and allow you to build confidence.

### Outline your Answers

Many essay questions have several parts. Jot down each part. Some instructors grade by assigning specific numbers of points to specific parts of the essay. Whether or not this is the case with your instructor, you will probably get more credit for your answer if you specifically address each point in your answer. It is probably a good idea to write a short heading and underline it for each part. This will force you to organize your answer in line with the question and it will also make grading easier for your instructor. He or she will see that you have answered all parts.

### Don't Add Irrelevant Material

The point of essay answers is not to write everything you know that is tangentially related to a topic. The point is to write what you know that is directly related to the topic. Going off on tangents won't impress the graders with your knowledge. Such extraneous material is likely to annoy them because they have to search for the correct answer. Make it easy for graders by just giving relevant information in an organized form.

### Don't Answer Questions that Weren't Asked

This is related to the irrelevant material discussed above. If you really know nothing about a topic, then you are in trouble and, chances are, you have not followed the guidelines listed above. Don't try to weasel out by answering some question other than what was asked. Write whatever you know about the topic and leave it at that. And study harder the next time!

### Write Legibly

Some instructors (including this one) simply give up if they have difficulty reading an answer (and they are unlikely to assume that the correct answer is really there without reading it). Thus, try to write as legibly as possible. If you have poor handwriting, try printing your answers or try to write larger than usual. Whatever you can do to make your handwriting more legible will help you in the long run.

## Taking Matching Tests

### Understand the Rules

The most important point here is to understand the rules of the matching tests. If your instructor did not tell you, then ask. (You do have a right to know the constraints on the test.) Is each alternative used only once, or can some be used multiple times? Is there, in fact, a match for each item? Find out these things before you start.

### Write in the Answers that You Know

The whole matching item might look overwhelming, but once you have written answers that you are sure of, you may do much better on the rest. This is much easier if each alternative is used only once. You can simply cross off those that you are sure of and you greatly reduce the number that you need to use for the remaining items. If alternatives can be used more than once, then you might look for items that are similar to those that you know and put in the same alternatives.

### Work with one item at a time

Take a single item on the matching test and compare it with each alternative individually. You might even put the number of the item beside an alternative if you think it might match. Then go through those that you have put the item number beside and make it a multiple-choice test. Mark out the alternatives that seem less likely until you are left with only one in ideal circumstances, or more in less-than-ideal circumstances. If you cannot decide among several alternatives, simply guess. You have already improved your chances by eliminating many of the potential match items.

## Learn from Your Errors

### Understand Your Wrong Answers

Always look over your test when you get it back (or go and look at the key if your instructor posts one). Check your test and make yourself aware of which items you have gotten right and which are wrong. Don't be "sick of it" and not look at a test after it's over and graded. The test provides a great learning experience, particularly if your instructor gives a cumulative final. The material that you missed will probably be back on the final, so keep your tests to study for the final exam.

### Use the Test Experience to Analyze Your Study Plan

If you met your goal on the test, then you know that you are studying appropriately. Keep doing what you have been doing; your study plan works! If you did worse than you realistically expected, then you either need to change your study plan, find more time for study, or change your goal. Changing your study plan should be the first step. Go back over your plan and see whether you could use some of your time more efficiently. Is your study group working or do they spend half the study time visiting? Are you really using those hours between classes? Are you following through on your study plan? For example, are you writing answers to questions or are you just looking at them and assuming that you know them? When you make an error on a question while studying, are you going back to really understand why you were wrong and why another answer is correct? If you really are giving the course all the time that you can and if you really have an efficient study plan that you are following, you may have to reset your goals. Perhaps, getting an A in the course is not realistic. Change your expectations to settle for a B (but don't settle for much less--there is always a way to improve your study plan).

## IF YOU HAVE PROBLEMS

There are a number of things to do if you find you are not doing as well on your tests as you wish. Visit your instructor or your teaching assistant during office hours. They may have some specific ideas about how you can do better in the course you are taking. Don't be afraid to go to your instructor's office during office hours. Even when they are teaching large classes, most instructors are alone during office hours. Students rarely go to see them. Even if things aren't going badly, you should always feel free to visit your instructor and discuss either your progress in the course or an issue that is of interest to you. If you still have problems with a course, try your university's counseling center. They have a staff who is trained to help you. Use them, even if your problem is not severe. You probably have an advisor who can help you also. Go and talk with him or her when you begin to have difficulty. Find out about your school's drop policy. Can you still drop the course that is causing the problems without penalty? If you are overloaded (which you should know before classes start when you make up your schedule), drop the excess courses immediately. Don't think that you will start with more courses than you have time for and later drop the worst one. By that time, you have already spread yourself too thin and hurt your performance in all of your courses. Set up a reasonable load and then stick with it.

## FINAL NOTE

It is true that all of this takes a long time. However, learning a great deal of new material, as is necessary in any college-level course, is not easy. The procedures suggested here will make you much more efficient than if you simply read and reread your text. These studying techniques will pay off, and as you get better at using them, they will become easier. The key point in all of this is to BE ACTIVE. The less time you spend passively reading and the more time you spend actively generating answers and testing yourself, the better you will do on tests in your course. And generating answers makes studying much more interesting than simply reading and reading and reading. The topics covered in this textbook are exciting and useful in everyday life. May you learn them well and use them for your entire lifetime!

## REFERENCES

Bahrick, H. P., Bahrick, L. E., Bahrick, A. S., and Bahrick, P. E. (1993). Maintenance of foreign language vocabulary and the spacing effect. *Psychological Science, 4*, 316-322.

Balch, W. R., Bowman, K., and Mohler, L. A. (1992). Music-dependent memory in immediate and delayed word recall. *Memory and Cognition, 20*, 21-28.

Bransford, J. D., and Johnson, M. K. (1973). Consideration of some problems of comprehension. In William G. Chase (Ed.), *Visual information processing*. New York: Academic Press.

Craik, F. I. M., and Tulving, E. (1975). Depth of processing and the retention of words in episodic memory. *Journal of Experimental Psychology: General, 104*, 268-294.

Craik, F. I. M., and Watkins, M. J. (1973). The role of rehearsal in short-term memory. *Journal of Verbal Learning and Verbal Behavior, 12*, 599-607.

Druckman, D., and Bjork, R. A. (Eds.). (1994). *Learning, remembering, believing: Enhancing human performance*. Washington, D. C.: National Academy Press.

Fischhoff, B., Slovic, P., and Lichtenstein, S. (1977). Knowing with certainty: The appropriateness of extreme confidence. *Journal of Experimental Psychology: Human Perception and Performance, 3*, 552-564.

Foos, P. W., Mora, J. J., Tkacz, S. (1994). Student study techniques and the generation effect. *Journal of Educational Psychology, 86*, 567-576.

Glover, J. A. (1989). Improving readers' estimates of learning from text: The role of inserted questions. *Reading Research Quarterly, 28*, 68-75.

Greenwald, A. G., Spangenberg, E. R., Pratkanis, A. R., and Eskenazi, J. (1991). Double-blind tests of subliminal self-help audiotapes. *Psychological Science, 2*, 119-122.

Haenggi, D., and Perfetti, C. A. (1992). Individual differences in reprocessing of text. *Journal of Educational Psychology, 84*, 182-192.

Jacoby, L. L. (1978). On interpreting the effects of repetition: Solving problems versus remembering solutions. *Journal of Verbal Learning and Verbal Behavior, 17*, 649-667.

Krueger, W. C. F. (1929). The effects of overlearning on retention. *Journal of Experimental Psychology, 12*, 71-78.

Krug, D., Davis, T. B., and Glover, J. A. (1990). Massed versus distributed repeated reading: A case of forgetting helping recall? *Journal of Educational Psychology, 82,* 366-371.

Linden, M., and Wittrock, M. C. (1981). The teaching of reading comprehension according to the model of generative learning. *Reading Research Quarterly, 17,* 45-57.

Locke, E. A., and Latham, G. P. (1990). *A theory of goal setting and task performance.* New York: Prentice-Hall.

McDaniel, M. A., Einstein, G. O., DeLosh, E. L., May, C. P., Brady, P. (1995). The bizarreness effect: It's not surprising, it's complex. *Journal of Experimental Psychology: Learning, Memory, and Cognition, 21,* 422-425.

Maki, R. H., and Serra, M. (1992). Role of practice tests in the prediction of test performance over text material. *Journal of Educational Psychology, 84,* 200-210.

Melton, A. W. (1970). The situation with respect to the spacing of repetitions and memory. *Journal of Verbal Learning and Verbal Behavior, 9,* 596-606.

Nitsch, K. E. (1977). Structuring de-contextualized forms of knowledge. (Doctoral dissertation, Vanderbilt University) as cited in J. D. Bransford. (1979). *Human cognition.* Belmont, Calif.: Wadsworth.

Paivio, A., Walsh, M., and Bons, T. (1994). Concreteness effects on memory: When and why? *Journal of Experimental Psychology: Learning, Memory, and Cognition, 20,* 1196-124.

Rusche, K. M. (1984). The effectiveness of study skills training for students of different personality types and achievement levels. (Doctoral dissertation, Loyola University).

Saufley, W. H., Jr., Otaka, S. R., and Bavaresco, J. L. (1985). Context effects: Classroom tests and context independence. *Memory and Cognition, 13,* 522-528.

Schraw, G., and Roedel, T. D. (1994). Test difficulty and judgment bias. *Memory and Cognition, 22,* 63-69.

Smith, S. M., Glenberg, A., and Bjork, R. A. (1978). Environmental context and human memory. *Memory and Cognition, 6,* 342-353.

Tulving, E., and Thomson, D. M. (1973). Encoding specificity and retrieval processes in episodic memory. *Psychological Review, 80,* 352-373.

Van Meter, P., Yokoi, L., Pressley, M. (1994). College students' theory of note-taking derived from their perceptions of note-taking. *Journal of Educational Psychology, 86,* 323-338.

# INTRODUCTION TO THE LANGUAGE ENHANCEMENT GUIDE

Teachers like myself have adopted Jim Kalat's Introductory Psychology textbook for many reasons. The main reason is that teachers as well as their students like the book. There are three reasons that I and my students like the book. First, Kalat makes sure that each sentence and paragraph is clear and understandable. Secondly, you will find that the topics he selects are interesting so you will want to read them. Third, he provides many study aids in the chapter to help you understand and memorize the material. One study aid consists of printing all new technical terms in bold face type. These words are then immediately defined and followed by examples you can understand. Other study aids include summaries and definitions of all new technical terms at the end of each chapter section.

There is also a major feature of the book that is based on a teaching objective that most teachers like myself share with Kalat. You will probably agree with this objective when you read about it. We want students to learn the habit of questioning claims made in textbooks, claims made by college professors, claims made in newspapers, claims made by TV news reporters, claims made by friends as well as claims that you make yourself. We want students to develop their critical thinking skills and look and ask for the evidence and reasons used to support a claim. We want students to look for and recognize errors in reasoning and in collecting evidence. We believe that mastery of a subject is much more than just memorizing technical terms, methods and principles. We believe that mastery involves active critical thinking and applying what you have learned to solving life problems.

Now there is a problem for some but not all students who have read Kalat's text. Kalat has written his textbook for college students with English as their native language. Kalat also uses a college level vocabulary that can be easily understood by students who can read at the 12th grade level. However, if you are not a native English speaker or do not have a 12th grade level or college level vocabulary Kalat's vocabulary may give you problems in understanding the material. You may find that you need to look up many words on each page of the textbook in a dictionary. Looking up words in a dictionary takes some students many extra hours of study and can be a frustrating experience. Students with this problem often drop my class and tell me that if they had a page of definitions for "problem words" it would save time, and make understanding the book easier. I have written this language enhancement study guide to meet this need.

## HOW TO USE THIS LANGUAGE ENHANCEMENT GUIDE

To use this language enhancement guide effectively you should know how it was designed and how you can use each section to help you better read and understand the text and increase your vocabulary.

The first section of each chapter of this Language Enhancement Guide is entitled, Vocabulary, Idioms and Cultural Concepts. This section consists of a list of 12th grade and college level words arranged in the order in which they appear in the text. Each word is followed by a brief definition or an explanation. Please note that Appendix A contains a dictionary of all terms in the Language Enhancement Guide.

The second section of each chapter is entitled, Vocabulary Building. This section contain tutorials and exercises to enhance vocabulary building. One type of enhancement will consist of explanations and drills to help the student learn common prefixes, roots and suffixes of technical and non technical words used in the book.

Each chapter in this study guide matches the corresponding chapter in the text book and has two kinds of study aids. The first study aid is called Vocabulary, Idioms and Cultural Concepts. This study aid consists of a list of college level words used on each text page and their definitions. Each definition contains the meaning of the word as used by Kalat on the page indicated. There are a number of different ways the list can help you. One way is to find the meaning of the word you do not know on the list. This will save you the time and effort of looking them up in a dictionary. All the words on the page will not be on the list. Technical words defined by Kalat can be found in the text glossary at the end of the book. College level non-technical words that are used several times in the book are defined only the first few times they appear. All the college level words used in the book are found in a short dictionary at the end of this study guide. We will discuss several other ways to use the list later in the introduction.

The second section of each chapter is called Vocabulary Building. This aid is based on the fact that many words in the English language are made up of separate parts that have been borrowed from many other languages such as Latin, Greek, Spanish, German, French, etc. When you can break up a word into its parts and you know the meaning of each part you can then determine the possible meanings of the word. The exercises in this section will help you master the common parts of words so you will be able to figure out the meaning of many words without needing to look them up in a dictionary

## VOCABULARY BUILDING AND THREE LEVELS OF VERBAL PRECISION

The major goal of this guide is to help you build (increase) your vocabulary. Why is building your vocabulary so important? A large working vocabulary and skill in using words at the correct level of precision is essential for effective communication, thinking and mastery of a scientific field of knowledge like Psychology. College text books, newspapers, news magazines and professional journals require a college level vocabulary. When you apply for a job that requires a college education you will be judged by your pronunciation, your vocabulary and how you use words to express your thinking. Therefore, a major goal of a college education and of this class is to increase your vocabulary and improve your communication skills.

Words can be classified into three levels of usage and precision: 1. Every day words, Slang and common Idioms, 2. Standard Dictionary and Cultural References and 3. Professional Technical. As we move from Slang to the Professional level, the degree of precision increases and vagueness and uncertainty decreases. Now let's take a close look at the details of each level of precision and how this study guide will help you better understand the text and help you develop a larger vocabulary.

## Level 1. Slang, Idioms and the Every Day Vocabulary

### Slang

Slang is the everyday level at which many people talk. "Hi. How ya' doin. Pretty darn good. How's about you? Not so good. I bombed on my last exam." If you are a native English speaker you have learned English at this level. This level is "good enough" for everyday use when we don't need to be very precise and accurate. After all, we use slang everyday, and you "kinda know what I'm sayin. don't ya?" The problem with slang is that it varies from one region of the country to another. Kalat's book avoids slang.

### Idioms

An idiom consists of words or phrases that are not directly translatable into other languages. Native English speakers immediately know the meaning of these phrases. People who are not native speakers and even some who are native speakers are confused by them. Kalat uses many common idioms in the book. Here are a few. How many of them do you know?

- lead to a deeper
- had its roots
- only once in a while
- deal with an issue
- fruitful
- pitfalls
- knock-down-argument

- far-fetched
- had any tips
- use on people
- in its extreme form
- a little more noble
- at issue
- branch of medicine

- is governed by
- to the whole enterprise
- plot out a route
- was put together
- in a sense
- great strides
- willing to admit

It's not always easy to guess the meanings of idioms in context (that is, as a part of the whole sentence or paragraph in which they occur). There are many of these expressions throughout the text. The most difficult in each Chapter are listed the first study aid, **Vocabulary, Idioms and Cultural Concepts.** Many idioms have more than one meaning. The definition accompanying each idiom corresponds to the way the author uses the expression in the paragraph.

### Level 2. Standard Dictionary English Vocabulary and Cultural References

The term "Standard Dictionary English Vocabulary" refers to words that students at the 12th grade to college level and above are expected to know. Native English speakers with limited vocabulary and reading skills must look them up in a dictionary. Here are some sample words that are used in the text book. How many of them do you know?

- ascertain
- advent
- allegedly
- alluded
- anarchist
- ascertain
- aspire
- conceal
- deception

- detour
- emerge
- eminent
- exaggerate
- gullibility
- inadvertent
- pertinent
- pharmacological
- phenomenon
- peripheral

- presume
- prolific
- prone
- refute
- scrutinize
- stratagem
- subtly
- syndrome
- skeptical
- telepathic

At the level of Standard English, you can find the various meanings and pronunciation of each word in a "general" dictionary. A "general" dictionary is a very useful tool to find out the meanings of new words that are used by educated people as they speak and write in magazines, newspapers, novels, TV and text books like Kalat's Introduction to Psychology.

Kalat's textbook makes use of many Standard Dictionary English Level words. If you do not have a vocabulary at least at the 12th grade level, you may not be able to understand much of the text, tests and lecture. Fortunately, the Kalat text and your instructor use many of these college level vocabulary words over and over in the book and in the lectures. Once you learn these words, your understanding of the text and the lecture will get easier. This study guide will help you by providing you with dictionary definitions of twelfth grade and college level words used in the text and lecture. The sooner you memorize these words the better you will understand of the text and lectures.

### Cultural References

These are names of people, places, objects and historical events that may not be familiar to non-native speakers. Even native speakers may not be fluent with historical events and people. For example, the following Cultural References Terms are used in the first two chapter. How many of them do you know?

| | | |
|---|---|---|
| • psychic | • nutritional deficiencies | • juvenile delinquent |
| • overeducated society | • welfare | • scientific revolution |
| • Renaissance | • health provider settings | • cyborg |

The first study aid, **Vocabulary, Idioms and Cultural Concepts**, will present and define the meaning of many college level standard dictionary English words and Cultural References.

## Level 3. Technical Professional Vocabulary

The Professional Level includes scientists, philosophers, language specialists, medical doctors, college professors, lawyers, engineers and other professionals. Technical Professional words are used to deal with the subject specialties such as economics, psychology, physics, engineering, law, medicine etc. Every occupation and profession has its own special vocabulary. Scientists and professionals need words that have precise and exact definitions to be used without vagueness or ambiguity. Many professional and text books provide a glossary with precise definitions for the technical words used.

You may be thinking, "Why do we need a glossary? Why not use a general dictionary?" The problem is that a general dictionary provides many brief definitions for thousands of common words but very little or nothing at all about very special words used by scientists and professionals. When used by professionals some of the everyday and slang meanings of a word or even the standard dictionary meaning may be either stripped away or changed. This can be confusing at first to the nonprofessional. However, with study of the definitions the confusion clears up. Therefore, if you want to improve the quality of your use of words and ability to think critically, you must take the time to master the use of precisely defined professional terms. Let us now look at the ways that Kalat helps you learn the meaning of new words.

As you read the first chapter did you notice that Kalat defines all technical words that appear in bold face type in the sentence following the word. He then repeats that definition in the section summary and again in the terms glossary and again in the glossary in the back of the book. A **Glossary** is a dictionary of technical words with the author definition. For example find the first bold faced word in the text on page 7. The word is **determinism**. Notice that the word is followed by a short dash line and a definition. Kalat then defines the word again in the section summary. Look for the word **determinism** on page 18. All the bold faced terms in each section of the chapter are then listed and defined at the end of the summary in a section called **TERMS**. Look for the word **determinism** on page 19. These bold faced words are very important and you are expected to learn their meanings. Ruth Maki's study guide that precedes each Language Enhancement section text will help you memorize these technical words. Kalat will used these technical words other places in the text. **The Vocabulary, Idioms and Cultural Concepts list does not include the technical words found on each page of the textbook.** If you see these words again and you forget their meaning you can look them up in Kalat's Glossary at the back of the text book. Look up the word **determinism** in the glossary.

Step 1: Do a quick review of the assigned chapter. Familiarize yourself with the contents by reading heads, subheads, picture captions, and marginal text. Don't read the chapter word-for-word, and use the dictionary as little as possible at this point. This is the Survey part of SPAR.

Step 2: Read through the corresponding material in this Language Enhancement Guide in the **Vocabulary, Idioms and Cultural Concepts** section; find items in your text using the page references and study their contexts. This will familiarize you with the non technical vocabulary. Then read the assigned page of the textbook. As you read the page if you find a non technical word that you do not understand look for it on the **Vocabulary, Idioms and Cultural Concepts** list for this chapter or in Appendix A that defines many non technical words found in the textbook.

Step 3: Now do a careful, word-for-word reading of the chapter. This is the P̲rocess Meaningfully part of SP̲AR.

Step 5: Read the text carefully a second time. After this reading, do the Comprehension Checks, Short Answer Essay questions, and Multiple Choice in the study guide preceding the Language Enhancement section. This will help you to complete the A̲sk Questions part of SPA̲R.

Step 4: Complete the remaining exercises in this guide.

Step 6: Prepare a 3" x 5" note card with the **Vocabulary, Idioms and Cultural Concepts** you need to learn and carry them with you. At various moments of the day just look at the note cards and see how many words you can define. You can also do this with the technical words in the chapter. This would be part of the R̲eview and Self-Test part of SPAR̲.

# CHAPTER 1  WHAT IS PSYCHOLOGY?

**OBJECTIVES**

Understand that:

I.  The theme of this book is "Ask for evidence"  (p. 4)

**Goals of Psychologists**

II.  Psychology had its start in philosophy, and some philosophical issues are still important in psychology  (p. 6)
    A.  Free will vs. determinism  (pp. 6-7)
        1.  Does behavior have predictable physical causes or are some choices unpredictable?  (p. 7-8)
    B.  Mind-brain problem  (p. 8)
        1.  How does brain activity relate to behavior and experience?  (pp. 8-9)
    C.  Nature-nurture issue  (pp. 9-10)
        1.  Are differences in behavior due to heredity or environment?  (p. 10)
III.  What psychologists do  (pp. 10-11)
    A.  Different types of psychologists emphasize different issues  (pp. 10-12, Table 1.2)
        1.  Clinical psychologists are interested in helping troubled people  (p. 10)
        2.  Psychiatrists are medical doctors  (p. 11)
        3.  Psychoanalysts emphasize the methods of Freud  (p. 11)
    B.  Psychologists work in academic institutions, clinics, businesses, and schools  (p. 13, Fig. 1.4)
    C.  At present, women are well represented in psychology, but the proportion of minorities is small  (p. 13)
IV.  Psychologists use several approaches  (p. 14, Table 1.3, p. 15)
    A.  Psychologists with a quantitative approach use tests  (p. 14)
        1.  Tests don't explain performance  (p. 14)
    B.  Biopsychologists are interested in genetics, effects of brain damage, and drugs  (pp. 14-16)
    C.  Behavioral psychologists believe that behavior depends on its consequences  (p. 16)
    D.  Cognitive psychologists study how people think and acquire knowledge  (pp. 16-17)
    E.  Social psychologists study how thoughts and behavior are affected by other people  (p. 17)
    F.  Clinical psychologists look for explanations in terms of emotional influences  (p. 17)
    G.  Approaches to psychology overlap  (pp. 17-18)

**Psychology Then and Now**

V.  The early era of psychology was 1879 to 1920  (p. 20)
    A.  Wundt founded the first psychology laboratory in 1879  (p. 20)
        1.  Psychological experience is composed of compounds  (pp. 20-21)
    B.  Titchener asked observers to describe the elements of experience  (pp. 21-22)
    C.  William James focused on the actions that the mind performs  (pp. 22-23)
    D.  Early psychologists studied psychophysics, the relationship between perceived stimulus intensity and actual physical intensity  (p. 23)
    E.  Darwin's theory spurred the study of animal intelligence  (pp. 23-24)
    F.  Galton focused on human intelligence  (pp. 24-25)
    G.  Mary Calkins and Margaret Washburn were early female psychologists  (p. 25)
VI.  Behaviorists dominated psychology from about 1920 to 1970  (p. 25)
    A.  John B. Watson argued that psychology should be totally objective  (p. 26)

B. Clark Hull tried to create an equation to account for maze learning  (pp. 26-27)
VII. Psychologists still investigate many questions  (p. 27)
    A. There is increasing interest in human diversity  (pp. 27-28)
    B. Sometimes approaches are unsuccessful, but often they lead to better questions and better answers (p. 28)

## COMPREHENSION CHECK

Answer these questions soon after reading the chapter.  Circle the best alternative.  Check your answers on pp. 5-7 of the study guide.  If you gave a wrong answer, try to write why it was wrong.  Understanding your wrong answers can be a better learning experience than giving the right answer.  Check your reasons on pp. 5-7 of the study guide.

### Goals of Psychologists

1. The theme of this book is:
    a. everything you read in textbooks must be true
    b. you should disbelieve everything you read or hear
    c. phrases that start with "They say..." are based on common sense and usually true
    d. professors are absolutely certain about most conclusions
    e. ask for the evidence when you hear or read something

Correct _____  If wrong, why? _____

2. Psychology is the systematic study of:
    a. conscious thought
    b. human behavior
    c. abnormal behavior
    d. behavior and experience
    e. techniques for manipulating and tricking people

Correct _____  If wrong, why? _____

3. According to determinism:
    a. choices cannot be predicted
    b. unpredictability implies a lack of causes
    c. everything people do has a physical cause
    d. much of human behavior is caused by random factors
    e. physical events have natural causes, but human decisions are guided by free will

Correct _____  If wrong, why? _____

4. Chaos theory proposes that:
    a. events aren't unpredictable; they could be predicted if we knew the many small causes
    b. unpredictability comes from a lack of causes
    c. human behavior results from indeterminism
    d. only large influences affect final outcomes
    e. human behavior is beyond the reach of the natural sciences

Correct _____  If wrong, why? _____

5. What do research studies, such as those using PET scans, say about the mind-brain problem?
    a. they show how mind controls the brain
    b. they constrain the answers that philosophers can give to this problem
    c. they show that mind and brain are two names for the same thing
    d. they indicate the independence of mind and brain
    e. they show that brain activity causes thoughts

Correct _____ If wrong, why? _____

6. A researcher attempts to determine whether a personality trait is inherited or learned. Which philosophical issue is she addressing?
    a. nature vs. nurture
    b. chaos theory versus indeterminism
    c. free will vs. determinism
    d. mind-brain problem

Correct _____ If wrong, why? _____

7. Which type of psychologist would try to help a person with a history of compulsive gambling?
    a. ergonomist
    b. psychometrician
    c. clinical psychologist
    d. school psychologist
    e. environmental psychologist

Correct _____ If wrong, why? _____

8. Dr. Psyche has an M.D. degree and his specialty is helping people with emotional problems. He sometimes prescribes drugs for his patients. He is a:
    a. clinical psychologist
    b. psychiatrist
    c. psychoanalyst
    d. experimental psychologist

Correct _____ If wrong, why? _____

9. Women constitute:
    a. 11.4% of all psychologists
    b. just over 80% of all graduate students in psychology
    c. over 50% of all graduate students in psychology
    d. less than 30% of all psychologists, and the number is declining

Correct _____ If wrong, why? _____

10. Dr. Bates uses a large number of tests in order to assess children's abilities. Her approach is:
    a. social
    b. biological
    c. behavioral
    d. quantitative

Correct _____ If wrong, why? _____

11. What does a biopsychologist study?
    a. the influence of the nervous system, drugs, genetics, and evolutionary pressure on behavior
    b. thinking and acquiring knowledge
    c. whether or not tests measure what they are supposed to
    d. the influence of consequences on behavior

Correct _____ If wrong, why? _____

12. A psychologist taking which approach would argue that "people differ from one another because some of them know more than others about a particular topic"?
    a. social
    b. clinical
    c. behavioral neuroscientist
    d. cognitive

Correct _____ If wrong, why? _____

13. A child's parents constantly tell him that he is dumb. He does poorly in school. To what would the social approach attribute the child's failure?
    a. the child is living up to (or down to) the expectations of his parents
    b. the child's conflicts with his parents make him perform poorly
    c. the child has been rewarded for failure in the past
    d. the child has some subtle damage in a specific part of the brain

Correct _____ If wrong, why? _____

14. A quantitative psychologist has given Timmy a test and found that his IQ is much lower than normal. Does this mean that Timmy does poorly in school because of his low IQ?
    a. yes, low IQs cause poor school performance
    b. yes, low IQs predict poor school performance
    c. no, poor school performance actually causes low IQs because children who don't study in school do poorly on IQ tests
    d. no, there must be a reason for both the low IQ and the poor school performance; tests don't explain poor performance

Correct _____ If wrong, why? _____

**Psychology Then and Now**

15. Wundt's main question was:
    a. what are the components of experience?
    b. can questions about mind be answered philosophically?
    c. how does the mind produce useful behavior?
    d. how do the consequences of behavior strengthen behavior?
    e. why do some men become eminent?

Correct _____ If wrong, why? _____

16. How did Darwin's theory affect psychology?
    a. his work showed Hull that mathematical equations could be used to describe learning
    b. his finding that physical stimuli and perceived stimuli are not directly proportional began the study of psychophysics
    c. his work implied that animals have intelligence, and comparative psychologists began to study it
    d. his work showed that it was easy to measure animal intelligence
    e. women were finally allowed to earn Ph.D. degrees because of his theory

Correct _____ If wrong, why? _____

## ANSWERS AND EXPLANATIONS FOR COMPREHENSION CHECK

First, cover the Other Alternatives section and write the correct answer beneath each question. If you are correct, great! If not, write why you think your answer is wrong in the blank below the question. The page where the topic is covered is given. Look at your book to see why you were wrong. Finally, look at the explanation given below and see how correct you were. You might also want to look at why the other answers are wrong to further your understanding. The Objective (pp. 1-2) related to each question is also given.

<u>Correct Answer</u>                 <u>Other Alternatives Are Wrong Because:</u>

1. e (p. 4)                    a. not necessarily; look for good evidence
    Obj. I                     b. no, just ask how the conclusions were drawn
                               c. such phrases are often not true
                               d. absolute certainty is fairly rare, even among professors

2. d (p. 6)                    a. unconscious thought is studied too, especially by psychoanalysts
    Obj. II                    b. animals are studied, especially by biological psychologists
                               b. animals are studied, especially by biological psychologists
                               c. normal behavior is studied too, e.g., do people have several kinds of memory
                               e. psychologists try to understand why people act as they do, not to develop techniques for tricking them

3. c (pp. 6-7)       a. if enough could be known, choices would be predictable
   Obj. II-A         b. many small causes may result in complex effects that seem
                        unpredictable
                     d. causes are not random; they are orderly and can be known
                     e. determinism says that human behavior results from predictable
                        causes

4. a (pp. 7-8)       b. events appear unpredictable because they result from many
   Obj. II-A            small causes
                     c. all natural events result from many small causes
                     d. many small influences affect outcomes
                     e. this is the free-will position, not chaos theory

5. b (pp. 8-9, Fig. 1.2)   a,c,d,e.  wrong because research cannot resolve the mind-brain
   Obj. II-B                            problem

6. a (pp. 9-10)      b. asks whether apparently unpredictable events result from many
   Obj. II-C            small causes
                     c. asks whether behavior has identifiable causes
                     d. studies the relationship between mind and brain

7. c (p. 10, Table 1.2, p. 12)   a. redesigns machines to make them easier to use
   Obj. III-A-1                  b. measures intelligence, personality, and interests
                                 d. works with children with academic difficulties
                                 e. studies the influence of environmental conditions on behavior

8. b (p. 11, Table 1.1)   a. an M.D. is needed to prescribe drugs; a clinical psychologist
   Obj. III-A-2               has a Ph.D.
                          c. no indication that he trained at a psychoanalytic institute
                          d. experimental psychologists don't help people with emotional
                             problems; they study perception, learning, memory, and thinking

9. c (pp. 13-14)     a. only 11.4% of the doctorates in clinical psychology are
   Obj. III-C           awarded to ethnic minorities
                     b. just over 50% of graduate students are women
                     d. over 50% with the percentage increasing

10. d (p. 14,        a. the emphasis here is on tests, not on the influence of others
    Table 1.3, p. 15)   b. she isn't explicitly studying the brain
    Obj. IV-A        c. usually don't rely on tests; they observe behavior

11. a (pp. 14-16, Table 1.3)   b. cognitive psychologist
    Obj. IV-B                  c. quantitative psychologist
                               d. behavioral psychologist

12. d (pp. 16-17)    a. would emphasize influence of others, not knowledge
    Obj. IV-D        b. emphasizes emotional influences, not knowledge
                     c. would emphasize biological influences, not knowledge

13. a  (p. 17)
    Obj. IV-E

b. a clinical psychologist's explanation in terms of emotions

c. a behaviorist explanation in terms of consequences

d. this is a biological explanation

14. d  (p. 14)
    Obj. IV-A-1

a. tests don't explain poor performance

b. tests predict performance, but performance isn't low because of the test score

c. a third factor may cause both poor performance and low test scores, but it's not necessarily studying

15. a  (pp. 20-21)
    Obj. V-A-1

b. asked by philosophers prior to Wundt; Wundt tried to answer the questions experimentally

c. asked by the functionalist, William James

d. asked by the behaviorists

e. asked by Francis Galton

16. c  (pp. 23-24)
    Obj. V-E

a. Darwin influenced Hull's use of animals, but not Hull's use of mathematics

b. Darwin didn't study sensations

d. later psychologists tired to do this but not very successfully

e. Darwin's theory did not help to improve the lot of women in psychology

## LECTURE MATERIAL

Write a brief outline of the topics that your instructor covered in lecture. Be sure that you understand each topic; if not, ask your instructor or your teaching assistant to explain it to you. Be sure to process your lecture notes meaningfully. Write comments directly on your notes. Then write questions over the major concepts.

-----------------------------------------------------------------------------------------------------

WAIT AT LEAST 24 HOURS BEFORE PROCEEDING.
LET FORGETTING OCCUR--IT WILL!!

-----------------------------------------------------------------------------------------------------

## SHORT-ANSWER ESSAY QUESTIONS

Write brief answers to each of the following. The answers are on pp. 9-10, but do try to write the answers yourself before looking at them.

### Goals of Psychologists

1. The theme of this book is "Ask for the evidence." What does this mean?

2. Explain how chaos theory can explain apparently unpredictable events.

3. Research studies cannot solve the mind-brain problem, but they can shed light on it. How?

4. Some psychological disorders are more common in large cities than in the country. Describe how the nature and the nurture viewpoints might explain this.

5. Your friend says that all psychologists are shrinks (which he explains means psychiatrists) and they all psychoanalyze you. Explain why he is wrong.

6. How do biopsychologists and cognitive psychologists differ?

7. Describe how the acceptance of women in psychology has changed from the 1890s to today.

8. Describe the types of settings in which psychologists work.

9. Quantitative psychologists use tests to measure individual differences. However, those tests do not explain, they only measure. Explain why.

10. How does the behavioral approach differ from the approach taken by social psychologists?

**Psychology Then and Now**

11. Describe the approach taken by most psychologists from about 1920 to 1970.

12. Why did early psychologists study sensation?

*******************************************************************************
Find the questions that you wrote over lecture material and write answers to them.
*******************************************************************************

## ANSWERS TO SHORT-ANSWER ESSAY QUESTIONS

1. Don't accept conclusions unless you understand how and why someone came to the conclusion. Draw your own conclusions based on evidence. (p. 4)

2. Many tiny influences can result in very different patterns of responses. Each small event has a cause and may such small events can add up to very different outcomes. So, as indicated in the text, each bounce of a golf ball is caused by physical principles but the final location of the ball appears unpredictable because we can't identify the small influences for each bounce. (pp. 7-8)

3. Researchers can look for links between behavior and brain activity. For example, studies using PET scans show that different tasks result in different types of behavior. This puts constraints on how philosophers should think about the mind-body problem. (pp. 8-9)

4. *Nature:* People have a genetic predisposition to the psychological disorder. As the disorder worsens, they move to the big city to find a job and use the welfare services.
   *Nurture*: Life in crowded, impersonal cities causes the psychological disorder. (pp. 9-10)

5. Psychologists with Ph.D. degrees may concentrate in many different areas. One type of psychologist, a clinical psychologist, usually works with people who have emotional problems. Psychiatrists have M.D. degrees, but they are only psychoanalysts if they complete specialized training at an institute of psychoanalysis. Relatively few clinical psychologists and psychiatrists are psychoanalysts. (pp. 10-12)

6. The biological psychologist looks for relationships between the nervous system and other biological systems and behavior. The cognitive psychologist studies the specific thought processes and knowledge necessary to perform various tasks. (pp. 14-17)

7. In 1895, Mary Calkins completed her graduate work at Harvard University, but they would not grant a Ph.D. to a woman. Today, over 50% of the graduate students in psychology are women. (pp. 13, 25)

8. The largest percentage (about 40%) of psychologists work in settings that provide health care, such as hospitals, clinics, and independent private practices. A little over 33% work in academic institutions, including colleges, universities, and medical schools. Others work in a variety of settings: businesses, government, schools, and counseling centers. (p. 13, Fig. 1.4)

9. Children may score poorly on tests and perform poorly in school for many different reasons. The test scores predict that the children will do poorly in school, but they say nothing about why. (p. 14)

10. The behaviorist is interested in studying observable behavior. Behavior occurs because of its consequences in a given situation. The social psychologist stresses the role of others in influencing behavior. Social norms and expectations are important. (pp. 16-17)

11. Behaviorism was the dominant school of psychology. The idea was that observable behavior, rather than elements of mind, should be studied. The main research question was: What do people and other animals do under various conditions. (pp. 26-27)

12. The philosophical reason was that they wanted to understand mental experience, and experience is primarily composed of sensations. The strategic reason was that they wanted to create a scientific psychology, and they began with questions that could be answered. (p. 23)

## POSTTEST

Take this test with all of your books and notes out of sight. This should give you a good idea of how well you understand the material. The answers are on pp. 13-14.

### Matching

Put the letter of the approach on the right in the blank beside the description on the left.

1. _____ studies how people think and acquire knowledge

2. _____ gives tests to measure individual differences; determines validity of tests

3. _____ looks for relationships between factors that affect body functioning and behavior

4. _____ looks for emotional reasons for behavior

5. _____ emphasizes the effects that other people have on an individual's behavior

6. _____ stresses consequences of behavior

A. cognitive

B. biological

C. clinical

D. behaviorist

E. quantitative

F. social

**Multiple-Choice**

Circle the best alternative.

Goals of Psychologists

1. Psychology is best defined as the study of:
   a. abnormality
   b. social influences
   c. consciousness
   d. human behavior
   e. behavior and experience

2. Popular claims about psychology that begin with "They say..." are:
   a. usually valid
   b. almost always wrong
   c. best evaluated based on evidence
   d. always so nonsensical that we can't even evaluate their truth
   e. partly valid under most circumstances

3. Prof. R is engaged in a debate with Prof. S.  Prof. R argues that people are free to make choices and that their choices are unpredictable.  Prof. S argues that choices are made because of past experience and that each choice could be predicted if we knew enough.  Prof. R's arguments support
   _____ and Prof. S's arguments support _____.
   a. free will; determinism
   b. mind controls brain; brain controls mind
   c. determinism; free will
   d. brain controls mind; mind controls brain
   e. nurture; nature

4. Boys generally spend more time playing with toy guns and trucks than girls do.  Which of the following reasons for this is consistent with the nature point of view?
   a. boys watch more violent television shows than girls do
   b. boys like to do what their fathers do and many fathers use guns and trucks
   c. boys have genes that make them prefer such toys
   d. society discourages girls from playing with such toys
   e. boys are given such toys so they have more opportunities to play with them

5. African Americans, Hispanics, Asian Americans, and other minorities constitute about:
   a. 11% of all doctorates awarded in clinical psychology
   b. 50% of all psychologists
   c. 25% of all clinical psychologists; 50% of all others
   d. 50% of all doctorates awarded in clinical psychology
   e. 5% of all psychologists today, but the percentage is declining

6. A clinical psychologist is:
   a. the same as a psychiatrist
   b. the same as a psychoanalyst
   c. any psychologist with a Ph.D.
   d. a psychologist who helps people with emotional problems
   e. any psychologist who administers and interprets tests

7. A psychoanalyst:
   a. is the same as a clinical psychologist
   b. is the same as a psychiatrist
   c. adheres to Freud's methods and theories
   d. has fewer years of formal training than a clinical psychologist
   e. always hold the Ph.D. degree

8. How is a psychologist different from a psychiatrist?
   a. there is no difference
   b. psychiatrists deal with helping people; psychologists do research in universities
   c. psychiatrists have M.D. degrees; psychologists have Ph.D. degrees
   d. psychologists use methods developed by Freud; psychiatrists do not
   e. psychologists can prescribe drugs; psychiatrists cannot

9. A child scores poorly on an IQ test, and his parent is told that he is doing poorly in school because of this. Which of the following is true about this conclusion?
   a. this is correct; poor IQ scores predict poor school performance
   b. the test says nothing about why the child performs poorly
   c. it is wrong; IQ scores and school performance are unrelated
   d. measuring individual differences is essentially the same thing as explaining them, so the conclusion is appropriate

10. Which type of psychologist would be most interested in the genetic makeup of an individual?
    a. cognitive
    b. behaviorist
    c. biological
    d. psychoanalytic
    e. clinical

11. A child is constantly in trouble at school for disrupting the class. How would a behaviorist view this situation?
    a. there is conflict in the child's home, and he unconsciously wants to hurt his parents
    b. the child may have damage to a specific part of his brain
    c. the child's diet is lacking in essential minerals and vitamins
    d. the child only receives attention (which is reinforcing) when he is disruptive
    e. other students expect the child to be disruptive, so he is

12. A psychologist believes that differences between males and females are due to society's expectations about how boys and girls behave. This psychologist takes which viewpoint?
    a. social
    b. cognitive
    c. physiological
    d. clinical
    e. behaviorist

13. Which of the following is true about the approaches of psychology?
    a. they are distinct, and each psychologist takes only one
    b. all study the same phenomena; they just come up with different explanations
    c. the approaches listed in the text include all possible approaches
    d. psychologists who take different approaches often study different aspects of behavior

Psychology Then and Now

14. What was Wundt's most lasting impact on psychology?
    a. his discovery that it takes time to shift attention
    b. he set the precedent for studying psychological questions with scientific data
    c. he correctly described the elements of mind
    d. he made self-observation into an exact science
    e. he mapped out the psychophysical functions relating psychology to physical stimuli

15. Mary Calkins, the first woman psychologist:
    a. received her Ph.D. degree from Harvard
    b. was never allowed to attend graduate classes
    c. performed poorly on her final examination for the Ph.D., so she never received her Ph.D.
    d. never received her Ph.D. because Harvard would not grant a Ph.D. to a woman
    e. completed a Ph.D. at Harvard, but was unable to find a job because she was a woman

16. How does the psychology advocated by the behaviorists differ from the psychology advocated by the structuralists?
    a. the behaviorists were more interested in sensation than the structuralists
    b. the behaviorists emphasized the study of animal intelligence, and the structuralists developed a psychology of human intelligence
    c. the behaviorists developed mathematical models of intelligence, and the structuralists developed nonmathematical models
    d. behaviorists emphasized learning, and the structuralists emphasized sensation

## ANSWERS TO POSTTEST

| Correct Answer | Questions Testing a Similar Concept | |
| --- | --- | --- |
| | Comprehension Check | Short-Answer |

**Matching**

(See Table 1.3, p. 15 for all)

| | | |
| --- | --- | --- |
| 1. A  (pp. 16-17) | 12 | 6 |
| 2. E  (p. 14) | 10,14 | 9 |
| 3. B  (pp. 14-16) | 10b,11 | 6 |
| 4. C  (p. 17) | 7c,8a,12b | 5 |
| 5. F  (p. 17) | 10a,12a,13 | 10 |
| 6. D  (p. 16) | 10c, 11d, 13c | 10 |

**Multiple-Choice**

| | | |
|---|---|---|
| 1. e (p. 6) | 2 | -- |
| 2. c (p. 4) | 1 | 1 |
| 3. a (pp. 6-8) | 3,4 | 2 |
| 4. c (pp. 9-10) | 6 | 4 |
| 5. a (pp. 13-14) | 9a | -- |
| 6. d (pp. 10-11, Table 1.1) | 7,8a,12b,13b | 5 |
| 7. c (p. 11) | 8c | 5 |
| 8. c (pp. 10-11, Table 1.1) | 7c,8 | 5 |
| 9. b (p. 14) | 14 | 9 |
| 10. c (pp. 14-16, Table 1.3) | 10b,11,12c,13d | 6 |
| 11. d (p. 16) | 10c,11d,13c | 10 |
| 12. a (p. 17) | 10a,12a,13 | 10 |
| 13. d (pp. 17-18) | -- | -- |
| 14. b (pp. 20-21) | 15 | -- |
| 15. d (p. 25) | -- | 7 |
| 16. d (pp. 21-22, 25-27) | 10c,11d,13c | 10,11,12 |

# CHAPTER 1 LANGUAGE ENHANCEMENT GUIDE

## I. VOCABULARY, IDIOMS AND CULTURAL CONCEPTS

### Instructions

As you read the text refer to the following list of words and their definitions. The words are listed in the order in which they appear in the chapter. The definitions presented contain the meaning of the word as used by Kalat on the textbook page indicated.

Remember that these words like all words can have different meanings in other sentences. If you do not find a non-technical word on this list it may have been defined on a previous page or chapter of this study guide. The definition of non-technical words may be found in Appendix A at the end of this study guide. Kalat defined each new technical word as it first appears on a page and these may be found in Kalat's summary at the end of the section and in the Glossary at the end the textbook.

### The Goals of Psychologists

suppose (6) = think; believe
accomplish = do; achieve
tips (had any tips) = suggestions
seduction = get sexual favors
devote = to give or apply time and effort to a specific activity
techniques = methods
manipulate = to manage; to control to one's own advantage; to exploit, maneuver or trick.
Renaissance = the start of the modern development of art, science and literature that originated in Italy in the 14th century and later spread throughout Europe
derives its roots = beginning, origin
Scientific Revolution = a major growth in science that started during the Renaissance
profound = very serious; far-reaching; thoughtful
phenomena = observable events

analyze (7) = to break down something into its parts
assumption = a belief without supporting evidence
accomplish = to succeed in doing, to complete
the point of = the main goal or idea
is a product = is the result of
merely(mere) = nothing more than
vague = unclear; a word or statement with several meanings and the intended meaning is unknown
way beyond reach = cannot be studied
natural sciences = science like physics, biology, psychology
ultimately = the end result; finally
empirical = relying on or based on observation or experiment
suppose = briefly think something is true or real
hazardous = dangers to life or health
in its extreme form =
you are on your way =
impaired = to lose ability, strength, value, or quality
hearing-impaired = unable to hear sound
eventually (8) = occurring at an unspecified time in the future
discrepancy = distance or differences between objects; can also refer to differences or deviations
 between claims, ideas theories, etc.
cumulative = increasing, growing or getting bigger by getting things added
concede = yield; acknowledge; admit
would support = provide evidence for
concept = idea
not refute = not reject; not disprove; not prove false
conceivable = imaginable; thinkable

conceive (conceivable) = to form an idea in the mind
nonphysical entity
physical = refers to the body as distinguished from the mind or spirit.
entity = something that exists, such as an object or people.
philosophical issue =
philosophy = love and pursuit of wisdom by intellectual means and moral self discipline; a system of
 inquiry; Inquiry into the nature of things based on logical reasoning rather than empirical methods.
tomography see the surrounding text

they would submit (9) = they would suggest
we are far from understanding = we are just beginning to understand
get along without it = do without it
are not about to resolve = solve
constrain = to limit; hold back
seriously entertain = think about
ultimate = the last in a series or process; the final point, a fundamental fact, solution or principle

abuse (10) = to misuse and cause illness or injury to one's self or others
less prevalent = not accepted or practiced by many people
genetic differences = difference due to heredity
genes = thousands of hereditary units located in every cell of the body that determines each characteristic
 in an organism.

predisposition = likely to be influenced; habit, tendency, inclination, or susceptibility

the relative contribution of heredity = the amount given by heredity

the whole enterprise of psychology = all of psychology

distinguish = to see or show how things are different

branch of medicine (11) = a sub field or area of specialization in medicine

client = a person who seeks the help of or uses the professional services of a doctor, clinical psychologist, or lawyer, etc.

overmedicated = the use of drugs even when not needed

explicit = fully and clearly expressed; specific


health provider settings (13) = places like hospitals and medical clinics

independent practice = psychologists who are self-employed

constitute = to be a part of

recruit = to supply or find new members or employees


quantity (quantitative) (14) = ;refers to the numerical amounts of something on a scale of measurement or a frequency count. For example weight, age, IQ score, number of dreams per night, number of miles per gallon, etc.

quality (qualitative ) = A characteristic of an object event or person. For example, gender(male, female), marital status(married, single, divorced), etc.

neuroscience = branch of biology that studies the brain and the nervous system


ruptured (15 )= broken or open

prolonged malnutrition = not eating enough food for many days or weeks

toxic = poison that can cause injury or death

enormously = a very large amount


alter behavior (16) = change behavior

amphetamine = a drug used to stimulant the brain

nutritional deficiencies = not enough food or vitamins

consequences = the results or effects of a behavior

disruptive behavior = behavior that causes confusion or disorder

giggle = repeated short laughs

distinction = difference

moreover = in addition


in short (17) = in summary; briefly

acquire = to get

expectation = to look forward to something; anticipate

subsequently = following in time or order; succeeding

emerge = to come into existence

willing to admit to themselves = to tell themselves

stratagem = method

oversimplified = made too easy

constitutes one way of = is one of many methods

**Psychology Then and Now**

enthusiastic (20)= showing a lot of excitement or interest in a subject or cause

will you address = will you study

what constitutes a good question = what are the characteristics of a good question

novelist = a person who writes books with long fictional imagined stories

profound = very deep, thoughtful and wise

fruitful = very productive

great strides = much progress

components = parts or elements of something

compound = to produce or create by combining two or more ingredients or parts, something that is made of two or more parts

musings (21) = thinking

demonstrate = to show

prolific = very productive; doing a lot of work

shrug = to raise the shoulders as a gesture of doubt

simultaneously (22) = at the same time

introspective = thinking about and reporting one's own experience

vertebrate (23) = animal with a back bone like dogs, cats and monkeys

presuming = assuming; accepting

implication = interpretation, suggestion, effects, consequences

compare (comparative) (24) = to study and show differences and similarities between things

eminent = outstanding; famous; distinguished

fascinated = showing great interest in something

substantial period = a long time

era (27) = a period of time characterized by a major event or person

deal with = covers; presents

postbehaviorist = the period of time after behaviorism when it was no longer a ruling point of view

broadened their scope = enlarged to include more topics to study

dominance = having the most influence or control

find out what = to learn or discover

in short = in summary; briefly

fascinating = very interesting

in practical consequences = useful in daily life

## II. VOCABULARY BUILDING

### Prefixes, Suffixes, and Roots

Many words in the English language are made up of separate parts that have been borrowed from many other languages such as Latin, Greek, Spanish, German, French, etc. The process of breaking up something to study its parts and the relationship among the parts is called **analysis**. When you can analyze a word and you know the meaning of each part, you can then determine the possible meanings of the word. When you combine the possible meanings of a word with the way the word is used in the sentence, you can often determine the author's meaning. Each part of the word is given a name. The part of the word that you read first is called the **prefix**. The part that is at the end of the word is called the **suffix**. Word that can stand alone with prefixes or suffixes attached to them are called **roots**.

For example, the word psychology has two parts- "psych" and "ology." Words that begin with the prefix *psyche* have to do with the "soul" and "mind." The suffix *ology* comes from the Greek word "logos" that means "study" or "word." When you combine the prefix and suffix, the word can be translated to mean the study of the mind. This meaning comes close to Kalat's definition of psychology. Kalat defines psychology as, "the systematic study of behavior and experience." Kalat used the term experience to refer to activities of the mind such as thinking, feeling, and remembering, etc.

## Why Must Word Structure and Context be Combined?

Did you notice with the word psychology that when you figure out the meaning of a word based on the prefix and suffix you only come close to the meaning that the author intends? For many words knowing the prefix and suffix is not enough. You must also know how the word is used in the sentence and how the sentence fits into the paragraph. However, knowing how to break up words into their parts can help you determine as well as help you remember their meaning. Examine the next box for another example of how knowledge of prefixes and suffixes can help you determine the meaning of words.

| Suffix | Meaning |
|--------|---------|
| ologist | one who studies |
| ological | the adjective form of ology |

psychologist = one who studies psychology
psychological research = research that focuses on topics that make up psychology.

There are a number of sciences that are related to psychology that Kalat will talk about in the text. Here are the prefixes and suffixes for each of these sciences.

| Prefix | Meaning |
|--------|---------|
| Anthro | human, refers to human cultures and societies |
| Socio | society, refers to culture and society |
| Bio | life, refers to the anatomy and physiology of living things |

Now you provide a definition for each term.

| Word | Meaning |
|------|---------|
| Anthropology | |
| Sociology | |
| Biology | |

### Word Analysis

In each chapter you will be given a list of roots, prefixes and suffixes and their definitions to learn. Then you will be asked to analyze words made up from them to determine their meanings . The words will be selected from the text book and from words that a college educated person is expected to know. You will find that memorizing these roots, prefixes and suffixes and using them to figure out the meaning of words will help you increase your reading vocabulary, speed up your reading rate and improve your understanding of the text book. Here is an example.

## Instructions

1. Study the meaning of the prefixes, roots and suffixes listed below.
2. Break each word in the table into its prefixes, suffixes and roots.
3. Guess the meaning of the word based on the meaning of its parts.
4. Find the word on the text page indicated in the brackets and redefine the word based on the context of the sentence, paragraph and chapter.
5. Look up the definition of the word in the VOCABULARY, IDIOMS AND CULTURAL CONCEPTS section above or in a college level dictionary.

Study the following list of common roots and suffixes and then write in the meaning of the words below. Remember to consider the content of the chapter.

## Exercise 1. Humanism

**Suffix _____ism = belief / practice / doctrine / theory / system**

| Word | Meaning |
|------|---------|
| Human | An organism that has the characteristic of human beings. |
| Behavior | The observable measurable actions or reactions of organisms. |
| Function | The duty, activity, purpose or role of something. |
| Structure | The way in which parts are arranged or put together to form something |

Compare your answers for the following terms with Kalat's definition on text pages 28 to 29

| Word | Meaning |
|------|---------|
| Humanism | |
| Behaviorism | |
| Functionalism | |
| Structuralism | |

## Exercise 2. Humanistic

**Suffix _____ic = characteristic / having to do with**

| Root | Meaning |
|------|---------|
| bio | life |
| alcohol | alcoholic beverages or chemicals |
| ideal | The idea of something in its perfect. A worthy principle or goal. |
| real | Occurring in fact or actuality. Genuine and authentic; not artificial |

| Word | Meaning |
|------|---------|
| biotic | |
| alcoholic | |
| idealistic | |
| realistic | |
| Humanistic | |
| Behavioristic | |
| alcoholism | |
| racism | |

# CHAPTER 2  SCIENTIFIC METHODS IN PSYCHOLOGY

## OBJECTIVES
Understand that:

### Science and the Evaluation of Evidence

I. Scientists generally agree on how to evaluate competing theories  (p. 33)
   A. There are ordered steps for gathering evidence  (pp. 33-34, Fig. 2.1)
      1. Making a hypothesis  (p. 34)
      2. Devising a method to test the hypothesis  (p. 34)
      3. Measuring the results  (p. 34)
      4. Interpreting the results  (p. 34)
   B. Experiments should be replicable  (pp. 34-35)
   C. The goal of research is to establish theories  (p. 35)
      1. Theories should fit known facts, make new predictions, and be
         falsifiable  (p. 35)
   D. Theories should be parsimonious  (pp. 36-37)
      1. A parsimonious explanation for Clever Hans' arithmetic skills that he watched his trainer and
         received cues  (pp. 37-38)
      2. There is no scientific evidence for extrasensory perception   (pp. 38-39)
         a. Evidence is often based on anecdotes  (p. 39)
         b. Psychic stage performers use tricks and illusions  (pp. 39-40)
         c. Experiments have produced mixed results and positive results may not be replicable
            (pp. 40-41)

### Methods of Investigation in Psychology

II. Research follows some general principles  (p. 43)
   A. Variables should be operationally defined  (pp. 43-44)
   B. Samples should be representative and random  (pp. 44-45)
      1. Cross-cultural studies pose special sampling problems  (p. 45)
   C. Observers and subjects should be "blind"  (pp. 45-46, Table 2.1)
III. There are many different types of research designs  (p. 46, Table 2.2, p. 47)
   A. Naturalistic observation involves careful observation under natural conditions  (p. 46)
   B. Case histories involve detailed studies of an individual  (pp. 46-48)
   C. Surveys involve giving questionnaires to samples of individuals  (p. 48)
      1. People may express opinions even if they know little about a topic  (p. 48)
      2. Results depend upon how a question is asked  (p. 48)
      3. The surveyor may intentionally bias the questions to get a desired answer  (p. 49)
   D. A correlational study examines the relationship between two variables, without manipulating them
      (p. 49)
      1. Correlation coefficients are statistical measures of the relationship that range from -1 to +1
         (pp. 49-50, Fig. 2.12, p. 51)
      2. Correlations observed in everyday life may be illusory  (pp. 50-51)
      3. Correlation does not imply that one variable causes the other  (pp. 51-52, Fig. 2.13)
   E. The investigator manipulates variables in experiments  (p. 52)
      1. Independent variables are manipulated and dependent variables are measures of behavior
         (p. 52, Fig. 2.14)

2. Experimental groups receive the treatment and control groups do not (p. 53, Fig. 2.15)
      3. Subjects are randomly assigned to groups (pp. 53-54)
  F. An example of an experiment is an investigation of the effects of televised violence on aggressive behavior (pp. 54-55)
      1. Adolescent boys were randomly assigned to watch violent films or not (p. 54)
      2. Boys who watched violent films were more aggressive than those who didn't (p. 54)
IV. Experiments sometimes go wrong (p. 55)
  A. Demand characteristics may produce self-fulfilling prophecies (pp. 55-56)
      1. Double-blind studies can reduce these (p. 56)
  B. Experimenter bias may result in distorted procedures or results (p. 56)
  C. Selective attrition can affect conclusions (p. 56)
V. Generalization of results to other people or circumstances may not always be possible (p. 57)
VI. Some experiments raise ethical issues (pp. 57-58)
  A. Participants in research should give informed consent (p. 58)
  B. Research with nonhuman animals raises special ethical issues (pp. 58-59)

**Measuring and Reporting Results**

VII. Descriptive statistics are mathematical summaries of results (pp. 62-63, Fig. 2.20)
  A. There are several measures of the central score (p. 63)
      1. Mean is the arithmetic average (p. 63)
      2. Median is the middle score in a set of ordered scores (p. 63)
      3. Mode is the most common score (p. 63)
  B. Measures of variation refer to the spread of the scores (p. 64)
      1. Range is the distance from the top to the bottom score (p. 64)
      2. Standard deviation measures the distance of scores from the mean (p. 64, Fig. 2.22)
VIII. Inferential statistics show whether results are statistically significant (p. 65, Fig. 2.24, p. 67)
  A. If a result is statistically significant, it probably did not occur by chance (p. 66)
      1. $p$ values indicate how often results would occur by chance (p. 66)
      2. The lower the $p$ value, the more convincing the results (p. 66)

## COMPREHENSION CHECK

Answer these questions soon after reading the chapter. Circle the best alternative. Check your answers on pp. 25-27. If you gave a wrong answer, try to write why it was wrong. Check your reasons on pp. 25-27.

**Science and the Evaluation of Evidence**

1. Which of the following is not an appropriate order for steps involved in gathering and evaluating evidence?
  a. gather the data, then make up a hypothesis
  b. make up a hypothesis, then devise an appropriate method
  c. interpret the results, then try to replicate them
  d. gather the data, then think of alternative explanations

Correct _____ If wrong, why? _____

2. If a result is replicable, it:
    a. may be found by a few investigators, but many investigators cannot get the same results
    b. is not falsifiable
    c. is interpreted so that everyone agrees with the interpretation
    d. can be found by anyone who repeats the same procedures

Correct _____ If wrong, why? _____

3. What are the criteria for good scientific theories?
    a. predict new discoveries and be vague
    b. not falsifiable, but parsimonious
    c. be stated so that all types of evidence would fit
    d. make accurate predictions and be parsimonious
    e. change a few simple facts into complex ones and fit known facts

Correct _____ If wrong, why? _____

4. Clever Hans was actually:
    a. able to add and subtract but not multiply or divide
    b. able to do simple arithmetic of all types and was also able to identify musical notes
    c. able to respond to subtle cues given by the examiner
    d. better at answering questions when the examiner was out of sight

Correct _____ If wrong, why? _____

5. Anecdotes are not good scientific evidence for ESP because they:
    a. usually involve prediction before the event
    b. show that accurate predictions could not be coincidental
    c. produce accurate predictions when the predictions were very specific and precise
    d. usually involve selective memory; people remember when predictions come true but not when they don't

Correct _____ If wrong, why? _____

**Methods of Investigation in Psychology**

6. Which of the following is the best operational definition of aggression?
    a. the number of times one person strikes another person during a 30-minute period
    b. how much physical force and verbal abuse is contained in a 30-minute period
    c. how much violence there is
    d. assaultive, offensive, and combative behavior

Correct _____ If wrong, why? _____

7. If a researcher conducts a survey of all the customers at an expensive restaurant, she has:
   a. selected a representative sample of the entire population
   b. used a random sample of the entire population
   c. conducted a cross-cultural study
   d. conducted single-blind study
   e. conducted study that will have limited generalizability

Correct _____ If wrong, why? _____

8. A news columnist asked readers to write in and indicate the importance of sex in their marriages. The responses were tallied and published. The columnist conducted:
   a. a correlational study
   b. an experiment
   c. a case history
   d. a survey

Correct _____ If wrong, why? _____

9. A researcher found that grade-point averages of college students are related to their family incomes. High GPAs generally go with higher incomes and low GPAs go with lower incomes. This study is:
   a. an example of an illusory correlation
   b. an experiment
   c. a correlational study
   d. a double-blind study

Correct _____ If wrong, why? _____

10. Generally the weight of clothing that people wear goes down as the outdoor temperature goes up. This relationship would produce a:
    a. negative correlation
    b. zero correlation
    c. very high positive correlation
    d. very low positive correlation

Correct _____ If wrong, why? _____

*Questions 11 to 14 refer to the following:*
An experiment was conducted to determine whether a new approach to psychotherapy (interactive scream therapy) is effective in helping couples with marital problems. Couples who came to a clinic were randomly assigned to two groups--one group was given the new interactive scream therapy for 6 months and he other was placed on a waiting list and given no treatment. After 6 months, couples in both groups rated their marital happiness and therapists rated the adjustment of each couple.

11. What is the dependent variable?
    a. the therapy program
    b. the couples
    c. the ratings
    d. the clinic

Correct _____ If wrong, why? _____

12. What is the term for the group who received the therapy program?
    a. the experimental group
    b. the dependent variable
    c. the independent variable
    d. the control group

Correct _____ If wrong, why? _____

13. Why did the experimenter use random assignment?
    a. to be sure that the subjects in the experiment were represented in the same proportions as subjects in the population
    b. to reduce the possibility that the two groups differed in the beginning
    c. to avoid demand characteristics
    d. to avoid selective attrition

Correct _____ If wrong, why? _____

14. Instead of using random assignment, the researcher obtained ratings from couples who had signed up for and completed the new therapy and those who did not sign up. She found better adjustment in the therapy group. What type would the study be and what conclusion could be made?
    a. experiment; the improvement is caused by the therapy
    b. correlation; interactive scream therapy "cures" marital problems
    c. experiment; there is a relationship between signing up for this therapy and adjustment
    d. correlation; there is a relationship between signing up for this therapy and adjustment

Correct _____ If wrong, why? _____

15. A researcher studied the effect of drugs on learning in rats. Rats received three doses of a drug supposed to help memory. Originally there were 12 rats in each group but some rats died, so in the end there were 11 in the low-dose group, 9 in the medium-dose group, and 6 in the high-dose group. The high-dose rats learned faster. Which of the following is most likely?
    a. the rats in the high-dose group performed well because of demand characteristics
    b. selective attrition may explain why rats in the high-dose group were better (the poorer ones may have died)
    c. experimenter bias because the experimenter expected the low dose rats to perform the best
    d. the rats in the high-dose group probably had ESP and performed better
    e. the high dose acted like a placebo

Correct _____ If wrong, why? _____

16. Which of the following would be <u>unethical</u> in conducting research?
    a. an experiment uses mild shock; subjects were informed about the shock and agreed to participate
    b. an experiment involves eating disgusting things (such as cockroaches) but subjects are told they are eating shrimp
    c. an experiment uses small doses of marijuana that has been approved by the Human Subjects Committee
    d. an experiment in which behavior is manipulated

Correct _____ If wrong, why? _____

**Measuring and Reporting Results**

17. A group of scores is 5, 6, 4, 8, 1. What is the median?
    a. 4
    b. 4.8
    c. 8
    d. 5

Correct _____ If wrong, why? _____

18. The researcher finds a difference between a therapy group and a control group that is statistically significant at $p < .01$. This means:
    a. the difference would occur by chance more than 1% of the time
    b. the probability that the difference was due to therapy is 1/100
    c. the explanation that therapy helped is parsimonious
    d. the difference would occur by chance less than 1% of the time

Correct _____ If wrong, why? _____

## ANSWERS AND EXPLANATIONS FOR COMPREHENSION CHECK

| <u>Correct Answer</u> | <u>Other Alternatives Are Wrong Because</u>: |
|---|---|
| 1. a (pp. 33-34, Fig. 2.1)<br>   Obj. I-A | b-d. the question asked for orders that are not appropriate; each of these is appropriate |
| 2. d (pp. 34-35)<br>   Obj. I-B | a. this would be considered replicated because a few investigators found it, but not replicable because most did not<br>b. refers to theories, not results; theories are falsifiable if some set of observations would disconfirm them<br>c. everyone may not agree with the interpretation, even though they can replicate the results |
| 3. d (pp. 35-36)<br>   Obj. I-C-1, I-D | a. theories should be precise, not vague<br>b. they should be falsifiable<br>c. should be able to imagine evidence that would falsify the theory<br>e. parsimony suggests that simple is better; shouldn't make simple things complex |

4. c (pp. 37-38)
   Obj. I-D-1

a. he probably wasn't doing any arithmetic; c is more
   parsimonious
b. he probably couldn't do either; c is more parsimonious
d. the examiner needed to be in the horse's sight

5. d (p. 39)
   Obj. I-D-2-a

a. specific predictions are not usually made
b. coincidence can explain many apparently accurate predictions
c. predictions are usually not specific or precise

6. a (pp. 43-44)
   Obj. II-A

b. how would physical force and verbal abuse be measured?
c. how is violence measured?
d. what is meant by assaultive, offensive, combative?

7. e (pp. 44-45, 57)
   Obj. II-B

a. it may be representative of people who eat in expensive
   restaurants, but not of the population
b. everyone in the population didn't have an equal chance of being
   selected, so it is not random
c. refers to comparing people from different societies
d. not used for surveys; refers to a situation in which either the subject
   or experimenter doesn't know the participant's group

8. d (p. 48)
   Obj. III-C

a. specific relationships were not studied
b. no independent variable was manipulated
c. not an in-depth study of an individual

9. c (p. 49)
   Obj. III-D

a. the correlation is not illusory; it has been objectively observed
b. a relationship was noted, but no variables were controlled or
   manipulated by the researcher
d. we don't know whether the experimenter knew which subjects were
   from high- and low-income families; the participants probably knew

10. a (pp. 49-50,
    Fig. 2.12, p. 51)
    Obj. III-D

b. the variables are related; correlation cannot be zero
c. the variables do not increase together; one goes up and the
   other goes down
d. the relationship is pretty strong so the correlation should be high; see
   c for why it is not positive

11. c (p. 52)
    Obj. III-E-1

a. the researcher controls the therapy program  (gives it
   to some couples, not others), so it is the independent variable
b. the couples are the subjects or participants
d. the clinic is the site of the study, not a variable

12. a (p. 53)
    Obj. III-E-2

b. dependent variable is the measure of behavior, not a group
c. the therapy group is one level of the independent variable, not the
   independent variable itself
d. control group is the one that is not treated, i.e., the no-therapy group

13. b (pp. 53-54)  
    Obj. III-E-3

    a. this is a representative sample; random assignment refers to placing the sample into groups  
    c. demand characteristics could still be a problem if participants know they're supposed to improve  
    d. selective attrition could still occur if more are lost from one group than the other

14. d (pp. 51-52)  
    Obj. III-D,E

    a. not an experiment because who got the therapy was not controlled by the experimenter; people who sign up for therapy may be different from people who don't  
    b. correlational, but you cannot be sure that therapy is the only difference between the groups; the group who signed up may already be better adjusted or they may be more motivated  
    c. not an experiment because the groups already existed; experimenter did not randomly assign couples to therapy

15. b (p. 56)  
    Obj. IV-C

    a. unlikely that the rats knew the experimenter's expectations, but it is possible  
    c. experimenter bias makes results come out as the experimenter expects, not in the opposite direction  
    d. not a very parsimonious explanation  
    e. a placebo is an inert drug; the drug here probably had physiological effects

16. b (p. 58)  
    Obj. VI-A

    a. informed consent was obtained  
    c. the committee has judged that the specific procedures are ethical  
    d. all experiments attempt to manipulate behavior, but such manipulation is usually short-lived

17. d (p. 63)  
    Obj. VII-A-2

    a. scores must be rank ordered first, then the middle score is the median  
    b. this is the average or mean  
    c. highest score or top of the range

18. d (p. 66)  
    Obj. VIII-A-1

    a. < means less than 1%--it's a rare event  
    b. probability that difference is due to <u>chance</u> is less than 1/100  
    c. statistical significance is unrelated to parsimony; a difference could be significant and the explanation still might not be the simplest

## LECTURE MATERIAL

Don't forget to review your lecture material. Process each topic meaningfully. First, be sure that you understand the material in each lecture--if you don't, ask your instructor or teaching assistant. Associate the material with things that you already know and with your personal experiences. If you can make up mental images of any of the material, do so. Try to think of real-life applications of the concepts. Write comments on your notes. Then write questions to cover each concept.

---------------------------------------------------------------------------

WAIT AT LEAST 24 HOURS BEFORE PROCEEDING.  
LET FORGETTING OCCUR--IT WILL!!

---------------------------------------------------------------------------

## SHORT-ANSWER ESSAY QUESTIONS

Write brief answers to each of the following. The answers are on pp. 30-31, but do try to write the answers yourself before looking at them.

### Science and the Evaluation of Evidence

1. Describe two factors that would help you decide whether a theory is a good one.

2. Explain why things like coincidence and subtle cues are more parsimonious explanations for incidents such as anticipating what your friend will say than is extrasensory perception.

3. Explain why anecdotes do not provide very strong scientific evidence.

### Methods of Investigation in Psychology

4. Explain how a survey differs from a case history.

5. A researcher found that students who enrolled in a study skills class improved their GPAs more the next term than students who did not enroll. He concluded that GPAs increased because of the study skills class. What is wrong with this conclusion?

6. Describe how you would do a good experiment to see whether study skills classes help students. Indicate the independent and dependent variables.

7. Explain how a correlational study differs from an experiment both in terms of procedures and in terms of the types of conclusions that can be drawn.

8. Explain how demand characteristics might play a role in an experiment to test two types of therapy and how you might try to minimize them.

9. Explain why experimenter bias probably did not influence the results of the study on televised violence and aggression in the "What's the Evidence?" section.

10. Why would a researcher be concerned if eight participants drop out of the experimental group in a weight-reduction program, but only one drops out of the control group?

11. Explain what is meant by informed consent in experimental participation.

**Measuring and Reporting Results**

12. Describe how you would find the means in the study skills experiment you designed and explain what a statistically significant difference at $p < .05$ would mean.

\*\*\*\*\*\*\*\*\*\*\*\*\*\*\*\*\*\*\*\*\*\*\*\*\*\*\*\*\*\*\*\*\*\*\*\*\*\*\*\*\*\*\*\*\*\*\*\*\*\*\*\*\*\*\*\*\*\*\*\*\*\*\*\*\*\*\*\*\*\*\*\*\*\*\*\*\*\*\*
Find the questions that you wrote over
lecture material and write answers to them.
\*\*\*\*\*\*\*\*\*\*\*\*\*\*\*\*\*\*\*\*\*\*\*\*\*\*\*\*\*\*\*\*\*\*\*\*\*\*\*\*\*\*\*\*\*\*\*\*\*\*\*\*\*\*\*\*\*\*\*\*\*\*\*\*\*\*\*\*\*\*\*\*\*\*\*\*\*\*\*

## ANSWERS TO SHORT-ANSWER ESSAY QUESTIONS

1. Theories should make specific predictions that can be tested in experiments that are replicable. In other words, a theory should be falsifiable. Theories should be parsimonious so that their explanations use generally accepted scientific principles. (pp. 35-37)

2. Scientists do not know how humans might receive "extrasensory" stimuli. Because there is no accepted explanation for this, it is not parsimonious. We do know that people in the same situation will have similar thoughts with some probability and that people and animals can read nonverbal cues in people. (pp. 38-39)

3. Anecdotes rely on memory, which may not be accurate; the observer may exaggerate; coincidence may be the correct explanation; people generally remember when predictions came true and not when they didn't. (p. 39)

4. A survey involves asking questions of a lot of people; a case history involves a much more detailed study of one person. The survey should use a random sample, so that everyone in the population of interest has an equal chance of being selected. A case study selects a specific person because of some interesting characteristic. (pp. 46-49)

5. The researcher conducted a correlational study. Students who signed up for the study skills class may differ from those who didn't. The increase in GPA might have been due to something other than the class; perhaps those students were more motivated to improve and would have improved without the study skills class. (p. 49)

6. Take a large group of students who are having difficulty in college. Randomly assign half of them to the study skills class. Look at the grades of both groups before the study skills class and look after the study skills class. The experimental group (who took the study skills class) should show a larger increase in grades than the control group (who did not take the class). The independent variable is whether the study skills class was taken or not; the dependent variable is the students' grades. (p. 52-53, Fig. 2.15)

7. In an experiment, the researcher randomly assigns participants to specific groups. The groups should be equal in the beginning because of the random assignment. Any difference in the end should be due to the independent variable. The researcher has control over who gets which treatment. In a correlational study, the researcher compares existing groups, which may differ in more ways than the one the researcher is interested in. Differences might be due to any of these original differences. The researcher does not control who gets which treatment. (pp. 49-52)

8. People might improve simply because they expect the therapy to work and not because the therapy itself is effective. Some sort of "placebo" therapy could be used in a control group. Participants would be led to expect that it would help, but actually it would be ineffective. If the therapists rating improvement don't know who got which therapy, the experiment would be double blind. If the participants know whether they're getting therapy or not, but the raters don't, it's a single-blind experiment. (pp. 55-56, Table 2.1, p. 46)

9. The observers who recorded aggressive behavior in the boys were "blind." That is, they did not know which boys were watching the violent films each night and which boys were not. Thus, experimenter bias did not influence the dependent variable. The study was not double-blind because the boys knew whether they had watched the violent films or not. (pp. 54-55)

10. The participants who drop out are probably the ones who are not losing weight. So, if all of those who don't lose weight drop out of the experimental group, the mean weight loss would be greater than in the control group which still contains participants who didn't lose weight. This could lead to the conclusion that the experimental treatment was better when it really is not. (p. 56)

11. Participants should know what will happen in the experiment before they participate. In addition, they must be given the right to withdraw if they do not wish to participate once they know what will happen. (p. 58)

12. Add all the grade point averages (GPAs) of the students in a group and then divide by the number of students in that group. Do this for junior-year grades of the group that had the study skills class and for the group that did not. A significant difference at the .05 level would mean that the observed difference in grades between the groups would occur by chance less than 5% of the time. (pp. 63, 66)

## POSTTEST

Take this test with all of your books and notes out of sight. This should give you a good idea of how well you understand the material.

### Matching

Write the letter of the design on the right in the blank beside the description on the left.

Methods of Investigation in Psychology

1. _____ Ted has noticed that it seems to rain every time he has his car washed, but he hasn't collected precise data on this

2. _____ a psychologist studies all aspects of the memory of a person who has an exceptional memory

3. _____ the number of wrinkles was counted on people who smoke and people who don't smoke, and smokers were more wrinkled

4. _____ students were asked to answer questions about how much they use and plan to use microcomputers

5. _____ a random half of the participants in a weight-loss program were given exercise plans and half were not

6. _____ some students were given a marijuana brownie and others were given a placebo brownie; their social interactions were rated by observers who did not know who ate which

7. _____ one group of patients was given psychotherapy and the other was not; interviewers who did not know who received the therapy rated their adjustment

A. experimental study

B. correlational study

C. illusory correlation

D. double-blind study

E. survey

F. single-blind study

G. case history

**Multiple-Choice**

Circle the best alternative.

Science and the Evaluation of Evidence

1. Prof. R tried to repeat an experiment that he read about in a scientific journal using exactly the same procedures as the original experiment. His results were different. Therefore, the original experiment was not:
   a. double-blind
   b. parsimonious
   c. statistically significant
   d. replicable
   e. accurate in its predictions

2. You suggest a theory and your instructor says it is not parsimonious. She means that it:
   a. doesn't make sense
   b. would not lead to replicable experiments
   c. would not lead to statistically significant differences
   d. would lead to experiments with demand characteristics
   e. does not make simple scientific assumptions

3. How did Clever Hans solve arithmetic problems?
   a. with ESP
   b. by taking advantage of coincidence
   c. by watching the examiner for subtle cues
   d. by using his native abilities to do arithmetic
   e. by taking advantage of selective attrition

4. In one experiment, people who said they had ESP were tested over several days. Sometimes they performed above chance and sometimes below chance. The researcher concluded that ESP depends on mood--it can be either positive (above chance) or negative (below chance). What is wrong with the explanation?
   a. it is not parsimonious--performance will vary around chance
   b. it is too parsimonious--some factor other than ESP must be operating
   c. it is replicable--people should not vary around chance
   d. there are too many demand characteristics that force performance below chance
   e. differential attrition occurred, so chance performance dropped

5. Advertisers often use testimonials in which a single person tells how a product helped. Why are such reports not good evidence?
   a. they are replicable
   b. they involve objective observation
   c. they involve experimental-control group designs
   d. they ignore the cases where the product did not help
   e. improvement could not occur by coincidence

6. Experiments with ESP have:
   a. had a history of flawed procedures and nonreplicable results
   b. produced positive results that are easily replicated
   c. proved that ESP occurs for people who can read brain waves
   d. shown that most professional psychics have ESP

Methods of Investigation in Psychology

7. Sometimes an inert pill is given to experimental participants, but they are told that the pill is effective. This pill is called a:
   a. placebo
   b. dependent variable
   c. double blind
   d. mode

8. A random sample involves selecting:
   a. only those people who volunteer
   b. people so that the percentages in the sample match the percentages in the population
   c. people from one specific culture
   d. so that every individual has an equal chance of being chosen

9. It has been found that children who have encyclopedias in their homes get better grades in school than children without encyclopedias. Can you conclude that using an encyclopedia makes children do better in school?
   a. yes, this is an experimental study and encyclopedias are the independent variable
   b. yes, this is a correlational study and the correlation is a strong positive one
   c. no, this is a correlational study; something other than encyclopedias might help grades
   d. no, this is an experiment but there is no control group
   e. no, this is a survey and experimenter bias might affect the conclusion

10. If there is a high correlation between parents' use of physical punishment and children's aggressiveness, then we can conclude:
    a. physical punishment causes aggression
    b. aggressive children cause parents to use physical punishment
    c. a third factor in the family causes both
    d. both a and b must be true
    e. nothing can be said about causality

11. If a correlation between variables A and B is -1, then:
    a. there is no relationship
    b. A causes B
    c. increases in A are perfectly associated with decreases in B
    d. increases in A are perfectly associated with increases in B
    e. the mean of A is larger than the mean of B

12. A study was conducted to test a new hay fever drug. Patients were randomly assigned to experimental and control groups. For 6 weeks, experimental patients took the drug daily and control patients took nothing. Each patient recorded hay fever attacks. The drug users had fewer and less severe attacks. What is wrong with this study?
    a. the groups probably were not equal in the beginning
    b. demand characteristics may have caused the effect
    c. the experiment lacks a dependent variable
    d. random assignment wasn't used
    e. informed consent wasn't obtained

13. Which of the following would best improve the design in Question 12?
    a. use a placebo rather than a "nothing" group
    b. include an independent variable
    c. use more participants to increase selective attrition
    d. include a dependent variable
    e. avoid the use of random assignment

14. An experiment was conducted to test the effect of rewards on learning. One group of subjects was paid 10 cents for every word they memorized and the other group was not paid. Number of words memorized was measured. Which of the following is true?
    a. number of words memorized is the dependent variable
    b. payment or not is the dependent variable
    c. random assignment should ensure that the groups differ in the beginning
    d. number of words memorized is the independent variable

15. Student experimenters were told that a special diet makes rats learn faster. They also knew that the rats in Group A had the special diet and the rats in Group B had a regular diet. The students tested all the rats in a maze, counting how many errors they made. In fact, the scores showed that the rats in Group A had fewer errors than the rats in Group B. Which of the following problems is most likely to have influenced the results?
    a. experimenter bias
    b. the cross cultural nature of the study
    c. selective attrition
    d. the double-blind procedure
    e. demand characteristics

16. In the beginning of his course, Dr. Whoopee asked students how interested they were in psychology. The mean of the 60 students was 5.2 on a 10-point scale. At the end of his course, Dr. Whoopee asked the same question of the 40 students who were still enrolled. Now the mean was 7. Dr. Whoopee was pleased that he had increased student interest in psychology. The best alternative explanation for the increase is:
    a. a triple-blind effect
    b. experimenter bias
    c. a Clever Hans effect
    d. a negative correlation
    e. selective attrition

17. A good question for deciding whether an experiment is ethical or not is:
    a. would subjects have agreed to participate if they had known what was going to happen?
    b. will the subjects experience any discomfort?
    c. is there any manipulation of behavior involved?
    d. will any subjects agree to participate?
    e. would any subject withdraw from the experiment?

18. Participants in an experiment are often kept "blind" about the condition to which they've been assigned. This will help prevent:
    a. selective attrition
    b. an illusory correlation
    c. experimenter bias
    d. demand characteristics

## Measuring and Reporting Results

19. A researcher found that subjects who were paid for memorizing words remembered more than subjects who were not paid, $p < .01$. This means:
    a. the reward group recalled 1% more than the nonreward group
    b. the results were not statistically significant
    c. the results are not replicable
    d. the results may have occurred because of an illusory correlation
    e. a difference that large would occur less than 1% of the time by chance alone

20. A class of seven students received the following grades on a test: 65, 78, 90, 89, 64, 78, 60. Which is true?
    a. the mode is 90
    b. the mean is 63
    c. the median is 89
    d. the mode is 89
    e. the median is 78

## ANSWERS TO POSTTEST

| Correct Answer | Questions Testing a Similar Concept | |
|---|---|---|
| | Comprehension Check | Short-Answer |

**Matching**

| | | |
|---|---|---|
| 1. C (pp. 50-51) | 9a | -- |
| 2. G (pp. 46-48) | 8c | 4 |
| 3. B (p. 49) | 8a,9c,14 | 5,7 |
| 4. E (pp. 48-49) | 8 | 4 |
| 5. A (p. 52) | 9b,12,13,14 | 6,7 |
| 6. D (p. 46) | 9d | 8,9 |
| 7. F (p. 46) | 7d | 8,9 |

**Multiple-Choice**

| | | |
|---|---|---|
| 1. d (pp. 34-35) | 1c,2 | 1 |
| 2. e (pp. 36-37) | 3 | 1,2 |
| 3. c (pp. 37-38) | 4 | 2 |
| 4. a (pp. 38-39) | 3 | 2 |
| 5. d (p. 39) | 5 | 3 |
| 6. a (pp. 40-41) | 5 | 2 |
| 7. a (p. 46) | 15e | 8 |
| 8. d (pp. 53-54) | 7b,13 | 4 |
| 9. c (pp. 51-52) | 9,14 | 7 |
| 10. e (pp. 51-52) | 14 | 7 |
| 11. c (pp. 49-50) | 10 | -- |
| 12. b (pp. 55-56) | 7d,13c | 8 |
| 13. a (pp. 46, 56) | 7d | 8 |
| 14. a (p. 52) | 11 | 6 |
| 15. a (p. 56) | 15c | 9 |
| 16. e (p. 56) | 13d,15 | 10 |
| 17. a (p. 58) | 16 | 11 |
| 18. d (pp. 55-56) | 13c,15a | 8 |
| 19. e (p. 66) | 18 | 12 |
| 20. e (p. 63) | 17 | 12 |

# CHAPTER 2  LANGUAGE ENHANCEMENT GUIDE

## I. VOCABULARY, IDIOMS  AND CULTURAL CONCEPTS

### Instructions

As you read the text refer to the following list of words and their definitions.  The words are listed in the order in which they appear in the chapter.  The definitions presented contain the meaning of the word as used by Kalat on the text book page indicated.

Remember that these words like all words can have different meanings in other sentences.  If you do not find a non-technical word on this list it may have been defined on a previous page or chapter of this study guide.  The definition of non-technical words may be found in the dictionary in Appendix A of this study guide.  Kalat defined each new technical word as it first appears on a page and these may be found in Kalat's summary at the end of the section and in the Glossary at the end the textbook..

### Science and the Evaluation of Evidence

spectacular(32) = impressive, amazing, sensational, a big display
abduction  = to carry away by force
alien = from another planet
Age regression = to act as if you were a child
Francis Bacon = a famous English Philosopher
manuscript = a document, a book
alleged = to say something is true without providing evidence
preposterous = can't  be believed; not true; not reasonable; absurd

skeptical = doubtful; questionable; not to be believed
plausible = likely to be true; believable;
so far as we can = with great effort
claim = to state as true; to state as a fact

concede (33) = to accept a claim as true
constitutes = to be part of something
ethicist = a people who study the rules of morality -the goodness or badness of human behavior
assertion = to make a claim; to express with a strong feeling
unambiguous = a word or idea with a very clear meaning
ambiguous = a word or idea with many meanings and the reader doesn't know
which meaning is correct.

casual (34)= not serious; not careful; superficial;
violent = acting with great force that injures, hurts  or causes pain to others
appropriate  = suitable; acceptable
aggressive (aggressive behavior) = to behave in a hostile fashion
interpretation = to determine meaning; to think of different applications or uses
contradict = to state or express the opposite of (a statement).
abandon = to give up; to stop accepting
modify = to change
limitation = a use beyond which a study does not apply or is not effective
ultimate = final; best
hidden flaw = an error or mistake that was not seen

extracts (35) = material taken out of something (to extract = to take out or remove)
consistently replicable = to get the same results over and over again
criteria = a standard or rule used to make a judgment or decision
alluded = to refer to; to point to
comprehensive explanation = to explain everything about a behavior or event
phenomena = an event ; something that happens
natural phenomena = events in nature
reinforcer = a reward that strengthens  a habit or a behavior
vague = not clear in meaning or application
other things being equal = other conditions are the same

radically new (36) = very new and different
stick close = be similar to; not very different
open-minded = willing to listen to or accept new ideas
interstellar = between the stars in the sky

skeptical (37) = to doubt; to question
skepticism = a doubting or questioning attitude
spectacular  = impressive or sensational.
would seem to be = is likely to be
parsimonious(parsimony) = to look for the simplest assumption or explanation
assume = to accept an explanation or idea without evidence

intellectual powers (38) = ability to think, plan and solve problems

replicable = able to be copied, reproduced, or repeated
anticipation = to expect; to wait for
involuntary = acting or behavior without or against one's will
cue = a signal, such as a word or an action, used to prompt another event
telepathic powers = the ability to communicate through means other than the senses
apparent violation = breaking or deviating from
perceive = to see
inanimate objects = non moving things

fundamental tenets of physics (39) = basic principles or laws
hunch = An intuitive feeling or idea
coincidence = a sequence of accidental events that seems to have been planned or causally linked
exaggerate = to say something is greater or more than is actually the case
allegedly = to make a claim or prediction without any evidence
psychics = people who claim special abilities such as extrasensory perception and
mental telepathy
deception = to trick or to fool

eliminate (40) = to remove
dignitary = a person of high rank or position like a mayor or president
subtly = to be difficult to see, not immediately obvious
illusion = a misinterpreted sensation
to the contrary = opposite or opposing

decades (41) = many years (a decade is period of ten years)
inconclusive = no conclusion can be made ( conclusive = to put an end to doubt or uncertainty)
premature = too soon; too early
implications = meanings; consequence; outcomes; applications
tentative and subject to revision = temporary; to accept a claim only until more evidence is available
contradictory evidence = opposite evidence
abandon = stop accepting

## Methods of Investigation in Psychology

face some special problem (43) = study a problem
ponder = to think about; to consider with great care
devised = invented; developed
disregard = to ignore; to stop looking at something
pertinent = related to; relevant; can be applied to
duration of time = a period of time
more likely = probable; more frequently occurring

never mind (45) = disregard; do not pay attention to
vertebrate species = animals with a spine
resembles = to look alike; similar to
city residents = people who live in a city
census = a count of all the people who live in an area
and so forth = this expression indicates that other examples can be listed
dispute = to question; to argue about
aspects = characteristics; features; properties

some aspect = characteristics
engages = to be occupied; to participate in an activity

pharmacological effects (46) = the effects of drugs on the body
loses track = forgets
good deal of = many; much; a lot of
characteristics = a feature that helps to identify or describe something
as an outsider = a person who is not a member of the group
inability = not being able to do something

might have some bearing on (47) = can affect
is well suited to = appropriate; all right; OK
prevalence = widely or commonly occurring, existing,
deceptively = to deceive; to mislead; to cause to believe what is not true
was soundly defeated = completely defeated

follow-up question (49) = the next related question
harassed = to annoy; tease; torment; embarrass; bother
sponsoring = to take responsibility for another person or activity
explicitly = clearly expressed; leaving nothing implied

testosterone levels (50) = the amount of the male hormone
casual observations = not serious or careful ; superficial
persist = to continue
it first arose = it got started

people went crazy (51) = people acted foolishly
to wind up in  = to be sent to
mental hospital = a hospital for people with serious emotional and behavior problems

manipulate (52) = to change; control
investigator = a person who does a scientific study
presumably = to take for granted; suppose; assume
spends time = to uses the same amount of time

most prone to (53) = likely to
impulsive = to act quickly without thinking about the effects of the act

will engage in (54) = will do
juvenile delinquents =  young people who break the law.
cottage = a small house
poses some thorny problems = presents a difficult problem

act strange (55) = behave in an unusual way
deprivation = to take or keep something away from
apparatus = equipment; machines; tools
hallucination = false perception of objects or events; seeing things that are not there

interrogated (56) = questioned
to drop out  = to stop participating; to stop coming

will react pretty much the same way  (57) = act the same way
generalizing = to apply a finding from a few people to many or all people
despair = to lose all hope

ethical (58) = guidelines for right and wrong behavior
objectionable  = undesirable; not wanted
bear in mind = think about
to exert any long-lasting effects = cause changes that last a long time
prospective = likely or expected to
reputable institutions = having a good reputation; honorable
might not want to mention = does not want to say

animal welfare (59)  = prevent hurting animals

humanely (60) = acting with kindness, mercy, or compassion.
consider alternatives = look at two or more different way to act

**Measuring and Analyzing Results**

circumstances (63) = situations
approximately = almost exact or correct
roughly speaking = commonly speaking

curriculum (65) = material and procedures for teaching

## II.  VOCABULARY BUILDING

Remember that we pointed out in the last chapter that many words in the English language are made up of separate word parts that have been borrowed from many other languages such as Latin, Greek, Spanish, German, French,  etc.  This can create a problem  for word analysis when the same prefix or suffix is borrowed from different languages and have different meanings.  The prefix **in** for example can mean either **in** or **to** or **not** or **without**.  Here is a sentence from page 41 of the textbook with the word inconclusive underlined.

"Then ESP researchers admit that the previous research was <u>inconclusive</u> but claim that they now have a better procedure and better evidence."

When we break **inconclusive** into its parts we find the word following the prefix **in** is conclude (conclusive).  Conclude means to come to an end or close or reach a decision.  Which one of the several meanings that  the prefix **in** can  have is appropriate here?  To figure this out we must look at the context of the sentence and the discussion of ESP. Based on the context the best guess as to the meaning of **in** is **not** or **without**.  So inconclusive means **no conclusion** or **without a conclusion.**  It does not mean **in conclusion** or **to conclude.**  In the  context of the sentence it means no decision or conclusion  can be made about ESP based on past research on ESP. This is the meaning given in a dictionary and the meaning required in the sentence.  However, you must be cautious in your word analysis because as helpful as it is most of the time there will be times when you can and will make errors.  With practice and checking a dictionary when you are in doubt your word analysis skill will improve.

**Word Analysis**

<u>Instructions</u>

1. Study the meaning of the prefixes roots and suffixes listed.
2. Break each word in the table into its prefixes roots and suffixes.
3. Guess the meaning word based on the meaning of its parts.
4. Find the word on the text page indicated in the brackets and define the word based on the context of the sentence, paragraph and chapter .
5. Look up the definition of the word in the VOCABULARY, IDIOMS AND CULTURAL CONCEPTS section above , in Appendix A (indicated as A), in a dictionary, or in the textbook's glossary (G).

<u>Exercise 1.  Inanimate</u>

**Prefix:  in/im____ = in/to/on**
**Prefix:   spect____ = to look**
**Prefix :  anima____= moving**
**Suffix:  _____ or = one who**
**Suffix:  _____ ive , ate = tending to be; having the characteristic of**
**Suffix:  _____ent = being, having, doing,  performing**

| Word | Meaning |
|---|---|
| inanimate (A) | |
| investigator (A) | |
| interrogated (A) | |
| impaired (A) | |
| independent (A) | |
| introspective  (A) | |
| input | **to put in** |
| income | **money or wages earned,  money coming in** |
| impress | |
| impulsive (G) | |
| inhuman | |

<u>Exercise 2.  Inconclusive</u>

**Prefix  in_____ = not/without/into/in**
**Root  _____  conclude  = to an end; close;  reach a decision**

| Word | Meaning |
|---|---|
| inconclusive (A ) | |
| inability | |
| inferiority (G) | |

Exercise 3. Unambiguous

**Prefix: un_____ = not/opposite**
**Prefix: ambi _____ = two**
**Suffix: _____ ous = full of**

| Word | Meaning |
|---|---|
| unambiguous | without two meanings or interpretations, clear, certain |
| undo | |
| unnatural | |
| uneven | |
| unloved | |
| unconditional | |
| unfair | |
| unconscious (G) | |

Exercise 4: Degrade

**de _____ down/take away/lower**

| Word | Meaning |
|---|---|
| debug | to remove a hidden electronic device (called a bug), such as a microphone; to search for and eliminate malfunctioning elements or errors; to remove insects from, as with a pesticide |
| declassify | |
| deform | |
| degeneration | |
| degrade | |
| demote | |
| denial (G) | |
| depression (G) | |

# CHAPTER 3 THE BIOLOGICAL APPROACH TO BEHAVIOR

## OBJECTIVES

### Psychological Explanations at the Level of the Gene

I. Principles of Genetics (p. 73, Fig. 3.1-3.2, p. 74)
- A. Genes are transmitted from one generation to the next (p. 74)
  - 1. People are either homozygous or heterozygous for genes (p. 74, Fig. 3.3, p. 75)
  - 2. Genes are dominant or recessive (p. 74, Fig. 3.4, p. 75)
- B. Some genes are different from males and females (pp. 75-76)
  - 1. Sex chromosomes determine sex (p. 75, Fig. 3.5, p. 76)
  - 2. Sex-linked genes are found on the X chromosome (pp. 75-76, Fig. 3.6)
  - 3. Sex-limited genes affect one sex more than the other (p. 76)
- C. Specific genes can be identified and localized (p. 77)
  - 1. Huntington's disease is caused by a specific gene (p. 77)
  - 2. Genetic counseling can be given if genetic disorders are known (p.77)

II. Behavioral effects of genetics can be determined in several ways (p. 77)
- A. Monozygous and dizygous twins can be compared (p. 78)
  - 1. Adopted children can be compared with their biological and adoptive parents (p. 78)
- B. Genetics can influence many types of behavior (p. 79)
- C. Heredity and the environment interact (p. 77)
  - 1. Just because something is under genetic control doesn't mean that the environment can't alter it (p. 80)
    - a. PKU is a genetic disorder that can be altered by the environment (pp. 80-81)

III. Genes are a product of evolution (p. 81)
- A. Reproductive advantage is the key to evolutionary success (p. 81, Fig. 3.10)

IV. The role of genetics can be studied by comparing animal species (pp. 82-83)

V. Sociobiology is the study of social behaviors from a biological viewpoint (p. 83)

### Explanations of Behavior at the Level of the Neuron

VI. The nervous system is composed of neurons and glia (p. 87)
- A. A neuron consists of a cell body, dendrites, and an axon (p. 88, Figs. 3.15-3.16)
- B. Nerve impulses are called action potentials (p. 89)
  - 1. Inflow of sodium ions makes inside of axon positive (pp. 89-91, Figs. 3.18-3.20)
- C. Gaps between neurons are called synapses (p. 91, Fig. 3-21)
  - 1. Neurotransmitters are released from presynaptic endings (pp. 91-92, Fig. 3.22)
    - a. Neurotransmitters from one animal can affect another animal (p. 94)
- D. Different neurotransmitters have different effects on behavior (pp. 95-96, Table 3.1)
  - 1. Parkinson's disease occurs because neurons producing dopamine die (p. 96, Fig. 3.25)
- E. Chemicals can interfere with the function of neurons (p. 97)
  - 1. Lack of Vitamin $B_1$ will deprive the brain of glucose (p. 97)
  - 2. Some drugs block neurotransmitters at the synapses (p. 97)

### Explanations of Behavior at the Level of the Nervous System

VII. Neurons are organized into the brain and nervous system (pp. 99-100, Fig. 3.26)
- A. Spinal cord is connected to sensory and motor nerves (pp. 100-101, Fig. 3.28)
- B. Autonomic nervous system consists of sympathetic and parasympathetic nervous systems (p. 101)

C. Endocrine system produces hormones that are similar to neurotransmitters (pp. 101-102)

D. Hindbrain consists of the medulla, pons, and cerebellum (pp. 103-104, Fig. 3.31)

    1. Medulla and pons receive sensory input and control life-preserving functions (p. 104)

        a. The reticular formation serves an arousal function (p. 104)

    2. Cerebellum controls movement (p. 104)

VIII. Cerebral cortex is the "master area" of the brain (p. 104)

A. Cortex consists of left and right hemisphere (p. 104)

    1. Cortical hemispheres are made of cell bodies, gray matter (pp. 104-105)

    2. Axons covered with white insulation, called myelin, lie beneath the cortex (p. 105, Fig. 3.32)

B. Brain is full of separate systems operating in parallel (pp. 106-107)

    1. Damage to different areas of the visual cortex result in different deficits (pp. 107-108, Fig. 3.35)

    2. Damage to the parietal lobe can lead to neglect or inattention (pp. 108-109)

    3. A small amount of damage to the frontal lobe can results in loss of memory for a specific location (p. 109)

C. Cerebral cortex consists of four lobes (pp. 109-110, Fig. 3.36)

    1. Occipital lobe is specialized for vision (p. 110)

    2. Parietal lobe is specialized for body senses (p. 110)

        a. Primary somatosensory cortex senses touch in different body areas (p. 110, Fig. 3.40, p. 111)

    3. Temporal lobes are involved in hearing (p.110)

    4. Frontal lobes have several different functions (pp. 110-111)

        a. Primary motor cortex controls movement on opposite side of body (p. 110, Fig. 3.40, p. 111)

        b. Prefrontal cortex is critical for keeping track of memories and planning actions based on them (pp. 110-111)

D. Regional cerebral blood flow (rCBF) can be used to study brain activity (pp. 111-112)

IX. Split-brain operations involve cutting the corpus callosum (p. 113)

A. Helps epilepsy by stopping spread of seizures (pp. 113-114)

B. Fibers from each retina still go to each hemisphere (p. 114, Fig. 3.45, p. 115)

    1. Half of the optic nerves cross over to the other side of the brain (p. 114)

C. Cutting the corpus callosum creates two separate hemispheres (pp. 114-115)

    1. Information presented to the right visual field (left hemisphere) can be named, but information presented to the left visual field cannot (pp. 114-116, Fig. 3.46)

X. There are many misconceptions about the brain (pp. 116-117)

A. Although the right and left hemispheres are specialized, all tasks rely on both hemispheres (p. 116)

B. People use all of their brains; the idea that we only use 10% is a myth (pp. 116-117)

**COMPREHENSION CHECK**

Circle the best alternative. Check your answers on pp. 48-50. If you were wrong, look back at your text and write why you were wrong. Check your reasons and the reasons why other alternatives are wrong on pp. 48-50.

**Psychological Explanations at the Level of the Gene**

1. People who have the gene for Alzheimer's disease:
    a. will always develop the disease
    b. may develop the disease, depending upon the environment
    c. will develop the disease earlier than people who don't have the gene
    d. begin to develop the disease soon after birth

Correct _____ If wrong, why? _____

2. Neither F. Lat nor his wife can curl their tongue. How about their children?
    a. none of them will be able to curl their tongue
    b. half will probably be able to curl their tongue
    c. all should be able to curl their tongue
    d. either b or c, depending on whether F. Lat and his wife are heterozygous or homozygous

Correct _____ If wrong, why? _____

3. Men are much more likely to be color-blind than women because this is a sex-linked trait. This means that:
    a. the gene is sex limited; although both sexes carry it, it is more likely to show up in men
    b. it is not carried on a chromosome
    c. it is carried on the Y chromosome
    d. it is carried on the X chromosome

Correct _____ If wrong, why? _____

4. Huntington's disease:
    a. begins when individuals are teenagers
    b. can be prevented if the gene is found before the disease begins
    c. is caused by a single gene that can be identified
    d. results in progressive increases in memory loss

Correct _____ If wrong, why? _____

5. How could genetics affect people's preferences for dairy products?
    a. a single gene is directly responsible for the food preference
    b. genes control the ability to digest lactose
    c. genes produce differences in taste buds, which produce differences in food preferences
    d. genetics doesn't control this taste preference; it depends purely upon culture

Correct _____ If wrong, why? _____

6. Although people say evolution is the survival of the fittest, what really matters is not survival but:
    a. length of life
    b. environment
    c. health
    d. reproduction

Correct _____ If wrong, why? _____

7. According to sociobiology, why might women be less likely than men to have multiple sex partners?
   a. they have no need to pass their genes along
   b. by having multiple sex partners they are likely to have more trouble finding someone to help with rearing their children
   c. girls learn from an early age that they should take care of children
   d. it is part of a male plot to maintain their superiority

Correct _____ If wrong, why? _____

**Explanations of Behavior at the Level of the Neuron**

8. Which of the following is true?
   a. neurons are larger and more numerous than glia cells
   b. each neuron physically touches at least one other neuron
   c. neurons are all similar in shape and size
   d. neurons consist of a cell body, dendrites, and an axon
   e. neurons decrease dendritic branching with enriched experience

Correct _____ If wrong, why? _____

9. The action potential:
   a. occurs when positive sodium ions enter an axon
   b. becomes weaker as it travels down an axon
   c. can be speeded up by anesthetic drugs
   d. occurs when potassium enters the axon

Correct _____ If wrong, why? _____

10. What happens at the synapse between neurons?
    a. synaptic vesicles are released from postsynaptic endings
    b. presynaptic endings are destroyed by action potentials
    c. neurotransmitters are released from terminal buttons
    d. neurotransmitters excite the next neuron

Correct _____ If wrong, why? _____

11. Parkinson's disease:
    a. involves muscle twitches and hallucinations
    b. results from the death of axons that use dopamine
    c. can be helped by having the patient take dopamine
    d. results from a deficit in MPTP

Correct _____ If wrong, why? _____

12. LSD:
    a. is chemically similar to the neurotransmitter serotonin
    b. is chemically similar to dopamine
    c. stimulates the synapses that respond to endorphins
    d. blocks acetylcholine synapses and stimulates norepinephrine synapses
    e. results in a deficiency of Vitamin B$_1$, which is necessary for the brain to use glucose

Correct _____ If wrong, why? _____

## Explanations of Behavior at the Level of the Nervous System

13. John is about to give a speech and his heart is racing, he is breathing rapidly, and he has "butterflies in his stomach." What part of his nervous system is controlling this reaction?
    a. parasympathetic nervous system
    b. spinal cord
    c. endocrine system
    d. sympathetic nervous system
    e. sensory nerves

Correct _____ If wrong, why? _____

14. A person has damage to the hindbrain. Which of the following would be <u>least</u> likely?
    a. the person may have difficulty with memory because of damage to the hippocampus
    b. the person may have difficulty walking a straight line because of cerebellum damage
    c. the person may not show much arousal because of damage to the reticular formation
    d. the person may die because of damage to the medulla and pons

Correct _____ If wrong, why? _____

15. Which is the best statement about how the brain works?
    a. it works as a whole with all brain areas contributing equally to functions
    b. various areas of the brain funnel their information into association areas where the senses are integrated
    c. although the entire brain doesn't work as a whole, all visual input is integrated into one area of the brain
    d. there are many separate modules that act in parallel with each other

Correct _____ If wrong, why? _____

16. The primary somatosensory cortex is:
    a. located in the frontal lobe
    b. the receiving area for touch from the same side of the body
    c. located in the parietal lobe
    d. located behind the cerebral cortex

Correct _____ If wrong, why? _____

17. When regional cerebral blood flow (rCBF) is measured while a person is speaking, what happens?
    a. the right hemisphere turns red, showing increased activity
    b. the left hemisphere turns red, showing increased activity
    c. the occipital lobe turns purple showing increased activity
    d. the right temporal lobe turns purple, showing increased activity
    e. the right frontal lobe turns green, indicating increased activity

Correct _____ If wrong, why? _____

18. How does cutting the corpus callosum control the seizures of epilepsy?
    a. it removes the part of the brain that is damaged
    b. it prevents seizures from spreading to the other hemisphere
    c. it prevents visual input from reaching the brain
    d. it prevents axons from the retina from crossing at the optic chiasm

Correct _____ If wrong, why? _____

19. If a person with a split-brain operation closes her right eye and looks at a picture as long as she wants with her left eye, where does the picture end up in her brain?
    a. in her right hemisphere because the axons from the retina cross at the optic chiasm
    b. in her left hemisphere because the axons from the retina go straight back at the optic chiasm
    c. both hemispheres-axons from the left side of the eye go to left hemisphere; axons from the right side of the eye go to right hemisphere
    d. both hemispheres-axons from the right side of the eye go to left hemisphere; axons from the left side of the eye go to right hemisphere

Correct _____ If wrong, why? _____

20. A right-handed, split-brain patient sees a pen very briefly in her left visual field. What will happen when she is asked to identify it?
    a. she will say it is a pen, and pick it out from among other objects with either hand
    b. she will not be able to say what it is, but she will pick it up with her right hand
    c. she will say it is a pen, and will be able to pick it up with her left hand
    d. she will not be able to say what it is, but she will pick it up with her left hand

Correct _____ If wrong, why? _____

## ANSWERS AND EXPLANATIONS FOR COMPREHENSION CHECK

| Correct Answer | Other Alternatives Are Wrong Because: |
| --- | --- |
| 1. b (p. 73)<br>   Obj. I | a. some may not, depending upon the environment<br>c. people who don't have the gene won't develop the disease<br>d. it develops in old age, following a normal life |

2. a (p. 74, Fig. 3.4, p. 75)
   Obj. I-A-1,2

   b. would occur if one was heterozygous and the other
      homozygous for not curling; one can't be heterozygous
      because curling is dominant
   c. would occur if both carried two genes (homozygous) for tongue
      curling; can't be because neither can do it
   d. because tongue curling is dominant, it would show up with one gene;
      they must both have two recessive genes for an inability to curl

3. d (pp. 75-76)
   Obj. I-B-2

   a. located on the X chromosome; capable of altering either
      sex
   b. all genes are carried on chromosomes
   c. the Y chromosome is smaller and does not carry this gene at all; that
      is why a male is color-blind if he gets the gene from his mother

4. c (p. 77)
   Obj. I-C-1

   a. begins in middle-aged people
   b. as yet, it can't be prevented although research may someday
      lead to this possibility
   d. results in loss of voluntary muscle control eventually leading to
      death; Alzheimer's disease shows progressive memory loss

5. b (p. 79, Fig. 3.8, p. 80)
   Obj. II-B

   a. genes control the taste preference indirectly, not directly
   c. differences in taste buds don't explain this
   d. cultures do differ in their preference for milk products, but this is
      genetically controlled

6. d (p. 81)
   Obj. III-A

   a. not how long one lives, but how many offspring one has
   b. may determine reproductive success, but not evolution
   c. health doesn't matter; it's number of offspring

7. b (p. 84)
   Obj. V

   a. according to sociobiology, reproduction is the key to survival
   c. probably true, but not the sociobiologists' explanation
   d. unlikely; sociobiologists emphasize spreading of one's own genes

8. d (p. 88, Fig. 3.16)
   Obj. VI-A

   a. glia cells are more numerous
   b. neurons do not actually touch each other
   c. neurons differ in shape, depending on how many sources of
      information they have and where their impulses travel
   e. studies with rats show that enriched environments result in an
      increase in dendritic branching

9. a (pp. 89-90)
   Obj. VI-B-1

   b. the impulse remains at the same intensity
   c. anesthetics prevent action potentials
   d. potassium ions leave the axon as sodium enters

10. c (pp. 91-92, Fig. 3.22)
    Obj. VI-C-1

    a. released from <u>presynaptic</u> endings
    b. endings are part of structure; not destroyed
    d. postsynaptic neurons may be <u>either</u> excited or inhibited

11. b. (p. 96, Fig. 3.25)  a. movement problems and depression, not hallucinations
    Obj. VI-D-1          c. dopamine does not cross blood-brain barrier, must use L-DOPA
                         d. a chemical that causes symptoms similar to Parkinson's

12. a (p. 97)            b. LSD is similar to serotonin
    Obj. VI-E            c. heroin and morphine stimulate the endorphin synapses
                         d. common cold remedies do this to decrease the flow of sinus fluids
                         e. chronic alcoholism is associated with this, not LSD

13. d (p. 101)           a. has the opposite reactions; "calms" body down
    Obj. VII-B           b. part of nervous system that controls internal organs lies just outside
                            of spinal cord
                         c. not part of nervous system; secretes hormones
                         e. carry sensory information to spinal cord

14. a (pp. 103-104, Fig. 3.31) b-d. each of these is a function of hindbrain, so they are likely
    Obj. VII-D

15. d (pp. 106-107)      a. Lashley believed this but he worked with complex behavior
    Obj. VIII-B          b. this was believed in early 1900s, but modern research shows it
                            isn't true
                         c. specific aspects of vision, e.g., shape, color, and motion, are
                            processed in different areas of the brain

16. c (p. 110)           a. it is in parietal lobe
    Obj. VIII-C-2        b. from the opposite side of body
                         d. it is part of cerebral cortex

17. b (pp. 111-112,      a. speech results in more <u>left</u> hemisphere activity
    Fig. 3.42)           c. occipital lobe is involved in vision; not so much increased
    Obj. VIII-D             activity here
                         d,e. left lobe shows greatest increase; higher activity is red

18. b (pp. 113-114)      a. connection between hemispheres, not site of damage, is cut
    Obj. IX-A            c. visual input still goes to one hemisphere, but not to both
                         d. optic chiasm is not interfered with in split brain

19. c (p. 114, Fig. 3.45,  a. only axons from the right half of the left eye cross to
    p. 115)                 the right hemisphere
    Obj. IX-B            b. only axons from the left half of the left eye go straight back to
                            the left hemisphere
                         d. reversed-axons from the right side of an eye go to the right

20. d (pp. 114-115)      a. only the right hemisphere "knows" the object; she needs to
    Obj. IX-C-1             use her left hand
                         b. she'll pick it up with her <u>left</u> hand
                         c. she won't be able to say what it is; speech is in the left hemisphere
                            and "pen" is in the right hemisphere

## LECTURE MATERIAL

Don't forget to review your lecture material. Process each topic meaningfully. First, be sure that you understand the material in each lecture--if you don't, ASK your instructor or teaching assistant. Associate the material with things that you already know and with your personal experiences. If you can make up mental images of any of the material, do so. Try to think of real-life applications of the concepts. Put comments on your notes. Then write questions to cover each concept.

------------------------------------------------------------------------------

WAIT AT LEAST 24 HOURS BEFORE PROCEEDING.
LET FORGETTING OCCUR--IT WILL!!

------------------------------------------------------------------------------

## SHORT-ANSWER ESSAY QUESTIONS

Write brief answers to each of the following. The answers are on pp. 53-54, but do try to write the answers yourself before looking at them.

### Psychological Explanations at the Level of the Gene

1. What are the advantages of locating specific genes that are related to specific characteristics?

2. What have studies involving monozygous and dizygous twins shown about the role of genetics in behavior?

3. Genetics and environment interact. What is meant by this?

4. Give an example of an animal behavior that is controlled by genetics.

### Explanations of Behavior at the Level of the Neuron

5. Describe how nerve impulses travel through neurons and describe what happens when an impulse reaches the end of a neuron.

6. Describe how chemicals can interfere with neural transmission.

**Explanations of Behavior at the Level of the Nervous System**

7. Describe the autonomic nervous system. How is it similar to the endocrine system?

8. How does the brain integrate information from all the different senses?

9. Name the four lobes of the cerebral cortex and describe the function of each.

10. How does a split-brain operation help epilepsy, and what are the major consequences of such an operation?

11. Describe the path of the nerve fibers from each eye to the two hemispheres of the brain.

12. "They say that we only use 10% of our brain." What does the textbook say about this?

\*\*\*\*\*\*\*\*\*\*\*\*\*\*\*\*\*\*\*\*\*\*\*\*\*\*\*\*\*\*\*\*\*\*\*\*\*\*\*\*\*\*\*\*\*\*\*\*\*\*\*\*\*\*\*\*\*\*\*\*
Find the questions that you wrote over
lecture material and write answers to them.
\*\*\*\*\*\*\*\*\*\*\*\*\*\*\*\*\*\*\*\*\*\*\*\*\*\*\*\*\*\*\*\*\*\*\*\*\*\*\*\*\*\*\*\*\*\*\*\*\*\*\*\*\*\*\*\*\*\*\*\*

## ANSWERS TO SHORT-ANSWER ESSAY QUESTIONS

1. Finding a specific gene for a genetic disorder such as Huntington's disease would allow a person to know that they will develop the disease and to plan accordingly. The person may not want to have children. If genes can be identified, researchers may be able to develop a treatment to undo the damage. Problems may be preventable before they begin. (p. 77)

2. Monozygous twins, who share the same genetics, are more similar in characteristics such as having a predisposition toward schizophrenia, depression, and alcohol abuse than dizygous twins, who are less similar genetically. Even monozygous twins separated at birth and reared apart are very similar. They often share interests and hobbies. These similarities aren't conclusive evidence for genetics because the twins shared the prenatal environment. (pp. 77-78)

3. Although something is controlled by genetics, it doesn't mean that it can't be modified by the environment. Phenylketonuria (PKU) is a good example of a genetic disorder that is under environmental control. People who are homozygous for PKU are unable to break down a substance called phenylalanine. Phenylalanine accumulates in the brain and causes mental retardation. However, if the child stays on a diet that is low in phenylalanine, the child does not become mentally retarded. Thus, the environment (the diet) modifies the genetic condition. (pp. 80-81)

4. The Kittiwake, a type of gull that lays its eggs on narrow ledges, shows many behaviors that must be genetic, including fighting over territory, using mud to form a barrier for its nest, and remaining motionless as a chick until it can fly. These behaviors are well adapted to life on narrow ledges and they occur even when nests are built on the ground, suggesting a genetic cause for the behaviors. (pp. 82-83)

5. Nerve impulses travel through the axons of neurons. The impulse is a positive charge inside an axon that occurs because sodium ions rush in. The impulse continues from the cell body end of the axon to the presynaptic ending, where the impulse causes neurotransmitters to be released into the synapse. (pp. 89-93, Fig. 3.23)

6. A deficiency in vitamin B-1 can interfere with the brain's ability to use glucose, one of the few fuels it can use. Common cold remedies block the synapses that promote the flow of sinus fluids, along with the blocking of other synapses that use the same neurotransmitter. Novocain blocks the sodium gates which prevents the occurrence of action potentials. Hallucinogenic drugs, like LSD, act on synapses either to block or to stimulate them; that is, they either work like neurotransmitters or prevent neurotransmitters from working. (p. 97)

7. The autonomic nervous system lies just outside the spinal cord and it consists of two parts: sympathetic and parasympathetic. The sympathetic nervous system prepares the body to "fight or flee" by increasing heart and breathing rates and decreasing digestive processes. The parasympathetic nervous system does just the opposite; it decreases heart and breathing rates and increases digestion. The endocrine system consists of glands that secrete hormones that can function like neurotransmitters. Epinephrine is a hormone that does the same thing as the sympathetic nervous system. (pp. 101-102)

8. In the early part of the 20th Century, people believed that there were association areas that integrated information from the various senses. The parts of the brain were thought to funnel their specific information to association areas. But these areas were never found. Karl Lashley argued that the brain operates as a whole and that information did not need to be funneled to any one spot. However, he studied complex learning tasks. Today it is known that small areas of the brain specialize in different functions and each area works in parallel with other areas. Brain damage to specific areas produces different types of deficits that are as specialized as involving only shape, color, motion. attention, and very specialized memory loss. (pp. 105-107)

9. Occipital: Vision, although specific areas contribute to different aspects of visual coding, including motion, shape, and color
   Parietal: Body senses, including touch, pain, temperature, and awareness of body part location. Primary somatosensory cortex is here
   Temporal: Hearing, emotional behavior, language comprehension.
   Frontal: Primary motor cortex controls fine movement; prefrontal area contributes to organization and planning of movements; left frontal lobe involved in language production. (pp. 109-111, Fig. 3.36, p. 108)

10. The corpus callosum is cut so there are no connections between right and left cerebral hemispheres. This prevents seizures from spreading between the hemispheres. People generally behave normally, but if information is presented very briefly to one visual field, it gets into the opposite hemisphere. Right hemisphere cannot say what was seen but it can identify objects with the left hand. Left hemisphere can say what was seen but it is poor at spatial tasks. (pp. 113-115)

11. Information presented to each visual field gets into both eyes. For example, information in the left visual field goes onto the right side of each retina. The optic fibers on the nose side (right) of the left eye cross to the right hemisphere, and the fibers on the temple side (right) of the right eye go back to the right hemisphere. Hence, information from the left visual field goes to the right hemisphere and information from the right visual field goes to the left hemisphere. (If this is unclear, review pp. 114-115 and Fig. 3.45)

12. First of all, no statement should be accepted without evidence. Who is "they"? We could not lose 90% of our brains and operate normally. More than 10% of the neurons in the brain are active at any given time. We use all of our brain, even if we don't seem to be thinking very well. In the 1920s, the function of the so-called "association areas" was not clear to researchers so they may have imagined those areas did nothing. The brain does include many small neurons. Early observers may have thought that those were immature and would develop later. There is no scientific evidence for the 10% claim. (pp. 116-117)

## POSTTEST

Take this test with all of your books and notes out of sight. This should give you a good idea of how well you understand the material.

**Matching**

Write the letter of the structure on the right in the blank beside the description on the left.

Explanations of Behavior at the Level of the Neuron

1. _____ tiny gap between one neuron and another

2. _____ widely branching structure of neuron that receives information

3. _____ contains nucleus of neuron

4. _____ spherical packets that contain neurotransmitters

5. _____ place where neurotransmitters are released from axon

6. _____ single, long, thin straight part of a neuron

7. _____ insulate neurons and remove waste products from brain

A. axon

B. glia

C. cell body

D. synaptic vesicles

E. synapse

F. terminal button

G. dendrite

**Multiple-Choice**

Circle the best alternative.

Psychological Explanations at the Level of the Gene

1. Neither Jane nor her husband Jim can taste PTC. Will their children be able to taste this bitter substance?
   a. about half will and half will not
   b. all should be able to taste PTC
   c. none of their children will be able to taste PTC
   d. either a or b, depending upon whether Jane and Jim are heterozygous or homozygous for the gene

2. If a gene shows its effects more in one sex than the other because certain hormones activate it, the gene is said to be:
   a. sex limited
   b. recessive
   c. dominant
   d. sex linked
   e. chromosomal

3. In order for a gene to be favored in evolution, it must affect the:
   a. health of the organism
   b. reproductive success of the organism
   c. appearance of the organism
   d. behavior of the organism

4. Which of the following statements would be most conclusive?
    a. similarities in monozygotic twins raised apart must be genetic
    b. lack of resemblance in some trait for monozygotic twins indicates a non-genetic influence
    c. similarities between adopted children and their adoptive parents indicates a genetic influence
    d. preferences and attitudes cannot be genetic because they are psychological
    e. if something is under genetic control, it cannot be modified by the environment

5. Which of the following fits with principles of sociobiology the <u>least</u>?
    a. sexual customs vary greatly from culture to culture
    b. reed bunting males help incubate the eggs more if the female hasn't mated with a neighboring male
    c. male lions kill young lions after driving off an old male
    d. women devote more effort to child care than men
    e. a goose that sees a hawk overhead utters an alarm call to warn other geese

Explanations of Behavior at the Level of the Neuron

6. Action potentials:
    a. occur when potassium ions enter the axon of a neuron
    b. make the inside of an axon negative relative to the outside
    c. become weaker as they travel down an axon
    d. generally travel away from the cell body
    e. can be increased in strength with anesthetic drugs

7. How does one neuron send its signal to another neuron?
    a. its terminal button touches the next neuron
    b. the two axons touch so that the action potential is passed from one to the next neuron
    c. the positively charged ions from one neuron stimulate the axon of the next
    d. the postsynaptic neuron receives stimulation directly from the dendrites of the presynaptic neuron
    e. neurotransmitters diffuse across the synapse and attach to receptors of the postsynaptic neuron

8. Loewi collected fluid around the heart after stimulating axons that slowed down the heart and then transferred the fluid to the heart of a second animal. What happened?
    a. nothing; fluid from one animal had no effect on another animal
    b. the second animal's heart sped up; that is, the fluid produced the opposite effect on the second animal
    c. neurotransmitters contained in the fluid stimulated the second animal's heart to slow
    d. myelin contained in the fluid stimulated the second animal's heart to slow
    e. axons contained in the fluid stimulated the second animal's heart to slow

9. Parkinson's disease can be helped by:
    a. taking pills that contain dopamine
    b. taking pills that contain MPTP
    c. injections of epinephrine
    d. injections of serotonin
    e. taking pills that contain L-DOPA

10. Jack has just taken LSD and is having hallucinations. Why?
    a. LSD prevents the use of endorphins by the brain
    b. LSD stimulates serotonin synapses
    c. LSD decreases the activity at acetylcholine synapses
    d. LSD prevents action potentials by attaching the axon membranes
    e. LSD causes damage to the cerebellum

## Explanations of Behavior at the Level of the Nervous System

11. The sympathetic nervous system:
    a. lies at the very top and very bottom of the spinal cord
    b. controls the peripheral nerves that communicate with the skin and muscles
    c. transmits impulses from the central nervous system to the muscles and glands
    d. increases heart rate and breathing rate
    e. increases digestive activities

12. Hormones differ from neurotransmitters in that hormones:
    a. affect the organs, neurotransmitters affect the nervous system
    b. affect only the cells close to where they are released; neurotransmitters are diffused throughout the body
    c. are released into the blood stream; neurotransmitters are released adjacent to the cell they are to excite or inhibit
    d. have only short-lived influence; neurotransmitters can have long-term influences
    e. have no effect on behavior; neurotransmitters can have large behavioral effects

13. Damage to which of the following is most likely to be fatal?
    a. cerebellum
    b. spinal cord
    c. medulla
    d. midbrain
    e. limbic system

14. The idea that all kinds of information is funneled to association areas of the cerebral cortex is:
    a. supported by recent research
    b. supported by the finding that prosopagnosia occurs with damage to specific parts of the inferior temporal cortex
    c. similar to Lashley's theory that behavioral function depends on all brain areas equally
    d. supported by the idea that the two hemispheres operate independently
    e. challenged by the finding that different sensory systems seem to operate independently and in parallel

15. A person who shows unilateral neglect:
    a. has a sensory deficit so that things in one visual field are not seen
    b. is unable to detect movement
    c. may lose spatial memory for just one specific location
    d. has a loss of attention rather than a loss of sensation
    e. is also unable to detect shape and color

16. What is concluded in your text about the relationship between brain and mind?
    a. they are inseparable; if a part of the brain is lost, that part of behavior and experience is lost
    b. "mind" is the central area where all sensations are funneled and organized
    c. because all areas of the brain are integrated, the loss of any one specific part of brain will cause total disorganization of "mind"
    d. loss of large parts of the brain has little effect on "mind"; they seem to be separate
    e. both b and c are true

17. The primary somatosensory cortex is:
    a. in the temporal lobe
    b. the part of the brain that controls fine motor movement
    c. organized with a larger area devoted to more sensitive parts of the body
    d. in the occipital lobe
    e. contributes primarily to the organization and planning of movements

18. A person who has epilepsy has a split-brain operation. Which of the following is true?
    a. the person's corpus callosum has been cut
    b. seizures will increase
    c. seizures will occur more often than before the operation, but they will be less severe
    d. the fibers from each retina will only go to one hemisphere
    e. the person's optic chiasm has been cut

19. A right-handed split-brain patient sees the word cupcake presented very briefly such that cup is in the left visual field and cake is in the right visual field. Which of the following will occur?
    a. she will say that she saw the word "cup"
    b. she will pick out a cup with her left hand
    c. she will say that she saw the word "cupcake"
    d. she will pick out a cake with her left hand
    e. both a and d

20. In Question 19, the word "cup" will fall on the:
    a. right side of both retinas and go to the left hemisphere
    b. left retina only and go to the right hemisphere
    c. left side of both retinas and go to the left hemisphere
    d. right side of both retinas and go to the right hemisphere
    e. right side of the left eye and left side of the right eye and go to both hemispheres

21. The idea that some people are right-brained and some people are left-brained:
    a. is correct; some people use their left hemisphere for all tasks and some use their right
    b. is wrong because most people only use 10% of their brains and that 10% is almost always in the left hemisphere
    c. is correct and based on the fact that small neurons are constantly maturing so that only 10% of the neurons in only one hemisphere are mature at any given time
    d. is wrong; all people are left-brained; the right hemisphere is virtually useless
    e. is wrong because all tasks involve both hemispheres to some extent

## ANSWERS TO POSTTEST

| Correct Answer | Questions Testing a Similar Concept | |
| --- | --- | --- |
| | Comprehension Check | Short-Answer |

**Matching**

| Correct Answer | Comprehension Check | Short-Answer |
| --- | --- | --- |
| 1.  E  (p. 91) | 10 | 5,6 |
| 2.  G  (p. 88) | 8d,8e | -- |
| 3.  C  (p. 88) | 8 | -- |
| 4.  D  (p. 91) | 10a | 5 |
| 5.  F  (p. 91) | 10 | 5 |
| 6.  A  (p. 88) | 8,9 | 5 |
| 7.  B  (p. 87) | 8a | -- |

**Multiple-Choice**

| Correct Answer | Comprehension Check | Short-Answer |
| --- | --- | --- |
| 1.  c  (p. 74) | 2 | -- |
| 2.  a  (pp. 75-76) | 3a | -- |
| 3.  b  (p. 83) | 6 | -- |
| 4.  b  (pp. 80-81) | -- | 2 |
| 5.  a  (pp. 83-84) | 7 | -- |
| 6.  d  (pp. 89-91) | 9 | 5 |
| 7.  e  (pp. 91-92) | 10 | 5 |
| 8.  c  (p. 94) | -- | -- |
| 9.  e  (p. 96) | 11 | -- |
| 10.  b  (p. 97) | 12 | 6 |
| 11.  d  (p. 101) | 13 | 7 |
| 12.  c  (pp. 101-102) | 10 | -- |
| 13.  c  (p. 104) | 14d | -- |
| 14.  e  (pp. 105-107) | 15b | 8 |
| 15.  d  (pp. 108-109) | 15a,c | 8 |
| 16.  a  (p. 109) | 15 | 8 |
| 17.  c  (p. 110) | 16 | 9 |
| 18.  a  (pp. 113-114) | 18 | 10 |
| 19.  b  (p. 114) | 19,20 | 11 |
| 20.  d  (pp. 114-115) | 19,20 | 11 |
| 21.  e  (p. 116) | -- | 12 |

# CHAPTER 3  LANGUAGE ENHANCEMENT GUIDE

## I. VOCABULARY, IDIOMS AND CULTURAL CONCEPTS

### Instructions

As you read the text refer to the following list of words and their definitions.  The words are listed in the order in which they appear in the chapter.  The definitions presented contain the meaning of the word as used by Kalat on the text book page indicated.

Remember that these words like all words can have different meanings in other sentences.  If you do not find a non-technical word on this list it may have been defined on a previous page or chapter of this study guide.  The definition of non-technical words may be found in the dictionary at the end of this study guide.  Kalat defined each new technical word as it first appears on a page and these may be found in Kalat's summary at the end of the section and in the Glossary at the end the textbook.

### Psychological Explanations at the Level of the Gene

a great deal (72) = much; a large amount
underestimate =  to make too low an estimate of the quantity, degree, or worth of something
keep-up-to-date = keep current
highlights = the main ideas; the most important facts
bogged down = to focus too much time or effort on something

interaction (73) = two or more events effecting each other
enormous = a very large number; very large; many
hallucinations = a sensory experience that does not correspond to reality
delusion = false and improbable beliefs
apparently = obvious; easily seen or understood
predisposition = tendency, inclination, or susceptibility.
ultimately = the end result; finally

transmission (74) = sending; passing on

contributes  (75) =  to give or supply

localizing (77) =  to confine or restrict to a specific location
deterioration =  to grow or to get  worse; degenerate; to lose strength or effectiveness
to cope with = to manage; to live with
undesirable =  not wanted; not  pleasing; objectionable.
earlier intervention = to take action between two points of time
conceivably =  a possible idea
discriminate against =  to act or state  unreasonable judgments  against  a group of people
seemed inclined = wanted to
schizophrenia =   a group of psychological disorders usually characterized by withdrawal from reality, illogical thinking, delusions, and hallucinations.
resemblance = to look alike

genetic tendencies (79) = characteristics partly controlled by inherited genes

apparently = obvious; easily seen or understood

religious devoutness = devoted to religion or to religious duties

optimistic = expecting and focusing on the most hopeful aspects of a situation.

pessimistic = expecting and focusing on the worst aspects of a situation

implausible = not likely to be true; not credible

multitude = many

presumably = assumed; taken for granted; a reasonable guess


consumption (80) = eating; using up

interacts = two events effecting each another

intervention = an action or influence on another event


like begets like (81) = children are similar to their parents

disadvantageous = not beneficial; not favorable;


constituted an explanation (83) = acceptable as an explanation

ferociously = extremely savage; fierce; vicious or merciless; brutal


invariably (84) = not changing or subject to change; constant

in driving off = chase away

sticks together = stay together; to form a group

speculative = guessing or making a risky claim without much evidence

### Explanations of Behavior at the Level of the Neuron

skeptical (84) = doubtful; questionable; not to be believed

controversial = a dispute between sides holding opposing views


estimate (87) = to guess or calculate the approximate amount, extent, magnitude, position, or value
   of something

physically merged = combined


excitatory (88) = increase

inhibitory = decrease


is not fixed throughout life (89) = remaining the same; constant

disrupt = disturb; change


contemplate (94) = to think about

radioactivity labeled chemicals =

investigator = a person who carries out a research study

elaborate equipment = special tools used to carry out a research study


distinct (95) = easily seen as different from other things; distinguishable from all others; discrete impairment (96) = to diminish or reduce the strength, value, or quality of something

facilitates movement = helps movement

converted = changed from one thing to another

appears promising = looks like it would work

toxic substances = poison things that can cause injury or death

deficient = missing an essential quality or element

deteriorate = to diminish or lessen in quality, value or amount; to grow worse; degenerate

## Explanations of Behavior at the Level of the Nervous System

components (101) = parts or elements of something

peripheral = located in, or forming an outer boundary


adjacent (102) = close to; lying near.

diffuses = to spread out or scatter; disseminate; to make less bright; soften

migration = moving from one country or region and settling in another


can still make (104) = can make

frankly = openly, directly, honestly

insulation = preventing the passage of heat, electricity, or sound into or out of something, especially
     by surrounding with a nonconducting material


funneling (106) = to direct or guide; to move through or as if through a funnel

acting in parallel = acting together at the same time


neglect (108) = to fail to do or carry out a task; to fail to pay attention to something


localized (109) = confine or restrict to a specific location

inseparable = cannot be separated


anesthetized (111) = loss of sensation, due to disease, injury or an anesthetic, such as chloroform

unanesthetized = not anesthetized


feedback loop (114) = the return of information about the result of a process or activity

resume = to start over again


severed (115) = cut


specialization (116) = to focus on a particular activity or product

## II. VOCABULARY BUILDING

### Word Analysis

<u>Instructions:</u>

1. Study the meaning of the prefixes, roots and suffixes listed.
2. Break each word in the table into its prefixes, roots and suffixes.
3. Guess the meaning of the word based on the meaning of its parts.
4. Find the word on the text page indicated in the brackets and redefine the word based on the context of the sentence, paragraph and chapter.
5. Look up the definition of the word in the VOCABULARY, IDIOMS AND CULTURAL CONCEPTS section above, in Appendix A (marked by A) or in a college level dictionary. If the word is followed by letter G look it up in the text Glossary.

<u>Exercise 1. Quantities</u>

**Prefix : mono/uni** _____ = single, one
**Prefix : di /bi** _____ = double/two
**Prefix : tri** _____ = three/triple
**Prefix : poly/multi** _____ = many
**Word: zygote** =
**Word: lateral** = side
**Root: chroma** = color
**Root: soma** _____ = body
**Suffix** _____ic = characteristic / having to do with

| Word | Meaning |
|------|---------|
| monozygotic (G) | |
| dizygotic (G) | |
| unilateral | |
| bilateral | |
| multilateral | |
| monotone | |
| trimester | |
| monochromatic | |
| trichromatic (G) | |
| chromosome (G) | |

<u>Exercise 2. Same and Different</u>

**Prefix : hetero** _____ = different, other
**Prefix : homo** _____ = same
**Suffix:** _____ ous = full of, characterized by
**Root** ___ gamy ____ = marriage

| Root | Meaning |
|---|---|
| heterozygous (G) | |
| homozygous (G) | |
| heterogeneous (G) | grouping that puts different kinds of people or things together |
| homogenous | grouping that puts similar kinds of people or things together |
| dangerous | |
| monogamy | |
| bigamy | |

Exercise 3.  Parasympathetic

**Prefix: para** _____ **= beside/resembling**
**Prefix: sym** _____ **= with/together**
**Prefix: gen** _____ **= become/produce/bear**
**Root:** _____ **pathy** ____ **= feeling/sorrow/suffering**
**Root:** ____ **soma/physio** _____ **= body**
**Suffix:** _____ **= characterized by/having the nature of/like/**
                       **belonging to**

| Word | Meaning |
|---|---|
| parasympathetic(G) | |
| sympathetic(G) | |
| sympathy | |
| paramedic | |
| psychometric (G) | |
| physiological | |
| genetic | |
| psychosomatic( G) | |

Exercise 4.  Away, Apart and Without

**Prefix : dis** ____ **= away from/ apart/ not/ without/**

| Root | Meaning |
|---|---|
| disadvantageous (A) | |
| discomfort | |
| discard | |
| dissolve | |
| disassociate | |
| disown | |
| disbelief | |

**Prefix: un _____ = not, the opposite of**
**Suffix: _____ able, ible = able to, able to make**

| Word | Meaning |
|---|---|
| undesirable (A) | |
| unanesthetized (A) | |
| uncooperative | |
| uncomfortable | |

Exercise 6. Potent Power

**Root : _____ potent _____ = power**
**Prefix: Im_____ = without**
**Suffix: _____ al = like/being**

| Word | Meaning |
|---|---|
| potential | power or ability existing as a possibility |
| impotent | without power |
| musical | being musical, having musical talent or skills |
| comical | |
| seasonal | |

Exercise 7:  Transmit

**Prefix: trans _____ = send or carry across/beyond**
**Prefix: neuro _____ = nerve**
**Suffix: _____ tion/ion = the process or act of**
**Suffix: _____ er =**

| Word | Meaning |
|---|---|
| transmit (A) | |
| transmission (A) | |
| transform | |
| transplant | |
| neurotransmission (G) | |
| neurotransmitter (G) | |

Exercise 8:  Pre and Post

**Prefix: pre _____ = before/before/ahead**
**Prefix: post _____ = after**
**Root: _____dict_____ = speak/ say**

| Word | Meaning |
|---|---|
| postsynaptic  (G) | |
| presynaptic (G) | |
| prehistoric | |
| postgraduate | |
| predict (A) | |

Exercise 9. Unfold

**Prefix: un _____ = reversal, removal of**

| Word | Meaning |
|------|---------|
| unbutton | |
| unfold | |
| unbutton | |
| unfold | |

Exercise 10. Sensitivity

**Suffix: _____ tion = condition**
**Suffix: _____ ate = to do**
**Suffix _____ al = having the qualities of**
**Suffix _____ ly = in this manner**
**Suffix _____ ment = cause/means/ result (of an action)**
**Suffix _____ ness = condition/quality/degree**
**Suffix _____ ity = the quality of/ an example of**
**Suffix _____ ic = having the qualities of**

| Word | Meaning |
|------|---------|
| adaptation | |
| demonstration | |
| visual | |
| excitedly | |
| treatment | |
| loudness | |
| sensitivity | |
| characteristic | |

# CHAPTER 4 SENSATION AND PERCEPTION

**OBJECTIVES**

Understand that:

I. Sensation is the conversion of energy into nervous system responses (p. 122)

**Vision**

II. Vision involves reception of radiated energy (p. 123, Fig. 4.1)
    A. Receptors are specialized cells that convert energy (p. 123)
    B. Light passes through the cornea, pupil, and lens (p. 124, Fig. 4.2)
        1. Elongated eyeballs cause nearsightedness; flattened eyeballs cause farsightedness (pp. 124-125, Fig. 4.4)
        2. Glaucoma is increased pressure in the eyeball which can damage the optic nerve (p. 125)
        3. The lens becomes cloudy with cataracts (pp. 125-126)
    C. Receptors are located on the retina (p. 126)
        1. Rods are sensitive in dim light (p. 126, Table 4.1, p. 127)
        2. Cones are sensitive to color and give detailed vision (p. 126, Table 4.1, p. 127)
            a. Fovea consists of cones (p. 126)
    D. Dark adaptation occurs for both rods and cones (pp. 127-128, Fig. 4.7)
    E. Neural impulses travel through the bipolar cells, ganglion cells, and optic nerve to the brain (p. 128)
        1. The blind spot is where the optic nerve leaves the retina (pp. 128-129, Fig. 4.9, p. 130)
III. Color vision depends on cones (p. 129)
    A. Young-Helmholtz theory or trichromatic theory -- three types of cones (pp. 129-131, Fig. 4.10)
    B. Opponent-process theory -- three two-color systems (pp. 131-132, Fig. 4.12)
        1. Can explain negative afterimages (p. 132, Fig. 4.13)
    C. Retinex theory -- retina and cortex interact to determine color vision (pp. 133-134, Fig. 4.15)
        1. Can explain color constancy (p. 133)
    D. Color blindness occurs because of a deficiency in the cones (pp. 134-136)

**Nonvisual Senses**

IV. In hearing, sound waves are translated into neural impulses (pp. 138-139)
    A. Path is eardrum, three tiny bones, cochlear fluid, basilar membrane, hair cells which are the receptors (p. 139, Fig. 4.19)
        1. Conduction deafness occurs when sound waves aren't properly transmitted to the cochlea (p. 139)
        2. Nerve deafness occurs because of damage to the cochlea, hair cells, or auditory nerve (pp. 139-140)
    B. Pitch perception depends on three mechanisms (p. 140, Fig. 4.20, p. 141)
        1. Neurons fire in synchrony for low frequencies (p. 140)
        2. Groups of neurons fire in synchrony for middle frequencies (volley principle) (p. 140)
        3. Different parts of basilar membrane vibrate for high frequencies (p. 140)
    C. A few individuals with absolute pitch can identify notes perfectly (p. 141)
    D. Sound is localized by differences in loudness and time of arrival at the two ears (pp. 141-142, Fig. 4.21)

V. Receptors for vestibular senses are in inner ear  (pp. 142-143, Fig. 4.22)
  A. Semicircular canals detect acceleration  (p. 142)
  B. Otolith organs detect tilt of the head  (pp. 142-143)
VI. The cutaneous senses depend upon receptors in the skin  (pp. 143-144, Fig. 4.23)
  A. Receptors are dense on fingertips, lips, and other sensitive areas  (p. 144)
  B. Pain receptors are bare nerve endings  (p. 144)
    1. Intensity of pain depends on other sensory experiences  (pp. 144-145)
      a. Gate theory of pain suggests that pain message pass through a gate which can be open or closed  (p. 145)
      b. Endorphins  (endogenous morphine) decrease pain  (pp. 145-146, Fig.  4.26)
      c. Capsaicin causes a burning sensation followed by a reduction in pain  (p. 146)
VII. Chemical receptors are responsible for taste and smell  (p. 147)
  A. Taste receptors are taste buds on the tongue  (p. 147, Fig. 4.27)
    1. Traditionally, the four primary tastes are sweet, sour, salty, and bitter  (pp. 147-148)
      a. There is evidence for distinct receptors  (p. 148)
  B. Olfactory  (smell) receptors are on mucous membranes at rear of nose  (p. 148, Fig. 4.28, p. 149)
    1. The nose has at least 100 different receptors.  (p. 148, Fig. 4.28, p. 149)
    2. Animals identify each other by pheromones  (p. 149)

**The Interpretation of Sensory Information**

VIII. The perceived world is created from the real world  (p. 153)
  A. A threshold is the minimum intensity that a person can detect half the time  (pp. 153-154, Fig. 4.31)
    1. Sensory adaptation can change the threshold  (p. 154)
      a. The absolute threshold is found when adaptation is maximal  (p. 154)
    2. Observers' willingness to make false alarms can affect threshold  (p. 154)
      a. This is studied in signal-detection theory  (pp. 154-155)
  B. Subliminal perception occurs below the conscious threshold  (p. 155)
    1. Subliminal messages don't do many things they are claimed to do  (pp. 155-156)
      a. They don't cause people to buy things  (pp. 155-156)
      b. Backward messages aren't understood  (p. 156)
      c. Subliminal audiotapes don't cause behavioral changes  (p. 156)
    2. There is some evidence that stimuli that aren't conscious are processed  (pp. 156-157)
      a. Subliminal messages may cause weak behavioral changes that are short-lived  (p. 157)
IX. People are very good at recognizing what things are  (p. 157)
  A. Feature detectors break patterns into simple components  (pp. 157-158)
    1. Cells that detect specific features have been found in animals  (pp. 158-159, Fig. 4.35)
    2. Fatigued feature-detector cells produce illusions  (pp. 158-159, Fig. 4.36)
  B. More complex identification depends on context  (pp. 159-160)
  C. Gestalt psychology suggested that we actively construct overall patterns  (p. 161)
    1. Reversible figures are evidence for active organization  (pp. 161-162, Fig. 4.41)
    2. The Gestalt principles of proximity, similarity, continuation, closure, and good figure help to explain the organization of stimuli  (pp. 162-163, Fig. 4.42)
  D. Gestalt principles also apply to hearing  (pp. 164-165)
  E. Feature detection is "bottom-up" and Gestalt is "top-down" processing  (p. 165)
    1. Both types of processing probably occur  (p. 165)

F. Preattentive processes allow the detection of many features automatically and in parallel (pp. 168-166, Fig. 4.45)

X. Distance and movement are interpretations of changes on the retina  (p. 167)
  A. Objects are perceived as constant in size and shape  (p. 167, Fig. 4.47)
  B. Movement of an object doesn't occur when the eyes move  (pp. 169-170)
    1. Induced movement occurs when the background moves and the object is stationary (pp. 167-168)
    2. Stroboscopic movement occurs when stationary images are presented (p. 168)
  C. Several cues are used to perceive distance  (p. 168)
    1. Retinal disparity occurs because the two retinas receive different images  (pp. 168-169, Fig. 4.50)
    2. The eyes must converge more to focus on close objects  (p. 169, Fig. 4.51, p. 170)
    3. Other monocular cues involve only one eye  (pp. 169-170, Fig. 4.52)
      a. Object size, linear perspective, detail, interposition, texture gradients, and shadows can be used to judge distance in pictures  (pp. 170-171, Fig. 4.52-4.53)
      b. Motion parallax involves relative movement and requires real scenes  (p. 171)
  D. Illusions occur because of misinterpretations  (pp. 172-173, Fig. 4.54)
    1. Sometimes changes in distance are interpreted as size changes  (pp. 173-174, Fig. 4.55, 4.56)
    2. Interpreting two-dimensional drawings as three-dimensional can cause depth perception errors (pp. 174-175, Fig. 4.57, 4.58, 4.59)
  E. People misjudge loudness when apparent distance changes also  (p. 175)
  F. The strength of illusions may differ across cultures, depending on experience with objects (pp. 175-176, Fig. 4.60)
  G. The moon looks much larger on the horizon than high in the sky  (pp. 176-177)
    1. There are several theories of the moon illusion, but none explains completely  (pp. 176-177)

## COMPREHENSION CHECK

Answer these questions soon after reading the chapter. Circle the best alternative. Check your answers on pp. 73-75. If you gave a wrong answer, try to write why it was wrong. Check your reasons on pp. 73-75.

### Vision

1. The nervous system:
    a. builds a copy of the external stimulus in the brain
    b. registers the exact intensity and direction of every stimulus
    c. uses receptors to interpret information and to extract meaning
    d. translates external stimuli into internal representations

Correct _____ If wrong, why? _____

2. Prof. Quaalude is myopic. He:
    a. is farsighted
    b. has an eyeball that is flattened
    c. has a cornea that is too round
    d. has a faulty optic nerve
    e. has an eyeball that is elongated

Correct _____ If wrong, why? _____

3. John is a night watchman. He thinks he hears someone outside in the dim light. In order to see this as clearly as possible, he should:
    a. look slightly to the side of the fovea so rods will be stimulated
    b. look through his widened pupil so cones will be stimulated
    c. make the image fall on his fovea so cones will be stimulated
    d. be sure that the entire electromagnetic spectrum falls on his retina
    e. try to get the image into his blind spot so that his cornea will be clear

Correct _____ If wrong, why? _____

4. Dark adaptation takes much longer if you stare at a faint light while another light flashes in the periphery of your vision than if you just stare at the first light. Why?
    a. having the two lights stimulates more cones
    b. the second light stimulates cones, which take longer to adapt
    c. the second light stimulates rods, which take longer to adapt
    d. having two lights stimulates the ganglion cells as well as the bipolar cells
    e. the second light moves the stimulation from the first light from the blind spot

Correct _____ If wrong, why? _____

5. According to the opponent-process theory, we see green when:
    a. the medium wavelength cone is more active than the other two
    b. the cortex synthesizes a color from active areas of the retina
    c. particular ganglion cells are inhibited and others are excited
    d. we have a negative afterimage of a yellow light

Correct _____ If wrong, why? _____

**Nonvisual Senses**

6. Which of the following is the correct path of sound waves to the receptors for hearing?
    a. eardrum, cochlea, three tiny bones, hair cells, basilar membrane
    b. eardrum, three tiny bones, cochlear fluid, basilar membrane, hair cells
    c. three tiny bones, cochlear fluid, basilar membrane, eardrum, hair cells
    d. three tiny bones, basilar membrane, hair cells, eardrum, cochlear fluid

Correct _____ If wrong, why? _____

7. How does the human ear encode a tone of 10,000 hertz?
    a. the basilar membrane vibrates in synchrony; hair cells send impulses at that frequency
    b. the basilar membrane vibrates in synchrony with it, and groups of hair cells volley impulses in synchrony with the tone
    c. by the difference in time and loudness at the two ears
    d. the basilar membrane vibrates maximally at a specific location; those hair cells send impulses

Correct _____ If wrong, why? _____

8. If you have damage to your semicircular canals:
   a. you may have trouble with balance
   b. your vestibular sense would be poor
   c. your free nerve endings would not send impulses
   d. both b and c
   e. both a and b

Correct _____ If wrong, why? _____

9. Jalapeño peppers cause somewhat painful sensations because they result in the release of:
   a. endorphins
   b. capsaicin
   c. sodium lauryl sulfate
   d. substance P
   e. pheromones

Correct _____ If wrong, why? _____

10. The olfactory sense in humans:
    a. is very poor because the receptors are not sensitive
    b. is particularly important because of the role played by pheromones
    c. results from receptors that are called taste buds
    d. is limited to only four tastes: sweet, sour, bitter, and salty
    e. is stimulated by gaseous molecules that we inhale

Correct _____ If wrong, why? _____

**The Interpretation of Sensory Information**

11. An observer might often detect stimuli that are below the absolute threshold because:
    a. dark adaptation has occurred, lowering the threshold
    b. thresholds are defined as 50% detection, so observers will detect below-threshold stimuli half the time
    c. observers set a stringent criterion and make few false alarms
    d. evidence for subliminal perception can be found easily and such perception has been shown to have long-lasting influences on behavior

Correct _____ If wrong, why? _____

12. The feature-detector approach differs from the Gestalt approach because the feature-detector approach:
    a. suggests that we break stimuli down into components; the Gestalt approach argues that we perceive "wholes"
    b. relies on the measurement of thresholds; the Gestalt approach emphasizes optical illusions
    c. points out the importance of visual constancies; the Gestalt approach emphasizes reversible figures
    d. argues that aftereffects should not be found after fatiguing specific feature detectors; Gestalt approach argues that they should

Correct _____ If wrong, why? _____

13. Many computer printers produce letters that consist of unconnected small dots. Yet we see the patterns as complete letters. Which Gestalt principle is operating here?
    a. separation of figure and ground
    b. similarity
    c. closure
    d. reversible figure
    e. proximity

Correct _____ If wrong, why? _____

14. The brain decides that a T is a T because the points make up a vertical line and another set of points make up a horizontal line and these join just below the center of the horizontal line. This type of processing is called:
    a. bottom-up
    b. backward masking
    c. top-down
    d. preattentive

Correct _____ If wrong, why? _____

15. When a rectangular door is slightly open, it projects a trapezoidal image on the retina, yet you see it as rectangular. Why?
    a. size constancy makes it appear the same
    b. visual constancies cause you to interpret changes on the retina as actual changes in the size and shapes of objects
    c. shape constancy tells you that it has changed position, not shape
    d. convergence tells you that its shape has not changed
    e. because a door is a door even if it's ajar

Correct _____ If wrong, why? _____

16. Which depth cue could not be used by a person with one eye?
    a. size
    b. closer objects overlap farther objects
    c. amount of detail in objects
    d. convergence
    e. motion parallax

Correct _____ If wrong, why? _____

17. Jack, who is standing perfectly still, says that there is some wind because the leaves on the trees are moving; Jill, who is riding up the hill, says "No, the leaves aren't moving." How can this discrepancy be explained?
    a. Jill's vestibular system tells her that she is moving
    b. induced movement tells Jack that the leaves are moving
    c. Jack is having an illusion similar to the Mueller-Lyer illusion
    d. the background is stationary to Jill

Correct _____ If wrong, why? _____

18. The moon illusion:
    a. is not an illusion at all; the moon is larger when it is close to the horizon
    b. occurs because light rays bend differently near the horizon
    c. occurs because we interpret the horizon as being farther away than the overhead sky
    d. occurs because we are likely to compare the moon's size with objects at the horizon
    e. both c and d may be partly correct, but the moon illusion is difficult to explain

Correct _____ If wrong, why? _____

## ANSWERS AND EXPLANATIONS FOR COMPREHENSION CHECK

| Correct Answer | Other Alternatives Are Wrong Because: |
|---|---|

1. d  (p. 122)
   Obj. I

   a. the internal representation may not resemble the external stimulus in any way
   b. internal representations are related to external stimuli, but they aren't the same
   c. this is perception; receptors are responsible for sensation

2. e  (pp. 124-125, Fig. 4.4)
   Obj. II-B-1

   a. myopic means nearsighted; presbyopia means farsighted
   b. this occurs in farsightedness
   c. cornea shape is unrelated to nearsightedness
   d. optic nerve goes from ganglion cells to brain

3. a  (p. 126,
   Table 4.1, p. 127)
   Obj. II-C-2a

   b. cones cannot see well in dim light; a widened pupil makes it more likely that rods will be stimulated
   c. cones cannot respond in dim light
   d. the entire spectrum is not visible, only part of it
   e. blind spot is where axons leave retina; nothing can be seen there

4. c  (pp. 126-127, Fig. 4.7)
   Obj. II-D

   a. second light would only stimulate rods
   b. rods take longer to adapt than cones
   d. both lights would stimulate both types of cells
   e. nothing can be seen in the blind spot; a second light wouldn't affect where the first one falls

5. c  (pp. 131-132, Fig. 4.12)
   Obj. III-B

   a. Young-Helmholtz theory  (emphasis on cones)
   b. retinex theory  (emphasis on cortex)
   d. blue would produce a yellow afterimage

6. b  (p. 139, Fig. 4.19)
   Obj. IV-A

   a. three tiny bones are between eardrum and cochlea
   c. eardrum comes before three tiny bones
   d. eardrum comes first, cochlear fluid before basilar membrane

7. d  (p. 140,
   Fig. 4.20, p. 141)
   Obj. IV-B-3

   a. for low tones, below 100 hertz
   b. for medium tones, 100-5000 hertz
   c. this is how sound is localized

8. e (pp. 142-143)
   Obj. V-A

a. correct, but so is b
b. correct, but so is a
c. free nerve endings are receptors for pain and temperature, not vestibular sense
d. b is correct, but c is incorrect

9. d (p. 146, Fig. 4.26)
   Obj. VI-B-1-c

a. neurotransmitters that inhibit the release of substance P
b. this is the chemical in the jalapeños that causes the release of substance P
c. a chemical that weakens the response to sweet tastes
e. odorous chemicals released by mammals

10. e (p. 148)
    Obj. VII-B

a. each receptor is sensitive; we just don't have as many as other animals
b. less important for humans than other animals
c. taste buds are for taste, not smell
d. olfactory means smell, not taste

11. b (pp. 153-154,
    Fig. 4.31)
    Obj. VIII-A

a. the absolute threshold is measured when dark adaptation is complete; it's the lowest measurable threshold
c. a stringent criterion would result in more misses and fewer false alarms
d. evidence for subliminal perception is not always found and, when it is, it is short-lived

12. a (pp. 159-164)
    Obj. IX-A

b. feature detection emphasizes components, but not necessarily thresholds; Gestalt relies on more than illusions
c. visual constancies not particularly relevant to features; reversible figures are one demonstration
d. such fatigue is evidence <u>for</u> feature detectors

13. c (pp. 162-163)
    Obj. IX-C-2

a. involves picking out object from background
b. tendency to see similar things as going together
d. tendency to see parts as either figure or ground
e. tendency to see things that are close as going together

14. a (p. 165)
    Obj. IX-E

b. refers to a second visual stimulus erasing the first one; not to the identification of single stimuli
c. the opposite; refers to starting with expectation and then seeing parts based on it
d. this would be automatic and in parallel; the present case sounds more attentive and serial

15. c (p. 167, Fig. 4.47)
    Obj. X-A

a. shape is emphasized here, not size
b. we do not interpret changes as actual changes in objects
d. convergence is a cue to distance
e. a bad joke, but that's what shape constancy suggests

16. d (pp. 169-170,  a-c. all can be seen with one eye
    Fig. 4.51)      e. differential movement across retina can be seen with one eye,
    Obj. X-C-3          although not in a picture

17. a (p. 171)       b. occurs when background moves and object doesn't;
    Obj. X-B             object is moving here
                      c. seeing lines with outward arrowheads as longer than lines with
                         inward arrow heads; not relevant here
                      d. background would be moving to Jill since she is moving

18. e (pp. 176-177)  a. moon is same size
    Obj. X-G         b. it is a psychological, not a physical effect
                     c,d. both are possibly correct, but see e

## LECTURE MATERIAL

Don't forget to review your lecture material. Process each topic meaningfully. First, be sure that you understand the material in each lecture--if you don't, ask your instructor or teaching assistant. Associate the material with things that you already know and with your personal experiences. If you can make up mental images of any of the material, do so. Try to think of real-life applications of the concepts. Put your own notes on your lecture notes. Then write questions to cover each concept.

-------------------------------------------------------------------------
### WAIT AT LEAST 24 HOURS BEFORE PROCEEDING.
### LET FORGETTING OCCUR--IT WILL!!
-------------------------------------------------------------------------

## SHORT-ANSWER ESSAY QUESTIONS

Write brief answers to each of the following. The answers are on p. 77-78, but do try to write the answers yourself before looking at them.

### Vision

1. What is the function of receptors? How are they involved in the relationship between the external and internal worlds?

2. Describe three differences between rods and cones other than their shapes.

3. Contrast the Young-Helmholtz, opponent-process, and retinex theories of color perception.

4. Explain what occurs in the cones when people are color-blind.

**Nonvisual Senses**

5. Explain how pitch is perceived for sounds of different frequencies.

6. According to the gate theory of pain, why do reports of pain differ so much, even when the physical damage is similar?

7. Describe evidence that suggests there are different receptors for different tastes.

**The Interpretation of Sensory Information**

8. How does the signal-detection approach to detection differ from the threshold approach?

9. What are the problems in studying subliminal perception? What does modern research suggest about the possibility of subliminal perception?

10. Contrast the Gestalt and the feature-detector approaches to perception.

11. Explain how Gestalt principles apply to hearing.

12. Assume that you have a negative afterimage of the U.S. flag. Describe what would happen if you looked at a white screen that is very close to you and then at one that is very far away. Use this example to explain how size and distance are related.

\*\*\*\*\*\*\*\*\*\*\*\*\*\*\*\*\*\*\*\*\*\*\*\*\*\*\*\*\*\*\*\*\*\*\*\*\*\*\*\*\*\*\*\*\*\*\*\*\*\*\*\*\*\*\*\*\*\*\*\*\*\*\*\*\*\*\*\*\*\*\*\*\*\*\*\*\*\*\*
Find the questions that you wrote over lecture material and write answers to them.
\*\*\*\*\*\*\*\*\*\*\*\*\*\*\*\*\*\*\*\*\*\*\*\*\*\*\*\*\*\*\*\*\*\*\*\*\*\*\*\*\*\*\*\*\*\*\*\*\*\*\*\*\*\*\*\*\*\*\*\*\*\*\*\*\*\*\*\*\*\*\*\*\*\*\*\*\*\*\*

## ANSWERS TO SHORT-ANSWER ESSAY QUESTIONS

1. Receptors convert physical energy into nerve impulses, or stimuli in the external world into internal stimuli. The internal experience is lawfully related to the external stimuli, but they are not perfectly related. (p. 123)

2. Rods are sensitive in dim light; cones are sensitive only in bright light. Rods are color-blind; cones respond to color. Cones are concentrated on the fovea at the center of the retina; rods are on the periphery. (p.126, Table 4.1, p. 127)

3. Young-Helmholtz theory holds that there are three types of cones that respond maximally to different colors. Opponent-process theory holds that higher-level cells are excited (speeded up) to one color and inhibited (slowed down) to another. Retinex theory stresses interpretation of color by the cortex. (pp. 129-134)

4. Usually, there is an abnormality in either the red or green cones (although other types of colorblindness also occur). If the problem is in the green cones (medium-wavelength), it is called deuteranopia; if it is in the red cones (long-wavelength), it is called protanopia. The abnormal cones don't respond properly to the red or green light, so the person has difficulty discriminating red from green. (pp. 134-135)

5. For low sounds (under 100 Hz), the basilar membrane vibrates in synchrony with the sound and nerve impulses are sent in synchrony. Middle sounds (100-5000 Hz) are coded in a similar manner, except that individual hair cells cannot send impulses that fast, so groups of cells volley and, as a group, send impulses that are in synchrony with the sound. High sounds (over 5000 Hz) cause maximum vibration at certain places on the basilar membrane, and only those hair cells send impulses to the brain. (p. 140, Fig. 4.20, p. 141)

6. According to Melzack and Wall's gate theory, pain messages pass through a gate in the spinal cord. The brain can send messages to the spinal cord to open the gate and let the pain impulses through or to close the gate and block the pain. Although some of the details of this gate theory are wrong, the basic idea that the brain facilitates or inhibits the transmission of pain messages is correct. Distraction may help to close the gate, or distraction may cause the release of endorphins, which are natural painkillers that work in the brain. (p. 145)

7. Cooling the tongue reduces sensitivity to sweet tastes, but not to other tastes. Chemicals such as sodium lauryl sulfate (an ingredient in toothpaste) weakens sensitivity to sweet and increases sensitivity to sour and bitter. (pp. 147-148)

8. Thresholds are found by determining the lowest-intensity stimulus that can be detected half of the time. Thresholds will vary depending upon other factors, such as degree of dark adaptation. Using signal-detection theory, both the ability to detect a stimulus and the observer's criterion are taken into account. An observer may detect more stimuli under some conditions, but if she also makes a lot of false alarms (detecting the stimulus when it isn't present), detection isn't any better; the criterion is simply less stringent (strict). (pp. 154-155)

9. One problem is identifying whether stimuli are really subliminal (below threshold) because subjects may or may not report seeing or hearing them, depending upon how cautious they are about their responses. There is evidence that the nervous system processes stimuli even though we are unaware of them, but these effects don't last very long. These can influence our perception of other stimuli, but there is no evidence that subliminal messages influence buying behavior or have any effect on breaking bad habits. (pp. 155-157)

10. The feature-detector approach argues that people break stimuli down into components, such as lines and angles. The brain then analyzes the components to decide what a stimulus is. The Gestalt approach argues that we take in whole stimuli rather than breaking them into components. (pp. 157-164)

11. There are reversible figures in sound as well as in vision. For example, a clock can sound like "tick, tock, tick, tock" or "tock, tick, tock, tick." People also lock onto one interpretation of a sound and cannot hear the other one. If they organize the words in a sentence in one way, they may organize the words in the next sentence in the same way until they discover that the organization doesn't make sense. (pp. 164-166)

12. The negative afterimage has a certain size on your retina. If you look at a white piece of paper near your eyes, you will see a small image. If you look at a piece of paper far away, you will see a large image. In the far case, you assume that the actual size must be quite large for the afterimage to be that big on your retina and that far away. In the close case, you assume that the actual size is small because the distance is close. (pp. 132, 169-170)

## POSTTEST

Take this test with all of your books and notes out of sight. This should give you a good idea of how well you understand the material.

## Matching

Put the letter of the structure on the right in the blank beside the description on the left.

The Eye and the Ear

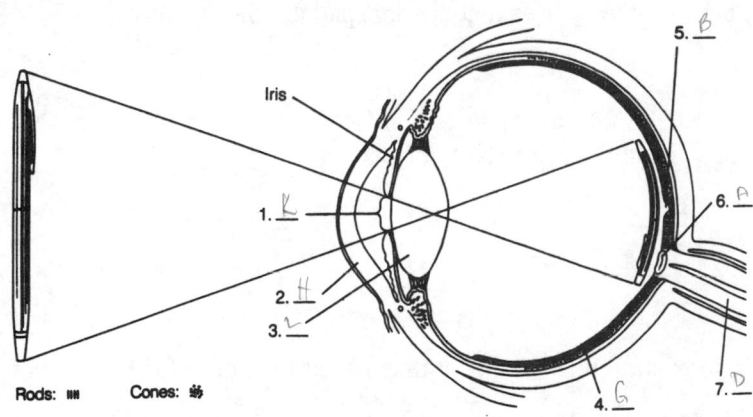

A. blind spot

B. fovea

C. semicircular canals

D. optic nerve

E. stirrup

F. eardrum

G. retina

H. cornea

I. hammer

J. anvil

K. pupil

L. lens

M. oval window

N. cochlea

O. round window

P. auditory nerve

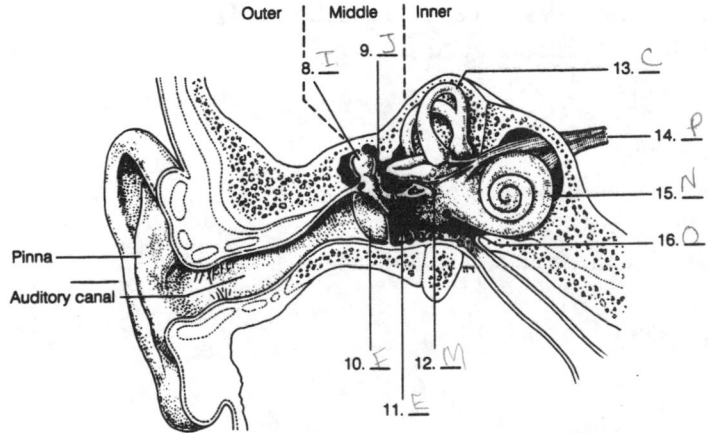

. Figure of ear adapted from *Human Information Processing: An Introduction to Psychology*, Second Edition, by Peter H. Lindsay and Donald A. Norman, copyright © 1977 by Harcourt Brace & Company, reproduced by permission of the publisher.

**Multiple-Choice**

Circle the best alternative.

<u>Vision</u>

1. What is the relationship between what we sense and what is really there?
   a. there is a perfect relationship between external events and our internal representations
   b. models of external stimuli are created in the brain
   c. they are physically identical
   d. external stimuli are translated into a neural "language"
   e. for vision, internal copies are made but for other senses that are nonspatial, other types of representations are formed

2. When a person is farsighted:
   a. the lens does not become thin and flat as it should for distant objects
   b. he or she has myopia
   c. the eyeball is elongated
   d. the eyeball is flattened
   e. both b and c

3. Why can you see fine detail better if you look straight at an object than if you look out of the corner of your eye?
   a. the object falls on the fovea, where there are many rods
   b. the object falls on the periphery, where there are many cones
   c. the object falls on rods, many of which send impulses to the same ganglion cell
   d. the object falls in the blind spot, where detailed vision is good
   e. the object falls on the fovea, where there are many cones

4. Why does everyone have a blind spot in each eye?
   a. there are no rods or cones where the optic nerve leaves the retina
   b. there are no cones on the periphery of the retina
   c. the retina is organized with rods and cones at the front and ganglion cells at the rear
   d. the fovea contains no rods
   e. the rods on the far periphery contain no photopigments

5. Which of the following best supports retinex theory?
   a. negative afterimages occur in the opposite color
   b. people are usually red-green color-blind
   c. different cones show different levels of responding to different colors
   d. three different colors of light can be mixed to make all other colors
   e. the apparent color of an object depends upon the colors of the objects around it

6. Colorblind people:
   a. usually cannot distinguish any colors
   b. see green objects as red
   c. most often have trouble distinguishing yellow from blue
   d. most often have trouble distinguishing red from green
   e. do not have any photopigments in their cones

## Nonvisual Senses

7. What happens to the basilar membrane when a low tone (below 100 Hz) is sensed?
    a. a very small area of it vibrates; the rest is relatively stationary
    b. it vibrates in synchrony with the sound waves
    c. it volleys in synchrony with the sound waves
    d. the left basilar membrane responds faster than the right one
    e. it will respond to more reflected sounds than with a higher tone

8. When a sound comes from directly overhead, it is difficult to localize because:
    a. it reaches one ear earlier than the other
    b. the basilar membrane is unable to respond to such a sound
    c. it sounds louder in one ear than the other
    d. it reflects off objects too much
    e. it reaches the two ears at the same time and with the same intensity

9. Why is it easier to read when your head is moving than when the page is moving?
    a. the vestibular system keeps your eyes focused when your head moves but not when the book moves
    b. the basilar membrane vibrates when your head moves, but not when the book moves
    c. the somatosensory system keeps your eyes focused when your head moves but not when the book moves
    d. the gate in the spinal cord prevents stimulation to the brain when your eyes move, but the signal gets through the gate when the book moves
    e. capsaicin is released when the head moves; this causes the release of substance P, which keeps the eyes focused when the head moves

10. Endorphins are:
    a. drugs made from the opium poppy that are similar to morphine
    b. neurotransmitters that cause the release of substance P and decrease pain
    c. used to decrease the sensitivity of the olfactory system
    d. neurotransmitters that occur naturally and are similar to morphine
    e. naturally occurring substances that cause the release of capsaicin in the body

11. The four types of taste buds are:
    a. scattered uniformly across the tongue
    b. are important for sensing the location of the substance on the tongue
    c. are interrelated, so that if one of them is affected by some chemical, all are affected
    d. are located almost exclusively along the sides of the tongue
    e. are unrelated to heat and cold so that changing the temperature does nothing to the taste

12. Pheromones:
    a. are used by animals to recognize one another
    b. are very important in human sexual behavior
    c. do not exist in humans
    d. are neurotransmitters that help to reduce pain
    e. cannot be detected by the human olfactory system

13. Which of the following claims about subliminal perception is true?
    a. people choose a picture that was presented subliminally more often than one that wasn't presented
    b. subliminal messages presented backward in songs can make people believe in the devil
    c. subliminal messages in movies influence people to buy snacks
    d. subliminal tapes can make people change their behavior; they are especially effective for increasing self-esteem

14. Which of the following supports the feature-detector model of pattern recognition?
    a. Hubel and Wiesel found that some brain cells responded only to angles
    b. some figures are reversible so that the background becomes the object
    c. things which are close together tend to be grouped into a unit
    d. we tend to "hear" missing syllables in speech
    e. stimuli are identified in context such that additional stimuli can either help or hurt identification

15. Gestalt psychologists:
    a. try to break stimuli into their basic components
    b. believe that perceptions depend on overall configurations
    c. argue that perception is simply the passive reception of energy
    d. emphasize the study of feature detectors
    e. believe in the theories of their founder, B. F. Gestalt

16. K   K   K   K   K
    K   K   K   K   K
    K   K   K   K   K
    K   K   K   K   K

    Why are you more likely to see the above as columns of Ks rather than rows of Ks?
    a. figure-ground principle
    b. closure
    c. proximity
    d. continuity
    e. similarity

17. Often people can pay attention to many things at once. This is the result of:
    a. preattentive processes that occur intentionally
    b. attentive processes that occurs intentionally
    c. preattentive processes that occur in parallel
    d. attentive processes that occur in parallel

18. Which of the following is not a cue for distance?
    a. convergence of the two eyes
    b. different views seen by the two eyes
    c. haziness of objects
    d. curvature of the cornea when focusing
    e. size of objects

19. As the $100 bill that you just won blows away from you in the wind, you do not perceive it as becoming smaller. Why?
    a. you have size constancy
    b. you are not responding to visual constancies
    c. your eyes compensate by converging more and more to focus
    d. your lens is unable to change fast enough to notice the size change
    e. you assume that objects in the distance are moving closer

20. The Mueller-Lyer illusion is:
    a. seeing the moon as larger when it is closer to the horizon than when it is high in the sky
    b. seeing lines as longer when arrowheads point inward than when they point outward
    c. stronger for people who live in cities and more technological societies than for people from more rural cultures
    d. only experienced by people who have lots of experience with drawings of objects
    e. larger for adults than for children

## ANSWERS TO POSTTEST

| Correct Answer | Questions Testing a Similar Concept | |
|---|---|---|
| | Comprehension Check | Short-Answer |

**Matching**

(See p. 124, Fig. 4.2)

| | | |
|---|---|---|
| 1. K | 3b | -- |
| 2. H | 2c, 3e | -- |
| 3. L | -- | -- |
| 4. G | 3d | -- |
| 5. B | 3a, 3c | -- |
| 6. A | 3e, 4e | -- |
| 7. D | 2d | -- |

(See p. 139, Fig. 4.19)

| | | |
|---|---|---|
| 8. I | 6 | -- |
| 9. J | 6 | -- |
| 10. F | 6 | -- |
| 11. E | 6 | -- |
| 12. M | -- | -- |
| 13. C | 8 | -- |
| 14. P | -- | -- |
| 15. N | 6 | -- |
| 16. O | -- | -- |

**Multiple-Choice**

| | | |
|---|---|---|
| 1. d (p. 123) | 1 | 1 |
| 2. d (pp. 124-125, Fig. 4.4) | 2a,b | -- |
| 3. e (p. 126) | 3c | 2 |
| 4. a (pp. 128-129) | 3e,4e | -- |
| 5. e (pp. 133-134) | 5b | 3 |
| 6. d (pp. 134-135) | -- | 4 |
| 7. b (p. 140) | 7a | 5 |
| 8. e (pp. 141-142) | 7c | -- |
| 9. a (p. 142) | 8b | -- |
| 10. d (pp. 145-146, Fig. 4.26) | 9a | 6 |
| 11. d (pp. 147-148, Fig. 4.27) | -- | 7 |
| 12. a (pp. 149-150) | 10b | -- |
| 13. a (pp. 156-157) | 11d | 9 |
| 14. a (pp. 158-159) | 12,14 | 10 |
| 15. b (p. 161) | 12 | 10 |
| 16. c (p. 162) | 13e | 10 |
| 17. c (pp. 165-166) | 14d | -- |
| 18. d (pp. 168-171) | 16 | -- |
| 19. a (p. 167) | 15a,b | 12 |
| 20. c (pp. 175-176) | 17c | -- |

# CHAPTER 4  LANGUAGE ENHANCEMENT GUIDE

## I.  VOCABULARY, IDIOMS  AND CULTURAL CONCEPTS

**Instructions:**

As you read the text refer to the following list of words and their definitions.  The words are listed in the order in which they appear in the chapter.  The definitions presented contain the meaning of the word as used by Kalat on the text book page indicated.

Remember that these words like all words can have different meanings in other sentences.  If you do not find a non-technical word on this list it may have been defined on a previous page or chapter of this study guide.  The definition of non-technical words may be found in the dictionary in Appendix A of this study guide.  Kalat defined each new technical word as it first appears on a page and these may be found in Kalat's summary at the end of the section and in the Glossary at the end the textbook.

**Vision**

fundamentally (122) = basically; very important
conversion = to change; sorting one form to another form
gives rise to = produces

are packed with  (123) = many things grouped together
fall into the trap = accept
hard to shake the idea = change
to get away from = escape
continuum = a range of values

rigid (124) = not flexible; difficult to bend
transparent = material, like glass, that you can see through

peripheral (125)= seeing near the outer edges of the retina.
filters out = removes
artificial = man made; not natural

make little use (126) = seldom used
drops sharply = rapidly decrease
pool their resources = combines their ability or powers
can hardly see = can not see clearly
overwhelmingly = mostly

roughly (129) = approximately

relative rate (130) = speed or amount

repulsive-looking (132) = ugly

illuminated (133) = to brighten with light
synthesize a color = to combine to form a new color
deals with different aspects = to focus on different parts of a process

apparently (134) = easy to understand,
relatively insensitive = does not respond to
distinguishing = recognizing

to lack (135) = to have something missing
rare = very few; uncommon
stare at = look at
fatigued = decreased ability to respond

arbitrary (136) = determined by chance or by individual judgment

**The Nonvisual Senses**

to be taken literally (138) = exactly as stated
abstract = difficult to understand
concept = an idea formed in the mind that can represent an object or event
let us deal with = consider
mammalian = warm-blooded animals with hair and the females nurse their young with milk.

displace (139) = move from side to side
compensate = to counterbalance; to make up for; to replace
impairment = to make worse; to decrease worth, value or strength; reduction; lessening

synchrony (140)= together

consistent (141) = unchanging
refined the ability = improved

relative distance (142) = approximate or almost exact distance
absolute distance = exact distance
acceleration = speeding up or slowing down
jiggling = shaking; rapid movement

axis (143) = a straight line about which the body turns

broader term (144) = a more general or abstract word
densely packed = many things grouped together
scattered more widely = spread over a wide area
everyday object = a common object
a scale model = a small model of a large object
irritating = mild pain
suffer exposure = be exposed to
peculiarity (145) = an unusual or unexpected characteristic
alerts us to = signals us to
insensitive = not responding to; not aware of
considerable = a large amount; many
prolonged = a longer time

put the breaks on (146) = to stop
paradoxically = a statement or claim that sounds contradictory or false but may be true
inducing = starting
ancient = hundreds to millions of years old

has solid evidence (148) = evidence supported by scientific research
taste preferences = a persons choice
in principle = is possible; in fact
had the technology to = had the research equipment
spend a lifetime = take many years of study

synchronized (150) = occur together
menstrual cycle = taking place on a monthly basis

**The Interpretation of Sensory Information**
overall pattern (153) = total pattern
constitutes = is part of
enormous = a very large number
bombarded = received many stimuli at one time
extremely weak = very weak

split second (155) = less than a second of time
plausible = probably true;   acceptable; credible

have been so wild (156) = uncontrolled
they would flock = gather together in a group
satanic message = messages from the devil
allege = to claim
plainly visible = can be easily seen

refinements (157)= improvements
short-lived = lasting a few minutes

fatigue (158) = physical or mental tiredness resulting from exertion.
illusion = a.  an error  in the perception of reality.  b.  an erroneous concept or belief

stare (159) = to look at
we soon encounter (160) = we soon have
context = the part of a text or statement that surrounds a particular word or passage and determines its meaning.; the circumstances in which an event occurs; a setting.
flanking = to the right or left side of
fixation point = point of focus
blot out = to hide

erase (161) = to remove; to destroy
configuration = arrangement of parts or elements
component  = a part of something
instantaneously = quickly; without any delay

lock into (162) = pay attention to

symmetrical (165) = a figure where the left and right sides of a dividing line are the same
adores = loves or likes

spot the vertical (166) = see the vertical
distracters = something that turns attention away  from the original focus

hardly ever (167) = seldom; not very often; rarely
stationary = not moving

split second later (168) = less than a second
blink on and off = turn on and off
discrepancy = difference

extraordinary (172) = more than ordinary; exceptional; remarkable
misinterpretation = to interpret or explain with errors
deduce = to reach a conclusion by reasoning;  to infer from a general principle

apparently (174) = clearly or obviously
bewildering = To confuse with many different parts
misestimate = to guess with an error

most convincing (175) = easy to believe
vast terrain = a large land area

prevail upon (177) = persuade; force
bit far fetched = not likely to be true
what "is out there" = the real world

## II. VOCABULARY BUILDING

**Word Analysis**

<u>Instructions:</u>

1. Study the meaning of the prefixes roots and suffixes listed.
2. Break each word in the table into its prefixes, roots and suffixes.
3. Guess the meaning word based on the meaning of its parts.
4. Find the word on the text page indicated in the brackets and redefine the word based on the context of the sentence, paragraph and chapter.
5. Look up the definition of the word in the VOCABULARY, IDIOMS AND CULTURAL CONCEPTS  section above, in Appendix A (marked "A"), or in a college level dictionary. If the word is followed by letter "G"  look it up in the text Glossary.

<u>Exercise 1.  Synthesis</u>

**Prefix : syn/sym _____ = with/together**
**Prefix : metri _____ = measure**
**Suffix: _____ al = being like/relating to/belonging to/characterized by
/connected to/process/condition/result  of**

| Word | Meaning |
|---|---|
| synthesize (A) | |
| synthesis | |
| psychometric (G) | |
| symmetrical (A) | |
| symphony | sounding together in harmony |
| arrival | |
| approval | |
| international | |

<u>Exercise 2.  Illuminate</u>

**Prefix : il, in, ir _____ = in/into/within/not/without**

| Word | Meaning |
|---|---|
| illuminated (A) | |
| illusory (G) | |
| illogical (G) | |
| illness (G) | |
| illustrated | |
| incision | |
| incise | |
| insight | |
| irrational | |
| irreversible | |

Exercise 3.  Insensitivity

**Prefix : in/im _____ = not/without**

| Word | Meaning |
|------|---------|
| inactive | |
| imperfect | |
| inadequate | |
| incompetent | |
| immoral | |
| incompatible | |
| insensitivity (A) | |

Exercise 4.  Perception

**Prefix:  per _____ = through/throughout/**
**Prefix: im _____ = not/without**
**Prefix: per _____ = through/completely**
**Prefix: fect _____ = making/doing**
**Root: _____ ceptive _____ = aware/see**

| Word | Meaning |
|------|---------|
| perception(A) | |
| perceptive | |
| perfect | |
| imperfect | |
| imperfection | |
| impair (A) | |

Exercise  5.

**Prefix: auto _____ = self**
**Root: _____ mobile _____ move/change position/ to affect emotions**
**Root: _____ vis/vid = see**
**Suffix: _____ ced(e) = go/move/surrender**
**Suffix: _____ sequ/secu = follow**
**Suffix: _____ tech = skill**
**Suffix: _____ vers = turn**
**Suffix: _____ ence = quality/state/condition/act/means/results**

| Word | Meaning |
|------|---------|
| automobile | |
| vision | |
| precede (A) | |
| consecutive (A) | |
| technique | |
| reverse | |
| autokinetic (G) | |
| autonomic (G) | |
| autonomy (G) | |

# CHAPTER 5  ALTERED STATES

**OBJECTIVES**

Understand that:

**Sleep and Dreams**

I. Rhythms of activity and inactivity are called circadian rhythms  (p. 183)
   A. People go to bed and get up at about the same time every day even in an unchanging environment  (p. 183)
      1. Some people are morning people and some are evening people  (p. 184)
   B. West-shift  (going to bed later) is easier than east-shift  (going to bed earlier)  (p. 184, Fig.  5.3, p. 185)
II. Sleep must serve some function  (p. 185)
   A. Repair and restoration might be one function  (pp. 185-186)
      1. There are several weaknesses in this theory  (pp. 186-187)
         a. People don't need much more sleep after a day of extreme activity  (p. 186)
         b. Some people get by with very little sleep  (p. 186)
         c. People who go intentionally without sleep don't need much to be recovered  (pp. 186-187)
   B. Evolutionary theory suggests that sleep protects from danger  (p. 187)
      1. Species vary in how much they sleep, but all sleep some  (p. 188, Fig. 5.7)
III. Main stages of sleep are REM and non-REM  (NREM)  (pp. 188-189)
   A. There are four stages of  (p. 189, Fig.  5.9)
   B. A cycle through the stages takes 90-100 minutes  (p. 189)
   C. Dreaming occurs during REM sleep  (pp. 189-191)
      1. Deprivation of REM sleep leads to anxiety, irritability, and impaired concentration  (pp. 191-192)
      2. REM sleep may improve memory storage and new learning may prompt extra REM sleep  (pp. 192-193)
IV. The content of dreams is usually related to experiences of the day  (p. 193)
   A. The activation-synthesis theory suggests that the brain is active during sleep and that the brain tries to make sense of these sensations  (p. 194)
      1. Major postural muscles are paralyzed during REM sleep  (p. 194)
      2. Blind people who could see at one time have visual dreams; those who have never seen or who have damage to the visual cortex don't see dreams  (p. 194)
      3. People report color in their dreams half the time; colors in other dreams may not be memorable  (p. 194)
V. Abnormalities of sleep  (p. 195)
   A. There are three types of insomnia  (p. 195)
      1. Onset insomnia means trouble falling asleep  (p. 195)
      2. Termination insomnia means awakening too early  (p. 195)
      3. Maintenance insomnia means awakening several times during the night  (p. 195)
   B. People with sleep apnea awaken because they cannot breathe while asleep  (p. 196)
   C. People with narcolepsy fall asleep during the day  (p. 196)
   D. Sleep talking, sleepwalking, nightmares, and night terrors are fairly common  (p. 196)
      1. Sleep talking is common and nothing to worry about  (p. 196)
      2. Sleepwalking usually occurs in children  (p. 196)
         a. Walking sleepwalkers poses no problems  (p. 196)

3. Night terrors are accompanied by extreme panic  (p. 196)
    a. These are more common in children  (p. 196)
  E. Periodic limb movement disorder or restless leg syndrome can cause poor sleep  (pp. 196-197)

## Hypnosis

VI. Hypnosis is a state of increased suggestibility  (p. 199)
  A. Mesmer founded hypnotism, calling it animal magnetism  (p. 199)
  B. It can be induced in several different ways  (p. 200)
    1. Hypnotic experiences are not much different from other experiences in which attention is captivated  (pp. 200-201)
VII. Hypnosis can do a number of things  (pp. 201-202)
  A. The distress of pain can be reduced  (pp. 201-202)
  B. Posthypnotic suggestions can help people to change their habits  (p. 202)
VIII. Hypnosis cannot do other things that are claimed for it  (pp. 202-203)
  A. Hypnotized people "remember" actual facts, but they mix in fantasies  (pp. 202-203)
  B. Hypnotized people don't relive childhood  (p. 203)
  C. Hypnosis doesn't lead to recall from previous lives  (p. 203)
  D. People under hypnosis may do strange (and dangerous) things, but so do people who are pretending to be hypnotized  (pp. 204-205)
IX. Hypnosis can result in distortions of perception  (pp. 205-206)
  A. People may claim that they don't hear or see stimuli, but those stimuli can still influence behavior  (pp. 205-206)
X. Hypnotized people and people pretending to be hypnotized show some different behavior (but there are lots of similarities too)  (pp. 206-207)
  A. Hypnotized people are puzzled by seeing double realities; pretenders don't report seeing double realities  (pp. 206-207)
  B. Criminal defendant Kenneth Bianchi was faking hypnosis, according to expert Martin Orne  (pp. 207-208)

## Drugs and Their Effects

XI. There are many different types of abused drugs  (pp. 209-210, Table 5.1)
  A. Alcohol acts as a relaxant  (p. 210)
    1. Excessive use impairs judgment, memory, and motor control  (pp. 210-211)
    2. Alcohol abuse is more common among Native Americans and African Americans than among people with European ancestry; people with Asian ancestry are lowest  (p. 211)
  B. Tranquilizers help people to relax and fall asleep  (p. 211)
    1. Barbiturates facilitate the neurotransmitter GABA  (p. 211)
  C. Opiates bind to synapses that use endorphins  (pp. 211-212)
    1. Morphine is used as a pain killer in controlled doses  (pp. 211-212)
  D. Marijuana intensifies sensory experiences  (p. 212)
    1. THC, the active ingredient, attaches to receptors mostly in the hippocampus  (p. 212)
  E. Stimulants heighten alertness and increase activity  (p. 213)
    1. Caffeine can result in dependency  (p. 213)
    2. Nicotine increases heart rate and blood pressure, but decreasing breathing rate  (p. 213)
    3. Cocaine increases heart rate but it decreases brain activity  (p. 213)
      a. Crack is cocaine that can be smoked  (p. 213)
      b. Crack is very habit-forming  (p. 214)
  F. Hallucinogens induce sensory distortions  (p. 214)
  G. Designer drugs are synthetic drugs that aren't illegal yet  (pp. 214-215)

XII. Withdrawal effects and drug tolerance occur with extended use of drugs (p. 215)
    A. Withdrawal symptoms occur when habitual use ceases (pp. 215-216)
        1. Specific effects depend upon the drug (p. 215)
        2. Effects are often the opposite of those of the drug (p. 215)
    B. Drug tolerance means that more and more drug is required to get the same effects (p. 216)
        1. Tolerance may result from both automatic chemical changes and psychological effects (p. 216)

## COMPREHENSION CHECK

Answer these questions soon after reading the chapter. Circle the best alternative. Check your answers on pp. 95-97. If you gave a wrong answer, try to write why it was wrong. Check your reasons on pp. 95-97.

### Sleep and Dreams

1. Which of the following provides evidence that our 24-hour sleep-waking cycle is the result of a built-in mechanism?
    a. some people sleep only 5-6 hours a night; others sleep 7-8 hours
    b. only a little more sleep is needed after a day of exertion than after a day of little activity
    c. people who live in an environment in which everything is constant still go to sleep and wake at about the same time each day
    d. prisoners who are forced to stay awake for long periods of time develop severe health problems

Correct _____ If wrong, why? _____

2. Jet lag occurs whenever you change time zones quickly. Which type of trip will result in the most difficult adjustment?
    a. Flying from Los Angeles to New York
    b. Flying for 1 1/2 hours but staying in the same time zone
    c. Flying from New York to Chicago
    d. Flying from New York to Los Angeles

Correct _____ If wrong, why? _____

3. Which of the following is evidence for the repair and restoration theory of sleep?
    a. the body increases its rate of cell division during sleep
    b. species that are less likely to be attacked sleep longer
    c. people can survive without sleep for 10 or 11 days
    d. people need only a little more sleep following a day of extreme activity than following a day of inactivity

Correct _____ If wrong, why? _____

4. The evolutionary theory of sleep predicts which type of animal should sleep the least? One that is:
    a. unlikely to be attacked by other animals
    b. sleeping in a familiar environment
    c. able to complete its eating in a short time
    d. likely to be attacked by other animals

Correct _____ If wrong, why? _____

5. The high-school student who stayed awake for several days:
    a. was near death by the time he slept
    b. slept for many days when he finally went to sleep
    c. didn't fully recover until he had several nights of normal sleep
    d. slept longer than usual when he did go to sleep, but was fully refreshed upon awakening

Correct _____ If wrong, why? _____

6. REM sleep is also called paradoxical sleep because:
    a. the brain is very active, but heart rate, breathing rate, and temperature fluctuate greatly
    b. the brain is relatively inactive and the heart rate is very low
    c. the large muscles are very active but the temperature is very low
    d. the large muscles are relaxed and heart rate is low
    e. dreams occur here yet the times are much shorter than the perceived length of dreams

Correct _____ If wrong, why? _____

7. Electroencephalograph (EEG) waves:
    a. are similar when a person is in stage 4 sleep and awake
    b. become shorter and choppier as a person moves from stage 1 to stage 4 sleep
    c. become larger as a person goes into deeper sleep because a larger proportion of the active neurons
       are active at the same time
    d. are the largest when a person is very awake because the brain is most active

Correct _____ If wrong, why? _____

8. Which of the following is the proper order of sleep stages in a cycle?
    a. 1 (NREM), 2, 3, 4, 1 (REM), 2, 3, 4
    b. 1 (REM), 2, 3, 4, 1 (REM), 2, 3, 4
    c. 1 (REM), 2, 3, 4, 3, 2, 1 (REM)
    d. 1 (NREM), 2, 3, 4, 3, 2, 1 (REM)

Correct _____ If wrong, why? _____

9. Dreams:
    a. only occur in REM sleep
    b. may occur in NREM sleep but they are less vivid and visual than in REM sleep
    c. are almost always in color
    d. may occur in REM sleep but they are less vivid and visual than in NREM sleep
    e. never occur in blind people

Correct _____ If wrong, why? _____

10. People who have been selectively deprived of REM sleep:
    a. have difficulty waking up in the morning and falling asleep at night
    b. become very depressed
    c. often show REM rebound
    d. can die if they are not allowed to sleep without interruption
    e. develop narcolepsy

Correct _____ If wrong, why? _____

11. Which of the following is not true?
    a. Dreams last about as long as REM sleep does
    b. Sleep talking occurs only during REM sleep
    c. People who have the same dream over and over report more anxiety, depression, and stress than
       do other people
    d. Night terrors are common among young children and usually occur during stages 3 and 4
    e. Restless leg syndrome is a common cause of poor sleep in people over 50

Correct _____ If wrong, why? _____

**Hypnosis**

12. The state of hypnosis is best described as a:
    a. condition of heightened suggestibility
    b. trance state that is similar to sleep
    c. power emanating from the hypnotist's body
    d. state in which the mind and body become separated

Correct _____ If wrong, why? _____

13. A well-established effect of hypnosis on perception is:
    a. the elimination of certain illusions as a result of suggestion
    b. the ability to become deaf
    c. a reduction in the distress of pain
    d. a large reduction in the intensity of pain

Correct _____ If wrong, why? _____

14. There are many myths about hypnosis. Which of the following is actually true?
    a. People can remember things very accurately that they cannot remember without hypnosis
    b. Hypnotized people can become stiff as a board
    c. People under hypnosis will do strange things that nonhypnotized people would never do
    d. Posthypnotic suggestions cause long-term behavior change
    e. Hypnotized people can remember most events from childhood

Correct _____ If wrong, why? _____

15. Orne detected that Kenneth Bianchi was faking because Bianchi:
    a. denied seeing a person that Orne suggested was sitting in the chair opposite him
    b. developed another personality after Orne told him that most multiple personalities have three, not two, personalities
    c. couldn't remember how the filter of his cigarette got torn off
    d. saw an imagined person and the whole chair in which the person was sitting at the same time

Correct _____ If wrong, why? _____

**Drugs and Their Effects**

16. Which drugs boost energy, heighten alertness, and increase activity?
    a. hallucinogens
    b. alcoholic beverages
    c. barbiturates
    d. stimulants
    e. opiates

Correct _____ If wrong, why? _____

17. Research has shown that the relationship between brain receptors and THC is that THC:
    a. attaches to specialized receptors, found mostly in the hippocampus
    b. doesn't attach to receptors but modifies neuronal membranes
    c. may attach to a few receptors but those are rare in the brain
    d. attaches to the same receptors as endorphins do

Correct _____ If wrong, why? _____

18. In rats, it has been shown that the coordination of rats after 24 injections of alcohol is better at the end if they have been tested after each injection. This shows that:
    a. alcohol is not addictive
    b. alcohol produces strong withdrawal symptoms
    c. tolerance results from more than simple repeated exposures to the drug
    d. drug tolerance depends on purely automatic chemical changes

Correct _____ If wrong, why? _____

**ANSWERS AND EXPLANATIONS FOR COMPREHENSION CHECK**

| Correct Answer | Other Alternatives Are Wrong Because: |
|---|---|
| 1. c (pp. 183-184)<br>    Obj. I-A | a. they still may have a 24-hour cycle<br>b. problem for repair-restoration theory but not evidence for cycles<br>d. but those who stay awake on their own usually don't; not evidence for 24-hour cycles |
| 2. a (p. 184)<br>    Obj. I-B | b. this should not cause jet lag because time doesn't change<br>c,d. going west is not as bad as going east; it's easier to go to bed later than earlier |
| 3. a (pp. 185-186)<br>    Obj. II-A | b. evidence for evolutionary theory<br>c, d. weakness of repair-restoration theory |

4. d (p. 188, Fig. 5.7)       a. an animal that is a predator will sleep a lot
   Obj. II-B                   b. should increase sleeping; no need to fear attack
                               c. and, therefore, can afford to sleep a lot

5. d (p. 186)                  a. consequences are not that serious
   Obj. II-A-1-c               b. sleep only a few more hours than normal
                               c. usually recover after one night's sleep

6. a (pp. 188-189)             b. brain is active; heart rate fluctuates
   Obj. III-C                  c. large muscles are very relaxed; temperature and heart rate fluctuate
                               e. subjective time for dreams is about the same as REM periods

7. c (p. 189,                  a. stage 4 waves are much larger and slower
     Fig. 5.9, p. 190)         b. they become longer and less choppy with sleep
   Obj. III-A                  d. when the brain is active, neurons are out of synchrony and they
                                  cancel each other

8. d (p. 189)                  a,b. goes from 4 to 3, not to 1
   Obj. III-B                  c. the first stage is 1,NREM; REM later replaces Stage 1

9. b (pp. 189-190)             a. some dreaming occurs in NREM sleep
   Obj. III-C                  c. maybe, but people report color only about half the time
                               d. NREM dreams are less vivid and visual
                               e. visual dreams occur in people who had vision and lost it; people who
                                  never had vision dream about touch

10. c (pp. 191-192)            a. characteristics of jet lag
    Obj. III-C-1               b. this can improve mood in depressed people
                               d. there is no evidence for death from REM deprivation
                               e. they show more REM the next night; they don't fall asleep suddenly
                                  during the day

11. b (p. 196)                a,c,d,e are correct statements so they are not correct answers to
    Obj. V-D                      the question which asked you to select the statement that was
                                  not true
                               b. statement is wrong; occurs during non-REM also

12. a (p. 199)                 b. in terms of ability to move about and respond to stimuli,
    Obj. VI                       hypnosis is more like waking
                               c. being a hypnotist requires no unusual personality traits
                               d. people just become more suggestible under hypnosis

13. c (p. 201-202)             a. illusions still occur, even when their cause is supposedly
    Obj. VII-A                    not perceived
                               b. the behavior of hypnotized people suggests that they still hear, even
                                  when they say they don't
                               d. the intensity of pain is changed only a little

14. b (p. 202)
   Obj. X

    a. many memories that come out under hypnosis are wrong
    c. nonhypnotized "pretenders" do strange things too
    d. usually change is short-lived, but if there is long-term change, it's probably due to the person's resolve and not the hypnotic suggestion
    e. many such "memories" are not accurate

15. b (p. 207-208)
   Obj. X-B

    a. he didn't deny it; he actually shook hands with the person--a rare response for a hypnotized person
    c. he said he couldn't remember which would be appropriate for a hypnotized person, but he repeated this three times for other hypnotists
    d. actually hypnotized people do this; pretenders don't

16. d (p. 213)
   Obj. XI-E

    a. causes hallucinations and sensory distortions actually a relaxant
    b. may appear to stimulate because it inhibits some brain areas
    c. results in sleep, a sedative
    e. analgesics; these reduce pain

17. a (p. 212)
   Obj. XI-D-1

    b. scientists used to think this, but specific receptors have been found
    c. THC receptors may be among the most numerous in the brain
    d. opiates do this; anandamide is the neurotransmitter that binds to the same receptors as THC

18. c (p. 216)
   Obj. XII-B

    a. alcohol is an addictive drug
    b. alcohol does produce withdrawal symptoms, but this drug tolerance example doesn't show this
    d. if tolerance was purely automatic, then practice would have no effect

## LECTURE MATERIAL

Don't forget to review your lecture material. Process each topic meaningfully. First, be sure that you understand the material in each lecture---if you don't, ask your instructor or teaching assistant. Associate the material with things that you already know and with your personal experiences. If you can make up mental images of any of the material, do so. Try to think of real-life applications of the concepts. Write your own notes on your lecture notes. Then write questions to cover each concept.

-------------------------------------------------------------------
WAIT AT LEAST 24 HOURS BEFORE PROCEEDING.
LET FORGETTING OCCUR--IT WILL!!
-------------------------------------------------------------------

## SHORT-ANSWER ESSAY QUESTIONS

Write brief answers to each of the following. The answers are on pp. 99-100, but do try to write the answers yourself before looking at them.

### Sleep and Dreams

1. Describe evidence that supports the idea that humans have built-in mechanisms that produce a 24-hour wake-sleep cycle.

2. Briefly describe the repair and restoration theory of sleep. Discuss two weaknesses of the theory.

3. Explain the evolutionary view of sleep.

4. Describe the stages of sleep including the EEG activity that accompanies them. Discuss two characteristics of REM sleep.

5. What are the effects of REM sleep deprivation?

6. Describe the three types of insomnia and discuss two possible causes of insomnia.

7. What is narcolepsy? How does it differ from insomnia?

8. Discuss sleep talking, sleepwalking, and night terrors.

**Hypnosis**

9. Describe the modern view of hypnosis. How does it differ from Mesmer's view?

10. Describe how people imitating hypnosis are similar to and different from people who are actually hypnotized.

**Drugs and Their Effects**

11. Explain how crack differs from cocaine both in terms of the substance itself and in terms of its effects.

12. Explain how drug withdrawal symptoms might work to keep someone using the drug.

\*\*\*\*\*\*\*\*\*\*\*\*\*\*\*\*\*\*\*\*\*\*\*\*\*\*\*\*\*\*\*\*\*\*\*\*\*\*\*\*\*\*\*\*\*\*\*\*\*\*\*\*\*\*\*\*\*\*\*\*\*\*\*\*\*\*\*\*\*\*\*\*\*\*\*\*\*\*\*\*
Find the questions that you wrote over lecture material and write answers to them.
\*\*\*\*\*\*\*\*\*\*\*\*\*\*\*\*\*\*\*\*\*\*\*\*\*\*\*\*\*\*\*\*\*\*\*\*\*\*\*\*\*\*\*\*\*\*\*\*\*\*\*\*\*\*\*\*\*\*\*\*\*\*\*\*\*\*\*\*\*\*\*\*\*\*\*\*\*\*\*\*

## ANSWERS TO SHORT-ANSWER ESSAY QUESTIONS

1. Two people spent several weeks in a cave in which the temperature was constant and they controlled their own lighting. They tended to go to sleep and awaken at their usual times even though there were no cues in the environment. (pp. 183-184)

2. The body needs sleep in order to repair and restore itself from the day's exertions. Cell division and the rate at which the body produces new proteins increase. One weakness is that we do not seem to need more sleep after a day of extreme activity than after a day of inactivity. Another weakness is that people vary greatly in the amount of sleep that they need. (Other weaknesses exist; see pp. 185-187)

3. Sleep may have a restorative function, but it also occurs at a time when the animal is likely to be inefficient. How often and how long an animal sleeps depends upon whether it is a predator and can afford lots of sleep or a prey and can afford little sleep. It also depends upon whether meals are short or whether the animal must eat constantly. (pp. 187-188)

4. Stage 1 (NREM) - stage 2 - stage 3 - stage 4 - stage 3 - stage 2 - stage 1 (REM). The cycle takes about 90 min. Brain waves go from short, choppy waves to long, slow waves at stage 4. During REM sleep, the person's EEG shows short, choppy waves; postural muscles are relaxed; and the person is hard to awaken. (p. 189, Fig. 5.9, 190)

5. People who are deprived of REM show anxiety, irritability, and difficulty in concentrating. When participants are allowed to sleep undisturbed, REM rebound occurs; they spend more time in REM than usual. Because REM sleep facilitates memory storage, deprivation of REM sleep may also slow down learning, at least in animal studies. (pp. 191-193)

6. Onset insomnia refers to trouble falling asleep. Termination insomnia refers to waking up too early. Maintenance insomnia refers to awakening repeatedly during the night, although people with this condition can get back to sleep. An out-of-synch circadian rhythm (wanting to sleep and wake at the wrong times) is one cause of insomnia. Overuse of tranquilizers can cause insomnia. Sleep disorders, such as apnea (failure to breathe while sleeping) and periodic limb movement disorder (repetitive leg movements while sleeping) may also cause people to awaken and have insomnia. (p. 195)

7. Narcolepsy is a condition in which people fall asleep, often going into REM sleep, in the middle of the day. This is the opposite of insomnia. The person with insomnia cannot fall asleep at night; the person with narcolepsy falls asleep during the day. (p. 196)

8. Most people talk in their sleep sometimes. It occurs both during REM and NREM sleep and is not abnormal. Children are more likely to sleepwalk than adults. It occurs during stage 4 sleep because the muscles are too relaxed during REM sleep. Night terrors are fairly common in young children. The child usually awakens in an extreme state of panic and has a very high heart rate. These occur in sleep stages 3 and 4. (p. 196)

9. Hypnosis is considered to be a state of heightened suggestibility. People who are hypnotizable are likely to do what the hypnotist tells them without question. In terms of ability to move about and to respond to stimuli, it is more like waking than sleeping. Mesmer thought that the powers were within him, the hypnotist. In fact, hypnotizability seems to be due more to the subject's willingness to accept suggestions than to the hypnotist. (pp. 199-200)

10. People who are imitating hypnosis will tolerate pain without flinching, recall old memories, make their bodies stiff as a board and lie between two chairs, and show physiological changes when told to experience an emotion. However, they are not as inconsistent as actually hypnotized people who will report seeing a person sitting in a chair and also report seeing the entire chair. Real hypnotized people report seeing two images of the same person, but pretenders don't. (p. 206-207)

11. Cocaine can be sniffed or injected, but not smoked. In order to smoke it, the drug must have the hydrochloride removed, turning it into "freebase" cocaine, commonly called crack. Crack enters the brain more rapidly than cocaine, so it is more likely to be addictive. It is also more likely to    lead to mental confusion, heart attacks, lung disease, and neglect of daily activities. (pp. 213-214)

12. Drugs usually provide the stimulus for pleasant emotional states. As drugs wear off, however, the user moves into the opposite state. Because drugs produce tolerance effects, initial highs grow weaker and weaker with use. Finally, users may need to take the drugs to avoid the negative, opposite states produced as the effects of drugs wear off. (pp. 215-216)

**POSTTEST**

Take this test with all of your books and notes out of sight. This should give you a good idea of how well you understand the material.

**Matching**

Put the letter of the term in the blank beside the description.

Sleep and Dreams; Drugs and Their Effects

1. _____ medical condition in which people
   fall asleep suddenly in middle of day

   A. sleep apnea

   B. insomnia

2. _____ tranquilizers that are less habit forming

   C. narcolepsy

3. _____ bind to endorphin synapses in brain

   D. hallucinogens

4. _____ induce distortions of experience

   E. benzodiazepines

5. _____ habit-forming tranquilizer that can
   be fatal in overdose

   F. opiates

6. _____ trouble breathing while asleep

   G. barbiturate

7. _____ difficulty in sleeping

**Multiple-Choice**

Circle the best alternative.

Sleep and Dreams

1. What happened to the sleep cycles of the people who spent a few weeks in Mammoth Cave?
   a. they spontaneously adapted to a 28-hour day
   b. they slept for about 4 hours and stayed awake for about 4 hours
   c. they could not keep a set cycle; sleeping and waking times varied greatly from day to day
   d. they kept a 24-hour cycle, waking up and going to sleep at about the same time each day
   e. they were sleepy in the morning, but not at night

2. Sleep deprivation for a period of several days results in:
   a. dizziness, slurred speech, and hallucinations in everyone
   b. a loss of skill, such as that needed to play arcade games
   c. the need to sleep for 24 hours or more before recovery can occur
   d. minimal effects in some people who have control of the situation
   e. a total loss of ability to concentrate; even the simplest tasks cannot be completed

3. Which of the following is consistent with the repair and restoration theory of sleep?
   a. some people need much less sleep than other people
   b. only a little more sleep is needed after a day of exertion than after a day of inactivity
   c. people who stay awake are sleepier at night than in the morning
   d. people can go for 10 or more days without sleep
   e. the body increases the rate of cell division and new protein production during sleep

4. According to the evolutionary theory of sleep, some animals sleep more than others because they:
   a. are more active
   b. must expend more energy to kill their prey
   c. eat such low-calorie food that they must rest often
   d. are less vulnerable to attack
   e. have higher metabolic rates

5. Why is it better to shift work schedules from an eight-to-four shift to a four-to-midnight shift than the other way around?
   a. the body is better able to repair and restore when sleep occurs later than earlier
   b. it is like flying east--going toward the sunrise makes it easier to fall asleep than going away from it
   c. the direction of the shift is irrelevant as long as the lights are kept dim for the night shift
   d. it is like flying west--it is easier to go to bed later than usual
   e. this type of shift makes you feel safer in your bedroom, so you sleep better

6. Sam Snore volunteered for a psychology experiment in which he slept for two nights in the laboratory. On the first night, he was awakened every time he entered REM sleep. The result was that he had almost no REM sleep during that night. His EEG on the next night would show:
   a. more stage 4 sleep than usual
   b. more stage 2 sleep than usual
   c. less REM sleep than usual
   d. less stage 4 sleep than usual
   e. more REM sleep than usual

7. Bob seems to be deeply asleep, yet his brain waves resemble those of an alert, waking state. Bob is now in _____ sleep and just before this he was in _____.
   a. REM; a drowsy, awake state
   b. REM; stage 2 sleep
   c. Stage 4; stage 2 sleep
   d. Stage 2; stage 1 sleep
   e. paradoxical; stage 4 sleep

8. REM sleep:
   a. has been shown to help memory storage
   b. lasts longer during the first than during the second half of the night
   c. is the time when sleepwalking is most likely to occur
   d. is the only stage in which dreams occur at night
   e. is absolutely necessary; even a few nights of deprivation can cause death

9. The content of dreams is influenced by:
   a. experiences of the past day
   b. stimuli being experienced during sleep
   c. spontaneous brain activity
   d. all of the above

10. Why is it impossible for sleepwalking to occur during REM sleep?
    a. the postural muscles are so relaxed that they would not support a person
    b. the heart rate is so slow that there would not be enough blood flowing to the large muscles
    c. the part of the brain that is responsible for movement becomes inactive
    d. the EEG shows too much spontaneous activity for specific muscles to be stimulated
    e. the eye movements use so much energy that there is little left for coordinated movement

11. Which of the following is <u>false</u>?
    a. night terrors usually occur during Stage 3 or Stage 4 sleep
    b. most people talk in their sleep, at least some of the time
    c. the activation-synthesis theory of dreams suggests that the brain is actively organizing sensory information during dreams
    d. sleepwalking occurs in adults more often than in children
    e. dream content is often related to the day's activities

12. Narcolepsy involves:
    a. a failure to breathe while sleeping that may results in awakening many times each night
    b. very unpleasant dreams that keep children awake
    c. prolonged creepy-crawly sensations in the legs
    d. frequent awakenings during the night
    e. sudden attacks of extreme sleepiness during the day

<u>Hypnosis</u>

13. Mesmer's animal magnetism:
    a. worked because magnets redirected patients' flow of blood
    b. made physicians and scientists associate hypnosis with eccentrics
    c. was based on the idea that hypnosis is a state of enhanced suggestibility
    d. induced hypnotic trances, which redistributed brain activity
    e. worked with actual magnets, but not without them

14. Scientific studies have most strongly supported the contention that hypnosis can:
    a. reduce the distress of pain, although it reduces the intensity of pain only slightly
    b. make people totally deaf
    c. eliminate illusions if the hypnotist says to ignore the contextual stimuli
    d. give you physical strength that you would not have otherwise
    e. make you do things that you would never do otherwise

15. Hypnosis has been used to help people remember things. These memories:
    a. are extremely accurate
    b. often include things that the hypnotized person has made up
    c. are quite accurate under hypnosis, but become mixed with fantasy when the person comes out of hypnosis
    d. are very accurate if they involve the person's childhood; otherwise they are not accurate

16. Which of the following is true of people who are actually hypnotized as compared with people who are pretending?
    a. pretenders cannot tolerate pain without flinching
    b. when asked to sit down, pretenders look for a chair first; hypnotized people do not
    c. when told to experience anger, hypnotized people show physiological reactions, pretenders do not
    d. hypnotized people will imagine seeing someone sitting in a chair and also see the entire chair; pretenders do not report seeing the chair
    e. pretenders will report seeing a single individual in two places; hypnotized people will not report seeing the same person in two places

Drugs and Their Effects

17. Marijuana:
    a. is chemically similar to crack
    b. causes sexual debauchery
    c. facilitates transmission at synapses using GABA
    d. can help relieve glaucoma
    e. is gone from the body within 3 hours after use

18. Cocaine:
    a. increases heart rate, but decreases overall brain activity
    b. has no anesthetic properties
    c. has less of an effect after it is treated with ether
    d. is called a designer drug because people from high society use it
    e. is not addictive

19. Symptoms of withdrawal from opiate drugs include:
    a. sweating, sleeplessness, and possibly hallucinations and seizures
    b. nervousness and sleeplessness
    c. anxiety and heightened sensitivity to pain
    d. only mild withdrawal symptoms or no withdrawal symptoms occur

20. How are drug withdrawal and drug tolerance related?
    a. both are purely physiological effects
    b. both are purely psychological effects
    c. together they lead to decreased use of a drug
    d. increased tolerance makes a drug less effective so users may take more of the drug to fight withdrawal effects
    e. increased tolerance makes a drug more effective, so less of the drug is needed to eliminate withdrawal effects

## ANSWERS TO POSTTEST

| Correct Answer | Questions Testing a Similar Concept | |
| --- | --- | --- |
| | Comprehension Check | Short-Answer |

**Matching**

| Correct Answer | Comprehension Check | Short-Answer |
| --- | --- | --- |
| 1. C (p. 196) | 10e | 7 |
| 2. E (p. 211) | -- | -- |
| 3. F (pp. 211-212) | 16e | -- |
| 4. D (p. 214) | 16a | -- |
| 5. G (p. 211) | 16c | -- |
| 6. A (p. 196) | -- | 6 |
| 7. B (p. 195) | -- | 6,7 |

**Multiple-Choice**

| Correct Answer | Comprehension Check | Short-Answer |
| --- | --- | --- |
| 1. d (pp. 183-184) | 1 | 1 |
| 2. d (p. 186) | 3d,5 | 2 |
| 3. e (pp. 185-186) | 3 | 2 |
| 4. d (p. 188) | 4 | 3 |
| 5. d (pp. 184-185) | 2 | -- |
| 6. e (pp. 191-192) | 10 | 5 |
| 7. b (p. 189) | 8 | 4 |
| 8. a (pp. 191-193) | 6 | 5 |
| 9. d (pp. 193-194) | 11c | -- |
| 10. a (p. 196) | 6d | 4,8 |
| 11. d (p. 196) | 11 | 8 |
| 12. e (p. 196) | 10e | 7 |
| 13. b (pp. 199-200) | 12 | 9 |
| 14. a (pp. 201-202) | 13, 14 | -- |
| 15. b (pp. 202-203) | 14a,e | 10 |
| 16. d (pp. 206-207) | 14, 15 | 10 |
| 17. d (p. 212) | 17 | -- |
| 18. a (pp. 213-214) | 16 | 11 |
| 19. c (pp. 211-212) | 16e,17d | 12 |
| 20. d (pp. 215-216) | 18 | 12 |

# CHAPTER 5 LANGUAGE ENHANCEMENT GUIDE

## I. VOCABULARY, IDIOMS AND CULTURAL CONCEPTS

**Instructions:**

As you read the text refer to the following list of words and their definitions. The words are listed in the order in which they appear in the chapter. The definitions presented contain the meaning of the word as used by Kalat on the text book page indicated.

Remember that these words like all words can have different meanings in other sentences. If you do not find a non-technical word on this list it may have been defined on a previous page or chapter of this study guide. The definition of non-technical words may be found in the dictionary at the end of this study guide. Kalat defined each new technical word as it first appears on a page and these may be found in Kalat's summary at the end of the section and in the Glossary at the end the textbook..

### Sleep and Dreams

altered (182) = to change or make different; modify.
states = conditions of conscious awareness
irrelevant = not related to
constitutes = to be part of; compose
inference = An inference is a conclusion about an event or condition that we did not directly see. Inferences are claims that must be supported by observations.
observation = The opposite of an inference would be directly observing, seeing, hearing, touching, measuring the object or event so you could make a description of it.

hibernate (183) = to sleep through winter
encounter = a meeting that is unexpected or brief.
migrate = to move from one country or region and settle in another
Mammoth Caves = very large and deep dark caves in the state of Kentucky
humidity = refers to air with a high amount water vapor

intermediates (184)= lying or occurring between two extremes or in a middle position
synchrony = occurring at the same time
jet lag = refers to the difficulty people have staying awake or falling asleep when they fly long distances across time zones
akin to = similar to
disproportionate = very large

restoration (186) = an act of repairing, or recovering
get by with = to recover; to adjust
confirmed = to support a claim; verify
brainwashing = the process of changing a person's beliefs by torture and sleep deprivation combined with teaching methods
prodding = to jab or poke with a pointed object
apparently = it appears so
declined = decreases; reduced in amount

deprivation = the process of taking something away from someone
progressive = doing something in a steady step-by-step manner
deterioration = a reduction in the amount, quality, character, or value of something
in short = in summary; briefly
evidently = the evidence shows

solar-powered (188) = powered by the suns heat energy
for instance = for example

paradox (189) = two claims with opposite predictions; an apparent contradiction
out of synchrony = not occurring at the same time
synonymous = having the same or a similar meaning
bizarre = very unusual in appearance; odd

consecutive (191) = following one after another without interruption

foretold (192) = to predict an event before it occurs

maintained (193) = to claim something as true
a fair amount = a large amount

synthesis (194)= combining of separate elements to form a new whole
spontaneous = happening without apparent external cause; self-generated
to make sense = to understand; to make meaningful
zombies = a dead person with supernatural power who comes to life to frighten people

speculation (195) = an opinion based on guessing with limited information
paralyzed = made unable to move or act
irresistible = not able to resist or stop
intrusion = to force in without an invitation or permission
indistinct = not clear
grunt = a low pitch sound or words that can't be understood
clearly articulated = clear understandable words
prolonged = to lengthen time
periodic = an event that is repeated over time

**Hypnosis**
fascinating (199) = very interesting
superficial = not carefully analyzed or thought about
dispense = stop using; get rid of
eccentric = a person of odd or unconventional behavior.
charlatan = a person who makes fraudulent claims such as having supernatural powers or skill; a
    quack or fraud.
practitioners of hocus-pocus = people who claim to have magical powers

emanating from (200) = coming or sending out from
monotonous = spoken in an unchanging tone
captivated = to be attracted by skill, excellence, charm or beauty

involuntary (201) = acting against one's will or without self control
anesthesia = loss of sensation or pain
anesthetic = a drug that stops pain

distress (202) = to cause or experience anxiety or suffering

astounding (203) = surprising and hard to believe

extraordinary (204) = much more than ordinary or usual; exceptional

susceptible (205) = easily influenced or persuaded

concede (206) = to yield or accept a claim as true
pretend = make believe; play-act
for instance = for example

defendant (207) = the accused person or criminal in a court of law
pick up a few tricks = learn new symptoms
in the course of = during
cultivated = developed
skepticism = a doubting or questioning attitude

## Drugs and Their Effects

blurry (209) = unclear; difficult to see
discourage = to persuade (a person) not to do something
exaggerated = to claim something as more than is actually the case; overstate
predominantly = most common or important

consumed (210) = ate or drank
social lubricant = helps reduce difficulty or conflict
impairment = to reduce or damage
abstinence = the act of permanently stopping from doing something

abuse (211) = to misuse or wrongly use something
speculative = uncertain; open to question
facilitating = making something easier or less difficult

bind to (212) = hold on to
suppresses = puts and end to; stops
tremor = shaking or vibrating movement

lucrative (214) = profitable; money making

chronic (215) = lasting for a long period of time

abstention (216) = to stop using or doing something
"cold turkey" withdrawal effect = the painful physical symptoms that occur when a person suddenly
    stops using a drug

## II. VOCABULARY BUILDING

### Word Analysis

Instructions:

1. Study the meaning of the prefixes, roots and suffixes listed.
2. Break each word in the table into its prefixes, roots and suffixes.
3. Guess the meaning of the word based on the meaning of its parts.
4. Find the word on the text page indicated in the brackets and redefine the word based on the context of the sentence, paragraph and chapter.
5. Look up the definition of the word in the VOCABULARY, IDIOMS AND CULTURAL CONCEPTS section above, in Appendix A (marked A) or in a college level dictionary. If the word is followed by letter G look it up in the text Glossary.

Exercise 1. Intermediate

**Prefix : inter_____ = among/between**
   Caution: inter can mean to bury (in the ground)

**Word: ____ mediate ____ = middle/**
**Word: ____ cede ____ = yield/give/assign/transfer**
**Suffix: _____ ate = having/resembling// having or holding an office**
   Caution: "ate" is a suffix with many other meanings that depend on the context.
**Suffix: _____ cede/ceed/cess = to go/to yield**

| Word | Meaning |
|---|---|
| intermediate (A) | |
| intercede | to act between two people to help them solve problems |
| international | |
| interference (G) | |

Exercise 2. Disproportionate

**Prefix : dis/di _____ = away/not**
**Word: ____ proportion _____ = part of a whole**
**Suffix: _____ ate = having/resembling// having or holding an office**
   Caution: "ate" is a suffix with many other meanings that depend on the context.

| Word | Meaning |
|---|---|
| disproportionate (A) | |
| discouraged (A) | |
| dispense (A) | |
| discounting | |
| disequilibrium (G) | |
| disorganize | |
| displacement (G) | |
| dissociation (G) | |
| digress | |
| distrust | |
| distract | |

Exercise 3.  Declined

**Prefix : de** _____ = down/take away/remove
**Suffix:** _____ ion = the act/means/results of
**Word: institution = a public organization i.e.  a college or hospital**
   Caution: The word institution can have other meanings in other contexts.

| Word | Meaning |
|---|---|
| declined (A) | |
| defendant (A) | |
| deprivation | |
| deterioration | |
| deinstitutionalization (A) | |

Exercise 4.  Abstinence

**Prefix : ab/abs** _____ = away/away from

| Word | Meaning |
|---|---|
| abstinence (A) | |
| abstention (A) | |
| abnormal | |
| abstract (A) | |

Exercise 5.  Restoration

**Prefix : re** _____ = back to a earlier condition/again/repeatedly
**Suffix:** _____ tion/ion = the act/means/result of

| Word | Meaning |
|---|---|
| restoration (A) | |
| restore | |
| reconstruction (G ) | |
| repay | |
| rehear | |
| redraw | |
| reappear | |
| recombination | |
| recall (G ) | |
| replace | |
| reaction (A) | |
| reflex (G) | |
| regression (G) | |
| reinforcement (G ) | |

# CHAPTER 6  LEARNING

## OBJECTIVES

Understand that:

### Behaviorism

I. Behaviorists study measurable, observable behaviors  (p. 221)
- A. Radical and methodological behaviorists differ in the degree to which they believe that  mental processes exist and can be inferred  (p. 221)
  - 1. Early behaviorists explained behavior in terms of stimulus-response connections  (p. 222)
- B. Behaviorists made several assumptions (pp. 222-223)
  - 1. All behavior is caused (determinism)  (p. 223)
  - 2. Mental explanations do not explain causes of behavior  (p. 223)
  - 3. Behavior is molded by the environment  (p. 223)

### Classical Conditioning

II. Pavlov first described classical conditioning  (pp. 225-227)
- A. Unconditioned stimuli (UCS) produce unconditioned responses (UCR)  (p. 226, Fig 6.3, p. 227)
  - 1. A neutral stimulus (CS) paired with the UCS causes a similar response (CR)  (p. 226, Fig.6.3)
- B. Many  phenomena are associated with conditioning  (pp. 228-230, Fig. 6.4)
  - 1. Acquisition occurs when the CR is strengthened following UCS and CS  pairings  (p. 228)
  - 2. Extinction occurs if the CS is  presented often without the UCS  (pp. 228-229)
  - 3. Spontaneous recovery occurs when extinguished responses return temporarily after a delay  (pp. 229-330)
  - 4. Stimulus generalization has occurred if CRs are made to stimuli that are similar to the CS  (p. 230)
  - 5. Discrimination has occurred if the animal responds to some stimuli but not others  (p. 230)

III. Drug tolerance can be explained by classical conditioning  (p. 231)
- A. Stimuli that  precede the drug become CSs for a defense reaction by the body   (p. 231)
- B. The drug has weaker effects because of this conditioned response  (p. 231)

IV. There are differing explanations of classical conditioning  (pp. 232-336)
- A. Pavlov thought that temporal contiguity caused conditioning  (p. 232, Fig. 6.8)
- B. CSs are reacted to as signals, not as if they were UCSs  (p. 232)
- C. Temporal contiguity is not the entire explanation  (pp. 233-235)
  - 1. Animals respond more to a first than to a second CS  (pp. 233-234; Fig. 6.9)
  - 2. Animals don't learn about a CS if the UCS often occurs without it  (p. 234)
- D. Both contingency and contiguity are important  (p. 235)
- E. Taste-aversion learning can occur with long delays between UCS and CS   (pp. 235-236, Fig. 6.11)
  - 1. Some CSs work better than others; e.g., tastes condition more to illness than lights and noises  (p. 236, Fig. 6.12)
- F. Learners actively  process information to determine what  predicts what  (p. 237)

### Operant Conditioning

V. Thorndike first studied operant  (instrumental) conditioning  (pp. 239-240)
- A. Reinforcement increases the  probability of a response  (p. 240)

1. The law of effect states that a response that is followed by favorable consequences will be more likely in the future  (p. 240)
2. Classical conditioning applies mostly to visceral responses; operant conditioning applies to skeletal responses, although the distinction sometimes breaks down  (p. 240)
   B. Extinction, generalization, and discrimination occur in operant conditioning also  (pp. 240-242)
   C. Some responses are more easily learned than others  (p. 242)
   1. Some stimuli and responses show belongingness  (p. 242)
VI. B. F. Skinner first demonstrated shaping  (pp. 243-245)
   A. Shaping involves reinforcement of responses that become closer to the final response  (p. 244)
   B. In chaining, each response is reinforced by an opportunity to  perform the next response (pp. 244-245)
VII. Response frequencies can be both increased and decreased  (pp. 245-246,  Table 6.2)
   A. Reinforcement increases response frequency  (pp. 245-246, Table 6.2)
   1. Event that increases behavior is added in  positive reinforcement  (p. 245)
   2. Unpleasant event is removed in negative reinforcement  (p. 246)
      a. Also called escape or avoidance learning  (p. 246)
   B. Punishment decreases response frequency  (p. 246, Table 6.2, p. 245)
   1. Event that decreases behavior is added for  punishment  (p. 246, Table 6.2, p. 245)
      a. Also called  passive avoidance learning  (p. 246)
      b. Effective only if it is  prompt and consistent, and if an alternative response is available (p. 247)
   2. Behavior removes that  positive event is negative  punishment  (p. 246)
      a. Also called omission training  (p. 246)
   C. A reinforcer is anything that increases responses  (p. 247)
   1. Drive-reduction theory argues that reinforcers satisfy drives  (p. 248)
   2. Premack  principle states that more frequent responses can serve as  reinforcers for less frequent responses  (p. 248)
   3. Disequilibrium  principle states that activities are reinforcing if we have spent less than our usual time on them  (p. 248)
   4. Unconditioned reinforcers meet biological needs  (p. 249)
   5. Conditioned reinforcers have been associated with unconditioned reinforcers  (p. 249)
   6. Individuals learn what leads to what  (p. 249)
   D. Reinforcement does not follow every response when a schedule is used  (pp. 250-251, Table 6.3)
   1. Reinforcement is given after some set number of responses in fixed ratio  (p. 250, Table 6.3)
   2. Reinforcement is given on the average after some number of responses in variable ratio  (pp. 250-251, Table 6.3)
   3. Reinforcement is given for the first response after some time  period in fixed interval  (p. 251, Table 6.3, p. 250)
   4. Reinforcement is given on the average after some time  period in variable interval (p. 251, Table 6.3, p. 250)
   5. Extinction takes longer following intermittent reinforcement than following continuous reinforcement  (p. 251)
VIII. Operant conditioning has  practical applications  (pp. 251-253)
   A. Animals are trained through shaping and reinforcement  (pp. 251-253)
   B. Reinforcements can be used to  persuade  people  (p. 252)
   C. Applied Behavior Analysis can modify  problem behaviors  (p. 253)
   D. Bad habits can be broken with operant conditioning  (p. 253)

**Social Learning**

IX. Much learning occurs from observing others, according to social-learning theory  (pp. 256-258)
   A. People model their behavior after others' behavior; they imitate  (pp. 256-257)
   B. Some behaviors occur or do not occur because similar behaviors in other  people have been reinforced (vicarious reinforcement) or punished (vicarious punishment)  (p. 258)
      1. Vicarious punishment doesn't work as well as vicarious reinforcement  (p. 258)
   C. Self-efficacy may be necessary for imitation  (pp. 258-259)
      1. Much behavior is maintained through self-reinforcement  (pp. 259-260)

## COMPREHENSION CHECK

Answer these questions soon after reading the chapter.  Circle the best alternative.  Check your answers on pp. 116-118.  If you gave a wrong answer, try to write why it was wrong.  Check your reasons on pp. 116-118.

### Behaviorism

1. Which of the following is not a basic assumption of behaviorists?
   a. behavior should be explained by internal motivations
   b. behavior is molded by the environment
   c. explanations based on internal states are not useful
   d. determinism is the appropriate philosophy

Correct _____  If  wrong, why? _____

### Classical Conditioning

2. Every time the toilet in a neighboring apartment is flushed, your shower becomes very hot and you jump back.  Soon you learn to jump back at the sound of the flushing even before the water gets hot.  Which of the following is correct?
   a. pulling back from a painful stimulus is a conditioned reflex
   b. the flushing sound is the UCS
   c. jumping back at the sound is the UCR
   d. the flushing sound is the CS
   e. jumping back from the hot water is the CR

Correct _____  If  wrong, why? _____

3. Which of the following would produce the best classical conditioning?
   a. an unfamiliar sound presented 1 sec. before the UCS
   b. a familiar sound presented 1 sec. before the UCS
   c. presentation of the CS many times without the UCS
   d. presentation of the CS immediately after the UCS

Correct _____  If  wrong, why? _____

4. A child named Albert learned to fear a rat because the sight of it was paired with a loud, frightening sound. Later the child also showed fear of his mother's fur coat. Why?
   a. there was no contingency between the noise and the rat
   b. he formed a discrimination for the situations when the UCS would and would not occur
   c. stimulus generalization occurred from the furry rat to the similar coat
   d. extinction probably caused him to associate the coat with the noise
   e. spontaneous recovery occurred following extinction of the fear

Correct _____ If wrong, why? _____

5. An individual always takes a drug injection in his small, cramped room. One reaction of his body to the drug is an increase in heart rate. The conditioned response in this case is likely to be:
   a. a decrease in heart rate
   b. an increase in heart rate
   c. things in the small, cramped room
   d. the injection of the drug itself
   e. the injection procedure

Correct _____ If wrong, why? _____

6. If you eat a new food and then get sick because of the flu, you might dislike that food and avoid it in the future. Which of the following is true?
   a. you would also avoid the type of plate upon which the food was served
   b. classical conditioning could not have occurred because the delay between the taste and illness would be too long
   c. a conditioned taste aversion was acquired; the association between taste and illness is easily learned
   d. a conditioned taste aversion developed with taste as the UCS for illness

Correct _____ If wrong, why? _____

**Operant Conditioning**

7. Thorndike's cats learned to escape the puzzle box because:
   a. positive reinforcement followed the correct response
   b. their learning curves showed a gradual increase
   c. visceral responses were changed by instrumental conditioning
   d. skeletal responses were changed by classical conditioning

Correct _____ If wrong, why? _____

8. How does extinction occur in <u>operant</u> conditioning?
   a. present the CS many times without the UCS
   b. present the CS many times without the UCS; then wait for a day and present the CS again
   c. withhold positive reinforcement following a correct response
   d. set up the situation so that the opportunity to make the next response is the reinforcement for each response

Correct _____ If wrong, why? _____

9. The lion in a circus stands up on a chair and from there jumps through a hoop that is on fire. No reinforcement is given until it goes to the center of the stage and stands on its hind legs. How was this animal trained?
   a. by shaping
   b. by reinforcing each successive approximation to the response
   c. by chaining the shaped responses
   d. by first giving positive reinforcement only when the entire sequence was correct
   e. a, b, and c

Correct _____ If wrong, why? _____

10. Many cars have loud, obnoxious buzzers that continue until the driver buckles the seat belt. Buckling the belt turns off the buzzer. This is an example of which type of operant conditioning?
   a. positive reinforcement
   b. negative punishment
   c. punishment
   d. negative reinforcement

Correct _____ If wrong, why? _____

11. What do psychologists currently believe about punishment?
   a. it is effective in the short run but not in the long run
   b. punishment can be effective if it is immediate and very severe
   c. punishment can be effective if it is immediate and there is an alternative response available
   d. punishment is never effective and should be avoided at all costs
   e. punishment sometimes reduces the behavior because attention is reinforcing

Correct _____ If wrong, why? _____

12. Your father promises you your own credit card if you do well in your first year at college. The credit card is:
   a. an unconditioned reinforcer
   b. valuable because you have been shaped to appreciate it
   c. a conditioned reinforcer
   d. an example of fixed-ratio reinforcement

Correct _____ If wrong, why? _____

13. Jake, a fly fisherman, finds that he gets an average of five bites per 50 casts. If getting bites is reinforcing, he is:
   a. on a fixed-ratio schedule of reinforcement
   b. on a fixed-interval schedule of reinforcement
   c. in a negative reinforcement situation
   d. on a variable-ratio schedule of reinforcement
   e. on a continuous reinforcement schedule

Correct _____ If wrong, why? _____

14. Jake, from question 13, goes fishing with Bud who, in the past, has gotten a bite with every cast. They go to a river where there are no fish and they get no bites. How long will each continue to cast?
    a. Jake will continue longer than Bud because he had been on intermittent reinforcement
    b. Bud will continue longer than Jake because he had been on intermittent reinforcement
    c. both will continue the same time because they are in a punishment situation
    d. Bud will continue longer because he was on a variable-interval schedule before and that prolongs extinction

Correct _____ If wrong, why? _____

15. A girl with a developmental disability is being taught to comb her hair, to brush her teeth, and to be generally neat and clean every day. She receives tokens that can be traded for goods and privileges. At first, almost any attempt at neatness earns a token, but later she must do more to earn a token. The girl is:
    a. being reinforced by the Premack principle
    b. receiving negative punishment
    c. receiving unconditioned reinforcers
    d. in an applied behavior analysis program
    e. being forced into disequilibrium by her behavior

Correct _____ If wrong, why? _____

**Social Learning**

16. John was able to stop smoking after seeing that his racquetball partner was able to play better and not become short of breath after he stopped. John:
    a. was able to stop because of his poor self-efficacy
    b. changed his behavior because of vicarious reinforcement
    c. began to change his behavior because of positive reinforcement
    d. changed his behavior because of vicarious punishment

Correct _____ If wrong, why? _____

17. If you have received vicarious reinforcement for a behavior, you are likely to be successful at executing the behavior if you:
    a. have poor self-efficacy
    b. have doubts about your ability but are willing to try anyway
    c. use appropriate self-reinforcement
    d. have high self-efficacy
    e. both c and d

Correct _____ If wrong, why? _____

**ANSWERS AND EXPLANATIONS FOR COMPREHENSION CHECK**

| Correct Answer | Other Alternatives Are Wrong Because: |
|---|---|
| 1. a (pp. 222-223)<br>Obj. I | a. the emphasis was on observable behavior, not on unobservable internal states<br>b-d. these are basic assumptions of behaviorists |

2. d (p. 226)
Obj. II-A-1

a. pulling back from a painful stimulus is an <u>un</u>conditioned reflex
b. flushing sound is CS; response to it is learned (conditioned)
c. jumping back from sound is CR; it is learned
e. jumping back from hot water is UCS; it is not learned

3. a (p. 226)
Obj. II-A-1

b. it is more difficult to learn CRs to familiar stimuli
c. this will produce extinction if conditioning has already occurred; otherwise no learning will occur
d. CS must precede the UCS for good conditioning

4. c (p. 230)
Obj. II-B-4

a. there was a contingency; the appearance of the rat predicted the noise
b. no; he responded in the new situation rather than discriminating it and not responding
d. extinction refers to the reduction of CRs to a CS, not to responding to other stimuli
e. the original fear was not extinguished; rat was not presented alone many times

5. a (p. 231, Fig. 6.7)
Obj. III-A

b. unconditioned response due to the drug itself; an opposite defense reaction is conditioned
c. would be part of the conditioned <u>stimuli</u>
d. this is the <u>unconditioned stimulus</u>
e. part of the conditioned <u>stimuli</u>

6. c (p. 236)
Obj. IV-E-1

a. visual stimuli are not easily associated with illness
b. this type of long-delay learning does occur
d. taste is the CS

7. a (p. 240)
Obj. V-A

b. curves plot the course of performance, they don't cause it; errors decreased
c. visceral responses are usually automatic and classically conditioned; not relevant to cats' behavior
d. skeletal responses are usually voluntary muscle movements and operantly conditioned

8. c (pp. 240-242)
Obj. V-B

a. extinction in classical conditioning
b. would lead to spontaneous recovery in classical conditioning
d. chaining; can be done without extinction

9. e (pp. 244-245, 246)
Obj. VI-A,B; VIII-A

a,b. different terms for reinforcing small parts of the response
c. this is how the different responses would be linked
d. the whole sequence would never occur spontaneously, so reinforcement would never be given

10. d (p. 246, Table 6.2)
Obj. VII-A-2

a. the buckling response removes an unfavorable consequence; it doesn't add a favorable one
b. the buckling response does not remove a favorable consequence
c. the buckling response does not add an unfavorable consequence

11. c (p. 247)
Obj. VII-B-1-b

    a. this was Skinner's view; however, if an alternative
        response is available, punishment can work
    b. very severe punishment is not necessary
    d. it can be effective, and may be necessary to stop dangerous behavior
    e. punishment is sometimes reinforcing because it is accompanied by
        attention; however, this increases the behavior, not decreases it

12. c (p. 249)
Obj. VII-C-5

    a. doesn't satisfy a basic biological need, unless you
        eat and digest plastic
    b. shaping refers to responses, not reinforcements
    d. you aren't being reinforced for a set number of responses

13. d (pp. 251-252,
Table 6.3)
Obj. VII-D-2

    a. he doesn't get a bite every 10th cast; it's on the average
    b. number of casts, not time, is specified
    c. refers to increasing a response because an unfavorable stimulus is
        removed; not relevant here
    e. continuous means reinforcement for _every_ response; not true here

14. a (pp. 250-551)
Obj. VII-D-5

    b. Bud has been on continuous reinforcement and that will produce
        faster extinction
    c. refers to addition of an unfavorable stimulus; not relevant here
    d. Bud has not been on any intermittent reinforcement schedule; he has
        been on continuous reinforcement

15. d (p. 253)
Obj. VIII-C

    a. tokens are reinforcers; she isn't being allowed
        to do a preferred behavior
    b. no favorable stimuli are being removed if she is not neat
    c. tokens are conditioned, not unconditioned, reinforcers
    e. disequilibrium refers to the fact that any behavior that has been
        engaged in less often than usual can be reinforcing;
        getting her to increase hygiene isn't doing this

16. b (p. 258)
Obj. IX-B

    a. he must have thought he was able to stop; he probably had high
        self-efficacy
    c. the positive benefits on his own health would be positive
        reinforcement, but at first he stopped because he saw his partner
        being reinforced
    d. the partner had a favorable, not an unfavorable, outcome

17. e (pp. 259-260)
Obj. IX-C,1

    a. must have high self-efficacy; think you can do it
    b. this is low self-efficacy; not likely to succeed
    c. correct, but high self-efficacy is important too
    d. correct, but probably need self-reinforcement as well

## LECTURE MATERIAL

Don't forget to review your lecture material. Process each topic meaningfully. First, be sure that you understand the material in each lecture--if you don't, ask your instructor or teaching assistant. Associate the material with things that you already know and with your personal experiences. If you can make up mental images of any of the material, do so. Try to think of real-life applications of the concepts. Write your own comments on your lecture notes. Then write questions to cover each concept.

------------------------------------------------------------------------

### WAIT AT LEAST 24 HOURS BEFORE PROCEEDING.
### LET FORGETTING OCCUR--IT WILL!!

------------------------------------------------------------------------

## SHORT-ANSWER ESSAY QUESTIONS

Write brief answers to each of the following. The answers are on pp. 121-122, but do try to write the answers yourself before looking at them.

### Behaviorism

1. Describe the three assumptions of behaviorism.

### Classical Conditioning

2. Describe how a person might come to feel frightened at a corner after having had an auto accident at that corner.

3. John's girlfriend is trying to get him to wink on command. She blows a puff of air into his eye and then says "Hi ya." After doing this many times, John still doesn't blink to "Hi ya." Explain why not.

4. Garcia and Koelling paired shock or illness with taste or lights and noise. Describe what they found.

5. Describe one example of evidence that classical conditioning is not simply the result of temporal contiguity.

## Operant Conditioning

6. Design an operant conditioning program to get a dog to press a lever to turn on a light.

7. Explain how negative and positive reinforcement differ.

8. Describe Skinner's view of punishment and also describe the more current view.

9. Describe the four schedules of reinforcement and describe the effect of intermittent versus continuous reinforcement on extinction.

10. Explain how shaping could be used to get prisoners to say things publicly that they don't believe.

## Social Learning

11. How would a social-learning theorist explain a child's learning to smoke cigarettes?

12. Describe the roles of self-efficacy and self-reinforcement in learning.


```
************************************************************
```
Find the questions that you wrote over lecture material and write answers to them.
```
************************************************************
```

## ANSWERS TO SHORT-ANSWER ESSAY QUESTIONS

1. 1) All behavior has a cause that can be understood with scientific methods; 2) explanations based on internal causes and mental states are not useful; explanations should be based on external, observable events; 3) the environment molds behavior, and we are influenced by our surroundings (pp. 222-223)

2. Classical conditioning could explain this. The fear at the sight of the corner is a conditioned response. Fear at the time of the accident is the unconditioned response to the unconditioned stimuli of loud noise and pain. The particular corner is the CS, but other corners may also produce fear through generalization. If only that corner produces fear, discrimination has occurred. (pp. 225-227)

3. For conditioning to occur, the CS ("Hi ya") needs to precede (predict) the UCS (puff of air). Simple contiguity is not enough; the UCS should be contingent upon the CS (the puff of air should only occur following the "Hi ya" stimulus). She should present the CS a second before the UCS and then John might wink on command. (pp. 232-233)

4. Rats that became ill learned to avoid the taste of the water, but they did not avoid the lights or noise. Rats that were shocked learned to avoid the lights and noise but not the taste. Animals seem predisposed to associate illness with tastes and shock with what they have seen or heard. (p. 236)

5. If a CS has already been conditioned to a UCS, then a second, simultaneous, CS is not learned about because it is redundant and not informative. This is true even though it has temporal contiguity with the UCS. Another piece of evidence is that conditioning doesn't occur when the UCS occurs alone frequently without the CS, even though presentations of the CS are always followed by the UCS. (pp. 233-234)

6. The dog would have to be shaped. First, a food reinforcement should be given whenever the dog looks toward the lever, then only when he moves toward it, and later when he touches it. Next, the dog would have to push the lever slightly to be rewarded. Finally, he would have to push it hard enough to turn on the light. (pp. 243-245, 251-252)

7. In positive reinforcement, the consequence of the behavior is that a favorable event occurs after the response. For example, money is given contingent upon some behavior. The goal is to increase the behavior that led to the positive event. In negative reinforcement, the behavior results in the removal of a negative event. For example, a shock is turned off as a result of a behavior. In negative reinforcement, the goal is to increase the likelihood of the behavior that led to the removal of the negative event. (pp. 245-246, Table 6.2)

8. Skinner argued that punishment may temporarily suppress a response, but that it is of no use in the long run. However, his animals were not given a response alternative. If an alternative response is available and if the punishment is immediate and consistent, punishment can be effective in the long run. (p. 247)

9. <u>Fixed ratio</u>: Reinforcement is given after a set number of responses; e.g., FR 10 means reinforcement after every 10 responses.
   <u>Variable ratio</u>: Reinforcement after some number of responses, but the number is an average; e.g., VR 10 means reinforcement is given after an average of 10 responses, but not after the 10th, 20th, etc.
   <u>Fixed interval</u>: Reinforcement is given for the first response following some time interval; e.g., FI 5 sec. means that the first response after 5 sec. has passed would be reinforced.
   <u>Variable interval</u>: Reinforcement is given after a time interval, but it is an average interval; e.g., VI 5 sec. means that the intervals would average 5 sec., but would vary. Responding will continue longer without reinforcement after one of these schedules than after reinforcement following every response (continuous). (pp. 250-251)

10. This happened during the Korean War. The Chinese Communists ran essay contests, and soldiers who wrote the best essays won extra food or privileges. Soldiers who wrote negative comments about the United States were asked to elaborate on them. Many prisoners ended up denouncing the United States, making false confessions, and even revealing military secrets. Basically, a shaping process with positive reinforcements was used. (p. 252)

11. Much human learning occurs through imitation. The child sees his or her parents, other children, and TV personalities smoking, and they seem to be enjoying themselves. Thus, the child receives vicarious reinforcement, so he or she imitates these people and tries the behavior. (pp. 256-258)

12. Even if a person has received vicarious reinforcement for some behavior, the behavior may not be imitated unless self-efficacy is high. That is, a person must think that he or she can succeed at the behavior before trying it. When the behavior is attempted, some self-reinforcement (self-administered praise or reinforcers) will probably be necessary for the execution of the behavior to continue. (pp. 258-260)

**POSTTEST**

Take this test with all of your books and notes out of sight. This should give you a good idea of how well you understand the material.

**Matching**

Put the letter of the stimulus or response in the blank beside the description.

Classical Conditioning

1-4. Paul's Aunt Molly gave him a new sweater that makes him itch. Now just the sight of the sweater makes him itch.

1. _____ sweater on the skin

2. _____ itching at the sight

3. _____ sight of sweater

4. _____ itching with sweater on

A. conditioned response (CR)

B. conditioned stimulus (CS)

5-8. Cryin' Bryan cringes when he sees lightning, although he has never been struck by lightning. The loud thunder that follows naturally makes him cringe.

5. _____ sound of the thunder

6. _____ cringing at thunder

7. _____ sight of lightning

8. _____ cringing at lightning

C. unconditioned response (UCR)

D. unconditioned stimulus (UCS)

**Multiple-Choice**

Circle the best alternative.

Behaviorism

1. Which of the following would most likely be a statement made by a radical behaviorist?
   a. learning is a change in an individual's response to a stimulus
   b. we can tell what people have learned by asking how well they think they know material
   c. having people describe thoughts and ideas is the only real way to observe learning
   d. behavior is often unpredictable because of free will
   e. both b and c

## Classical Conditioning

2. Our dog drools saliva whenever he hears the "doggy snacks" cupboard open. Which of the following is true?
    a. the sound of the cupboard is a UCS for salivating, which is the UCR
    b. the sound of the cupboard is the CS; the doggy snacks are the UCS
    c. salivating to the sound is the UCR; salivating to the snacks is the CR
    d. the snacks are the CS; salivating to the cupboard is the UCS
    e. the snacks are the UCS; salivating to the cupboard is the UCR

3. Which of the following is an example of spontaneous recovery?
    a. a dog hears a tone CS many times without the UCS
    b. a child who has learned to stop wetting the bed wakes up when he has stomach cramps as well as when he has a full bladder
    c. an alcoholic learns not to drink in the lab because he will become sick but learns that he can drink in the local bar
    d. a fear that was removed by presenting the object over and over without harm returns when the object hasn't been seen for weeks
    e. a dog salivates to the sound of any cupboard opening

4. Pavlov believed that the CS and UCS must be presented in temporal contiguity. What do psychologists believe today?
    a. temporal contiguity is even more important than Pavlov thought
    b. CS must predict the coming UCS
    c. long delays between CS and UCS make all learning impossible
    d. Presenting the UCS before the CS produces even stronger conditioning than presenting the CS first
    e. extinction will only occur if the UCS is presented without the CS

5. Rats that have been shocked while drinking sweetened water from a tube that produces loud noises and bright lights will later:
    a. avoid tubes with noises and lights
    b. avoid sweet-tasting water
    c. avoid both sweet-tasting water and tubes with noises and lights
    d. avoid all sweet-tasting substances
    e. completely stop eating and drinking

## Operant Conditioning

6. Which of the following is an example of operant conditioning?
    a. a child fears the sight of dogs because she was once bitten by one
    b. a cancer patient feels sick when she sees the hospital where she receives a strong drug treatment
    c. a rabbit blinks its eyelid to a tone that has been paired with shock
    d. a chimpanzee pulls the lever on a slot machine to get banana chips
    e. a boy learns to wake up before wetting the bed, because a full bladder has been paired with a loud noise

7. What procedure would you use to train your dog to go to the bedroom, pick up your slippers, carry them to your favorite chair, go to the door, get the newspaper, and bring it to you?
   a. shaping
   b. classical conditioning
   c. chaining
   d. both b and c
   e. both a and c

8. I have learned to open my umbrella in order to stop the rain from soaking me. What type of contingency led to this learning?
   a. positive reinforcement
   b. negative punishment
   c. punishment
   d. negative reinforcement
   e. omission training

9. Which of the following would increase the likelihood that punishment would be effective?
   a. make sure that there are no alternative ways of getting reinforcement
   b. make a child's punishment intense and with no explanation
   c. make a child's punishment mild and accompany it with an explanation
   d. give a child as little attention as possible, except when punishing him
   e. Punish a behavior that is strongly motivated and give the animal no other way to satisfy the motivation

10. Dogs are frequently trained with verbal praise, such as "Good boy," as the reinforcer. What type is it?
    a. an unconditioned reinforcer
    b. a negative reinforcer
    c. a punisher
    d. an instrumental reinforcer
    e. a conditioned reinforcer

11. The disequilibrium principle states that:
    a. any high-frequency behavior can be used to reinforce a low-frequency behavior
    b. any behavior that has been performed less often than usual can reinforce behavior
    c. rare behaviors can never be used to reinforce more frequent behaviors
    d. conditioned reinforcers are more powerful than unconditioned reinforcers
    e. individuals learn what leads to what rather than automatically increasing reinforced behaviors

12. Which of the following is an example of a variable-interval schedule?
    a. Bertha gets one chocolate-chip cookie for every 10 sit-ups she does
    b. A pigeon gets food the first time it pecks a key after 10 sec. have passed
    c. Freddie gets a dime each morning that he makes his bed
    d. A gambler wins on 3 out of 10 poker hands on the average
    e. A fisherman gets a bite once every 15 minutes on the average

13. The drive reduction theory of reinforcement states that reinforcers:
    a. must satisfy some drive which may be biological or not
    b. must satisfy biological needs
    c. are discovered by trial and error; if they increase behavior, they're reinforcing
    d. work is only if a behavior has occurred less often than usual
    e. really work because they allow one to engage in a preferred behavior

<u>Social Learning</u>

14. According to social-learning theory:
    a. we learn because of unconditioned reinforcement
    b.  we usually learn because we are classically conditioned by society
    c. much human learning occurs because of imitation
    d. operant conditioning is irrelevant for human learning
    e. society could be improved through operant conditioning

15. Vicarious punishment:
    a. works better than vicarious reinforcement
    b. involves actual physical consequences to the learner
    c. affects behavior less than vicarious reinforcement
    d. does not involve a model
    e. is probably an important reason for engaging in "safe sex"

16. Although it is clear that the gymnast was reinforced for her excellent tumbling routine, most people would not imitate her.  Why?
    a. vicarious reinforcement did not occur
    b. vicarious punishment occurred
    c. self-reinforcement doesn't work for gymnastics
    d. self-efficacy would be low for most people
    e. the gymnast would not be a good model

## ANSWERS TO POSTTEST

| <u>Correct Answer</u> | <u>Questions Testing a Similar Concept</u> | |
| --- | --- | --- |
| | Comprehension Check | Short-Answer |
| **Matching** | | |
| 1. D  (p. 226) | 2 | 2, 3 |
| 2. A  (p. 226) | 2 | 2, 3 |
| 3. B  (p. 226) | 2 | 2, 3 |
| 4. C  (p. 226) | 2 | 2, 3 |
| 5. D  (p. 226) | 2 | 2, 3 |
| 6. C  (p. 226) | 2 | 2, 3 |
| 7. B  (p. 226) | 2 | 2, 3 |
| 8. A  (p. 226) | 2 | 2, 3 |

**Multiple-Choice**

| | | |
|---|---|---|
| 1.  a  (pp. 221-222) | 1 | 1 |
| 2.  b  (p. 226) | 2, 3 | 2, 3 |
| 3.  d  (pp. 229-330) | 4e | -- |
| 4.  b  (pp. 233-235) | 3 | 3, 5 |
| 5.  a  (pp. 235-236) | 6 | 4 |
| 6.  d  (p. 240) | 7 | 6 |
| 7.  e  (pp. 244-245, 251-252) | 9 | 6 |
| 8.  d  (p. 246) | 10 | 7 |
| 9.  c  (p. 247) | 11 | 8 |
| 10.  e  (p. 249) | 12 | -- |
| 11.  b  (p. 248) | 15a,15e | -- |
| 12.  e  (p. 251, Fig. 6.3) | 14d | 9 |
| 13.  a  (p. 248) | 12a, 12c | -- |
| 14.  c  (pp. 256-258) | 16 | 11 |
| 15.  c  (p. 258) | 16d | 11 |
| 16.  d  (pp. 258-259) | 17 | 12 |

# CHAPTER 6  LANGUAGE ENHANCEMENT GUIDE

## I. VOCABULARY, IDIOMS  AND CULTURAL CONCEPTS

**Instructions:**

As you read the text refer to the following list of words and their definitions.  The words are listed in the order in which they appear in the chapter.  The definitions presented contain the meaning of the word as used by Kalat on the text book page indicated.

Remember that these words like all words can have different meanings in other sentences.  If you do not find a non-technical word on this list it may have been defined on a previous page or chapter of this study guide.  The definition of non-technical words may be found in the dictionary at the end of this study guide.  Kalat defined each new technical word as it first appears on a page and these may be found in Kalat's summary at the end of the section and in the Glossary at the end the textbook.

**Behaviorism**

suppose (220) = make believe
consecutive =  following one after another
confounding = complex; mixed up
distracted = to turn attention away from something; divert
ferocious = murderous; wanting to kill; violent; destructive

enduring (221) = long lasting
quite a range of = many different

context in which it arose (222) = time period in which it developed
mention = to refer to
surmised =  to infer something without much evidence

inconsistent (223) = not regular or predictable
ineffective = not effective
presumably = assumed; guessed
fruitful explanations = productive explanations
operational definition = a definition that specifies the process used to measure a variable or produce
    an event
internal states = physical conditions inside of the body
to be fair = without bias

## Classical Conditioning

furthermore (225) = in addition
conditioning = learning; training
to condition = to teach or train a response
orienting response = looking at or listening to changes in the environment

other things being equal (227) = other things being the same

prompted (228) = stimulated; motivated
practical concerns = a focus on useful activity or things
revealed = showed
to distinguish between = to see the difference between

pairing (231) = two stimuli that occur at the same time
temporal contiguity = being close together in time

appealed to (232) = attracted; was of interest
contrary = unfavorable; opposite in direction

aversion (235) = a very strong feeling of not liking along with avoidance or rejection of something
specialization = to develop a specific skill or function
saccharin = A white powder that tastes about 500 times sweeter than cane sugar, used as a calorie-
    free sweetener

deter (236) = stop
coyote = a small, wild dog-like animal that lives North America
built -in predisposition = a unlearned tendency or inclination

## Operant Conditioning

devised (239) = developed
a little sooner = earlier in time
eventually = occurring at an unspecified time

scowl (242) = to twist or move the eye brow to show anger or disapproval
virtually forever = a very long time
ardent practitioner = showing strong enthusiasm for doing something
parsimony = adoption of the simplest assumption in theory formulation or data interpretation
emerge = to rise from
successive = following in uninterrupted order
approximations = almost correct; closely resembling

intermediate (244) = occurring between two extremes or in a middle position

to engage in = to do the

"Star-Spangled Banner" (245) = the national song that refers to the American flag

needless to say = it is obvious that

is governed by = is controlled or influenced by

omission (246) = to not do something; to leave out; to neglect

to recap = to review

note that = remember that

apparatus (247) = equipment (in this case the Skinner box)

spank = to hit on the buttocks with a flat object or with the open hand,

slap = to hit with the open hand or with a flat object

going around in circles (248) = going from one definition to another definition with out being specific

equilibrium = a situation in which all influences are canceled by others, resulting in a stable, balanced, or unchanging system

concert (250) = a musical performance in a large room or theater

purely theoretical concerns (251) = focus on theory

confession (252) = admitting to or revealing secrets, sins or criminal behavior

approximate = almost correct; closely resembling

fatalities = deaths resulting from an accident

incompatible = two or more things (habits, behaviors) that cannot occur at the same time

drawing up a plan (253)= to make a plan

keep track of = to keep written records

## Social Learning

destination (256) = the place to which you are going

further reinforcement = more reinforcement

provoke = produce

customs (257) = patterns of behavior and rules of living followed by people of a particular group or region

soft drink = bottles or cans filled with flavored water; a non-alcoholic beverage

ads = advertisements

yell at = to give commands or criticize in a loud voice

adolescents = people between the ages of 13 to 18

quit your job = to leave a job; stop working

vicarious = substituting someone else's behavior for your own

blurting out (259) = to suddenly say something without thinking

## II. VOCABULARY BUILDING

### Word Analysis

Instructions:

1. Study the meaning of the prefixes, roots and suffixes listed.
2. Break each word in the table into its prefixes, roots and suffixes.
3. Guess the meaning of the word based on the meaning of its parts.
4. Find the word on the text page indicated in the brackets and redefine the word based on the context of the sentence, paragraph and chapter.
5. Look up the definition of the word in the VOCABULARY, IDIOMS AND CULTURAL CONCEPTS section above, in Appendix A (marked A) or in a college level dictionary. If the word is followed by letter G look it up in the text Glossary.

Exercise 1.    Consecutive

**Prefix : con _____ =  with/together**
**Prefix : sequ/secut _____ = follow**
**Word: ____ found _____ = mix/pour together/confuse**
**Word: _____ duct _____ = move/carry/lead/bring**
   Caution:  In other contexts, found can mean begin or start.

| Word | Meaning |
|---|---|
| consecutive (A) | |
| successive (A) | |
| confounding (A) | |
| conditioning (A) | |
| confession (A) | |
| induction | bringing or placing a person into an office or position; a form of reasoning |
| conduct | |
| sequel | one development or stage follows another; an installment |
| execute | to carry out a plan or order; to punish by death |
| consensus (G) | |
| consolidation (G) | |
| contingency (G) | |

Exercise 2.  Temper

**Suffix : _____ al  = relating to/belonging to**
**Suffix : _____ ment  =  the act/means/results of**
**Suffix : _____ ion = the act/ results of**
**Word: operate = to work/to perform/to act/to produce/**
**Word: temper = to adjust as the situation requires/toughen/harden/**
   Caution:  See time below

| Word | Meaning |
|---|---|
| operational (G) | |
| temperamental | |
| temperament (G) | |
| extinction (G) | |
| methodological | |

### Exercise 3.  Time

**Word:   temper = time**
**Word:   tempo = timing/rate of speed or motion as in music**

| Word | Meaning |
|------|---------|
| temporal (A) | |
| contemporary | of the same or current time period, modern, people of the same age |
| temporary | for a short period of time, not permanent |

### Exercise 4.  Inconsistent

**Prefix: in _____ = not/in/into**
**Suffix: _____ ent/ant = bing/having/doing/performing/showing**
**Suffix: _____ ive = tending  to (be)**
**Suffix: _____ ate = having/possing/being**
    Caution:  The suffix ate can have many other meanings.

| Word | Meaning |
|------|---------|
| inconsistent (A) | |
| ineffective (A) | |
| internal (A) | |
| intermediate (A) | |
| intermittent (A) | |
| incongruence (G) | |

### Exercise 5.  Reflex

**Prefix: re _____ = go back/ again and again**
**Word: flex = bend**
**Word: force = strength/energy/power**

| Word | Meaning |
|------|---------|
| reflex (A) | |
| reinforcement (A) | |
| reconstruct (A) | |
| regression (G) | |
| replicate results (G) | |
| resistance (G) | |

# CHAPTER 7 MEMORY

**OBJECTIVES**

Understand that:

**Types of Memory**

I. No one experiment characterizes all features of memory (pp. 265-266 )
   A. Ebbinghaus learned nonsense syllables and forgot quickly (p. 266)
      1. Ebbinghaus forgot faster than college students today because he learned so many lists (p. 267)
   B. Interference from earlier (proactive) or later (retroactive) learning can cause forgetting (p. 267)
   C. Meaningful material is remembered better than nonsense material (pp. 267-268)
   D. Distinctive material that stands out is remembered better than common material (p. 268)
      1. This is called the von Restorff effect (p. 268)
   E. How much one remembers depends upon the type of test (pp. 268-269, Table 7.5, p. 294)
      1. In recall, material must be produced from memory (p. 269)
      2. In cued recall, hints are given to help remember (p. 269)
      3. In recognition, several items are given and the person picks the correct one (p. 269)
      4. In savings or relearning, the person relearns the material and the time is compared to the time to learn it originally (pp. 269-270)

II. Information-processing model assumes that there are three basic types of memory (pp. 270-272, Fig. 7.8.)
   A. Sensory store holds a very brief image of stimuli (p. 271)
   B. Short-term memory is available only a short time; long-term memory can be available at any time (pp. 271-272, Fig. 7.10)
      1. Retrieval cues help to bring out long-term memories (p. 272)
   C. Short-term memory has a number of characteristics (pp. 273-275)
      1. Short-term memory capacity is limited (p. 273)
      2. Chunking can increase the amount of information that can be held in STM (pp. 273-274, Fig. 7.12)
         a. With practice, people can use larger and larger chunks (p. 274)
         b. These chunks may be stored in long-term memory (p. 274)
      3. Decay occurs in short-term memory if a person doesn't rehearse (pp. 274-275)
         a. Interference also causes forgetting from short-term memory (pp. 274-275)
   D. Information is transferred from short-term memory to long-term memory (p. 275)
      1. This is called consolidation (p. 275)
      2. Simply holding information in short-term memory won't put it in long-term memory (pp. 275-276)

III. The information-processing model needs some modification (p. 276)
   A. Working memory temporarily stores information, but it is also a system for working with information (p. 276)
      1. The central executive governs shifts of attention (p. 276)
      2. The phonological loop stores and rehearses speech (p. 276)
      3. The visuospatial sketchpad stores and manipulates visual and spatial information (p. 276)

IV. Psychologists make several other memory distinctions (p. 277)
   A. Semantic memory consists of factual information; episodic memory consists of specific events from a person's life (p. 277)

1. Source amnesia occurs when a fact is remembered but the person doesn't know where or how it was learned  (pp. 277-278)
　　B. Psychologists agree that memory consists of many processes  (p. 278)

## Memory Improvement

V. People remember events that were emotionally arousing, although such memories may not be accurate  (pp. 280-281)
　　A. The levels-of-processing principle states that how you store material will determine how long it is remembered  (p. 281, Table 7.3)
VI. Giving meaning to material results in a deep level of processing  (pp. 281-282, Table 7.3)
　　A. Putting things into categories helps memory  (p. 282)
VII. Learners must monitor whether they understand material  (p. 283)
　　A. People have some ability to predict future performance on text passages  (p. 283)
VIII. The timing of study of sets of material affects memory  (pp. 283-285)
　　A. The serial-order effect consists of a primacy effect and a recency effect  (p. 283)
　　　　1. The primacy effect is the tendency to remember things learned first  (p. 283)
　　　　2. The recency effect is the tendency to remember things learned last  (pp. 283-284)
　　B. Studying with time between repetitions increases long-term retention  (pp. 284-285)
　　C. How you study will determine how long you remember  (pp. 284-285)
　　　　1. To remember immediately, study close to test time and in conditions that are the same as the test conditions  (p. 284)
　　　　2. To remember for a longer time, study at various times and places with long intervals between studying  (pp. 284-285)
IX. Special coding strategies can help memory  (p. 285)
　　A.. The encoding specificity principle states that cues used during learning must be the same as the cues used for retrieval  (pp. 285-286, Table 7.4)
　　B. Mnemonic devices can help anyone to improve memory  (p. 286)
　　　　1. Stories linking items can help  (p. 286)
　　　　2. Method of loci involves imagining things in known places  (pp. 286-287)
　　　　3. With the peg method, you use rhymes of numbers instead of places  (p. 287)

## Memory Loss

X. Forgetting occurs normally for several reasons  (p. 289)
　　A. Forgetting occurs because of proactive and retroactive interference  (p. 289)
　　B. Memory traces may decay, although perhaps not from long-term memory  (p. 289)
　　C. Memories may be "forgotten" because the appropriate retrieval cues aren't used  (p. 289)
XI. Amnesia is a severe loss of memory following brain damage  (p. 290)
　　A. Damage to the hippocampus can cause amnesia  (p. 290, Fig. 7.22)
　　　　1. Anterograde amnesia is an inability to learn new things  (p. 290, Fig. 7.23, p. 291)
　　　　2. Retrograde amnesia is the forgetting of events that occurred before the damage  (pp. 290-291, Fig. 7.23)
　　　　3. Procedural memory may be spared in such amnesia  (p. 291)
　　　　　　a. The main problem is in memory for facts, declarative memory  (p. 291)
　　B. Damage to the frontal lobes produce a different type of amnesia  (pp. 291-292)
　　　　1. Korsakoff's syndrome occurs in chronic alcoholics who have a deficiency of vitamin $B_1$  (pp. 291-292)
　　　　2. These patients have severe retrograde and anterograde amnesia  (pp. 291-292 , Fig. 7.23)
　　　　3. They tend to fill in gaps in memory with confabulations  (p. 292)
　　　　　　a. They have trouble working with memory, or reconstructing memory  (p. 292)

C. Alzheimer's disease involves degeneration of many parts of the brain  (pp. 292-294)
   1. These patients have trouble remembering the recent past  (p. 293)
      a. They may show memory abnormalities before having recognizable symptoms  (p. 293)
D. Amnesic patients perform normally on implicit memory tasks, but not explicit tasks  (pp. 294-295)
   1. Implicit tasks don't require conscious recollection; explicit tasks do  (pp. 294-295, Table 7.5, Fig. 7.26)
E. Brain-damage amnesia shows that conscious awareness is not necessary for memory to influence behavior  (p. 296)

XII. Infant amnesia refers to the fact that most adults can't remember anything from before age 3 1/2  (p. 296)
   A. Freud argued that infantile memories are repressed  (p. 296)
   B. Early memories may be nonverbal and we later rely on language  (p. 296)
   C. The hippocampus may not be mature enough to store factual memories  (pp. 296-297)
   D. A sense of self may be necessary before permanent memories can be formed  (p. 297)

XIII. Elderly people experience some amnesia  (p. 297)
   A. Older people show the largest deficits on complex tasks  (p. 297)
      1. Most older people remember better in the morning  (p. 297)

**Reconstruction of Memory**

XIV. Memory is often reconstructed from bits of memory that remain  (p. 299)
   A. We use schemas to reconstruct stories  (p. 299)
      1. Typical events are often reconstructed  (p. 299)
      2. If material is highly schematic, unusual items may be better remembered, probably because they're distinctive  (p. 300)
   B. Hindsight bias refers to remembering events as consistent with the outcome  (pp. 300-302, Fig.7.28)
   C. Memory can be changed with suggestions  (pp. 302-304)
      1. Memory itself may not be distorted; it may depend upon how memory is tested  (p. 303)
      2. People may forget the source of their memory  (p. 304)

XV. Eyewitness testimony may be influenced by suggestibility  (p. 304)
   A. Lineups can be biased by the nature of the incorrect choices (foils)  (p. 304)
   B. Children can be more influenced by suggestion than adults  (p. 305)

XVI. Some psychologists warn that repressed memories for childhood sexual abuse may actually come from therapists' suggestions  (pp. 305-306)
   A. Freud defined repression as moving a memory into the unconscious  (p. 305)
   B. There is not good evidence that repression occurs  (pp. 305-306)

**COMPREHENSION CHECK**

Answer these questions soon after reading the chapter.  Circle the best alternative.  Check your answers on pp. 139-141.  If you gave a wrong answer, try to write why it was wrong.  Check your reasons on pp. 139-141.

**Types of Memory**

1. Oblivia Sue lost her bicycle lock and then bought a new one, which she used for several weeks. Finally, she found her old lock; but simply cannot remember its combination. What is the best explanation for her forgetting her old combination?
   a. the old combination is too distinctive
   b. proactive interference
   c. testing is by relearning rather than by recognition
   d. retroactive interference

Correct _____ If wrong, why? _____

2. After Ebbinghaus had been learning and recalling lists of nonsense syllables for months, he began to study forgetting. He learned a list and then tried to recall it after 24 hours. He forgot much more of the list than an average college student would. What is the best explanation for this?
   a. his declarative memory was fine, but his semantic memory was poor
   b. Ebbinghaus was probably less intelligent than the average student
   c. retroactive interference; the earlier lists caused rapid forgetting of the later lists
   d. proactive interference; the earlier lists caused rapid forgetting of the later lists
   e. Ebbinghaus had probably developed Alzheimer's disease

Correct _____ If wrong, why? _____

3. Which of the following is true about ease of memorizing?
   a. people who have more practice in memorizing similar things remember better
   b. distinctive events are easier to remember than less distinctive ones
   c. words that have little meaning are easier than words that are meaningful because there is less interference
   d. words that show the von Restorff effect are not well remembered

Correct _____ If wrong, why? _____

4. The questions in this exercise are using what method to measure your memory?
   a. recognition
   b. cued recall
   c. free recall
   d. savings
   e. relearning

Correct _____ If wrong, why? _____

5. Which memory store can only store images for less than a second?
   a. short-term memory
   b. long-term memory
   c. sensory store
   d. episodic memory store

Correct _____ If wrong, why? _____

6. You've just looked up a phone number and held it in memory while you dialed it. Now, the operator comes on and asks you what number you dialed and you are unable to tell her. What has happened?
   a. the number is still in your sensory store
   b. the number has faded from short-term memory
   c. the number is now in long-term memory
   d. the number was lost because you chunked it too much

Correct _____ If wrong, why? _____

7. Practice in short-term memory tasks can:
   a. expand short-term memory capacity
   b. actually hurt long-term memory
   c. help sensory memory as well as short-term memory
   d. improve the ability to chunk

Correct _____ If wrong, why? _____

8. Working memory:
   a. is broader than short-term memory involving a system of processing as well a storage
   b. occurs after a memory has been consolidated from short-term memory to long-term memory
   c. is the same thing as the phonological loop
   d. consists of memory for specific events in a person's life

Correct _____ If wrong, why? _____

9. Almost all memory researchers agree on which of the following?
   a. long-term memory should be divided into episodic and semantic
   b. source amnesia is the main cause of forgetting from long-term memory
   c. memory that stays in short-term store long enough is consolidated into long-term memory
   d. the visuospatial sketchpad is a separate system than the phonological loop
   e. memory is not a single store that we dump things into and later take them out

Correct _____ If wrong, why? _____

**Memory Improvement**

10. According to the levels-of-processing principle of memory, which of the following should be remembered best?
    a. a word that is repeated several times in short-term memory
    b. a word for which you produced a rhyme
    c. a word that you looked at to decide if it had an e in it
    d. a word for which you produced a synonym

Correct _____ If wrong, why? _____

11. If you want to remember something for a long time, what should you do?
    a. study it immediately before the test
    b. try to think about each individual item
    c. avoid self-monitoring of understanding
    d. study under exactly the same conditions as will be used in the test
    e. study several times with long intervals between studying

Correct _____ If wrong, why? _____

12. When you learned the word "spade," you thought of it as a type of card. Now you're trying to remember the word and you are given "shovel" as a cue, but it doesn't help you to remember. The best explanation is:
    a. encoding specificity principle
    b. working memory is different from reference memory
    c. depth-of-processing principle
    d. retroactive interference

Correct _____ If wrong, why? _____

13. The method of loci involves:
    a. avoiding mnemonic devices because they produce interference
    b. imagining what you want to remember in places that you already know
    c. use of the recency effect
    d. taking something that you know well, like the face of a coin, and using it to associate what you want to remember

Correct _____ If wrong, why? _____

**Memory Loss**

14. Damage to the hippocampus results in:
    a. in inability to learn new facts
    b. a loss of procedural memory
    c. anterograde, but no retrograde amnesia
    d. a total loss of all long-term memories developed before the damage
    e. total amnesia

Correct _____ If wrong, why? _____

15. A list of words is presented. Which would be an implicit test of the words?
    a. present a long list of words, half new and half old; ask subjects to say whether each word is old or new
    b. ask subjects to write down all the words they remember
    c. give the first three letters of the words and ask subjects to complete the stems with any word that comes to mind
    d. ask the subjects to relearn the words after some time period

Correct _____ If wrong, why? _____

16. Which of the following is true about the amnesia of normal old age?
    a. confabulation is common
    b. it may appear more severe in the afternoon because most older people are morning people
    c. older people don't show primacy effects
    d. procedural learning is the first to show the effects of amnesia
    e. it is particularly evident when the important parts of stories are tested

Correct _____ If wrong, why? _____

17. On which task would Korsakoff's patients do the best?
    a. describing their present life's situation, i.e., children's ages, length of marriage, location of present home
    b. describing what they had for dinner the night before
    c. remembering a list of words presented in the laboratory
    d. completing word stems with words that were previously presented
    e. describing what happened to them before age 3

Correct _____ If wrong, why? _____

**The Reconstruction of Memory**

18. After learning who was the murderer in a mystery novel, the reader thinks back and decides that she was pretty sure who actually did it after the very first chapter. This is an example of:
    a. savings
    b. retrograde amnesia
    c. von Restorff effect
    d. hindsight bias

Correct _____ If wrong, why? _____

19. Research has shown that incorrect suggestions given after a witnessed event:
    a. change memory for the original event
    b. can lead to incorrect answers about the original event
    c. affect adults, but don't affect children
    d. after memory when it is measured by lineups, but suggestions don't affect verbal memory

Correct _____ If wrong, why? _____

20. False memories:
    a. are controversial when they are remembered in therapy after having been "repressed"
    b. can occur for trivial events but not for emotional events such as sexual abuse
    c. are most controversial when the client has always known that she was abused
    d. may develop because children have little memory for traumatic events

Correct _____ If wrong, why? _____

# ANSWERS AND EXPLANATIONS FOR COMPREHENSION CHECK

<u>Correct Answer</u>       <u>Other Alternatives Are Wrong Because</u>:

1. d (p. 267)
   Obj. I-B

   a. distinctiveness helps, not hurts, memory
   b. the old combination would cause forgetting of the new one if it was proactive
   c. method of testing not relevant

2. d (p. 267)
   Obj. I-A-1,B

   a. Ebbinghaus measured declarative memory, and it was poor
   b. he was very creative for his times
   c. this is the reason, but it's <u>proactive</u>
   e. doubtful; his memory was generally good

3. b (p. 268)
   Obj. I-D

   a. the earlier material would cause proactive interference
   c. meaningful words are more easily associated
   d. refers to distinctive events; these are easier

4. a (p. 269,
   Table7.5, p. 296)
   Obj. I-E-3

   b. would give you cues but have you produce response
   c. would have you produce answers in any order
   d. would have you relearn material and compare with time to learn originally
   e. same as d

5. c (p. 271, Fig. 7.10,
   p. 272)
   Obj. II-A

   a. lasts for 20-30 sec. without rehearsal
   b. lasts indefinitely
   d. type of long-term memory for personal events

6. b (p. 272, Figure 7.10
   Obj. II-C-3

   a. moved out of sensory store before you could use it
   c. unlikely or you would remember it
   d. chunking allows you to remember more in short-term memory, not less

7. d (pp. 273-274)
   Obj. II-C-2-a

   a. more information can be learned, but capacity itself is not changed
   b. no evidence for this
   c. sensory memory is not affected by practice

8. a (p. 276)
   Obj. III-A

   b. is involved in consolidation; doesn't come after it
   c. the phonological loop is one part of working memory, not the whole concept
   d. this is episodic memory

9. e (p. 278)
   Obj. IV-B

   a-d. some theorists believe each of these statements, but there is wide agreement only on statement e

10. d (pp. 281-282,
    Table 7. 3)
    Obj. V-A, VI

   a. rote repetition does little good
   b. fairly superficial level of processing
   c. very superficial level of processing

11. e (pp. 284-285)
   Obj. VIII-C-2

   a. this will produce good performance in the short run, but not
        for the long-term
   b. learning is better is people look at relationships and sort things
        into categories
   c. self-monitoring of understanding is necessary for good learning
   d. same as a above

12. a (pp. 284-285,
     Table 7.4)
   Obj. IX-A

   b. this is a problem with retrieval cues, not differences in memory store
   c. the word should have been processed semantically; you can't retrieve
        it now
   d. no new learning occurred during the interval; it's a retrieval problem

13. b (p. 286)
   Obj. V-A-2

   a. method of loci is a mnemonic system
   c. very few people can remember detailed images; anyone can use
        method of loci
   d. people don't remember details on coins

14. a (pp. 290-291,
     Fig. 7.22)
   Obj. XI-A

   b. new skills can be learned
   c. some retrograde amnesia for memories occurring just before
        the brain damage
   d. some memories acquired long before the damage are normal
   e. no, because of b and d

15. c (pp. 294-295)
   Obj. XI-D-1

   a. recognition; an explicit test
   b. recall; an explicit test
   d. relearning; an explicit test

16. b (p. 297)
   Obj. XIII

   a. common in Korsakoff's syndrome  (frontal lobe damage)
   c. true of those who will soon develop Alzheimer's disease; not
        among the healthy elderly
   d. procedural learning is rarely affected by amnesia
   e. older people do as well as younger people on important parts of
        stories

17. d (pp. 291-292)
   Obj. XI-B

   a. they confabulate, mixing old memories with guesses
   b. such episodic memory is very poor
   c. word lists containing more than about seven items cannot be
        remembered
   e. they would not be able to do this because of infantile amnesia

18. d (pp. 300-302)
   Obj. XIV-B

   a. refers to faster relearning the second time; no relearning here
   b. forgetting of earlier material; material here is reconstructed
   c. memory for distinctive things; reconstruction occurred here

19. b (pp. 302-304)
   Obj. XIV-C

   a. original information can be retrieved if new information is not on test
   c. children are affected by suggestions
   d. incorrect suggestions can influence all types of memory

20. a (pp. 305-307)
    Obj. XVI

b. we don't know if such memories can be implanted by suggestion; it would be unethical to try

c. these cases probably involve real, not false, memories

d. children who have experienced traumatic events remember them fairly well

## LECTURE MATERIAL

Don't forget to review your lecture material. Process each topic meaningfully. First, be sure that you understand the material in each lecture--if you don't, ask your instructor or teaching assistant. Associate the material with things that you already know and with your personal experiences. If you can make up mental images of any of the material, do so. Try to think of real-life applications of the concepts. Put notes in the left margin of your lecture notes. Then write questions to cover each concept.

---
WAIT AT LEAST 24 HOURS BEFORE PROCEEDING.
LET FORGETTING OCCUR--IT WILL!!
---

## SHORT-ANSWER ESSAY QUESTIONS

Write brief answers to each of the following. The answers are on p. 143-145, but do try to write the answers yourself before looking at them.

### Types of Memory

1. Describe the research done by Ebbinghaus, including one of his findings.

2. Give one example of forgetting by retroactive interference and one example of forgetting by proactive interference.

3. Describe two characteristics of material that affect ease of memorizing, and give an example of each.

4. Describe two ways that short-term and long-term memory differ.

5. What are two problems with the traditional view that information moves from short-term memory to long-term memory following adequate time and rehearsal in short-term memory?

6. Describe working memory. How does it relate to reading comprehension?

**Memory Improvement**

7. Describe the effects of emotional arousal on memory.

8. According to the levels-of-processing principle, why is it useless to simply repeat a definition over and over?

9. Describe how the timing of study affects later memory.

10. Why does forgetting occur according to the encoding specificity principle?

11. Explain how you would use the method of loci to remember a grocery list.

**Memory Loss**

12. Discuss three reasons for normal forgetting.

13. What is the difference between retrograde and anterograde amnesia? From which type of amnesia did H. M. suffer?

14. Discuss the types of memory that are spared in most types of amnesia.

**The Reconstruction of Memory**

15. What is meant by reconstruction in memory? Give an example.

16. How is the suggestibility of memory related to the false memory controversy?

\*\*\*\*\*\*\*\*\*\*\*\*\*\*\*\*\*\*\*\*\*\*\*\*\*\*\*\*\*\*\*\*\*\*\*\*\*\*\*\*\*\*\*\*\*\*\*\*\*\*\*\*\*\*\*\*\*\*\*\*\*\*\*\*\*\*\*\*\*\*\*\*\*
Find the questions that you wrote over lecture material and write answers to them.
\*\*\*\*\*\*\*\*\*\*\*\*\*\*\*\*\*\*\*\*\*\*\*\*\*\*\*\*\*\*\*\*\*\*\*\*\*\*\*\*\*\*\*\*\*\*\*\*\*\*\*\*\*\*\*\*\*\*\*\*\*\*\*\*\*\*\*\*\*\*\*\*\*

## ANSWERS TO SHORT-ANSWER ESSAY QUESTIONS

1. Ebbinghaus wanted to study how associations are formed in memory. He used nonsense syllables because they had no prior associations (as he thought; it turns out that they do). He would memorize a list and then test himself. He measured how quickly he forgot a list of syllables. He found that he forgot rapidly, forgetting about half of the syllables after an hour and still more after 24 hours. (pp. 266-267)

2. <u>Retroactive interference</u>: Last week you studied theories of learning and this week you are studying theories of interference. You forget the theories of learning because you learned about interference. <u>Proactive interference</u>: Last week you learned how to use the NIFTY-1 word processing program and this week you learned how to use the SUPER-W program. Your memory for the SUPER-W program will be impaired, because the NIFTY-1 will interfere. (p. 267)

3. Things that are meaningful and have lots of associates are remembered better than things that are not. For example, you can remember material presented in your own language better than material presented in a language that you don't understand. Material that is distinctive is remembered better than material that is all similar. For example, an instructor's joke in the middle of a lecture may be remembered because it stands out from the rest of the lecture material. (pp. 267-270)

4. <u>Capacity</u>: Only about seven chunks fit in short-term memory; long-term memory capacity is unlimited. (p. 273)
   <u>Length of time that information is available</u>: Information is available for only a short time in short-term memory; it becomes less available after attention has shifted; information is potentially retrievable forever in long-term memory. (p. 272)

5. Rehearsing words in short-term memory for a shorter or a longer time has no effect on later memory for the words. Some brain damaged patients have very small short-term memory capabilities, yet they are able to form and retrieve long-term memories normally. (p. 276)

6. Working memory both stores information and works with current information. It may be thought of as one's present region of attention. The central executive governs shifts of attention. The phonological loop stores and rehearses verbal information. The visuospatial sketchpad stores and manipulates visual and spatial information. People who can't hold as much in their phonological loops have more trouble understanding complex sentences than people who have larger phonological loops. (pp. 276-277)

7. People often remember many details about arousing events, such as news of an assassination or some major disaster. Although the memories may be vivid and intense, they are not necessarily accurate. Exciting events may be remembered because certain norepinephrine synapses are stimulated and because the sympathetic nervous system is aroused. (pp. 280-281)

8. Rote repetition results in a very superficial level of learning. Studies have shown that simple repetition does not lead to an increase in later memory for the material. A deeper encoding in terms of meaning and understanding is necessary for later memory. Remember the SPAR system-- Process meaningfully. (pp. 281-282)

9. The serial order effect includes the primacy effect, which is the tendency to remember the first items of a list, and the recency effect, which is the tendency to remember the last items. Other timing effects have to do with spacing study over long periods of time, or learning right before a test. Spacing learning sessions over weeks results in slower learning than learning all in one session. However, the spaced learning will be remembered longer than the massed learning. Thus, to remember a long time, learning should be spaced over several sessions. (pp. 283-284)

10. The principle of encoding specificity argues that you must use retrieval cues that are similar to the way you originally thought about the material. If you place a word in memory in one way (e.g., thinking of ball as a dance) and try to pull it out in way (e.g., thinking of ball as a round, bouncy object), you won't retrieve it. (p. 285)

11. First, I would learn a list of 20 locations in order, buildings on a walk around campus, for example. Then I would imagine each item that I want to buy in one of those locations. For example, if the administration building comes first and I want to buy tomatoes, I would imagine tomatoes smeared all over the building. Then in the store, I would take an imaginary walk and "see" each thing that I want to buy. (pp. 286-287)

12. Interference is one explanation for forgetting. People forget specific information because of other similar information that they learned before it (proactive interference) or because of other information learned after it (retroactive interference). A second explanation is decay, that is, the traces fade away. This may be a better explanation of forgetting from working memory than from long-term memory. A third possibility is that information is not forgotten but that the retrieval cues are not appropriate at a given time. The material is potentially retrievable with different cues at a later time. (pp. 289-290)

13. Retrograde amnesia means a loss of memory for events that occurred before the onset of the amnesia. Anterograde means an inability to learn new things, or to form new long-term memories. H. M.'s biggest problem was anterograde amnesia; he couldn't learn new facts. Although he had some trouble remembering events that happened a few years before his operation, H. M. could generally remember things that occurred before his amnesia.
(pp. 290-291, Fig. 7.23)

14. People with amnesia generally perform normally on tests that do not require explicit remembering. These implicit memory tests ask participants to simply respond to some stimuli that they have experienced before, like giving words for word fragments. Generally, the people with amnesia give as many previously seen words as normal participants do. People with amnesia are usually normal on procedural memory tasks. They remember how to do things even though they may not remember having learned to do them. (pp. 294-295)

15. We tend to fill in the gaps of memories by inserting things that should be true. We omit or distort other details to fit with our expectations. For example, students remember a Native American folk tale as more consistent with their expectations than it really was. People may omit unexpected events and include events that should have happened even though they didn't when asked to recall stories. (pp. 299-300)

16. Experiments show that people will incorporate false information from questions about events into their memory of the events themselves. Whether the memories actually change, or whether people have trouble identifying the source of the suggested information is not clear. The false memory controversy surrounds clients' remembering childhood sexual abuse after having entered therapy. Some psychologists believe that certain therapeutic techniques suggest that abuse occurred when it did not and the client comes to believe this is an actual memory and not just a suggestion. (pp. 305-307)

## POSTTEST

Take this test with all of your books and notes out of sight. This should give you a good idea of how well you understand the material.

### Matching

Write the letter of the term on the right that best explains the forgetting in the description on the left.

1. _____ a person with Korsakoff's syndrome
   can't remember new things

   A. retroactive interference

2. _____ Mary remembers few facts about
   an important Civil War battle, so
   she just fills in the rest with what
   should have happened

   B. retrograde amnesia

   C. anterograde amnesia

3. _____ John forgot the Spanish that he learned
   in high school because he studied
   French in college

   D. encoding specificity

4. _____ When Amorfus learned the word *orange*,
   he thought of it as a color; now he can't
   remember it with *fruit* as a cue

   E. proactive interference

5. _____ Perplexity tried to memorize a
   definition by repeating it over and
   over; now she can't remember it

   F. reconstructive memory

   G. levels-of-processing

6. _____ Equivocus forgot his new address
   because of his old, similar address

7. _____ H. M. has a poor memory for things that
   happened within the 3 years before his operation

### Multiple-choice

Circle the best alternative.

Types of Memory

1. Susan learned German in college but she has not used it for two years. During this time, she has been studying French. Mary also learned German in college and she hasn't used it for two years either, but she has not learned any other languages in the two years. Who should remember German better and why?
   a. Mary; she will have less retroactive interference
   b. Susan; she will have less proactive interference
   c. Mary; she will have more retroactive interference
   d. Susan; she will have less retroactive interference
   e. Mary; she will have less proactive interference

2. Many students are dismayed because they feel that they have forgotten everything they learned in some courses. However, some weak memories are probably left. Which method would be most likely to show those weak memories?
   a. relearning
   b. cued recall
   c. recognition
   d. recall
   e. von Restorff effect

3. If you are given an English word and asked to give the French equivalent, your memory is being tested by:
   a. cued recall
   b. implicit test
   c. free recall
   d. recognition
   e. savings

4. If you meet someone and use her correct name immediately but cannot remember it a half-hour later, the name probably was in your:
   a. sensory store
   b. episodic memory
   c. short-term memory
   d. long-term memory
   e. semantic memory

5. If you glance at a bright scene on television and close your eyes and still see the exact image for less then a second, the image is in your:
   a. sensory store
   b. procedural memory
   c. long-term memory
   d. short-term memory
   e. episodic memory

6. Why can people hold about seven 5-letter words (35 letters) in short-term memory, but only seven unrelated letters?
   a. they use chunking so that each word is one unit
   b. words are tested by implicit memory; letters by explicit memory
   c. the seven letters are held in long-term memory, but the words are held in short-term memory
   d. the seven letters are held in short-term memory, but the words are held in long-term memory
   e. unrelated letters decay much faster than meaningful words

7. Why did Peterson and Peterson have subjects count backward during the delay interval in their experiment on short-term memory?
   a. to prevent passive decay
   b. to prevent rehearsal
   c. to prevent the use of visual imagery
   d. to interfere with the sensory store
   e. to increase the amount of proactive interference

8. The concept of working memory differs from the traditional concept of short-term memory in that working memory:
   a. does not store information, short-term memory is a storage system
   b. comes after the sensory store; short-term memory comes before it
   c. is forgotten because of interference; short-term memory forgotten because of decay
   d. has a limited capacity; short-term memory does not
   e. includes a processing system along with storage; short-term memory just stores information

Memory Improvement

9. According to levels-of-processing theory, which will lead to the best memory?
   a. repeating a word over and over for 5 sec.
   b. counting the number of vowels in a word
   c. looking to see whether a word contains an "e"
   d. producing a rhyme for a word
   e. producing a definition for a word

10. According to the encoding specificity principle, what type of cue will be best for the word *iron*, which you learned along with *sweep* and *wash*?
    a. metals
    b. i---
    c. had an "o"
    d. household chores
    e. rhymes with "my urn"

11. The Bahrick family studied foreign language vocabulary on a moderately frequent basis (every 2 weeks) or on an infrequent basis (every 8 weeks). The moderately frequent study led to:
    a. faster learning, but poorer retention
    b. slower learning, but better retention
    c. slower learning and poorer retention
    d. faster learning and better retention
    e. a total inability to learn

12. John needed to remember the last 10 presidents of the United States. He learned a rhyme beginning with "One is a bun" and then he changed the name of each president into something he could imagine. He imagined each modified name in the object paired with each number in his rhyme. John used:
    a. the method of loci
    b. the peg method
    c. a mnemonic device
    d. both a and c
    e. both b and c

Memory Loss

13. The patient H. M.:
    a. has damage to the cerebral cortex
    b. could not remember any information from before his operation
    c. has no short-term memory
    d. has great difficulty learning new facts
    e. cannot learn any new skills

14. People with Alzheimer's disease
    a. cannot remember things that happened long ago
    b. have problems with semantic memory, but episodic memory is normal
    c. usually develop Korsakoff's syndrome
    d. are very aware of their memory loss
    e. have trouble remembering new information

15. Infant amnesia occurs because:
    a. childhood memories are repressed
    b. the hippocampus is immature so long-term memories aren't stored
    c. infants and young children don't have a sense of self yet
    d. early memories are nonverbal and later memories are verbal
    e. all of the above may be true, but there are problems with each explanation

Reconstruction of Memory

16. Which of the following is likely to occur in our recall of an event?
    a. incorrect suggestions given after the event will wipe out memory for the original event
    b. details that don't fit in with the rest of the story will be omitted or distorted
    c. it is either recalled word-for-word or not recalled at all
    d. memory for other events leading to the recalled event are not influenced by the outcome of the event
    e. the middle part is likely to be remembered better than the beginning and the end

17. Which of the following shows a difficulty with source amnesia?
    a. a 20-year old cannot remember anything from when he was 2 years old
    b. An Alzheimer's patient remembers how to knit but she can't remember where she got the yarn she bought yesterday
    c. a woman can't remember her husband told her about a movie or whether she actually saw the movie
    d. a teenager remembers how to ride a bicycle but he can't remember the brand of his bike
    e. a Korsakoff's patient can give presented words when shown word fragments, but he can't any of them

18. A lineup measures memory in what way?
    a. recall
    b. cued recall
    c. savings
    d. relearning
    e. recognition

## ANSWERS TO POSTTEST

| Correct Answer | Questions Testing a Similar Concept | |
|---|---|---|
| | Comprehension Check | Short-Answer |

**Matching**

| | | |
|---|---|---|
| 1. C (pp. 291-292) | 14c | 13 |
| 2. F (p. 299) | -- | 15 |
| 3. A (p. 289) | 1 | 2 |
| 4. D (p. 285) | 12 | 10 |
| 5. G (p. 281) | 10 | 8 |
| 6. E (p. 289) | 1b, 2 | 2 |
| 7. B (p. 290) | 14c | 13 |

**Multiple-Choice**

| | | |
|---|---|---|
| 1. a (pp. 267, 289) | 1 | 2 |
| 2. a (pp. 269-270) | 4e | -- |
| 3. a (p. 269) | 4b | -- |
| 4. c (pp. 271-272) | 5a, 6 | 4 |
| 5. a (p. 271) | 5 | -- |
| 6. a (pp. 273-274) | 6d, 7 | -- |
| 7. b (pp. 274-275) | 6 | -- |
| 8. e (p. 276) | 8 | 6 |
| 9. e (pp. 281-282) | 10 | 8 |
| 10. d (p. 285) | 12 | 10 |
| 11. a (pp. 284-285) | 11 | 9 |
| 12. b (p. 287) | -- | -- |
| 13. d (pp. 290-291) | 14 | 13 |
| 14. e (pp. 292-293) | 16c | -- |
| 15. e (pp. 296-297) | 17e | -- |
| 16. b (pp. 299-300) | 19 | 15 |
| 17. c (p. 277) | -- | 16 |
| 18. e (p. 269) | 4 | -- |

## CHAPTER 7  LANGUAGE ENHANCEMENT GUIDE

### I. VOCABULARY, IDIOMS AND CULTURAL CONCEPTS

**Instructions:**

As you read the text refer to the following list of words and their definitions.  The words are listed in the order in which they appear in the chapter.  The definitions presented contain the meaning of the word as used by Kalat on the text book page indicated.

Remember that these words like all words can have different meanings in other sentences.  If you do not find a non-technical word on this list it may have been defined on a previous page or chapter of this study guide.  The definition of non-technical words may be found in the dictionary at the end of this study guide.  Kalat defined each new technical word as it first appears on a page and these may be found in Kalat's summary at the end of the section and in the Glossary at the end the textbook.

## Types of Memory

constraint (264) =  restricted or confined within required limits or rules

vanish = disappear, fade away

contestant = (265)  a person competing in a contest

runner-up = the person who finishes in second place in a contest

cramming = only studying the night before a test

tempted (267) = invited

incomprehensible (268) =  difficult or impossible to understand

distinctive = a characteristic that helps  identify and recognize individuals,  and members of a  group
    or category

haphazard collection (270) =   having no particular pattern, purpose or organization; due to chance

analogous to = similar to

split second (271)  = less than a second

it will fade = disappear,  vanish

retain = keep, store

small fraction - small part of

rates of decay (272) = speed of fading away

curiously = interesting to know

capacity (273) =  the total amount that can be  stored; ability to  perform,  produce or carry

transfer (275) = to carry form one place to another

contradict =  does not support; to say the opposite

sphere of attention (276) = focus of attention

sketchpad =  a peace of drawing paper

ambiguous (277) = a word or phrase that has two or more meanings

distinguishing between = recognizing the difference between

much more fragile  = more easily forgotten

retrospect (278) = reviewing the past; looking backward

## Types of Memory Improvement

trivial event (280) = not important; ordinary

arousing = emotionally exciting, stimulating

facilitates (281) =  to make an activity easy or easier

compensates =  offsets, counteracts, makes up for, balances

mobilizing =  activating, put into use

hesitation = delay, slow to respond

superficial =   trivial; insignificant; near the surface

monitoring (283) = to keep close watch over something; managing; supervising; controlling
periodically = every few minutes; at regular intervals; . recurring or reappearing, intermittent

specificity (287) = to state exactly with accuracy and precision

### Memory Loss

impair (289) = damage
encountered = to meet; to meet, unexpectedly
nevertheless = however; in spite of that

context (290)= the part of a text or paragraph that surrounds a word or phrase and determines its
    meaning; the situation in which an event occurs; a setting
deterioration = to get worse, to weaken or decay; degenerate
deficits = a weakening or loss in mental or physical functioning; an unfavorable condition or position;
    a disadvantage

impairments (292) = damages, a loss of ability, strength or value
terminology = the technical words used in a subject, science, sport or art; nomenclature

implicit = indirect

overlooked (297) = to fail to notice, see, or consider; miss ; disregard

### The Reconstruction of Memory

reconstruct (299) = restore, recover, rebuild

omit (300) = to take or leave out; drop, remove, eliminate, delete
incongruous = does not fit, inconsistent, clashing, conflicting, discrepant

sporadically (301) = occurring at irregular intervals; having no time pattern or order
indecisively = without an ending or conclusion; uncertain, tentative

recollection (302) = recalled memories
presuppose = to believe a claim is true before evidence in available; to accept something as fact
    without proof

witness (304) = a person who sees something happen; a person who gives evidence, testifies, in a
    court of law
alters = changes
ominous = indicating or warning of danger or misfortune; threatening
culprit a person charged with or is guilty of crime

induce (305) = to cause, influence, persuade
controversy = a dispute between two or more individuals or groups holding opposing views

fantasize (306) = imagine

Satanic = refers to Satan, the devil or evil

cult = a religious group considered to be extremist or false, with its followers often living in an unconventional way under the control of an authoritarian, charismatic leader

Satanic cult = a cult that worships the devil

ritual = the required order of a religious ceremony

traumatic = an emotional shock that produces lasting damage to the psychological development of a person

flashback = suddenly remembering a painful past experience

implant = to establish, to put

## II. VOCABULARY BUILDING

### Word Analysis

Instructions:

1. Study the meaning of the prefixes roots and suffixes listed.
2. Break each word in the table into its prefixes roots and suffixes.
3. Guess the meaning word based on the meaning of its parts.
4. Find the word on the text page indicated in the brackets and redefine the word based on the context of the sentence, paragraph and chapter.
5. Look up the definition of the word in the VOCABULARY, IDIOMS AND CULTURAL CONCEPTS section above, in Appendix A (marked A) or in a college level dictionary. If the word is followed by letter G look it up in the text Glossary.

Exercise 1.  Retrospect

**Prefix : pro _____ = forward/before**
**Prefix: retro _____ = back/backwards/behind**
**Root: _____ spect _____ = to look**
**Suffix: _____ ive = tending  to (be)**

| Word | Meaning |
|---|---|
| retrospect (A) | |
| proactive (G) | |
| retroactive (G) | |
| prospect | |
| promote | |
| prospective | |
| introspective | |
| projection (G) | |
| retrograde (G) | |

Exercise 2.  Amnesia

**Prefix: a/an _____ = not/without/lacking**
**Root: ____ mene ____ to recall/ to remember**
**Root: ____ esthe ____ sensation/feeling**
**Root: ____ orex ____ desire/appetite**
**Root: ____ alg ____ pain/suffering**
**Suffix: ___ ia = quality/condition /state/act/result of/process of**
**Suffix: ___ ic = characterized by/having the power to/belonging to**

| Word | Meaning |
|---|---|
| amnesia (A) | |
| anesthesia | |
| anorexia (G) | |
| anorexic (G) | |
| analgesia | |
| analgesic | |

## Exercise 3. Encode

**Prefix: en /in _____ = in/into/within**
**Word: code = a system of arbitrary symbols or signals used to**
**represent words or ideas/a system of laws, rules, ethics**
**Root: ____cyclopedia___ = education/knowledge**

| Word | Meaning |
|---|---|
| encode (A) | |
| enthusiasm | to be in excitement about something, inspired |
| encyclopedia | a summary of knowledge, books that summarize knowledge |

## Exercise 4.  Antiabortion

**Prefix: anti _____ = against/opposed to/the opposite of/ opposed to                     /without**
**Prefix: re _____ = back/again and again**
**Suffix: _____ ion = the act/means/results of**

| Word | Meaning |
|---|---|
| antiepileptic (A) | |
| antiabortion | |
| reconstruction (A) | |
| reconstruct | |
| repression (A) | |

## Exercise 5.  Incongruous

**Prefix: in _____ = not**
**Prefix:: contra _____ = against/opposite of/opposed to/contrary**
**Root: _____ congru____ = agreement/harmony/consistent/fitting**
**Root: _____ dict _____ = to say/to speak**
**Suffix: _____ ous = full of/characterized by**
**Suffix: _____ ent/ant = being/doing/having/performing/showing**
**Suffix: _____ ion = the act/means/results of**

| Word | Meaning |
|---|---|
| controversy (A) | |
| contradict | to express the opposite of (a statement or claim) |
| contradiction | |
| incongruous (A) | |
| congruent | |
| dictation | |

# CHAPTER 8  COGNITION AND LANGUAGE

**OBJECTIVES**

Understand that:

**Thinking and Mental Processes**

I. Cognitive psychologists study how people think and gain knowledge  (p. 311)
   A. People are unaware of their thought processes  (p. 311)
II. Categories are used to group similar things  (pp. 311-312)
   A. There are several different theories about the arrangement of categories  (pp. 312-315)
      1. Categories are organized around prototypical members  (pp. 312-313)
      2. Categories are arranged into levels  (pp. 313-314, Fig. 8.2)
      3 Related concepts activate each other in memory  (pp. 314-315)
III. Thinking can occur in series (one at a time) or in parallel (several at once)  (pp. 315-316)
   A. Subjects scan through lists of unrelated digits in a serial manner  (p. 316)
      1. They may search through simple, organized lists in parallel (all at once)  (p. 316)
   B. Measuring time to respond can help to understand cognitive processes  (p. 316)
IV. Attention limits people's abilities to perform several activities at once  (p. 316)
   A. If both tasks require some cognitive effort, they will interfere with each other  (pp. 316-317)
V. Mental images can be used to solve problems  (p. 317)
   A. Mental images are much like actual perceptions  (pp. 318-319)
      1. Blind people perform similarly to sighted so maybe images are spatial, not visual  (p. 319)
   B. Cognitive maps are mental representations of spatial locations  (pp. 319-320)
      1. Cognitive maps are often distorted to be more regular than actual locations  (pp. 319-320)

**Problem Solving, Expertise, and Error**

VI. Experts have a lot of practice in their fields  (pp. 323-324)
   A. Experts recognize common patterns in their fields quickly  (p. 324)
      1. They remember organized material from their areas easily   (p. 324)
   B. Experts solve problems quickly by selecting relevant information  (p. 324)
VII. Problem solving involves four phases  (p. 325, Fig. 8.13)
   A. Problems need to be understood and simplified  (p. 325)
   B. Hypotheses should be generated  (pp. 325-326)
      1. Algorithms generate all possibilities  (p. 326)
      2. Heuristics generate likely possibilities  (p. 326)
   C. Hypotheses should be tested and results checked  (p. 327)
   D. Solutions should be generalized to similar problems  (p. 327)
      1. People often fail to generalize to similar problems  (pp. 327-328)
VIII. Some problems are solved insightfully  (pp. 328-329)
   A. But people may still be making progress before a solution is found  (p. 329)
   B. Insights in mathematics and science may come to anyone who has the data available  (pp. 329-330)
   C. Creative people are probably only creative in their own fields  (pp. 330-331)
IX. People often base decisions on illogical reasoning  (pp. 331-332)
   A. People are often overconfident about their answers  (pp. 332-333)
   B. They don't consider alternative hypotheses  (pp. 333-334)
   C. They often use representativeness and don't use the base rate  (pp. 334-335, Table 8.1, p. 336)

D. People overuse availability in memory to judge frequency (pp. 335-337, Table 8.1)
    1. Illusory correlations can result from this (p. 336)
E. The way a question is worded affects its answer (pp. 337-338)
    1. People are more willing to take risks when dealing with a loss than with a gain (pp. 337-338)
X. Gambling can be understood via knowledge about cognition and learning (pp. 338-342)
    A. People overestimate the amount of control they have (pp. 339-340)
    B. People don't understand differences among long shot probabilities (p. 340)
    C. Gambling is reinforced on a variable-ratio schedule (p. 340)
    D. Vicarious reinforcement is received by seeing others win (p. 341)
        1. Seeing others lose doesn't do much because vicarious punishment isn't very effective (p. 341)
    E. Availability and representativeness heuristics play a role in gambling (p. 341)
        1. Gamblers' fallacy (the next one will be a winner) is an example of the representativeness heuristic (p. 341)
    F. Self-esteem may be attached to proving oneself a winner (pp. 341-342)

**Language**

XI. Language makes humans unique (p. 345)
    A. Some animals have learned rudimentary human language (pp. 346-347)
        1. Chimps use symbols but they don't show flexibility (p. 347)
        2. Pygmy chimps show more flexible use of language (p. 347)
XII. Language and thought influence each other (p. 348)
    A. A huge number of unique sentences are produced and understood (p. 348)
        1. Transformational grammar involves the rules for changing one surface structure into another (p. 348, Fig. 8.29)
    B. Whorf argued that language determines thought (pp. 349-351)
        1. There isn't much evidence for this (p. 349)
            a. The use of "he or she" may produce different images (pp. 350-351)
    C. Some disciplines have many ways of saying things; others do not (pp. 351-352)
XIII. Language comprehension is complicated, yet we do it easily (p. 352)
    A. Missing sounds in words are filled in by the brain (p. 353)
    B. People hear the same sounds differently, depending upon context (p. 353)
    C. Negatives are particularly difficult to understand (pp. 353-354)
XIV. Reading is important to society (p. 354)
    A. Eyes jump in saccades while reading (p. 355)
        1. Nothing can be seen while the eye is moving (p. 355)
        2. Readers take in about 11 letters per fixation (p. 356)
            a. Part of the next word is processed while each word is being read (p. 356)
    B. Whole words are read faster than individual letters (pp. 357-358)
    C. The connectionist model involves interactive activation of higher-order and lower-order units (p. 358, Fig. 8.36)
    D. The Stroop effect shows that reading can be automatic (pp. 358-359, Fig. 8.38)
    E. Good readers suppress irrelevant meanings faster than poor readers (pp. 359-360)

**COMPREHENSION CHECK**

Answer these questions soon after reading the chapter. Circle the best alternative. Check your answers on pp. 161-163. If you gave a wrong answer, try to write why it was wrong. Check your reasons on pp. 161-163.

**Thinking and Mental Processes**

1. The topic that would be least likely to be studied by a psychologist interested in cognition is how people:
   a. plan a vacation
   b. use their imagination to describe a scene
   c. change their behavior following reinforcement
   d. becomes experts on a new topic

Correct _____ If wrong, why? _____

2. Which of the following is an example of categorizing by levels?
   a. a dog must have lungs because it is a mammal; mammals are animals; animals have lungs
   b. a dog is an animal because it has fur, a tail, and lungs
   c. a dog is an animal because it is similar to an average animal
   d. a dog is an animal because I memorized that fact in childhood

Correct _____ If wrong, why? _____

3. Sternberg asked students to memorize one, two, or four numbers and then asked them if a number was among the memorized set. He found:
   a. a straight-line relationship between the number of items in memory and response time
   b. that mental activity occurred too fast to be measured
   c. that students could compare four numbers as fast as one
   d. that students searched in parallel
   e. both c and d

Correct _____ If wrong, why? _____

4. Doing two things at once is:
   a. not possible
   b. no problem; it's just as efficient as doing only one thing
   c. no problem, if one thing is so routine that it requires no attention
   d. no problem, if you can delay the response to the second task by 200 milliseconds

Correct _____ If wrong, why? _____

5. When people decide whether two objects that differ in orientation are the same or not:
   a. the difference in orientation has no effect
   b. they act as if they are watching a model rotate in their heads
   c. responses are faster if the two objects are in very different orientations than if they are in similar orientations
   d. people report that they do not use visual images

Correct _____ If wrong, why? _____

6. A common error in cognitive maps is:
    a. people align things along east-west and north-south axes more than they actually are
    b. people don't use higher-level categories in making location judgments
    c. street angles that are 90 degrees are distorted; people remember them as being more or less than 90 degrees
    d. they have many more details than actual maps

Correct _____ If wrong, why? _____

**Problem Solving, Expertise, and Error**

7. Experts:
    a. attend to relevant features and ignore irrelevant ones
    b are better at all types of memory tasks involving material from their area than novices
    c. are born with special talent
    d. solve problems better than novices almost entirely because they have more "tools" to use

Correct _____ If wrong, why? _____

8. Which of the following would be least useful in solving a problem that you can't answer quickly?
    a. try to answer a related question
    b. start to generate hypotheses
    c. try to solve a simpler version
    d. start with the assumption that the problem is not solvable

Correct _____ If wrong, why? _____

9. When people are asked to solve problems that are similar to just-solved ones, they:
    a. easily apply the same principles to the new problem
    b. apply the same principles if they've seen only one example, but don't if they've seen many examples
    c. sometimes use the prior experience if they had a variety of different examples
    d. can apply materials from a specific discipline, such as physics, to a more general discipline, such as math, but not vice versa

Correct _____ If wrong, why? _____

10. Creative problem solving is:
    a. a talent; either you have it or you don't
    b. unrelated to prior knowledge; discoveries are made without reliance on accumulated data
    c. similar to insight in that it is sudden and unrelated to a gradual move toward a solution or a discovery
    d. based, in part, on the availability of prior data
    e. both b and c

Correct _____ If wrong, why? _____

11. A patient shows most of the symptoms of a very rare disease and many of the symptoms of a common one. The doctor decides that it must be the very rare disease. In her decision, she has ignored:
    a. base-rate information
    b. the similarity of the symptoms to those in each category
    c. the fact that there may be an alternative hypothesis
    d. a heuristic that would be useful in solving the problem

Correct _____ If wrong, why? _____

12. The availability heuristic would lead to which error?
    a. thinking that a test for a rare disease that is 99% accurate would call only a few well people "sick"
    b. taking a risk when a question is phrased in terms of loss but not in terms of gain
    c. deciding that a student is a math major because he wears glasses, carries a calculator in his pocket, and is sort of a nerd even though only 1% of all students are math majors
    d. thinking that you are more likely to die in a plane than in a car crash because you have read about so many plane crashes lately
    e. saying you are 99% sure you're correct when the actual likelihood is 70%

Correct _____ If wrong, why? _____

13. People generally:
    a. avoid taking risks when considering a loss
    b. avoid taking risks when considering a gain
    c. take risks when considering a gain
    d. avoid risks in all cases if lives are involved, but take them if money is involved

Correct _____ If wrong, why? _____

14. A correct explanation for gambling is that people:
    a. don't pay attention to the representativeness heuristic
    b. are much more willing to accept a certain loss than they are to accept a slim chance of winning
    c. continue a behavior that has been reinforced on a fixed schedule longer than a behavior that has been reinforced on a variable schedule, even when reinforcement has ended
    d. overestimate the control that they have in chance events
    e. are more influenced by vicarious punishment (losing) than by vicarious reinforcement (winning)

Correct _____ If wrong, why? _____

**Language**

15. The most recent attempts to teach language to animals have shown that:
    a. chimps can learn language and use it in the same way as children
    b. animals that supposedly understand and use language are really only using subtle cues
    c. young bonobos have shown evidence of actual language learning
    d. watching and imitating other animals who are being taught disrupts learning

Correct _____ If wrong, why? _____

16. "Visiting relatives can be tiresome" can either mean that the relatives are visiting you or you are visiting the relatives. Thus, this sentence has:
    a. two deep structures and one surface structure
    b. two surface structures and one deep structure
    c. deep structures that are identical to surface structures
    d. deep structures that are unrelated to surface structures

Correct _____ If wrong, why? _____

17. Some evidence for the Whorf hypothesis comes from:
    a. Eskimos' many words for snow and their concept of snow
    b. different images produced by gender-related words
    c. no understanding of concepts if the language lacks a word for the concept
    d. languages that use different gender endings for words result in different understandings of those concepts

Correct _____ If wrong, why? _____

18. Which of the following shows evidence that context affects our understanding of words?
    a. lecturers in scientific areas use fewer uhs and ers than lecturers in the humanities
    b. if there is a delay between a word with a missing first letter and the word that clarifies it (such as *ent and forest), people don't report the appropriate word (tent)
    c. adding a label such as "not cyanide" makes students less likely to select the container
    d. the word "rose" can refer to a flower or the past tense of rise depending on other words around it

Correct _____ If wrong, why? _____

19. During a fixation in reading, people:
    a. take in less than during a saccade
    b. can take in long sentences
    c. keep their eyes stationary for about seconds
    d. take in a window of about 11 characters

Correct _____ If wrong, why? _____

20. Which of the following is an example of the Stroop effect?
    a. when asked to name the color of ink, students take a long time to say green when the word "red" is written in green ink
    b. seeing the letter 'O' in JOIN is faster than when students focus on the whole word than when they focus on the spot where the letter appears
    c. letters activate units in memory and the pattern of activation allows identification of the word
    d. poor readers keep several meanings of ambiguous words active for a longer time than good readers

Correct _____ If wrong, why? _____

# ANSWERS AND EXPLANATIONS FOR COMPREHENSION CHECK

<u>Correct Answer</u>                    <u>Other Alternatives Are Wrong Because:</u>

1. c  (p. 311)
   Obj. I
    a. planning is part of cognition
    b. imaging is part of cognition
    d. acquiring knowledge is part of cognition

2. a  (pp. 313-314, Fig. 8.2)
   Obj. II-A-2
    b. using features to categorize
    c. prototype view of categorization
    d. true, but how is that fact represented in memory?

3. a  (pp. 315-316, Fig. 8.4)
   Obj. III-A
    b. the time to respond was measured
    c. four numbers took longer at 35 msec. per number
    d. parallel means comparing several as fast as comparing one; search was serial, not parallel
    e. c and d mean the same thing; both wrong

4. c  (p. 316)
   Obj. IV
    a. possible if one task requires no attention
    b. doing two things takes more attention unless one is very routine
    d. responding to a second stimulus 200 ms after a first one results in poor performance on the second stimulus

5. b  (pp. 317-318, Fig. 8.6)
   Obj. V-A
    a. the larger the difference in orientation, the longer the time
    c. the closer together the orientations, the shorter the time
    d. people say that they do compare images in this task

6. a  (p. 320)
   Obj. V-B-1
    b. use higher-level categories; for example, they say L.A. is west of Reno because California is west of Nevada
    c. angles that are <u>not</u> 90 degrees are remembered as being 90 degrees
    d. details are often omitted

7. a  (p. 324)
   Obj. VI-A, B
    b. not all memory tasks; they don't remember random arrangements better, just organized ones
    c. experts need to put in about 10 years of practice
    d. also know which "tools" to use and when to use them

8. d  (pp. 325-328)
   Obj. VII
    a-c. these should help problem solution
    d. not likely to help you see a solution, therefore, it is the least useful

9. c  (pp. 327-328)
   Obj. VII-D-1
    a. often the very same principles would work, but they are not used
    b. seeing several examples makes generalization <u>more</u> likely
    d. research shows just the opposite

10. d (pp. 329-330)
    Obj. VIII
        a. scientific discoveries may be based more on having available data than on talent
        b. access to prior data is important
        c. solutions to insight problems may first involve "getting warm"; creative discoveries may also be based on study of data and be gradual
        e. both b and c are incorrect

11. a (pp. 334-335)
    Obj. IX-C
        b. the similarity of the symptoms and the diseases was considered
        c. she did consider an alternative, the more common disease
        d. she doesn't need to simplify; the number of hypotheses is small

12. d (pp. 335-338)
    Obj. IX-D
        a. base-rate fallacy; ignoring how many people 1% of a large number actually is
        b. letting framing of questions affect decisions
        c. use of representativeness; ignoring base rate
        e. this is overconfidence

13. b (p. 337)
    Obj. IX-E-1
        a. they are willing to take risks when a loss is involved
        c. they tend to avoid risks if a gain is involved
        d. situations involving lives and money show similar effects

14. d (pp. 339-340)
    Obj. X-A
        a. do pay attention; the gamblers' fallacy is an example of the representativeness heuristic
        b. more willing to accept a slim chance of winning
        c. variable schedules lead to more persistence during extinction
        e. people are more influenced by vicarious reinforcement than vicarious punishment

15. c (p. 337)
    Obj. XI-A
        a. chimps' language wasn't as flexible as human children's language
        b. not true with the bonobos; they followed instructions given over headphones
        d. it probably helped young bonobos to learn

16. a (pp. 348-349)
    Obj. XII-A-1
        b. the sentence itself is the surface structure; there's only one
        c. deep structure is the meaning; different from surface structure
        d. they're not the same, but they're related

17. b (pp. 350-351)
    Obj. XII-B-1-a
        a. actually Eskimo languages don't have many more "snow" words than English
        c. actually most languages can express most concepts and people can think about those concepts
        d. could be, but there's no evidence

18. d (p. 353)
Obj. XIII-B

   a. not because of context but because there are fewer ways to say
       things in scientific areas than in the humanities
   b. this is an example where context <u>doesn't</u> affect understanding;
       context must come soon after an ambiguous word to clarify it
   c. evidence for the difficulty of understanding negatives; not necessarily
       evidence for context

19. d (p. 356)
Obj. XIV-A-2

   a. saccades are eye movements; nothing is taken in during them
   b. only about 11 characters
   c. fixations last from about 100 ms. to about 1 s

20. a (pp. 358-359,
Fig 8.38)
Obj. XIV-D

   b. this is the word superiority effect
   c. this is a simplified version of the connectionist model
   d. this is a difference between good and poor readers, but it is
      not called the Stroop effect

## LECTURE MATERIAL

Don't forget to review your lecture material. Process each topic meaningfully. First, be sure that you understand the material in each lecture--if you don't, ask your instructor or teaching assistant. Associate the material with things that you already know and with your personal experiences. If you can make up mental images of any of the material, do so. Try to think of real-life applications of the concepts. Go through each day's lecture and add your own notes. Then write questions to cover each concept.

-------------------------------------------------------------------------------
WAIT AT LEAST 24 HOURS BEFORE PROCEEDING.
LET FORGETTING OCCUR--IT WILL!!
-------------------------------------------------------------------------------

## SHORT-ANSWER ESSAY QUESTIONS

Write brief answers to each of the following. The answers are on pp. 166-168, but do try to write the answers yourself before looking at them.

### Thinking and Mental Processes

1. Behaviorists argue that thinking cannot be studied because there is no way to measure it. Give an example of an experiment which could be used to argue against that view.

2. Explain how a person would know that a robin is a bird according to the prototype view and according to the categorization by levels approach.

3. Discuss the conditions under which doing two things results in poorer performance than doing only one thing.

4. Describe an experiment that shows that mental images are similar to perceptions.

5. Cognitive maps are often distortions of actual spatial locations. Describe two ways in which they are distorted.

**Problem Solving, Expertise, and Error**

6. Describe two ways in which experts differ from novices.

7. Describe two things that a problem solver can do to understand a problem.

8. Explain the difference between an algorithm and a heuristic.

9. Discuss research on generalization of problem solution to other similar problems.

10. Discuss the characteristics of creative problem solving.

11. Under what conditions are people likely to be overconfident about their predictions?

12. Many people fail to consider alternative hypotheses when trying to solve a problem. Give one example of this.

13. Give an example of how rephrasing a situation involving risks would affect people's acceptance of risk.

14. Explain how gambling might be explained by understanding some principles of learning.

**Language**

15. Early attempts to teach language to non-human primates were not very successful, but later attempts have been more successful. Explain why.

16. What is the Whorf Hypothesis? What evidence is there for it?

17. What is known about the role of context in the understanding of words with missing phonemes?

18. Describe the word-superiority effect and explain how the connectionist model can handle it.

\*\*\*\*\*\*\*\*\*\*\*\*\*\*\*\*\*\*\*\*\*\*\*\*\*\*\*\*\*\*\*\*\*\*\*\*\*\*\*\*\*\*\*\*\*\*\*\*\*\*\*\*\*\*\*\*\*\*\*\*\*\*\*\*\*\*\*\*\*\*\*\*\*\*\*\*\*

Find the questions that you wrote over
lecture material and write answers to them.

\*\*\*\*\*\*\*\*\*\*\*\*\*\*\*\*\*\*\*\*\*\*\*\*\*\*\*\*\*\*\*\*\*\*\*\*\*\*\*\*\*\*\*\*\*\*\*\*\*\*\*\*\*\*\*\*\*\*\*\*\*\*\*\*\*\*\*\*\*\*\*\*\*\*\*\*\*

## ANSWERS TO SHORT-ANSWER ESSAY QUESTIONS

1. The time that thought processes take can be measured. More complex processes take longer than simple ones. For example, Sternberg did an experiment in which he presented one, two, or four numbers to be remembered. Then subjects decided whether a single number was in the memorized set. It took about 35 msec. to search each number in memory, suggesting that people compare the presented number against each one in memory. Sternberg concluded that the comparison processes was in series, not in parallel. (pp. 315-316)

2. The prototype view argues that people categorize by comparing objects with typical instances of categories. For <u>bird</u>, typical birds are robins and sparrows, so a person could quickly compare an actual robin with the prototypical bird, see the similarity, and call a robin a bird. The categorization by levels approach would argue that we determine that a robin is a bird by noticing that robin is subordinate to (beneath) bird in the hierarchy in memory. (pp. 312-314)

3. If one of the tasks is demanding, then doing both tasks at once will result in poorer performance than doing one alone. If people must identify two patterns that are presented 100-200 ms apart, they identify the second pattern more poorly than the first pattern. Apparently, it takes about half a second to shift attention from one stimulus to another. (pp. 316-317)

4. Shepard and Metzler presented pictures of three-dimensional objects and asked subjects if they were the same or different. Each pair of objects was in the same orientation, or one was turned some amount relative to the other. The time to say "same" depended upon the difference in orientation. It appeared that subjects actually imagined one of the pictures turning in their head and then matched the image with the other picture. The farther they had to turn it, the longer it took, just as it would if they were actually moving an object. (pp. 317-319)

5. People remember street angles as being 90 degrees (right and left turns), even when they are not 90-degree angles. They use higher-level categories to make judgments about lower-level locations, and sometimes these are incorrect. For example, Los Angeles is east of Reno even though California is generally west of Nevada. This type of error also results from people's tendencies to make locations fall more on north-south, east-west axes than they actually are. (pp. 319-320)

6. Experts recognize and remember organized patterns relevant to their expertise more quickly and accurately than novices. Experts know how to use their problem-solving tools appropriately, and immediately pick out relevant information and reject fruitless approaches. (p. 324)

7. Try to solve a simpler version of the problem. If there are many objects involved, try to solve it with only one or two. Even if you can't come up with an exact answer, see if you can make a decent estimate. Use what you know to estimate about what the answer should be. (pp. 325-328)

8. An algorithm is a mechanical, repetitive procedure that will eventually lead to a correct answer. It tests all possible hypotheses. Heuristics are strategies for simplifying a problem. They are "rules of thumb" for solving various problems that often lead to correct answers. (pp. 325-326)

9. People are often very poor at generalizing. They may be able to use probability to solve simple problems, such as those involving coin tosses, but they are poor at applying the same principles to real-world problems. People are better at generalizing if they have seen several different types of examples of problems than if they have only seen one type of example. Mathematics transfers to physics, but physics doesn't transfer to mathematics. We know that mathematics is applicable to many different areas, but we don't assume that this is true for physics. (pp. 327-328)

10. Creative contributions involve both good solutions to problems and the selection of appropriate problems. Guessing that problems are important and solvable is part of creative problem solving. The formation of great theories may depend on having the appropriate data and persistence to keep trying to solve the problem, and not on some special talent. Creative individuals often sense that the old ways are not quite right, and they throw themselves into the work. (pp. 329-330)

11. People tend to be overconfident when they predict events that are quite uncertain. This is particularly true about predictions of one's own performance. Students are overconfident about their performance in courses and athletes predict they'll have better seasons than they have. Government officials express great confidence in their predictions of future events, but they are actually no more accurate than people outside of the government. (pp. 332-333)

12. If subjects are told to find the rule for generating number sequences and are given 2,4,6 as an example, they immediately decide that the rule is "add 2" and ask if 6,8,10 or 190,192,194 fit the rule. They may not consider the alternative that any increasing sequence might be correct. (pp. 333-334)

13. People are more likely to accept a plan in which 200 out of 600 will live than a plan in which there is a one-third chance that all will live and a two-thirds chance you will save no one. However, if it is phrased as 400 out of 600 will die vs. a one-third chance that no one will die and a two-thirds chance that all will die, people prefer the second version. Phrasing in terms of gain (living) or loss (dying) changes people's willingness to accept risk. (pp. 337-338)

14. Gambling is reinforced on a variable-ratio schedule of reinforcement; occasionally a bet results in a win. Variable ratio schedules result in long persistence of responding in the absence of reinforcement. Gambling is also explained by social-learning theory. People tend to imitate behavior that they have seen reinforced in others, but they don't tend to stop behavior that was punished in others. Thus, hearing about someone winning the lottery will increase gambling. (pp. 338-342)

15. Very early attempts to teach spoken language to chimpanzees failed because chimpanzees do not have the appropriate vocal apparatus to speak. Later attempts to teach sign language or other symbols were more successful, although some scientists argued that the chimps simply imitated symbols used by their trainers. The chimps created nothing like a sentence. More recent attempts have used pygmy chimpanzees known as bonobos. These animals use symbols to describe objects and to relate past events. They make creative requests, but still they don't form full sentences. Bonobos may have greater language ability than other chimps, or learning by observation and imitation may be more effective than more formal training. (pp. 346-347)

16. Whorf (or Sapir and Whorf) suggested that language determines the way we think. People understand concepts to the extent that they have words for them. However, recent evidence has not shown much support for this hypothesis. People with large vocabularies do not think differently than people with smaller vocabularies. People speaking languages that have masculine and feminine words do not appear to think differently than people whose languages don't have gender endings. The one bit of evidence for the Whorf Hypothesis is that using the word "he" calls up a different image than using "he or she" or "they." (pp. 349-351)

17. Context can help to identify words with missing phonemes, but the appropriate context word must come soon after the word with missing sounds. Delayed context, however, can change your interpretation of a sentence, even if you have misinterpreted a word. (p. 353)

18. Letters can be identified in words faster than alone. According to the connectionist model, incoming letters activate units corresponding to the letters, which in turn activate higher-level word units. The letter units aren't activated enough to identify the letters. However, the word units increase the activation of the lower-level letter units, allowing the identification of the letters. (pp. 357-358)

## POSTTEST

Take this test with all of your books and notes out of sight. This should give you a good idea of how well you understand the material.

### Matching

Put the letter of the term in the blank beside the definition.

Problem Solving, Expertise, and Error

1. _____ strategy for simplifying a problem

2. _____ mechanical, repetitive procedure for solving a problem

3. _____ possibility that can be tested

4. _____ how rare or common something is

5. _____ assumption that events that haven't happened for a while are "due"

6. _____ item similar to category members belongs to it

7. _____ number of memories of an event indicates how common the event is

A. gamblers' fallacy

B. availability

C. heuristic

D. representativeness

E. base-rate information

F. hypothesis

G. algorithm

**Multiple-choice**

Circle the best alternative.

<u>Thinking and Mental Processes</u>

1. Mental activity can best be measured by:
    a. asking subjects what they are thinking
    b. directly observing it
    c. having people judge how long it would take them to do a task
    d. measuring how long it takes to answer questions
    e. none of the above; it cannot be measured and cannot be studied scientifically

2. Categories are:
    a. very similar from culture to culture
    b. absolute so that an object either is or is not a clear member of a category
    c. completely organized by levels such that each feature is stored at the highest possible level and not repeated at lower levels
    d. activated by related concepts
    e. clearly defined by critical features

3. According to the levels view of categorization, which would take longer to respond "true" to: "A blackpoll warbler can fly" or "A bird can fly"?
    a. "A bird can fly," because it is more general
    b. "A blackpoll warbler can fly," because you need to infer that a blackpoll warbler is a bird
    c. "A bird can fly," because it is a more typical statement
    d. "A blackpoll warbler can fly," because it is lacking some of the features of a typical bird

4. When Sternberg presented one to four digits to be memorized and then asked people if a single digit was in the memorized set, he found that:
    a. people tested the single digit against all of the memorized ones in parallel
    b. students could decide whether the single digit was one of four numbers faster than they could decide if it was one of two numbers
    c. about 35 msec. was added to the comparison time for each additional number in the memorized set
    d. the relationship between response time and number of digits was so irregular that he could not tell how people did the task
    e. the relationship between response time and number of digits was a U-shaped function--time first increased and then decreased

5. People can do two things as fast as one thing if:
    a. they are able to perform tasks in series, rather than in parallel
    b. one task is so routine that is requires no attention
    c. the response to one task follows the other one by 200 ms
    d. one task is difficult but the other task is easy
    e. both tasks require cognitive effort

6. In Shepard and Metzler's study in which students decided whether two drawings of blocks were the same or different, students:
   a. were more accurate in responding "same" than "different"
   b. took longer to say "same" when the two objects were many degrees different in orientation than when they were only a few degrees different
   c. took longer to say "same" when the two objects were only a few degrees different in orientation than when they were many degrees different
   d. made so many errors (over 97%) that reaction times were meaningless
   e. reacted as if they could not use mental images

7. Why do people respond incorrectly to the question "Is Rome north of Philadelphia"?
   a. people make geographical areas line up on north-south and east-west axes more than they actually do
   b. cognitive maps make angles closer to 90 degrees than they are
   c. central locations are more likely to be included in cognitive maps than less-central locations
   d. cognitive maps get more detailed with experience

## Problem Solving, Expertise, and Error

8. When chess experts were shown a chess board and asked to recall the pieces, they:
   a. recalled more poorly than novices; apparently their expertise got in the way
   b. remembered better than novices whether the pieces were arranged as in a game or randomly
   c. remembered more poorly than novices if the pieces were arranged as in a game, but better if they were arranged randomly
   d. remembered better than novices if the pieces were arranged as in a game, but about the same if they were arranged randomly

9. In which situation would a heuristic be most useful?
   a. you have no hypotheses about how to solve a problem
   b. you have committed yourself to one hypothesis
   c. you cannot think of a way to test a hypothesis
   d. you keep generating the same incorrect hypothesis
   e. you have too many hypotheses to test

10. Which of the following would be most useful in helping to understand a problem?
    a. try to answer a related question
    b. try to add complexity to the problem; think of many instances rather than just a few
    c. keep trying to retrieve the factual information; avoid making estimates of the answer
    d. sit back and try to use insight to solve the problem

11. Students who learned how to solve progression problems in physics were later asked to solve very similar math problems. They:
    a. solved them very quickly because they noted the similarity
    b. did not use their learning on the math problems; evidently they associated the solutions entirely with physics
    c. solved the math problems more quickly than students who learned math first and then were given physics problems
    d. gave correct solutions if the problems involved rigid things like guns and bullets, but not if water and hoses were used in the examples

12. Evidence that solutions to insight problems may involve a gradual progression toward the solution is shown by:
    a. people's inability to say whether or not they will be able to solve such problems
    b. people's ability to indicate whether or not problems have solutions, even without being able to solve them
    c. the fact that some people are never able to solve some insight problems
    d. the inability of students to calculate Kepler's results

13. Which of the following is an example of base-rate information?
    a. the population consists of 10,000 mosquitoes and 2 rare kwiny bugs
    b. the kwiny bug looks like a mosquito except it is a bit bigger
    c. the mosquito flies a bit faster than the kwiny bug
    d. a particular specimen looks exactly like a kwiny bug
    e. the bite of the kwiny bug soothes the skin rather than irritating it

14. You are quite sure that it rains every time you wash you car. In fact, this is probably not true, but it is most related to which heuristic?
    a. representativeness
    b. base-rate
    c. avoiding risk
    d. availability
    e. overconfidence

15. If you are like most people, which would you be more likely to select as your prize in a quiz show?
    a. win $5,000
    b. take a 25% chance of winning $20,000 with a 75% chance of winning nothing
    c. lose $2,000 that you've won
    d. take a 50% chance of winning $10,000 with a 50% chance of winning nothing
    e. all of the above are equally likely; people do not agree on their choices

## Language

16. Chimpanzees can:
    a. learn spoken language, but teaching them is very difficult
    b. learn to use many symbols in sign language
    c. not learn anything that resembles human language because they lack intelligence
    d. not learn sign language but they can learn spoken language
    e. learn and use language in the same way as children

17. "Mary chased the man" and "The man was chased by Mary" have:
    a. a unique transformational grammar
    b. two deep structures but only one surface structure
    c. totally arbitrary speech sounds
    d. two surface structures but only one deep structure

18. When students hear a sentence with part of a word missing, they report:
    a. exactly what was missing
    b. hearing a word that fits the sentence no matter when the relevant context word appears
    c. hearing the whole word, even the missing letter
    d. hearing the word with those sounds that occurs most frequently in the language, independently of context

19. Which of the following is consistent with the word-superiority effect?
    a. you can find letters faster by searching for letters rather than by reading words
    b. you can recognize the difference between C and J alone faster than in COIN and JOIN
    c. you can recognize the difference between C and J faster in XQCF and XQJF than in COIN and JOIN
    d. a single letter can be identified faster when people read the whole word than when they focus attention on the critical letter
    e. all of the above are consistent

20. The Stroop effect occurs because:
    a. it is very difficult to see the colors of ink
    b. people are so used to reading words that they cannot suppress the habit
    c. people do not take the frequency of things in the population into account
    d. people's thoughts are related to their categories

## ANSWERS TO POSTTEST

| Correct Answer | Questions Testing a Similar Concept | |
| --- | --- | --- |
| | Comprehension Check | Short-Answer |
| **Matching** | | |
| 1. C (p. 326) | 12 | 8 |
| 2. G (p. 326) | -- | 8 |
| 3. F (pp. 325-326) | 8b | 7 |
| 4. E (pp. 334-335) | 11a,12a,c | -- |
| 5. A (p. 341) | 14a | -- |
| 6. D (p. 334) | 12c,14a | -- |
| 7. B (pp. 335-337) | 12 | -- |
| | | |
| **Multiple-Choice** | | |
| 1. d (pp. 315-316) | -- | 1 |
| 2. d (pp. 314-315) | -- | -- |
| 3. b (pp. 313-314, Fig. 8.3) | 2,6b | 2 |
| 4. c (pp. 315-316, Fig. 8.4) | 3 | -- |
| 5. b (p. 316) | 4 | 3 |
| 6. b (pp. 317-318, Fig. 8.6) | 5 | 4 |
| 7. a (p. 320) | 6 | 5 |
| 8. d (p. 324, Fig. 8.10) | 7b | 6 |
| 9. e (p. 326) | -- | 8 |
| 10. a (pp. 327-328) | 8 | 7,9 |
| 11. b (pp. 327-328, Fig. 8.18) | 9 | 9 |
| 12. b (p. 329) | 10c | -- |
| 13. a (pp. 334-335) | 11,12a,c | -- |
| 14. d (pp. 335-337) | 12 | -- |
| 15. a (pp. 337-338) | 13 | 13 |
| 16. b (pp. 346-347) | 15 | 15 |
| 17. d (pp. 348-349) | 16 | -- |
| 18. c (pp. 352-353) | -- | -- |
| 19. d (pp. 357-358) | -- | 18 |
| 20. b (pp. 358-359, Fig. 8.38) | 20 | -- |

# CHAPTER 8 LANGUAGE ENHANCEMENT GUIDE

## I. VOCABULARY, IDIOMS AND CULTURAL CONCEPTS

**Instructions:**

As you read the text refer to the following list of words and their definitions. The words are listed in the order in which they appear in the chapter. The definitions presented contain the meaning of the word as used by Kalat on the textbook page indicated.

Remember that these words like all words can have different meanings in other sentences. If you do not find a non-technical word on this list it may have been defined on a previous page or chapter of this study guide. The definition of non-technical words may be found in the dictionary at the end of this study guide. Kalat defined each new technical word as it first appears on a page and these may be found in Kalat's summary at the end of the section and in the Glossary at the end the textbook..

**Thinking and Mental Process**

illusion (310) = a mistaken perception or belief

trivially easy (311) = very easy
coincidence = an accidental sequence of events that seems to have been planned or arranged
not coincidentally = not accidentally
in short = in conclusion
mimicking = to copy or imitate behavior, speech, expression, etc.
suits our purpose = is helpful
navigability = deep or wide enough to provide passage

take our (categories) for granted (312) = accept without question
loosely defined = vaguely defined

repentant (313)= apologetic, sorry, contrite, regretful
sarcastic = humorous, insulting statements that make its victim suffer emotional pain
toddler = a young child just learning to walk
hierarchy = a group of people, concepts or things arranged in order of rank, power or authority,
        complexity, abstractness, etc.

poses (316) = presents
a bit more = slightly more
deceleration = a decrease in speed
excitation = activation; elicit; arouse; stir to action

in other words (317) = another way to summarize this study

angular (318) = having a slanting or sloping direction

hail a cab (319) = call a taxi cab

**Problem Solving, Expertise, and Error**

aligned (320) = arranged in a line

granted (323) = accepted the idea that; acknowledged that

generally (325) = usually, typically, often
phase = a specific stage or step in a sequence
generating = producing, thinking of, creating
checking = evaluating, examining, inspecting, testing
you are facing = you have

suppose (326)= assume to be true or real for the following discussion or explanation
consider = think about
fast -food place = a restaurant like McDonaldís

plausible (327) = probably true,  likely to be valid; acceptable; credible
generalizing = extend to other ideas

check (328) = inspecting or test for accuracy or quality; examine
plausible = likely to be true; apparently valid or acceptable; credible
analogous = similar or alike in some way

groping (329) =  to search blindly or uncertainly;  feel one's way
addressed the right questions = asked the right questions

arbitrarily (330) = determined by chance and not by reason or principle
emerged = to come or rise from
should not fault = blame; criticize

atmosphere (331) = the social environment; the air in our physical environment
polishing the ideas = improving or perfecting the ideas
throws himself/herself = dedicates,  devotes time to
wholeheartedly = enthusiastically, with great energy
advocate =  to speak, plead, or argue in favor of a cause; a person who argues for a cause; a supporter
    or defender of a cause
err = to make a error, to make a mistake

virtually (332) = almost ; nearly; practically

contagious (337) = easily spread from one  person to another; infectious
breaks out = occurs suddenly

casino (338) = a public room or building used for gambling and entertainment
lotteries = a contest in which numbered tickets are sold; the winning numbers  are selected in a random
    drawing

affinity (340) = an attraction to or for something;  a feeling of kinship
long-shot = an event with a very low probability of occurring

vicarious (341) = another person's experience is felt as one's  own

**Language**

precursors (345) = anything that precedes and indicates someone or something to come; a forerunner or predecessor

transform (348) = to change the appearance or form of something

facilitate (349) = to make easy or easier

context (352) = the part of a paragraph or statement that surrounds a word or sentence and influences its meaning; the situation in which an event occurs

ambiguous (353) = open to more than one interpretation; words, sounds or events that have two or more meanings and the meaning is not clear

totalitarian (354) = a form of government in which the leaders have complete control over all aspects of life and opposing political points of view are suppressed; dictatorial, tyrannical, despotic

fixation = to focus one's eyes or attention on something;( to attach oneself to a person or thing in an immature or neurotic fashion)

monitor (355) = to keep track of something systematically; to collect information about an event

gibberish = nonsensical or meaningless talk or writing

eleemosynary (357) = relating to or dependent on charity; contributed to charity

metrorrhagia = very severe bleeding from the uterus

## II. VOCABULARY BUILDING

### Word Analysis

Instructions:
1. Study the meaning of the prefixes, roots and suffixes listed.
2. Break each word in the table into its prefixes, roots and suffixes.
3. Guess the meaning of the word based on the meaning of its parts.
4. Find the word on the text page indicated in the brackets and redefine the word based on the context of the sentence, paragraph and chapter.
5. Look up the definition of the word in the VOCABULARY, IDIOMS AND CULTURAL CONCEPTS section above, in Appendix A (marked A) or in a college level dictionary. If the word is followed by letter G look it up in the text Glossary.

Exercise 1.   Coincidentally

**Prefix : co _____ = with/together**
**Word: incident = a happening/an event/**
**Suffix: _____ ly = having the characteristics of/ happening at a specific time or period**
**Suffix: _____ ly = in the manner of/to the degree/in the direction of**

| Word | Meaning |
|---|---|
| coincidentally (A) | |
| incidental | a chance happening, a minor event |
| yearly | |
| daily | |
| generally | |
| badly | |
| northwardly | |
| cohort (G) | |

### Exercise 2. Representativeness

**Word: represent = to present/ to serve as a symbol for something else/to serve in a position for someone else/ to serve as an example**

**Suffix: _____ ive = tending to (be)/ inclined to (be)**

**Suffix: _____ ness = having the characteristic of/being**

| Word | Meaning |
|---|---|
| representativeness (A) | |
| passive | |
| active | |
| goodness | |

### Exercise 3. Recognition

**Prefix: pre _____ before/in front of/**

**Word: cognition = to think/to be aware/to know**

**Word: mature =**

| Word | Meaning |
|---|---|
| premature (A) | |
| precursor (A) | |
| precognition (G) | |
| preattentive (G) | |
| predictability (G) | |
| predisposition (G) | |
| preoperational (G) | |

### Exercise 4. Deceleration

**Prefix: de/ab/dis _____ = down/ off/away from/ out of/ reversal of/ undoing**

Caution: These prefixes have other meanings.

**Root: ____ celerate _____ = move/motion**

**Suffix: _____ ion = the act/means/result of**

| Word | Meaning |
|---|---|
| deceleration (A) | |
| depress | |
| depart | |
| deport | |
| detoxification (G) | |

## III. STRUCTURAL CLUES: TRANSITIONS

(This section is an adaptation of material developed by Laurie Blass)

Transitions are words (or phrases) that show a relationship between two ideas in a text. Transitions prepare you for information that is about to come; they let you know that the next idea may be a contrast, a conclusion, or an example of the previous idea. They appear between two parts of the same sentence, between two sentences, or between two paragraphs. Being able to recognize and understand transitional words and phrases will increase your reading speed and comprehension. Take a look at this example.

"If you went to work everyday and were exposed only to regular indoor lighting, your biological clock would take ten days to fully adapt. If, however, ..."

Without reading on, if you understand the function of the word however, you know that a contrasting idea is about to be presented. You can almost guess that the contrasting idea will have something to do with lighting. Now read the rest of the sentence reads:

"...you spent 6 to 8 hours of the first two days outside in bright sunlight, you would reset your biological clock and cause your circadian rhythm to be on local clock time."

The following table lists some common transitions and their functions:

| Transition | Function |
|---|---|
| however, but, on the hand, rather, by contrast | present a contrasting idea |
| for example, for instance, similarly, another example, to illustrate | present an example to illustrate the preceding idea |
| in addition, additionally | present another idea, similar to the preceding one |
| as a result, therefore, consequently | present a result or conclusion |
| in other words | present the same idea in fresh new words |

Find the following sentences in Chapter 8. Read the first sentence or paragraph. As soon as you come to the transition at the beginning of the following sentence or paragraph, stop and guess what will come next. Then read on to see if you were correct.

p. 311, paragraph 6, heading, "Categorization," beginning with: "An ancient Greek philosopher wrote that ..." ("However...")

p. 313, paragraph 5, heading "Thinking About Categories," beginning with: "One key point about..." ("For example...")

p. 314, paragraph 4, beginning with: "Your responses are not quite so simple..." ("Therefore...")

p. 317, paragraph 2, beginning with, " A second experiment..." ("In other words,....")

p. 317, paragraph 4, beginning with, "When people think about..." ("To illustrate...")

p. 323, paragraph 6, beginning with, "Hungarian author Laszlo Polgar..." and find next paragraph with "Similarly...."

# CHAPTER 9  INTELLIGENCE AND ITS MEASUREMENT

## OBJECTIVES
Understand that:

### Intelligence and Intelligence Tests

I. Defining intelligence is difficult, so we can't tell if the tests measure it  (p. 365)
  A. Original tests were developed to measure the ability to do well in school  (p. 365)
    1. This definition is too narrow  (p. 366)
  B. Spearman suggested that there is a general factor (*g*) in mental ability  (p. 366, Fig. 9.1, Table 9.1, p. 371)
  C. Cattell suggested that fluid and crystallized intelligence be distinguished  (pp. 367-368, Table 9.1, p. 371)
  D. Gardner argued that people have multiple intelligences  (pp. 368-369, Table 9.1, p. 371)
  E. Sternberg's triarchic theory has three components of intelligence  (pp. 369-370, Table 9.1, p. 371)
    1. Cognitive processes within an individual  (p. 370)
    2. Identification of situations that require intelligence  (p. 370)
    3. Relationship between intelligence and the outside world  (p. 370)
  F. Intelligence tests have little relationship to theories of intelligence  (p. 371)
II. Intelligence tests attempt to measure probable performance in school  (p. 372)
  A. The intelligence quotient (IQ) involves dividing mental age by chronological age  (p. 372)
  B. Stanford-Binet asks questions that can be answered at different ages  (pp. 372-373)
  C. Wechsler tests give scores on verbal and performance  (pp. 373-374)
  D. Raven's Progressive Matrices makes minimal use of language and facts  (pp. 374, 376-377)
  E. Scholastic Assessment Test predicts performance in college  (p. 377)
  F. Aptitude tests are supposed to measure ability; achievement tests measure learning in an area  (p. 378)
    1. All tests measure a complex mixture of abilities and knowledge  (p. 378)
  G. Test scores give overall summaries of abilities which can be useful  (p. 378)

### Evaluation of Intelligence Tests

III. Tests are standardized so that mean and standard deviation are set  (pp. 381-382, Fig. 9.10)
  A. Norms are established so that scores corresponding to percentiles can be determined  (p. 382)
  B. Tests are restandardized as society changes  (p. 382)
    1. Tests are harder today than they used to be  (pp. 382-383)
IV. Tests must be reliable and valid  (pp. 383-384)
  A. Reliability refers to the repeatability of the test  (p. 383, Figure 9.11; Table 9.4, p. 385)
    1. A correlation coefficient is used to measure reliability  (p. 383)
  B. Validity refers to whether a test measures what it claims to measure  (pp. 383-384, Table 9.4, p. 385)
    1. Content validity refers to whether questions accurately represent the information  (pp. 383-384)
    2. Construct validity refers to whether the test results correspond to theoretical expectations  (p. 384)
    3. Predictive validity refers to whether test scores predict behavior  (p. 384)
      a. Scores must vary over a substantial range for high predictive validity  (p. 384)
  C. Utility refers the practical usefulness of a test  (p. 385, Table 9.4)

D. Test scores can fluctuate, especially if reliability is low  (pp. 385-386)
V. Groups differ in mean performance on IQ tests  (pp. 386-387)
    A. Males and females have similar means, but males show more variability  (p. 386)
    B. There are some differences among ethnic groups on tests  (pp. 386-387, Fig. 9.12)
        1. Differences among European Americans are due to genetics and environment  (p. 387)
        2. Differences among ethnic groups may not have a genetic basis  (p. 387)
VI. Tests are biased against a group if they systematically underestimate abilities  (p. 388)
    A. Single items may be biased if they don't correlate with the whole test for a group of people  (pp. 388-389)
    B. Tests may be biased if they underestimate the performance of a group of people  (pp. 388-389)
    C. IQ tests predict performance in school equally well for minority groups and European Americans with the same test score  (p. 389)
        1. This doesn't mean there are differences in innate ability  (p. 390)
    D. Intelligence is influenced both by heredity and environment  (p. 390)
        1. People who are closely related have more similar IQ scores than more distant relatives  (p. 391, Fig. 9.15)
            a. IQs of identical twins are more similar than fraternal twins  (p. 391)
        2. Identical twins adopted into different families have similar IQs, but the environments are usually similar also  (pp. 391-392)
        3. Adopted children's IQs correlate with their biological parents' IQs  (p. 392, Fig. 9.16)
    E. It is not clear whether ethnic differences in IQ are influenced by genetics  (pp. 392-393)
        1. African-American children raised in European-American homes score only slightly higher than the average for African-American children  (pp. 393-395)
        2. The degree of European ancestry in African Americans does not predict IQ scores  (p. 395)
    F. The present research doesn't support either a genetic or an environmental reason for ethnic group differences  (pp. 395-396)

## COMPREHENSION CHECK

Answer these questions soon after reading the chapter. Circle the best alternative. Check your answers on pp. 182-184. If you gave a wrong answer, try to write why it was wrong. Check your reasons on pp. 182-184.

### Intelligence and Intelligence Tests

1. The *g* factor identified by Spearman:
    a. consists of tasks that girls excel in
    b. involves crystallized intelligence
    c. involves dealing with abstract concepts and perceiving relationships
    d. is all the knowledge that a person has acquired
    e. is evidence for defining intelligence as independent abilities

Correct _____ If wrong, why? _____

2. Which of the following is <u>not</u> part of Sternberg's triarchic theory?
    a. crystallized and fluid intelligence must be distinguished
    b. identification of situations that require intelligence
    c. relationship between intelligence and the outside world
    d. cognitive processes within an individual

Correct _____ If wrong, why? _____

3. A person who remembers all of the batting averages for major league baseball players over the last 5 years, but who can't remember a short grocery list, can best be explained by which theory of intelligence?
   a. Spearman's *g*
   b. Cattell's crystallized vs. fluid intelligence
   c. Gardner's theory of multiple intelligences
   d. Binet's intelligence quotient

Correct _____ If wrong, why? _____

4. IQ tests are:
   a. measures of innate potential
   b. explanations for why people do well or poorly in school
   c. useless for predicting school success
   d. not very reliable
   e. measurements of current performance

Correct _____ If wrong, why? _____

5. How do the Wechsler tests differ from the Stanford-Binet?
   a. the WISC-R has an average of 200; Stanford-Binet is 100
   b. WISC-R can be used with adults; Stanford-Binet cannot
   c. Wechsler tests give scores on more component abilities than the Stanford-Binet
   d. Wechsler tests don't involve factual information; Stanford-Binet test does
   e. Wechsler tests give only a single score; Stanford-Binet gives multiple scores

Correct _____ If wrong, why? _____

6. Scores on the Scholastic Assessment Test have just increased in 1995. Why?
   a. a smaller more select group of students took it than in previous years
   b. students can now take the test on the computer
   c. many students attend coaching classes which raise scores by 100 points or more
   d. the scores have been readjusted to bring the average back to 500

Correct _____ If wrong, why? _____

7. How are the Progressive Matrices different from the Wechsler tests?
   a. they require knowledge of more specific facts
   b. they can be used with blind people
   c. they make minimal use of language
   d. they provide scores on several distinct abilities
   e. they are not as "culture-fair"

Correct _____ If wrong, why? _____

8. Standard IQ and related tests:
    a. correlate positively with crude biological variables
    b. are inaccurate because they are not based on research
    c. focus on the ability to learn rather than on knowledge
    d. are useless because they don't correlate with how fast people process information

Correct _____ If wrong, why? _____

## Evaluation of Intelligence Tests

9. Susan, who is 10, performs better than 84% of the other 10-year-olds who took the Stanford-Binet. Her IQ would be:
    a. 84
    b. 16
    c. 100
    d. 116

Correct _____ If wrong, why? _____

10. To standardize a test means to:
    a. check to see if people get the same score twice
    b. establish the rules for administering the test and for interpreting its scores
    c. see if the test predicts what it is supposed to predict
    d. make sure that all items are very similar, so that if people get one correct, they will get all correct

Correct _____ If wrong, why? _____

11. I have designed a new test for admission to law school. I measure the size of a person's wrist, and if it is larger than 85% of the people's, the student is admitted. My test has:
    a. reliability but not validity
    b. validity but not reliability
    c. content validity but not reliability
    d. neither reliability nor validity
    e. both reliability and validity

Correct _____ If wrong, why? _____

12. If a test has construct validity, it means that the test:
    a. predicts a certain behavior in a setting outside of the test
    b. has utility
    c. contains questions that accurately represent the information that the test is supposed to measure
    d. measures a concept that corresponds to a theoretical expectation

Correct _____ If wrong, why? _____

13  Research has shown that IQ tests are biased against:
   a. females as compared to males
   b. twins who were reared apart and unrelated people
   c. African Americans and East Asians
   d. non-English-speaking immigrants to the U.S.

Correct _____ If wrong, why? _____

14. Identical twins are more similar in IQ scores than fraternal twins whether they were raised together or apart.  Which of the following is consistent with the conclusion that IQ is determined by heredity?
   a. twins whose parents thought they were identical but who really are fraternal are only as similar as other fraternal twins
   b. parents treat identical twins more similarly than they treat fraternal twins
   c. environments of twins reared apart are actually very similar
   d. twins are exactly the same age; random pairs of children are not

Correct _____ If wrong, why? _____

15. Which of the following provides evidence against genetics in the IQ difference between European and African Americans?
   a. there is no correlation between IQ scores and amount of European ancestry in African Americans
   b. African Americans consistently score lower than whites
   c. African-American children adopted into upper-middle class homes score only slightly higher on IQ tests than other African-American children
   d. African-American children's test scores do not improve when they are tested by an African-American tester using appropriate dialect

Correct _____ If wrong, why? _____

## ANSWERS AND EXPLANATIONS FOR COMPREHENSION CHECK

| Correct Answer | Other Alternatives Are Wrong Because: |
|---|---|
| 1.  c  (p. 366)<br>Obj. I-B | a. general intelligence, not gender-specific<br>b. part of intelligence--skills and knowledge one a already has; *g* argues for general factor<br>d. includes ability to acquire new knowledge also<br>e. Spearman argued that there is a general factor |
| 2.  a  (pp. 369-370)<br>Obj. I-E | a. Cattell's theory; not part of Sternberg's triarchic theory<br>b-d. general abilities included in triarchic theory |
| 3.  c  (pp. 368-369)<br>Obj. I-D | a. general ability; should be good at memory in general<br>b. memory ability should be more general; good at memorizing all types of things<br>d. IQ based on age appropriate questions; memory ability shouldn't |

4. e (p. 372)
   Obj. II-A

a. no reason to assume this
b. they don't explain performance, although they are reasonable predictors
c. predict school success fairly well
d. have high reliability

5. c (pp. 372-374)
   Obj. II-B, C

a. both have means of 100
b. WISC-R is the children's test
d. both test some factual knowledge
e. Wechsler tests give scores on several component abilities

6. d (pp. 377-378)
   Obj. II-E

a. a wider range of students have been taking the test in recent years
b. true, but this doesn't explain the change in scores
c. many students are coached but this only increases scores by 20-30 points

7. c (pp. 373-377)
   Obj. II-C, D

a. no specific facts are tested
b. neither test can be used with blind individuals
d. Matrices provide only one score
e. presumably they are more fair because they do not require many language skills and they do not test facts

8. a (p. 378)
   Obj. II-G

b. they are the product of decades of research
c. a criticism is that they focus too much on knowledge
d. they do show a positive correlation with information processing speed

9. d (pp. 381-382,
   Fig. 9.10)
   Obj. III-A

a. performs better than 84%; this is not her score
b. performed worse than 16%, this is not her score
c. this is average; she performed better than 50%

10. b (p. 381)
    Obj. III

a. test-retest reliability; not part of standardization
c. validity; not part of standardization
d. tests need a variety of items; items should be correlated with each other, but not all the same

11. a (pp. 383-384)
    Obj. IV

b. won't predict performance, but is reliable because I'd get about the same value every time
c. questions don't represent information a law student knows; is reliable, see b
d. it is reliable; see b
e. not valid-see b and c above

12. d (p. 384)
    Obj. IV-B-2

a. this is predictive validity
b. means that test is useful for practical purposes
c. this is content validity

13. d (p. 388)
   Obj. VI-B

a. females score about the same as males on IQ tests although males scores are more variable

b. genetics is irrelevant in bias

c. East Asians have higher than average scores and African Americans have lower than average scores but an intelligence test is only biased if it under predicts school performance

14. a (pp. 391-392)
   Obj. VI-D-1-a

b,c. environmental explanations for identical-twin similarities

d. explains why twins' IQs are more similar than random pairs, but not why identical twins are more similar than fraternal twins

15. a (p. 395)
   Obj. VI-E-2

b. doesn't say anything about genetics or environment because both differ

c. these results show a disappointingly small environmental influence; they don't argue against genetics they environment

d. doesn't argue against genetics

## LECTURE MATERIAL

Don't forget to review your lecture material. Process each topic meaningfully. First, be sure that you understand the material in each lecture--if you don't, ask your instructor or teaching assistant. Associate the material with things that you already know and with your personal experiences. If you can make up mental images of any of the material, do so. Try to think of real-life applications of the concepts. Write your own comments on your lecture notes. Then write questions to cover each concept.

-------------------------------------------------------------------------------
WAIT AT LEAST 24 HOURS BEFORE PROCEEDING.
LET FORGETTING OCCUR--IT WILL!!
-------------------------------------------------------------------------------

## SHORT-ANSWER ESSAY QUESTIONS

Write brief answers to each of the following. The answers are on pp. 186-187, but do try to write the answers yourself before looking at them.

### Intelligence and Intelligence Tests

1. Explain how the theories of intelligence of Spearman and Cattell are similar and how these two theories differ from Gardner's theory.

2. How does Sternberg's theory differ from those of Cattell and Spearman?

3. Describe the WISC-R and the WAIS-R and explain how they differ from the Stanford-Binet.

4. Explain why Raven's Progressive Matrices should be more "culture-fair" than the Stanford-Binet and the Wechsler tests.

5. Some have argued that we should do away with all aptitude tests because they measure achievement rather than aptitude. What are some arguments against this?

## Evaluation of Intelligence Tests

6. What does it mean to standardize a test? Why must tests be restandardized periodically?

7. Discuss the relationship between reliability and validity.

8. Discuss the differences between content, construct, and predictive validity. How do these concepts differ from utility?

9. What type of evidence would be necessary to decide that a specific test item is biased against a group of individuals?

10. Discuss whether IQ and other aptitude tests are biased against groups of people.

11. Describe how the role of genetics in a characteristic, such as IQ, can be studied.

12. Discuss evidence related to the role of environment in the differences in IQ between African Americans and European Americans.

\*\*\*\*\*\*\*\*\*\*\*\*\*\*\*\*\*\*\*\*\*\*\*\*\*\*\*\*\*\*\*\*\*\*\*\*\*\*\*\*\*\*\*\*\*\*\*\*\*\*\*\*\*\*\*\*\*\*\*\*\*\*\*\*\*\*\*\*\*\*\*\*\*\*\*\*\*\*\*\*
Find the questions that you wrote over lecture material and write answers to them.
\*\*\*\*\*\*\*\*\*\*\*\*\*\*\*\*\*\*\*\*\*\*\*\*\*\*\*\*\*\*\*\*\*\*\*\*\*\*\*\*\*\*\*\*\*\*\*\*\*\*\*\*\*\*\*\*\*\*\*\*\*\*\*\*\*\*\*\*\*\*\*\*\*\*\*\*\*\*\*\*

## ANSWERS TO SHORT-ANSWER ESSAY QUESTIONS

1. Spearman's and Cattell's theories assume that people use the same components of intelligence in tasks in different areas. Although they disagree on what or how many components of intelligence there are, they assume that the same components are used in different tasks. Gardner, on the other hand, assumes that there are different types of intelligence that are used for different tasks. (pp. 366-369, Table 9.1, p. 371)

2. Sternberg focuses less on the structure of intelligence and more on its function. He asks how people process information and engage in intelligent behavior. Sternberg's theory has three components: the cognitive processes that occur within an individual, the ability to identify repeated and novel situations and to make correct responses to them, and the ability to adapt to or change the environment. (pp. 366-371, Table 9.1)

3. The WISC-R is the children's version and the WAIS-R is the adult's version. They include a number of different parts to assess different types of knowledge and abilities. A score is given for each of the 12 sections and also for Verbal, Performance, and Total IQ. The Stanford-Binet yields an overall IQ score, along with three subscores. However, it doesn't report as many subcomponents as the Wechsler tests. (pp. 372-373)

4. The matrices involve very little language, so a person who does not understand English or who has poor verbal skills can still complete the tests (assuming they can understand the instructions). They also do not test specific knowledge, but rather ask people to look for relationships among nonverbal items, so they should be less dependent upon what a person has been taught than the other tests. (pp. 372-377)

5. It's true that aptitude tests measure how much students already know along with their ability to reason and learn new things. However, it can be argued that intelligent people learn more facts than less intelligent people. In addition, the tests are useful in predicting performance on school-like tasks. IQ tests also correlate with gross biological measures, such as brain volume and speed of information processing. (p. 378)

6. Standardization sets norms, or determines the mean performance and sets up the standard deviation. It also involves the selection of test items that test a variety of information but that all correlate to the total score. Over the years, some items become too easy, so they must be changed so that not everyone gets them correct. (pp. 381-383)

7. Reliability refers to the consistency of a test or how likely it is that a person will get the same score twice. A test can be very reliable (showing high consistency) but still not be useful or valid. A test that is not reliable, however, cannot be valid, because if the scores vary too much, they cannot predict performance. (pp. 383-384)

8. Generally, validity refers to whether a test measures what it is supposed to measure. A test has content validity if its questions represent the information that the test is supposed to measure. Construct validity refers to whether the test results are consistent with what would be expected from a theoretical construct. Predictive validity indicates that the test predicts behavior in a setting outside of the test. Utility refers to whether a test is useful, that is, whether its results can aid in improving selection or education. (pp. 383-385)

9. An item is biased if it systematically underestimates the abilities of one group relative to another, that is, if it is easy for individuals from one group but difficult for another group. An item may also be biased if it correlates with the whole test score better for one group than for another. For example, if an item using a football field is answered correctly more often by men than by women and if the item correlates with the entire test better for men than for women, then the item is probably biased against women and it should be replaced by another item. (pp. 388-390)

10. A biased test systematically underestimates the performance of a group, so a person should perform better than the test score would predict. This is true for immigrants who do not speak English as their first language. It is also true of older women who take college entrance tests. They do better in college than the tests predict. Some ethnic groups score higher on standardized tests than other ethnic groups. This does not necessarily mean the tests are biased, however, because they do tend to predict school performance for the ethnic groups. School grades, however, may be biased and unfair for someone from a culture other than the majority culture. (pp. 388-390)

11. The role of genetics can be estimated by comparing differences in IQ for people who are either very similar or different in genetics and environment. If the role of genetics is high, people who are very similar genetically (such as identical twins) should be very similar in IQ no matter how different their environments are. If the role of genetics is low, similarity in environment should predict similarity in IQ. (pp. 390-392)

12. African-American children adopted into upper middle-class European-American families have IQs that are slightly above the averages for non-adopted African-American children. However, the size of the environmental effect here is disappointing. The amount of European ancestry in African-American children does not predict their IQs; it should if genes associated with European Americans produce higher IQs. (pp. 393-395)

**POSTTEST**

Take this test with all of your books and notes out of sight. This should give you a good idea of how well you understand the material.

**Matching**

Put the letter of the test in the blank beside the description.

1. _____ general term for measure of person's probable performance in school

2. _____ nonverbal test in which patterns are completed

3 _____ another college entrance test, not discussed in chapter

4. _____ first practical intelligence test for English-speaking children

5. _____ intelligence test for adults that contains verbal and performance items

6. _____ college entrance test that has a theoretical mean of 500

7. _____ intelligence test for children that gives scores on subabilities

A. WAIS-R

B. SAT

C. Progressive Matrices

D. Stanford-Binet

E. IQ

F. WISC-R

G. ACT

**Multiple-choice**

Circle the best alternative.

Intelligence and Intelligence Tests

1. Which of the following is most consistent with Spearman's theory of intelligence?
   a. intelligence consists of a general ability to perceive and manipulate relationships, plus some specific abilities
   b. intelligence consists entirely of factual information
   c. intelligence consists of cognitive processes, identification of situations requiring intelligence, appropriate use of intelligence in the world
   d. intelligence consists of unrelated specific abilities
   e. intelligence consists of the ability to plan approaches to problems

2. Jimmy remembers things well and has learned skills taught in the first grade. However, he doesn't have much potential to go far beyond these very basic skills. Jimmy has:
   a. high fluid intelligence but low crystallized intelligence
   b. a high *g* factor but low crystallized intelligence
   c. a low *g* factor and high fluid intelligence
   d. high fluid intelligence and high crystallized intelligence
   e. high crystallized intelligence but low fluid intelligence

3. A 30-year-old adult who has an IQ of 130 did what on the Stanford-Binet?
    a. performed as well as the average 39-year-old
    b. performed better than half of the other adults
    c. performed toward the left end of the normal distribution
    d. performed better than most other adults
    e. performed as well as the average 23-year-old

4. If an adult tells you that her Verbal IQ is 110 and her Performance IQ is 120, she must have taken which test?
    a. WISC-R
    b. WAIS-R
    c. Raven's Progressive Matrices
    d. Stanford-Binet
    e. TAT

5. Theoretically, why should the Progressive Matrices test be more culture-fair than the Wechsler tests?
    a. the matrices have more subtests
    b. the matrices are balanced so that males and females score about the same
    c. the matrices call for no verbal responses and no specific information
    d. the matrices are more interesting than the Wechsler tests
    e. the matrices have much higher reliability than the Wechsler tests

6. SAT scores:
    a. can be improved by 100 points or more through coaching
    b. predict college performance much better than high school grades
    c. have increased recently because the students taking the test are much smarter than those who took earlier tests
    d. significantly improve the prediction of college success when combined with high-school grades
    e. cannot be changed through coaching

7. IQ tests:
    a. measure differences among people; they don't explain them
    b. probably measure a single quantity
    c. measure inborn limits and capacities
    d. are based on precise meanings of "intelligence"
    e. explain why some people do better in school than others

Evaluation of Intelligence Tests

8. To say that someone is in the 70th percentile on a test means that she:
    a. scored higher than 70% of the norm group
    b. is 2 standard deviations above the mean
    c. got 70% of the questions correct on the test
    d. falls within the "gifted" range of intelligence
    e. falls within the "retarded" range of intelligence

9. I have a test that accurately predicts who will learn statistics quickly. My test has:
    a. predictive validity but not reliability
    b. content validity but not predictive validity
    c. predictive validity and reliability
    d. neither validity nor reliability
    e. reliability but not predictive validity

10. Which of the following is evidence for a biased test item?
    a. a judge suggests that African-American children may respond differently than European-American children because of differences in their cultures
    b. the item is missed by most test-takers
    c. the item correlates well with the entire test
    d. the item correlates with the entire test better for one group than for another group

11. The Stanford-Binet and the Wechsler tests are biased against people who do not speak English well because:
    a. such people do better in school and on the job than their scores predict
    b. such people score lower than the average population
    c. such people do about the same in school as other people with the same score
    d. the tests do not have high content validity for them
    e. the tests are too reliable for them

12. The difference between the IQs of African- and European Americans:
    a. has been increasing in the last few years
    b. is about 25 points on the Wechsler tests
    c. predicts differences in their school grades
    d. is not caused by environmental differences
    e. is greater when African Americans who have more European ancestry are compared European Americans

13. If genetics plays no role in a trait, then:
    a. identical twins reared in very different environments should be more similar than unrelated people
    b. fraternal twins reared together should be much more similar than identical twins reared together
    c. adopted children should look more like their biological parents than their adoptive parents
    d. identical twins reared apart should be less similar than fraternal twins reared together
    e. disadvantaged children adopted in higher-income homes should perform the same as other disadvantaged children

14. Identical twins reared apart are more similar in IQ than fraternal twins reared apart. A researcher who believes in the influence of environment more than heredity might explain this in what way?
    a. identical twins are more similar genetically
    b. the environments of the identical twin pairs were more similar
    c. the identical twins were raised in genuinely different environments
    d. the adoptive parents of the fraternal twin pairs were more similar than the adoptive parents of the identical twin pairs
    e. both c and d

15. African-American children reared in upper middle-class European-American homes scored:
    a. higher than the average of European-American children on IQ tests
    b. about 15 points lower on IQ tests than the average of African-American children
    c. about the same as other African-American children in Minnesota
    d. much higher than the average African-American child in the United States
    e. much higher than European-American children adopted into the same homes

16. Performance on Raven's Progressive Matrices and amount of European ancestry in African-American children are:
    a. highly correlated, giving good evidence for the importance of environment in race differences in IQ
    b. highly correlated, giving good evidence for the importance of genetics in race differences in IQ
    c. uncorrelated, giving evidence that genetics may not be important in ethnic differences in IQ
    d. negatively correlated, giving good evidence for the importance of genetics in ethnic differences in IQ
    e. uncorrelated, giving good evidence for the importance genetics in ethnic differences in IQ

## ANSWERS TO POSTTEST

| Correct Answer | Questions Testing a Similar Concept | |
| --- | --- | --- |
| | Comprehension Check | Short-Answer |

**Matching**

| | | |
| --- | --- | --- |
| 1. E (p. 372) | 4 | -- |
| 2. C (pp. 374, 376-377) | 7 | 4 |
| 3. G (pp. 377-378) | -- | -- |
| 4. D (pp. 372-373) | 5 | 3, 4 |
| 5. A (pp. 373-374) | 5 | 3 |
| 6. B (pp. 377-378) | 6 | 5 |
| 7. F (pp. 373-374) | 5 | 3 |

**Multiple-Choice**

| | | |
| --- | --- | --- |
| 1. a (pp. 366-367) | 1 | 1, 2 |
| 2. e (pp. 367-368) | 1a,2 | 1, 2 |
| 3. d (pp. 372-373) | 5a,9c | 3 |
| 4. b (pp. 373-374) | 5 | 3 |
| 5. c (pp. 374, 376-377) | 7 | 4 |
| 6. d (pp. 377-378) | 6 | -- |
| 7. a (p. 372) | 4 | -- |
| 8. a (pp. 381-382) | 9 | -- |
| 9. c (pp. 383-384) | 11, 12 | 7, 8 |
| 10. d (pp. 388-389) | -- | 9 |
| 11. a (p. 388) | 13 | 9, 10 |
| 12. c (p. 389) | 15 | 12 |
| 13. d (p. 392) | 14 | 11 |
| 14. b (pp. 391-392) | 14 | 11 |
| 15. c (pp. 393-395) | 15 | 12 |
| 16. c (p. 395) | 15 | 12 |

# CHAPTER 9 LANGUAGE ENHANCEMENT GUIDE

## I. VOCABULARY, IDIOMS AND CULTURAL CONCEPTS

**Instructions:**

As you read the text refer to the following list of words and their definitions. The words are listed in the order in which they appear in the chapter. The definitions presented contain the meaning of the word as used by Kalat on the text book page indicated.

Remember that these words like all words can have different meanings in other sentences. If you do not find a non-technical word on this list it may have been defined on a previous page or chapter of this study guide. The definition of non-technical words may be found in the dictionary at the end of this study guide. Kalat defined each new technical word as it first appears on a page and these may be found in Kalat's summary at the end of the section and in the Glossary at the end the textbook..

### Intelligence and Intelligence Tests

controversy (365) = disagreement

misconception = incorrect interpretation; misunderstanding

analogy = a form of logical inference, based on the assumption that if two things are known to be alike in some ways, then they must be alike in other ways

tryout = athletes show their skills and the best performers are selected for the team

resemble = look like

imaginary = existing only in the mind; not real


cope (366) = to solve a problem; to manage

comprehend = understand

haphazard = having a random pattern without organization, or structure

deduced = to reach a conclusion by reasoning; to infer a general principle based on many examples

concepts = refer to words that label groups of objects or events that share common characteristics. Words like, dogs, animals, gender, intelligence and justice are concepts that label or name a group of objects or events that share common characteristics. Concepts can also be thought of as internal, mental representations of imagined or real objects, events and situations.

abstract = refers to a concept, symbol, picture or phrase that represents a large group of different items, behaviors or organisms that, though different, have one or more features in common. For example, the concept animal is more abstract than the concept mammals, and mammals is more abstract than dogs.

impairs = damages, harms, to reduced in strength or ability


amputation (367) = the cutting off of an arm or a leg due to accident or by surgery

modification = change


excel (368) = to do better than others

distinguish = to pay attention to differences between things

novel situations = unusual, unconventional, not typical, not ordinary


in one way or another (372) = in some way, by some means

overdoes = to use or do something when it is not needed

accommodate = to do a favor or service; to admit, hire, accept

foolhardy = foolish, stupid

deficiencies = not having required skills or abilities

retarded children = children with very low intelligence who cannot care for themselves or learn in
    school

administered = given

designated (373) = indicated, labeled, named, characterized by

assessment (377) = test

redundancy = repetition of message or idea

drifted downward = decreased

applicants = people that apply for a job or admission to college

supposed (378) = assumed to be true or real

persistent = continuing, lingering, prolonged

rough gauge = an approximation, almost exact or correct

as it may sound = appears to be

shortcomings = weaknesses, flaws, deficiencies

decade = a period of ten years

infallible (379) = without error, sure, certain, reliable, unfailing

### Evaluation of Intelligence Tests

norms (383) = descriptions of the frequencies at which scores on a test occur

exceeds = to be greater or better than; transcends, outdoes, surpasses, excels

designation (382)= naming or placing something into a category

an era of = a period of time characterized by particular events, or a famous person

via = by

penalized (383) = punished; lowered your test scores

much is at stake = there are serious consequences

dispute = argue, debate, question the truth of a claim

substantially = has a big influence

approximately = are almost exact or correct

construct (384) = concepts are called constructs when they are used to label and or explain cause-effect
    relationships. When we answer why questions with a single word, that word is typically a
    construct

substantial = a large

fluctuations (385) = irregular variations in the value or amounts of something; rising and falling in
    value

loading (386) = including more; packing, filling

bear in mind = remember

taboo (387) = not allowed, banned, forbidden, prohibited

presumably = to accept as true without evidence

discounted them (388) = disregarded them as untrustworthy

harassment = annoyance, bothering

systematically (389) = continually

underscores (390) = emphasizes
intimidated = threatened, inhibited

confounded (391) = distorted, biased, confused

## II. VOCABULARY BUILDING

### Word Analysis

Instructions:

1. Study the meaning of the prefixes, roots and suffixes listed.
2. Break each word in the table into its prefixes, roots and suffixes.
3. Guess the meaning of the word based on the meaning of its parts.
4. Find the word on the text page indicated in the brackets and redefine the word based on the context of the sentence, paragraph and chapter.
5. Look up the definition of the word in the VOCABULARY, IDIOMS AND CULTURAL CONCEPTS section above, in Appendix A (marked A) or in a college level dictionary. If the word is followed by letter G look it up in the text Glossary.

Exercise 1. Misconception

**Prefix : mis _____ = bad/wrong**
**Prefix : mis _____ = to hate/**
**Word: concept = a thought/a mental image of a thing/ (see your text)**
**Suffix: _____ ize =**
**Suffix: _____ ion = the act/the process /means/result of**
**Suffix: _____ ly = having the characteristics of/ happening at a specific time or period**
**Suffix: _____ ly = in the manner of/to the degree/in the direction of**
**Suffix: _____ al = relating to/characterized by/belonging to/**

| Word | Meaning |
|---|---|
| misconception (A) | |
| misconceive | |
| misunderstand | |
| mistake | |
| misogyny | to hate, fear or mistrust women |
| misandry | to hate, fear or mistrust men |
| misanthrope | to hate, fear or mistrust other human beings |
| conceptually | |
| conceptualize | |
| conceptualization | |
| conceptual | |

Exercise 2. Modification

**Prefix : moderate** _____ = to limit/ to regulate/ to keep within limits/to control/to alter/to change
**Suffix:** _____ ion = the act/the process /means/result of
**Suffix:** _____ ate = having/having been/ possessing/characterized by
**Suffix:** _____ ify = to make/ to become

| Word | Meaning |
|---|---|
| modification (A) | |
| moderate | |
| modify | |
| codify | |
| electrify | |

## III. STRUCTURAL CLUES: RHETORICAL QUESTIONS

You learned about the **SPAR** method of study. Recall that the "**P**" stands for processing text material. A good way to start would be to read the topic sentences of paragraphs. The main goal here is to understand the material in a meaningful way, that is, to process it deeply and produce a high level of learning. Another way to process text materials is to read the **rhetorical questions** that appear throughout the text before you read the text word-for-word. **Rhetorical questions,** sometimes called **advanced organizers,** are questions or problems placed in the chapter to stimulate your curiosity and start you thinking about what is coming next.

By reading these rhetorical questions, you get a pretty good idea of the information on that page. But don't just read them, try to answer these questions as best as you can before you start to read; then as you read, you can find out whether or not your answer was correct. It's tempting to skip them altogether, but they're there for a purpose -- to make the reading task easier and give your reading a purpose that makes reading easier.

For example, turn to page 366 and paragraph one of the text and you will find the following rhetorical question, "What would be a better definition? Before you read on stop and think of a better definition than the one preceding the question. After you have given this question some thought and generated your own answer, read on and compare your answer with the author's.

Practice using pre-reading questions to preview chapter material by finding the following questions on the pages indicated. Guess the answers before you read the material on the page. Then read the material word-for-word and see if your guesses were correct. Here are several rhetorical questions selected from Chapter 9 along with their page and paragraph numbers. Find each one in the chapter and examine how the author uses them to stimulate your interest in the text and start you thinking about the topic covered in the following paragraph or section. Whenever you find a rhetorical question start and think about the possible answers to that question. A number of research studies have found that students who pay attention to rhetorical question and try to answer them before they continue to read were able to able to recall more information with greater accuracy than students who ignored them.

1. p. 366 paragraph 1. "What would be a better definition?
2. p. 366 paragraph 6 "That is, the ability to do well on one task correlates with the ability to do well on other tasks, but why?"
3. p. 367 paragraph 2 "Now, which of these cases is more like intelligence?"
4. p. 374 paragraph 2 (Above figure 9.6) "Why not simply translate the test into other languages?"
5. p. 386 last paragraph " What accounts for the observed difference among ethnic groups?"

# CHAPTER 10 DEVELOPMENT

**OBJECTIVES**

Understand that:

**Early Development**

I. Prenatal development depends upon the health of the mother  (p. 402)
   A. Low birth weight babies may do poorly because of their environment after birth  (pp. 402-403)
   B. Fetal alcohol syndrome is marked by decreased alertness in newborns  (pp. 403-404)
II. Newborn's capacities are limited, but they do have some sensory and learning abilities  (p. 404)
   A. They spend more time looking at colorful objects and faces than at other objects  (p. 404, Fig. 10.6)
      1. Very young infants keep looking at the same object  (p. 405)
      2. Older infants shift their eyes but they keep looking back at the same object  (p. 405)
   B. Infants show a fear of heights soon after they begin to crawl  (p. 405)
   C. Young infants can discriminate one sound from another  (p. 406)
   D. Very young infants show learning and memory  (pp. 406-407)
      1. They respond more to their mother's than to an unfamiliar voice  (pp. 406-407)
      2. They can learn a response and remember it for days  (p. 407)
III. It is difficult to make inferences about what children are actually thinking  (pp. 408-409)
   A. Infants may display object permanence in the dark, even if they don't in the light  (p. 408)
   B. Why infants persist in looking for an object in its last hiding place is unclear  (pp. 408-409)

**Development of Thinking and Reasoning**

IV. Piaget studied how children's thought processes differ from those of adults  (pp. 410-411)
   A. Piaget uses some special terminology  (p. 411)
      1. Behavior is based on schemata that change with development  (p. 411)
      2. Development occurs through assimilation and accommodation  (p. 411, Fig. 10.14)
   B. Piaget proposed four stages of development  (p. 411, Table 10.2, p. 417)
      1. Sensorimotor stage lasts from birth to 1 1/2 years  (p. 412, Table 10.2, p. 417)
         a. Children begin to develop a concept of self  (p. 412)
      2. Preoperational stage lasts from 1 1/2 to 7 years  (pp. 412-416,Table 10.2)
         a. Early preoperational stage children accept that appearances are reality  (pp. 412-413, Fig. 10.15)
         b. Preoperational children tend to have egocentric thought  (p. 413)
         c. Preoperational children develop an understanding of other people's knowledge  (pp. 413-415)
         d. Concept of conservation is not understood  (pp. 415-416, Tables 10.1, 10.2, p. 417)
      3. Concrete operations stage lasts from 7 to 11 years  (p. 416, Table 10.2, p. 417)
      4. Formal operations stage begins at age 11  (pp. 416-417, Table 10.2)
   C. Children may have abilities related to later stages, but they may only be able to use them on simpler tasks  (p. 418)
   D. Vygotsky argued the children have a zone of proximal development that is important in education  (pp. 418-419)
V. Children learn new words very rapidly between ages 1 1/2 and 6  (p. 419)
   A. Children go through stages in language learning  (p. 420, Table 10.4)

1. Single words are used in the early phases, although some children start with phrases (pp. 420-421)
2. Children learn rules and apply them too generally (pp. 421-422)
   B. Speed of language development depends upon maturation (p. 422)
VI. Children's level of moral reasoning depends upon reasoning ability (p. 424)
   A. Kohlberg suggested that moral reasoning develops in stages (p. 423, Table 10.6, p. 424)
   B. Kohlberg has been criticized (pp. 425-427)
      1. Reasoning is just the beginning; does it lead to moral behavior? (pp. 425-426)
      2. Moral reasoning isn't as logical as Kohlberg proposed (p. 426)
      3. Kohlberg's studies looked at moral reasoning from a "justice" orientation, not a "caring" orientation (pp. 426-427)

**Social and Emotional Development**

VII. There are two main types of research designs for studying development (p. 429)
   A. Cross-sectional designs compare groups of different ages at one time (pp. 429-431, Table 10.8)
      1. Cohort effects refer to differences due to the time of growing up rather than age (pp. 430-431)
   B. Longitudinal designs compare the same individuals when they are at different ages (pp. 429-431, Table 10.8)
VIII. Erikson proposed eight stages of social and personality development (pp. 431-433; see Table 10.9 for stages)
   A. Basic trust vs. mistrust occurs first (p. 431)
   B. Autonomy vs. shame and doubt occurs from about ages 1 to 3 (pp. 431-432)
   C. Initiative vs. guilt occurs from about ages 3 to 6 (p. 432)
   D. Industry vs. inferiority is the conflict from ages 6 to 12 (p. 432)
   E. Adolescents fact a conflict between identity vs. role confusion (p. 432)
   F. Intimacy vs. isolation is the conflict of young adults (pp. 432-433)
   G. Generativity vs. stagnation occurs in middle adulthood (p. 433)
   H. The conflict in old age is between ego integrity vs. despair (p. 433)
IX. Infants develop attachments to their mothers (pp. 433-435)
   A. Harlow's studies with monkeys suggest that this is due to contact comfort (pp. 433-434)
   B. Deprivation of human contact is harmful to human infants (pp. 434-435)
X. Parents may be authoritative, authoritarian, or permissive (p. 435)
   A. The effects on children may differ in different ethnic groups (p. 435)
XI. Forming friendships is important for social and emotional development (p. 436)
   A. Children tend to be popular, rejected, or controversial (p. 436)
   B. Birth order may have some small effects on development (p. 436)
XII. Adolescence begins when the body shows signs of sexual maturation (p. 436)
   A. An identity crisis occurs as adolescents decide what kind of lives they will lead (pp. 437-438)
   B. Adolescents believe they are "special"; bad things won't happen to them (pp. 438-439)
      1. Teens often do not use contraceptives, thinking the won't become pregnant (pp. 438-439)
XIII. Young adulthood is the time to marry and choose a career (pp. 439-440)
   A. People gradually open up to each other as they date (p. 439)
      1. Many issues that cause friction in marriage are not discussed until the couple has decided to marry (p. 439)
   B. Both parents work in many families (pp. 439-440)
      1. Fathers and mothers have little time for anything other than work, house work, and child care (p. 440)

XIV. Middle adulthood includes highly productive years  (pp. 440-441)
   A. Most adults are satisfied with their jobs, but they could be more satisfied  (p. 441)
   B. People become aware that they won't accomplish their goals and have a midlife transition
      (pp. 441-442)
XV. A primary problem in old age is adjusting to retirement  (pp. 442-443)
   A. Older people desire to maintain control over their lives  (p. 443)
XVI. Death is a principal source of anxiety  (p. 443)
   A. Dying people may go through stages of adjustment  (p. 443, Table 10.11, p. 444)

**Growing Up the Same and Different**

XVII. Temperaments differ at birth and remain fairly consistent  (p. 446)
   A. Genetics plays a role because monozygotic twins are more similar in temperament than
      dizygotic twins  (p. 447)
   B. Environment also plays a role  (p. 447)
      1. Temperament may alter the environment, which affects temperament  (p. 447)
XVIII. The family plays a large role in children's social and emotional development  (p. 447)
   A. Effects of mothers' working on children may depend upon satisfaction with working  (p. 448)
   B. Nontraditional families don't produce children different from traditional families  (p. 448)
   C. Children have difficulty following divorce, especially in the beginning  (p. 449)
      1. Children who were well adjusted before the divorce and whose parents displayed minimal
         conflict did better  (p. 450)
XIX. There are relatively few, consistent sex differences  (pp. 450-451)
   A. Most sex differences emerge in social situations  (pp. 451-452)
      1. Boys' play is more competitive than girls'  (p. 451)
      2. Males and females have different styles and different needs  (p. 452)
         a. Men are more demanding; women are more cooperative  (p. 452)
         b. Men are concerned about status with other men  (p. 452)
         c. Women expect listeners to express sympathy about problems  (p. 452)
   B. Society teaches gender roles  (pp. 452-453)
      1. Children pass along gender roles to each other  (p. 453)
         a. Biology may provide dispositions to act in certain ways  (pp. 453-455)
XX. Minority children face different pressures than others  (p. 455)
   A. Immigrants undergo acculturation  (p. 455)
   B. Minority groups may show full assimilation to American culture or they may develop
      biculturalism  (pp. 455-456)

## COMPREHENSION CHECK

Answer these questions soon after reading the chapter. Circle the best alternative Check your answers on
pp. 203-206. If you gave a wrong answer, try to write why it was wrong. Check your reasons on pp.
203-206.

**Early Development**

1. Low-birth-weight babies typically show low achievement and often have behavior problems. The best
   reason for this is:
   a. impaired brain development
   b. that the mother is usually malnourished during pregnancy
   c. that the mother is usually unmarried
   d. that the mothers don't provide good environments

   Correct _____  If wrong, why? _____

2. Which of the following is a difference between infants and adults in terms of vision?
    a. adults look at human faces more than at other patterns but infants do not
    b. infants look at very different types of objects than adults
    c. infants shift their attention to new stimuli less than adults
    d. infants shift their attention from one stimulus to another much more than adults

Correct _____ If wrong, why? _____

3. When an infant sucks, the sound "ba" is produced. He increases his sucking rate and then decreases it as the sound is repeated. The experimenter then changes the sound to "pa." What is the infant likely to do?
    a. continue sucking at the same rate because he can't discriminate any speech sounds
    b. decrease his sucking rate because the new sound catches his attention
    c. continue sucking at the same rate because he can't discriminate "pa" and "ba"
    d. increase his sucking rate because he hears a new sound

Correct _____ If wrong, why? _____

4. Piaget interpreted infants' not reaching for a hidden object as a failure in object permanence. The correct explanation for this is that infants:
    a. don't know that objects continue to exist even when we can't see them
    b. may concentrate so much on seen objects than they ignore unseen ones
    c. quickly forget where things are hidden
    d. any of these could be correct; determining the correct explanation is difficult

Correct _____ If wrong, why? _____

**Development of Thinking and Reasoning**

5. An infant takes a new rubber ducky and immediately puts it in her mouth in exactly the same way as she sucks her rattle. Piaget would say that:
    a. accommodation of the ducky to the sucking schema has occurred
    b. assimilation of the ducky to the sucking schema has occurred
    c. the infant is in the preoperational stage
    d. the infant has added a new schema to handle the ducky

Correct _____ If wrong, why? _____

6. Children gain some concept of self during the first stage of development. What is the evidence for this?
    a. infants over 1 1/2 years touch a spot of rouge on their face when they see themselves in the mirror
    b. infants over 1 1/2 years touch the red spot on the mirror when they see themselves with rouge on their face
    c. 4-year-olds select the same cup as an informed adult rather than an uninformed adult
    d. children tend to draw a pile of blocks as they see them even when you ask them to draw the blocks as you see them from the other side

Correct _____ If wrong, why? _____

7. I take two equal-sized cans of Coke and pour one into a tall, thin glass and another into a shorter, fatter glass. Janie then tells me that there is more coke in the tall, thin glass. Janie is:
   a. in the concrete operations stage
   b. in the sensorimotor stage
   c. in the formal operations stage
   d. in the preoperational stage
   e. showing conservation

Correct _____ If wrong, why? _____

8. Several studies have been done to determine whether children who fail Piaget's tasks can pass the same tasks when they are set up more simply. After such practice, children can often pass the more difficult versions of the tasks. This shows that:
   a. the stages are distinct; children are either in one or the other
   b. the shift between the stages is sudden
   c. transitions from one stage to the next require a major reorganization of the child's way of thinking
   d. each stage seems to merge gradually into the next stage
   e. both a and b

Correct _____ If wrong, why? _____

9. Children learn grammatical rules:
   a. in elementary school after they have mastered speaking
   b. very early, although they often apply them too generally
   c. completely through formal training; if their parents do not teach them properly, they will not learn
   d. through formal teaching, but the type of teaching that is necessary depends on the culture

Correct _____ If wrong, why? _____

10. When infants first begin to learn language,
    a. they assume that words apply to all objects that are part of a common theme
    b. they use positives and negatives to refer to the same concept
    c. they utter single words that are meaningless
    d. they assume that words apply to types of objects or actions

Correct _____ If wrong, why? _____

11. John feels that he should be helpful to a new employee because one day that employee may become his boss and he would want his boss to owe him. John's moral reasoning is in which of Kohlberg's stages?
    a. social-contract legalistic
    b. universal ethical principle
    c. law and order
    d. instrumental relativist
    e. punishment and obedience

Correct _____ If wrong, why? _____

12. A weakness of Kohlberg's theory is:
    a. people often go back to earlier stages
    b. high-level moral reasoning does not necessarily go with moral behavior
    c. people progress through the stages in very different orders
    d. the differences between men's and women's moral reasoning are very great
    e. it emphasizes a "caring" approach to moral reasoning too heavily

Correct _____ If wrong, why? _____

**Social and Emotional Development**

13. An investigator wished to study the relationship between intelligence and age in adults. She started
    with a group of 40 20-year-olds and tested their intelligence. She (and later her students) continued
    to test this group every 5 years for the next 60 years. What type of study is this?
    a. longitudinal
    b. cohort
    c. cross-sectional
    d. a combination of longitudinal and cross-sectional

Correct _____ If wrong, why? _____

14. Perplexity is 16 years old. She is trying to decide whether she wishes to apply herself in school so
    that she can enter medical school or whether she wants to have fun in school and not bother about a
    career. Perplexity is in which of Erikson's stages?
    a. ego integrity vs. despair
    b. generativity vs. stagnation
    c. intimacy vs. isolation
    d. industry vs. inferiority
    e. identity vs. role confusion

Correct _____ If wrong, why? _____

15. Harlow reared infant monkeys with various types of artificial mothers. Which of the following is
    true?
    a. as long as the mother provided contact comfort, the infants developed normal sexual and social
       behavior
    b. infants spent more time clinging to a cloth mother, whether or not it provided nourishment
    c. infants developed a strong attachment to whichever mother provided nourishment
    d. infants who did not have a real mother were irreversibly harmed socially and sexually

Correct _____ If wrong, why? _____

16. An authoritarian parenting style is associated with:
    a. withdrawn children
    b. children who have a lack of self-control
    c. children who are socially cooperative
    d. withdrawn or assertive children depending upon the ethnic group
    e. African-American children doing well in school; European-American children doing poorly

Correct _____ If wrong, why? _____

17. Controversial children are those who are:
    a. popular with other children, but not with parents
    b. avoided by other children
    c. popular when young, but become rejected when they get older
    d. liked by some children, but rejected by others

Correct _____ If wrong, why? _____

18. Nick seems to be a different person at different times. Two months ago, he was a very serious
    student who wanted to become a lawyer. Now, he is a party-goer who couldn't care less about any
    career. Nick is showing:
    a. identity foreclosure
    b. identity achievement
    c. role diffusion
    d. a solution to his identity crisis

Correct _____ If wrong, why? _____

19. When both parents work,
    a. the more time the father spends with the child, the more he loves the mother
    b. the more time the father spends with the child, the less he loves the mother
    c. they seem to have more time for recreation and romance than when only one works
    d. women today are less likely to interrupt their careers than women in the 60s

Correct _____ If wrong, why? _____

20. Job satisfaction:
    a. generally decreases the longer one has worked at a job
    b. is high if people are asked if they are satisfied with their job, but lower if they are asked if they
       would seek the same job again
    c. is high if people are asked if they would seek the same job again, but lower if people are asked if
       they are satisfied with their job
    d. is unrelated to how satisfied people are with their life
    e. increases during the midlife transition

Correct _____ If wrong, why? _____

21. A dying person promises to leave all of his money to a worthwhile charity if God will save him.
    According to Kubler-Ross, he is in what stage?
    a. depression
    b. acceptance
    c. denial
    d. bargaining
    e. anger

Correct _____ If wrong, why? _____

**Growing Up the Same and Different**

22. Differences in temperament that exist in infancy are:
    a. largely gone by the time a child is 7
    b. due to the environment; genetics plays no role
    c. unrelated to measures of fear tested a few months later
    d. fairly consistent through childhood

Correct _____ If wrong, why? _____

23. Following divorce:
    a. almost all children act depressed for more than 5 years
    b. girls have more adjustment problems than boys, particularly if they live with their mother
    c. adjustment is best if children live with the opposite-sex parent
    d. African-American children have more adjustment problems than European-American children
    e. boys become aggressive toward other children

Correct _____ If wrong, why? _____

24. Gender roles are:
    a. gradually disappearing in today's society
    b. mostly defined by biology
    c. often learned from other children
    d. almost entirely learned from parents

Correct _____ If wrong, why? _____

## ANSWERS AND EXPLANATIONS FOR COMPREHENSION CHECK

| Correct Answer | Other Alternatives Are Wrong Because: |
|---|---|
| 1. d (pp. 402-403)<br>Obj. I-A | a. probably not, because when twins are compared in the same environment the low-birth-weight twin usually catches up to the higher-birth-weight one<br>b. true, but this isn't necessarily the cause of the poor development later<br>c. true, but mother's marital status per se doesn't cause the later problems |
| 2. c (pp. 404-405)<br>Obj. II-A | a. very young infants also look at human faces<br>b. both spend more time looking at more complex forms<br>d. they shift attention less; even later, infants may shift attention, but they move back to the original stimulus |
| 3. d (p. 406, Fig. 10.9)<br>Obj. II-C | a. infants can discriminate speech sounds<br>b. new sounds are novel and infants increase their sucking rate<br>c. infants do discriminate between "pa" and "ba" |
| 4. d (pp. 408-409)<br>Obj. III-A-B | a. Piaget's explanation; could be correct, but so could b or c<br>b. possibly correct, but so are a and c<br>c. possibly correct, but so are a and b |

5. b (p. 411)
   Obj. IV-A

a. an old schema was applied here because she sucked in exactly the same way; accommodation involves modifying an old schema
c. an infant is in the sensorimotor stage
d. an old schema, sucking, was used

6. a (p. 412)
   Obj. IV-B-1-a

b. this shows that they don't understand that it is themselves in the mirror; no concept of self
c. shows they understand other people's knowledge; not evidence for concept of self; 4-year old not in first stage of development
d. an example of egocentric thought

7. d (pp. 415-416,
   Table 10.1)
   Obj. IV-B-2-d

a. if so, she should know they are the same
b. if so, she shouldn't be able to talk
c. she would show conservation at this age
e. she is not showing con<u>serv</u>ation (notice the term is not con<u>vers</u>ation)

8. d (p. 418)
   Obj. IV-C

a. shows that the distinction is less certain; children appear to be in one stage on one task, but in the next stage on another task
b. the shift appears to be more gradual
c. Piaget's belief; this contradicts it; child shows thought patterns from both stages at same time
e. both a and b are wrong; they are Piaget's beliefs, which these results contradict

9. b (pp. 421-422)
   Obj. V-A-2

a. rules are learned before this
c. children learn rules without explicit teaching
d. no teaching is necessary in any culture

10. d (pp. 420-421)
    Obj. V-A-1

a. they just seem to apply words to specific objects, not related objects
b. they distinguish positive and negative, although they may create negatives incorrectly
c. single words can convey a great deal of meaning

11. d (p. 424, Table 10.6)
    Obj. VI-A

a. he's not arguing that it's best for society
b. he's not thinking about highest ethical principles
c. he's not doing it because it is the law
e. there are no immediate consequences

12. b (pp. 425-427)
    Obj. VI-B-1

a. people usually do not go back
c. people progress in the same order
d. there are some sex differences, but they are not great
e. Kohlberg's levels are based on a "justice" orientation

13. a (pp. 429-430,
    Table 10.8)
    Obj. VII-B

b. cohort effects refer to similarities in environment while growing up; occur with cross-sectional studies
c. would have tested different-age people all at once
d. purely longitudinal; same people tested many times

14. e  (p. 432, Table 10.9)
    Obj. VIII-E

a. during old age
b. during middle age
c. during young adulthood; she's only 14
d. during preadolescent years

15. b  (pp. 433-434)
    Obj. IX-A

a. neither male nor female isolates showed appropriate sexual
   behavior; females became poor mothers
c. nourishment was much less important than the contact comfort
   provided by the cloth mothers
d. infants raised with artificial mothers were fairly normal if they played
   with other infants

16. d  (p. 435)
    Obj. X-A

a. related to authoritarian European-American parents, but not
   African-American parents; d is a better answer
b. related to a permissive parenting style
c. related to an <u>authoritative</u> parenting style
e. related to an <u>authoritative</u> parenting style; it's European-American
   children who are likely to do well in school

17. d  (p. 436)
    Obj. XI-A

a. definitions refer to children's liking, not parents'
b. these are called "rejected" children
c. status tends to be fairly consistent from year to year

18. c  (p. 438)
    Obj. XII-A

a. child passively accepts role defined by parents; Nick doesn't
   have a stable role
b. deliberate decision about values, goals, and place in society; Nick
   hasn't found an identity yet
d. the crisis has not been solved yet

19. b  (p. 440)
    Obj. XIII-B-1

a. it's the opposite; more time with the child means less love for
   the mother
c. when both parents work, there is little time for recreation and
   romance
d. career opportunities weren't interrupted much then because there
   weren't many career opportunities for women

20. b  (p. 441)
    Obj. XIV-A

a. new employees are less satisfied than older ones
c. is high if asked about satisfaction, lower if asked about taking
   the same job again
d. people who are satisfied with their life are usually satisfied with their
   job and vice versa
e. tie when person learns that goals won't be met; not likely to increase
   job satisfaction

21. d  (pp. 443-444,
    Table 10.11)
    Obj. XVI-A

a. people lose hope in this phase
b. psychologically ready to die
c. people deny that death will occur
e. people grow abusive and ask "Why me?"

22. d (p. 446)
   Obj. XVII
   a. differences are still there at 7 1/2
   b. monozygotic twins are more similar than dizygotic, so genetics plays a role
   c. more difficult infants were more afraid later

23. e (p. 449)
   Obj. XVIII-C
   a. some did, but many felt better after a year or two
   b. boys had more problems
   c. generally better with same-sex parent
   d. it's the opposite; European-American children seem to have more problems

24. c (p. 453)
   Obj. XIX-B-1
   a. may be changing, but differences are still there
   b. a few aspects are, but most aren't biological
   d. also role models, television, other children

## LECTURE MATERIAL

Don't forget to review your lecture material. Process each topic meaningfully. First, be sure that you understand the material in each lecture--if you don't, ask your instructor or teaching assistant. Associate the material with things that you already know and with your personal experiences. If you can make up mental images of any of the material, do so. Try to think of real-life applications of the concepts. Write your own notes on your lecture notes. Then write questions to cover each concept.

------------------------------------------------------------------------------

WAIT AT LEAST 24 HOURS BEFORE PROCEEDING.
LET FORGETTING OCCUR--IT WILL!!

------------------------------------------------------------------------------

## SHORT-ANSWER ESSAY QUESTIONS

Write brief answers to each of the following. The answers are on pp. 208-210, but do try to write the answers yourself before looking at them.

### Early Development

1. Describe the relationship between low birth weight and later development.

2. For many years, it was thought that newborn infants could not learn. Describe some evidence that shows that infants can learn.

### Development of Thinking and Reasoning

3. Explain what Piaget meant by the terms "assimilation" and "accommodation."

4. Describe how a child in the concrete operations and a child in the formal operations stage would decide which two colors of paint would make a certain shade of brown.

5. Briefly describe the course of language development in children.

6. Describe what happens when children aren't exposed to any language at all.

7. Briefly describe Kohlberg's theory of moral development.

**Social and Emotional Development**

8. Explain how Harlow's studies with infant monkeys might be relevant to studies with human infants.

9. Discuss the "personal fable" of teenagers.

10. Describe the conditions under which people will open up to each other.

11. Describe the midlife transition.

12. Discuss how people adjust to retirement.

**Growing Up the Same and Different**

13. Briefly, describe the effects of a working mother and day care on the development of children.

14. Describe the situations in which sex differences are most likely to occur.

\*\*\*\*\*\*\*\*\*\*\*\*\*\*\*\*\*\*\*\*\*\*\*\*\*\*\*\*\*\*\*\*\*\*\*\*\*\*\*\*\*\*\*\*\*\*\*\*\*\*\*\*\*\*\*\*\*\*\*\*\*\*\*\*\*\*\*\*\*\*\*\*\*\*\*\*
Find the questions that you wrote over lecture material and write answers to them.
\*\*\*\*\*\*\*\*\*\*\*\*\*\*\*\*\*\*\*\*\*\*\*\*\*\*\*\*\*\*\*\*\*\*\*\*\*\*\*\*\*\*\*\*\*\*\*\*\*\*\*\*\*\*\*\*\*\*\*\*\*\*\*\*\*\*\*\*\*\*\*\*\*\*\*\*

## ANSWERS TO SHORT-ANSWER ESSAY QUESTIONS

1. Children who are born with low birth weight tend to have lower academic achievement and behavior problems later in life. This does not mean the low birth weight causes these problems, however. The postnatal environments of low birth weight children are often not very good. When twins who vary in birth weight are compared, the twin with low birth weight tends to catch up to the heavier twin, suggesting that low birth weight per se may not be the cause of later problems. (pp. 402-403)

2. Infants were rewarded with sugar water if they turned their head in the direction of a tickle on the cheek following a specific sound. They were not rewarded if they turned their head following a second sound. Newborns learned to turn their head more often in response to the sound that was paired with reward. (pp. 406-407)

3. Children try to use old ways of behaving in new situations. In Piaget's terms, they assimilate objects to a specific schema (an organized way of interacting with the world). Sometimes these old ways don't quite work, so they need to modify their behavior in order to interact with a new object. This modification of a schema is called accommodation. (p. 411)

4. The concrete operations child would haphazardly select two colors and mix them. This child might try some combinations twice and never try other combinations. The formal operations child would test pairs of colors systematically--mix #1 with #2, #3, #4, #5, #6, #7, and #8.Then she would mix #2 with #3, #4, #5, #6, #7, and #8. This systematic process would be continued until the correct combination was found. (pp. 416-417)

5. Children first babble; that is, produce sounds. By age 1 1/2, they begin     to speak in one-word sentences. Next, two-word phrases are used. (Some children go directly from babbling to producing

compressed phrases.) By age 2 1/2 to 3, children are speaking in sentences and learning grammatical rules, which they sometimes overuse, such as saying "foots" instead of "feet." By age 4, language is fairly well mastered although vocabulary is limited and some errors still occur. (pp. 420-422, Table 10.4)

6. Deaf children are sometimes not exposed to language. These children make up their own sign language. As they grow older, they often link signs together and use a consistent sign order. Most children teach their system or part of their system to one or both parents. (p. 422)

7. As children grow older, their moral reasoning becomes less related to immediate rewards and punishments and more related to abstract principles. There are six stages, with the highest level of morality based on ethical principles such as a respect for human life and justice. Kohlberg argues that these changes occur because the child becomes more and more able to reason abstractly. (pp. 423-424, Table 10.6)

8. Many orphanages in the early 1900s kept infants in cribs with almost no contact with caretakers or with other infants. A large percentage of these infants died, and those that survived were retarded in physical growth and mental development. They also were socially inept and had difficulty in getting along with their peers. Harlow's studies suggest that these effects may have been due to a lack of contact comfort and to social isolation. (pp. 433-435)

9. Teenagers are likely to believe that they are special and that bad things only happen to other people, not to them. This has been called the "personal fable"; it may lead to risky behaviors such as having sex without contraceptives. (pp. 438-439)

10. Dating couples open up very gradually and may never discuss important family issues until they decide to marry. Even couples who are happily married don't always "bare their souls" to each other, but couples who are having difficulty often do. In situations where there is nothing to lose, such as talking with a stranger on a train or plane, people are more likely to open up than in situations where there is more to lose. (p. 439)

11. People realize that they may never be able to meet some of the goals that they have not yet met. Illusions are discarded and people may become discontented. They may accept this and channel their energies into things they can accomplish or they may change their routine and modify their lives. Others may become depressed and turn to alcohol as a means of escape. (pp. 441-442)

12. People who had activities and interests outside of work adjust better than people without such outside interests. There is often a period immediately after retirement when people enjoy doing things they never had time for before. They may soon realize that they can't achieve all of their goals, and may set more realistic goals. Older people need to feel that they have control of their lives, even if their health begins to deteriorate. (pp. 442-443)

13. Mothers who enjoy working and do so because they want to are better parents than mothers who work because they have to and who resent it. If the child receives indifferent or unstable day care, he or she will probably be insecure. Children who spend much of the first year of life in day care may be "bossy," not obedient to their mothers, and somewhat aggressive. However, they also develop social skills and self-confidence in dealing with other children. (p. 447-448)

14. Important differences between males and females emerge in social situations. Boys compete with each other, whereas girls tend to cooperate. Boys exchange insults and make threats and boasts. Girls exchange compliments and make suggestions rather than demands. (pp. 451-452)

## POSTTEST

Take this test with all of your books and notes out of sight. This should give you a good idea of how well you understand the material.

### Matching

Write the letter of the term on the right in the blank beside the description on the left.

<u>Social and Emotional Development</u>

1. _____ awareness that decisions about life must soon be made

2. _____ awareness that many goals will never be reached

3. _____ trying out a number of different ways of living

4. _____ deliberate decisions about values, goals, and place in society

5. _____ passive acceptance of a role defined by one's parents

6. _____ belief that one is special; bad things only happen to other people

A. identity achievement

B. midlife transition

C. identity crisis

D. personal fable

E. identity foreclosure

F. role diffusion

### Multiple-choice

Circle the best alternative.

<u>Early Development</u>

1. Infants with low birth weight:
   a. may catch up in development to infants with higher birth weights if they experience similar environments
   b. have irreversible brain damage
   c. tend to be overachievers; have higher academic achievement than higher-birth-weight counterparts
   d. usually have environments that are similar to infants with higher birth weights
   e. have a lower risk of dying that heavier infants

2. Infants tend to shift their attention:
   a. much more often than adults; they have very low attention spans
   b. away from faces and other complex objects
   c. away from familiar things like their mother's voice
   d. toward objects that were previously seen and are now covered
   e. back toward objects they saw before

3. A toy is hidden several times on the left side of an 10-month-old infant, and she finds it there. If the toy is then hidden on the right, the infant will:
   a. continue looking on the left because she forgets where the object is hidden
   b. continue looking on the left because of a motor habit
   c. look on the right because infants frequently shift attention
   d. look on the right because infants know that hidden objects remain in their places
   e. continue to look on the left, but the exact reason is difficult to determine

## Development of Thinking and Reasoning

4. Which of the following is an example of egocentric thought, as Piaget described it?
   a. Johnny argues that his sister should not touch his toys
   b. Michael draws a pile of blocks as he sees them, even when ask to draw how they would look from your side
   c. Diane looks for the candy under the cup indicated by an "informed" adult
   d. Susie grasps at the new puppy and tries to shake him like a rattle
   e. Jamie doesn't hunt for Easter eggs because he assumes that hidden objects are gone

5. Susie in 4d above is showing:
   a. a lack of conservation
   b. assimilation
   c. concrete operational thought
   d. object permanence
   e. an inability to accommodate

6. A child in the formal operations stage can do which of the following that cannot be done by a child in the concrete operations stage?
   a. show conservation
   b. have the concept of object permanence
   c. be able to assimilate
   d. solve problems systematically
   e. distinguish between "pa" and "ba"

7. Piaget argued that children in the preoperational stage fail conservation tasks because they lack the necessary mental processes. More recent research has shown that:
   a. children understand relevant concepts; they just can't apply them to more complex tasks
   b. children who can show conservation of number with a few items fail when the number is increased
   c. giving children water to pour and balls of clay to squash speeds up their understanding of conservation
   d. Piaget overestimated the abilities of young children
   e. young children can easily deal with abstract conservation concepts, if they are presented properly

8. Why is the word "Mama" used so universally?
   a. "muh" is one of the first sounds uttered by infants
   b. most languages developed from a similar ancient language
   c. "muh" is the only sound that infants can utter until they are about a year old
   d. a natural adult response to an infant is to utter "muh" and infants imitate it

9. Children learn grammatical rules:
   a. because their parents correct their faulty grammar
   b. entirely by imitating adults
   c. without any predetermined assumptions
   d. in elementary school through explicit teaching
   e. by age 2 1/2 to 3, although they apply them too generally

10. The military overthrows a dictator because he gives rights to a minority and the law states that they have no rights. The military's moral reasoning is probably at what level?
    a. law and order
    b. punishment and obedience
    c. social contract
    d. interpersonal concordance
    e. universal principles

11. A weakness of Kohlberg's theory is that:
    a. people seem to progress through the stages in the same order
    b. people usually don't go back to earlier stages
    c. in societies throughout the world, people begin at Kohlberg's first stage
    d. differences between males and females are not great
    e. criminals often show high-level moral reasoning, but their behavior is not moral

Social and Emotional Development

12. Today's 20-year olds score higher on an IQ test than today's 60-year olds. To say that this is due to a cohort effect means that:
    a. IQ declines with age
    b. the groups of 60-year olds is a dull group and the 20-year olds are a bright group
    c. the effects are due to the longitudinal design
    d. there is a correlation, but cause cannot be determined
    e. the effects may be due to health and education differences while the groups were growing up

13. Michael is 21 and he is trying to decide whether to marry now or wait until he has finished graduate school. He is in which of Erikson's stages?
    a. intimacy vs. isolation
    b. identity vs. role diffusion
    c. ego integrity vs. despair
    d. generativity vs. stagnation
    e. identity foreclosure vs. identity achievement

14. When monkeys who had been reared with artificial mothers became mothers, they:
    a. were normal
    b. were overly attached to their infants and did not let them develop much independence
    c. were "super-moms," even better than normally reared mothers
    d. constantly clung to their infants, apparently trying to make up for the lack of contact in their own infancy
    e. they rejected their infants

15. Authoritative parents tend to have children who:
    a. lack a sense of social responsibility
    b. get mixed reactions from their peers, liked by some but rejected by others
    c. show self-reliance and self-control
    d. are withdrawn
    e. have serious identity crises

16. Adolescent outbursts of vandalism and delinquency:
    a. occur in all cultures
    b. are most common in teens who undergo identity foreclosure
    c. can be reduced by programs that discourage delinquent behavior
    d. occur only for teenagers who believe strongly in the personal fable
    e. are most common at age 16

17. J. Q. Med has just turned 40. He decides that his life isn't going anywhere. He has always wanted to sail around the world so he quits his job, buys a boat and takes off. J. Q. has experienced:
    a. a "honeymoon period"
    b. a failure in gender role identity
    c. an autonomy vs. shame and doubt crisis
    d. midlife transition
    e. an ego integrity vs. despair crisis

18. The "honeymoon period" of retirement refers to:
    a. the last few years before death, when marriage becomes more meaningful
    b. the desire of retirees to have close family ties
    c. the period following the loss of a spouse
    d. the period immediately following retirement in which the retiree tries to do all the things that he or she hasn't had time for
    e. the period early in retirement when both spouses are still living

19. M. N. has been told that he is dying of cancer. He becomes very abusive toward the doctor and the nurses. He is in which of Kubler-Ross's stages of death?
    a. bargaining
    b. acceptance
    c. depression
    d. denial
    e. anger

Growing Up the Same and Different

20. In which situation will the child of a working mother probably develop most normally?
    a. the mother works because she has to and she dislikes her job
    b. the child goes to a large day-care center where the staff is unstable
    c. the parents have just been divorced and the mother goes to work for the first time
    d. the mother likes her job and the child goes to a day-care center that is reasonably good
    e. none of the above; children of working mothers almost never develop normally

21. Gender roles:
    a. are entirely biologically based
    b. are learned, although some aspects have biological bases
    c. are learned entirely from parents and other adults who visit the home
    d. do not exist in most societies

22. If an immigrant to the United States is able to alternate between his native culture and that of the United States, he is showing:
    a. biculturalism
    b. total assimilation
    c. bilingualism
    d. difficulty with acculturation
    e. gender role identity

## ANSWERS TO POSTTEST

| Correct Answer | Questions Testing a Similar Concept | |
| --- | --- | --- |
| | Comprehension Check | Short-Answer |

**Matching**

| | | |
| --- | --- | --- |
| 1. C (pp. 437-438) | 18d | -- |
| 2. B (pp. 441-442) | 20e | 11 |
| 3. F (p. 438) | 18 | -- |
| 4. A (p. 438) | 18b | -- |
| 5. E (pp. 437-438) | 18a | -- |
| 6. D (pp. 438-439) | -- | 9 |

**Multiple-choice**

| | | |
| --- | --- | --- |
| 1. a (pp. 402-403) | 1 | 1 |
| 2. e (p. 405) | 2 | -- |
| 3. e (pp. 408-409) | 4 | -- |
| 4. b (p. 413) | -- | -- |
| 5. b (p. 411) | 5b | 3 |
| 6. d (pp. 416-417) | 7a,7c | 4 |
| 7. a (pp. 415-416) | 8 | -- |
| 8. a (p. 420) | -- | -- |
| 9. e (pp. 421-422) | 9,10 | 5 |
| 10. a (pp. 423-424, Table 10.6) | 11 | 7 |
| 11. e (pp. 430-431) | 12 | 7 |
| 12. e (pp. 430-431) | 13b | -- |
| 13. a (pp. 432-433, Table 10.9) | 14c | -- |
| 14. e (p. 435) | 15 | 8 |
| 15. c (p. 435) | 16 | -- |
| 16. e (p. 437, Fig. 10.30) | -- | -- |
| 17. d (pp. 441-442) | 20e | 11 |
| 18. d (pp. 442-443) | -- | -- |
| 19. e (p. 443, Table 1.11, p. 444) | 21 | -- |
| 20. d (p. 448) | -- | 13 |
| 21. b (pp. 452-453) | 24 | 14 |
| 22. a (p. 456) | -- | -- |

# CHAPTER 10 LANGUAGE ENHANCEMENT GUIDE

## I. VOCABULARY, IDIOMS AND CULTURAL CONCEPTS

**Instructions:**

As you read the text refer to the following list of words and their definitions. The words are listed in the order in which they appear in the chapter. The definitions presented contain the meaning of the word as used by Kalat on the textbook page indicated.

Remember that these words like all words can have different meanings in other sentences. If you do not find a non-technical word on this list it may have been defined on a previous page or chapter of this study guide. The definition of non-technical words may be found in the dictionary at the end of this study guide. Kalat defined each new technical word as it first appears on a page and these may be found in Kalat's summary at the end of the section and in the Glossary at the end the textbook.

### The Study of Early Development

overall  (401) = total
miscellaneous = made of many different characteristics or parts
devising = developing, inventing

tempted (402) = to be invited to do or believe something that is wrong, not correct
vertebrate = animals with a back bone
embryo =  an organism at any time before it is born or hatched
impaired = damaged
apparently = clearly  or obviously
seizures = sudden attacks, spasms, or convulsions
hyperactivity = behavior characterized by constant overactivity and sometimes difficulty paying
      attention or concentrating

apparently obvious (403) = easy to recognize
in short = in conclusion
not insurmountable = not  impossible to overcome
fetus = an unborn child from the end of the eighth week after conception to the moment of birth

remarkable (404) = worthy of notice
occasional =  periodic, occurring from time to time
impoverished = very poor
overcomes all odds = a successful outcome that is not expected; the occurrence of  a low probability
      event
maturation = the physical growth of the body and nervous system
haphazard ways = random ways
culminating = reaching the highest  or final level of development
insensitive to = not aware of

gaze back (405) = look back
may check = may look at
unable to inhibit = cannot prevent
immaturity of a path = lack of neural development

extensive = a lot of, much, a large  amount
coordination = harmonious activity of a  group of muscles in completing a movement
confined =  isolated, imprisoned

coordination (406) = a balanced combining of muscles to carry out movements
it might seem = it looks.  appears
aroused = excited, awake from sleep

## The Development of Thinking and Reasoning

profound (410)=  thoughtful; with many implications
rousing = something that produces enthusiasm or excitement
fascinating = very interested
mischievously = causing trouble

not merely  (411) = not just
until you hit on = find

approximate (412) = almost exact or correct, very close

perspective (413) = point of view

transition is not sharp (416) = the change is gradual

sophisticated abilities (417)  = complex and more adult-like abilities
bound to succeed = are likely to succeed
reverts to = goes back to

distinct (418) = easy to see differences between different things
revolutionary reorganization = a major change in organization

babbling (420) = sounds made by a baby
haphazard = occurring by chance

utterances (421) = spoken words
poorly articulated = poorly pronounced,  speech that is difficult to understand
imitative = copied
peculiarities = unusual characteristics
by the same token = in the same way

morality (moral)  (423) = social rules that are used to guide and judge behavior
analogous to = similar to
concede = acknowledge, accept
dilemma = a situation that requires a choice between two or more equally unfavorable or favorable
     alternatives
respondent = the person who  answers question

military junta (425) = a group of military officers ruling a country after overthrowing the government and taking power

progression = a movement from one step to the next on a continuous series or sequence

ultimate authority = final authority

## Social and Emotional Development

contestant (429) = a person taking part in a contest

overriding concern = a major problem, a major cause for anxiety or worry

face certain obvious = has easy to identify problems

practical difficulties = problems that occur when something is used

to make matters worse = to produce more problems

broaden their horizons (432) = to look for new experiences and challenges

makes a big mess = gets dirty

fantasize = imagine

plagued with = upset or disturbed with

artificial (433) = made by human beings rather than being natural

cling to = hold on to

woefully inadequate = very inadequate

merely = only

rear children (435) = bring up

tentatively = not fully worked out, not final

impose = to establish, apply, require

elicit = bring or draw out; produce

withdrawn = quiet, shy

assertive = outgoing, demanding

aggressive streak (436) = behaving aggressively from time to time

alleged = claimed as true without adequate evidence

disruptive (437) = to throw into confusion or disorder, to upset; to stop progress

delinquency = breaking the law or not doing what the law requires

reluctant (439) = not willing

to reveal themselves = to tell others about personal feelings and experiences

give-and-take process = sharing, each person makes a contribution

job discrimination (440) = not being given a job because of ones gender, age, race or ethnic identity

contemplate = think about, consider

reconcile (441) = to bring oneself to accept

plenty of time = enough time, lots of time

deteriorate (442) = weaken and grow worse

honeymoon period = a harmonious period in a relationship; a holiday or trip taken by a newly married couple

reborn hopes = renewed hopes

degrading = reducing in worth, moral, dignity or value
prospects = opportunities
fatal disease = an illness that lead to death

## Growing Up the Same and Different

unique (446) = being the only one of its kind; the only one in a particular category

inhibited (447) = to suppress or hold back a behavior, feeling, an impulse consciously or unconsciously

reasonably good (448) = adequate
dealing with = interacting with
so "right" = almost perfect
emerge = show up; to come out

endure prolonged conflict (449) = suffer conflict for a long time
upheaval = a sudden, violent change, disruption or upset
resorted to = started to
pouting = sticking the lips out to express unhappiness
exasperated = to become very angry, impatient and annoyed

overstated (451) = to claim more than the evidence justifies; exaggerated

episode (452) = an event that is part of a larger sequence of events
channels = directs

arbitrary (453) = determined by chance, or impulse, and not by reason, or principle; based on personal judgment or preference

## II. VOCABULARY BUILDING

### Word Analysis

In each of the past chapters the prefixes and suffixes used in each exercise were listed along with their meanings. Starting in this chapter you will be asked to analyze each term from memory. If you have any difficulty in remembering you can look up the terms in Appendix B that alphabetically lists and defines each prefix and suffix.

Instructions: (Note the new instructions.)

1. Break each word in the table into its prefixes, roots and suffixes. If you do not remember the meaning of a term look it up in Appendix B.
2. Guess the meaning of the word based on the meaning of its parts.
3. Find the word on the text page indicated in the brackets and redefine the word based on the context of the sentence, paragraph and chapter.
5. Look up the definition of the word in the VOCABULARY, IDIOMS AND CULTURAL CONCEPTS section above, in Appendix A (marked A) or in a college level dictionary. If the word is followed by letter G look it up in the text Glossary.

The following words  selected from this chapter  have prefixes and suffixes that have been covered in previous chapters.  How many can you define?

| Word | Meaning |
|---|---|
| aggressive (A) | |
| aggression | |
| aggressively | |
| assertive (A) | |
| autonomous (A) | |
| disruptive (A) | |
| generativity  (G) | |
| habituate (A) | |
| hyperactivity (G) | |
| implicate | |
| implication | |
| initiative (G) | |

Exercise 2. Review

The following words,  selected from this chapter,  have prefixes and suffixes that have been covered in previous chapters.  How many can you define?

| Word | Meaning |
|---|---|
| insensitive (A) | |
| insurmountable(A) | |
| mischievously (A) | |
| perspective (A) | |
| progression (A) | |
| prenatal (G) | |
| review | |

## III. STRUCTURAL CLUES:  PUNCTUATION

Skill in recognizing the uses of punctuation in a text can help you understand what you read. You should be familiar with a variety of punctuation types such as quotes, colons, semicolons, and commas.

Quotes have two uses in your text:

1.  To indicate direct speech.

Example:  The night after Tommy Smith's suicide, he (Jerry) told his mother, "I can't understand how anyone would commit suicide--that was the coward's way."

2.  To emphasize a special name or way of referring to something.

Example: As soon as the passion dies and the intimacy fades, the individuals no longer feel "in love" and go their separate ways.

Colons have two uses in your text:

1. To introduce lists.

Example: One such approach is Robert Sternberg's (1986) triangular theory of love, which divides love into three components: passion, intimacy, and commitment.

2. To introduce an idea that illustrates, clarifies, or gives further information on the preceding one. In this text, semi-colons have a similar use.

Example (colon): Researchers are no longer searching for what should occur (great emotional problems) but rather are studying what actually occurs: how adolescents change, adapt, and grow.

Example (semi-colon): Adolescence is a developmental period lasting from about ages 12 to 18 that marks the end of childhood and the beginning of adulthood; it is a transitional period of considerable biological, cognitive and social changes.

Commas separate a series of items.

Example: These individuals do well in school, develop rewarding friendships, and participate in social activities.

Practice using your knowledge of punctuation. First, read each of the following questions about material in your text. Locate the material in your text, and skim to find the punctuation clue.

1. What was Jerry's nickname (quotes)

2. What does Katherine Hepburn say about women's brains? (quotes)

3. According to the traditional view of gender roles, why does someone rated high on one pole of the continuum have to be low on the other? (colon)

4. What are the secrets of the Russians, Pakistanis, and Ecuadorians who tend to live to 100? (serial comma)

5. What is intimacy, and how does it develop? (semicolon)

As you read pay attention to the punctuation as part of your effort to be an active reader who processes the material deeply. As you learned in the memory chapter, the deeper you process the more you will remember and the greater the accuracy of your recall.

# CHAPTER 11  MOTIVATION

## OBJECTIVES
Understand that:

### General Principles of Motivation

I. There are many different types of definitions of motivation  (p. 461, Table 11.1, p. 465)
  A. Freud and Lorenz believed that instinctive energy compels behavior  (pp. 461-462)
  B. Drive-reduction theories propose that motivation is an internal state or irritation that energizes behavior  (p. 462)
    1. Homeostasis is the maintenance of biological conditions at an optimum level  (pp. 462-463)
  C. Incentive theories propose that incentives pull organisms  (p. 463)
    1. Intrinsic motivation involves engaging in a behavior for its own sake; extrinsic motivation includes rewards and punishments  (pp. 463-464)
II. People have many different types of motives  (p. 465)
  A. Primary motivations result from biological needs; secondary motivations result from learning  (pp. 465-466)
  B. Maslow proposed that motivations are arranged in a hierarchy of needs  (pp. 466-467, Fig. 11.3)
III. Motivated behaviors are goal-directed  (pp. 467-468)

### Motivation and Biological States:  The Case of Hunger

IV. Hunger is partly controlled by physiological mechanisms  (pp. 470-471)
  A. Hunger is controlled in the short run by glucose in blood stream  (p. 471, Fig. 11.6, p. 472)
    1. Insulin promotes movement of nutrients out of the bloodstream into cells  (p. 471)
      a. If insulin is low, as in diabetes, nutrients enter cells very slowly  (p. 471)
    2. Glucagon converts stored energy back into blood glucose  (p. 471)
      a. If insulin is consistently high, glucagon can't move glucose back into the bloodstream  (pp. 471-472)
  B. Satiety  (a full feeling) is controlled by stomach distention  (pp. 472-473)
  C. In the long run, the brain controls weight at a given set point  (pp. 473-474, Fig. 11.3)
V. Hypothalamus is important in regulating weight  (p. 474, Fig. 11.10)
  A. Lateral hypothalamus is critical for starting meals  (p. 474)
    1. Damage results in difficulty in digestion  (p. 474)
  B. Ventromedial hypothalamus controls the speed of digestion and insulin secretion  (p. 474)
    1. Damage results in rapid digestion and weight gain  (p. 474)
  C. Paraventricular hypothalamus is important for sensing stomach distention  (p. 474)
VI. Food selection depends upon physiological, social, and cognitive factors  (pp. 474-475)
  A. Some taste preferences are biologically based  (p. 475)
  B. People prefer familiar tastes  (pp. 475-476)
  C. Taste aversions develop to foods that preceded illness and to foods that evoke repulsive associations  (p. 476)
VII. Eating disorders occur when motivational mechanisms go awry  (p. 476)
  A. Obesity is an excessive accumulation of body fat  (p. 476)
  B. People sometimes overeat in response to emotional problems  (pp. 476-477)
      a. This probably isn't a cause of obesity  (p. 477)
  C. Genetics are involved in obesity  (pp. 477-478)
  D. Overweight people may expend less energy  (p. 478)

E. The best way to lose weight is to eat less  (p. 478)
   1. Increasing energy expenditure helps too  (p. 478)
F. Normal weight people  (especially women) often diet to become thinner  (pp. 478-479)
   1. People who are dieting may eat more after breaking their diets  (pp. 479-480, Fig. 11.18)
G. Anorexia nervosa involves steady weight loss  (pp. 480-481)
H. Bulimia involves eating binges  (pp. 482-483)
I. Motivations are controlled by a complex mixture of physiological, social, and cognitive forces  (p. 483)

**Sexual Motivation**

VIII. Sexual motivation depends upon physiological drive and incentives  (p. 485)
   A. Human sexual behavior shows great variability  (p. 486)
      1. People think that excessive means "more than they do"  (p. 486)
   B. Human sexual behavior varies across cultures  (p. 489)
   C. Sexual customs have changed over the years  (p. 488)
   D. AIDS has made couples more cautious in their sexual behavior  (pp. 489, 491)
IX. Sexual arousal involves four physiological stages  (pp. 492-493, Fig. 11.28)
X. Sexual orientation is a preference for male or female partners  (p. 493)
   A. The number of homosexuals is difficult to determine  (pp. 488, 494)
   B. Many homosexuals are well adjusted and content  (p. 494)
   C. A section of the anterior hypothalamus is smaller in homosexual men  (pp. 495-496)
XI. Rape is sexual contact obtained through violence, threat, or intimidation  (p. 496)
   A. In college, many rapes are date rapes  (pp. 496-497)
   B. Convicted rapists have a history of hostility and violence  (p. 497)

**Achievement Motivation**

XII. Need for achievement is striving for competitive success and excellence  (p. 500)
   A. The Thematic Apperception Test  (TAT) has been used to measure this  (pp. 501-502)
   B. People with a high need for achievement set moderately difficult goals  (p. 502)
      1. People dominated by fear of failure prefer very easy and very difficult tasks  (p. 502)
   C. High, realistic goals are the best motivators  (pp. 502-503)
XIII. Need for achievement varies with age and sex  (pp. 503-505)
   A. Preschool children don't show distress at failure  (p. 504)
   B. Women sometimes score lower on need for achievement than men  (pp. 504-505)
XIV. Need for achievement is different from other motives in that it is never satiated  (p. 505-506)

## COMPREHENSION CHECK

Answer these questions soon after reading the chapter.  Circle the best alternative.  Check your answers on pp. 226-228.  If you gave a wrong answer, try to write why it was wrong.  Check your reasons on pp. 226-228.

**General Principles of Motivation**

1. Which of the following is not consistent with a drive theory of motivation?
   a. libido accumulates and demands an outlet
   b. a hungry animal will seek food to achieve need reduction
   c. a rat will run faster to get tasty food than to get less-tasty food
   d. a thirsty child will produce many behaviors

Correct _____  If wrong, why? _____

2. Which of the following is an example of an extrinsically motivated behavior?
    a. you eat something quickly because it tastes so good
    b. a college student spends hours on a paper because the topic is so interesting
    c. a worker works extra hard because a bonus is expected soon
    d. a monkey figures out how to open a device "just for the fun of it"

Correct _____ If wrong, why? _____

3. According to Maslow's hierarchy of needs, a person who is desperately thirsty will try to satisfy:
    a. the need for self-actualization
    b. social needs
    c. needs at all levels
    d. physiological needs only
    e. secondary needs

Correct _____ If wrong, why? _____

4. If you eat because everyone else is eating, even though you're full from the dinner you've just finished, your eating is being controlled by:
    a. drive reduction
    b. incentives
    c. homeostasis
    d. libido

Correct _____ If wrong, why? _____

**Motivation and Biological States:  The Case of Hunger**

5. A person with uncontrolled diabetes has low insulin levels.  Which is most likely?
    a. a high percentage of what the person eats will be stored as fats
    b. the person probably has low glucagon levels
    c. the person has damage to the ventromedial hypothalamus
    d. a low percentage of each meal is converted to fats

Correct _____ If wrong, why? _____

6. A physician argues that overweight people have high set points and, therefore, cannot lose weight.  By this he means that:
    a. their brain mechanisms are maintaining a constant, high weight
    b. they are set in their ways and unlikely to change through diets
    c. they have damage to the lateral hypothalamus
    d. satiety occurs too quickly in overweight people

Correct _____ If wrong, why? _____

7. Damage to which structure will result in a rat that loses a lot of weight and then maintains a very low body weight?
   a. ventromedial hypothalamus
   b. lateral hippocampus
   c. lateral hypothalamus
   d. ventromedial hippocampus

Correct _____ If wrong, why? _____

8. Taste preferences in humans:
   a. develop during the 2nd year of life
   b. can be related to abnormal biological functioning
   c. are purely psychological; they aren't related to biology
   d. are almost always related to the amount of nutrition in food
   e. are very similar across ethnic groups

Correct _____ If wrong, why? _____

9. It has been argued that people become overweight because they eat to overcome emotional problems. Which of the following is true about this argument?
   a. it is true, because people "binge" when they are anxious
   b. it is probably not the reason for their being overweight, because overweight people do not have more emotional problems than normal-weight people
   c. it is probably true, because most overweight people have low self-esteem
   d. it is true, genetics has been linked to the increased anxiety and consequently to obesity

Correct _____ If wrong, why? _____

10. In the study in which subjects were either given a milkshake or not and then offered ice cream, the dieters:
    a. ate much less ice cream if they had a milkshake first, because they were not as hungry
    b. ate much less ice cream if they had a milkshake first, because of the "what-the-heck" effect
    c. ate the same amount or even more ice cream when they had a milkshake first, because of the "what-the-heck" effect
    d. didn't eat any ice cream if they had a milkshake first, because they had already exceeded the limits of their diets

Correct _____ If wrong, why? _____

11. Anorexia nervosa:
    a. results in very low energy levels
    b. is most common in women over 25
    c. is usually accompanied by a pathological fear of fatness
    d. occurs in women with poor self-control
    e. involves frequent episodes of binge eating

Correct _____ If wrong, why? _____

**Sexual Motivation**

12. How is the sex drive similar to hunger?
    a. both depend on physiological drives and incentives
    b. both drives are easily aroused in the absence of incentives
    c. incentives for both vary greatly, and people understand other people's preferences
    d. Masters and Johnson described four similar stages of arousal for both drives

Correct _____ If wrong, why? _____

13. In his pioneering research on sexuality, Kinsey found that:
    a. people agreed pretty much on what was excessive masturbation
    b. number of orgasms for an individual person declines with age
    c. the range of variation in male sexual activity was great; the range of variation in female sexual activity was very limited
    d. most people consider their behavior normal and anything above that to be excessive
    e. about 2.8% of the men reported themselves as being homosexual

Correct _____ If wrong, why? _____

14. Vaginal intercourse:
    a. is less likely to result in the transmission of the AIDS virus than anal intercourse
    b. will not lead to transmission of the AIDS virus, even if one partner is infected, so heterosexuals have nothing to fear
    c. has been less affected by the threat of AIDS than by the threat of other venereal diseases
    d. is safe between homosexual males if a condom is worn

Correct _____ If wrong, why? _____

15. Homosexuality in men:
    a. may occur because the mother secretes estrogen during pregnancy
    b. means that a man would prefer to be a woman
    c. was taboo in ancient Greek and Roman society
    d. appears to be related to genetics
    e. is caused by a part of the anterior hypothalamus being small

Correct _____ If wrong, why? _____

**Achievement Motivation**

16. How can the need for achievement be measured?
    a. have people tell stories about pictures in the Thematic Apperception Test
    b. ask people whether they are strongly motivated for success
    c. measure how much people achieve
    d. have people play a video game of a set difficulty

Correct _____ If wrong, why? _____

17. People with a strong fear of failure:
    a. put little effort into easy tasks
    b. put extraordinary effort into tasks if the goal is to "do your best"
    c. increase their efforts following feedback, no matter how they did
    d. react to feedback by reducing their efforts
    e. try harder when they're told they'll be evaluated

Correct _____ If wrong, why? _____

18. What has been found about young children's reactions to failure?
    a. they don't become discouraged; they assume they'll succeed next time
    b. they become discouraged very quickly, much quicker than adults
    c. they fear failure more than they seek success, even when they first enter school
    d. girls are encouraged to set higher personal goals than boys, so they fail more often and have more fear of failing

Correct _____ If wrong, why? _____

## ANSWERS AND EXPLANATIONS FOR COMPREHENSION CHECK

| Correct Answer | Other Alternatives Are Wrong Because: |
|---|---|

1. c (p. 462)
   Obj. I-B

   a,b,d. all consistent with drive theory
   c. tasty food should not reduce drive more than less tasty food; this is consistent with incentive theory

2. c (p. 463)
   Obj. I-C-1

   a,b,d. all intrinsically motivated; there is no external reward

3. d (pp. 466-467)
   Obj. II-B

   a. lower-level needs must be satisfied before the desire to fulfill one's potential motivates
   b. social needs are higher than physiological; they can't motivate until physiological are fulfilled
   c. lower-level needs must be met before higher-level needs can motivate
   e. won't satisfy secondary until primary are met

4. b (p. 463)
   Obj. I-C

   a. you're not hungry, so there's no physiological need
   c. refers to maintaining physiological factors constant; you're already full
   d. a kind of sexual energy; probably irrelevant here

5. d (p. 471)
   Obj. IV-A-1

   a. fats are stored when insulin is high
   b. has the opposite effect as insulin; not low in both
   c. this would produce high insulin levels

6. a (pp. 473-474)
   Obj. IV-C

   b. may be true, but it isn't what is meant by "set point"
   c. this would result in low body weight, not high
   d. satiety means feeling full, so this would result in low weight

7. c  (p. 474)  
   Obj. V-A

   a. damage to this structure increases insulin, which converts
      glucose to fat and makes an animal hungry; causes weight gain

   b,d. hippocampus is involved in memory

8. b  (p. 475)  
   Obj. VI

   a. some preferences are present at birth

   c. abnormal biological conditions can influence preferences, such as a
      need for salt if the boy excretes salt too quickly

   d. we often reject unfamiliar, nutritious foods

   e. ethnic groups may differ in their food preferences

9. b  (pp. 476-477)  
   Obj. VII-B

   a. people do binge, but this is not the cause of obesity; it usually
      happens in people who are dieting

   c. this is true for a minority of overweight people, but not the majority

   d. genetics plays a factor in obesity but it results in increased secretion
      of a protein and not in anxiety

10. c  (pp. 479-480,  
   Fig. 11.18)  
   Obj. VII-F-1

   a. this was true for nondieting people; dieters ate more

   b. the "what-the-heck" effect led them to eat more; they had
      already gone off their diets

   d. they ate ice cream following the milkshake, either as much as
      without the milkshake or more

11. c  (pp. 481-482)  
   Obj. VII-G

   a. energy levels tend to be very high

   b. most common in teenage years and early 20s

   d. anorexic women usually have high self-control

   e. bulimia; anorexics usually eat little food

12. a  (p. 485)  
   Obj. VIII

   b. for many people, the sex drive is only aroused in the presence
      of incentives; people get hungry whether or not they see food

   c. incentives probably vary more for the sex drive; people don't
      understand others' preferences

   d. they described the stages of sexual arousal

13. d  (p. 486)  
   Obj. VIII-A

   a. people varied greatly in what they thought was excessive

   b. can't tell; Kinsey's sample was cross-sectional so he interviewed
      different people at different ages

   c. females also showed a great deal of variability

   e. Kinsey actually reported that 13% were homosexual; a more recent
      survey found 2.8%

14. a  (p. 489)  
   Obj. VIII-D

   b. transmission can occur, although it is less likely than with
      anal intercourse

   c. AIDS has had more affect on sexual practices because it is life
      threatening

   d. only women have vaginas; two males cannot have vaginal intercourse

15. d (pp. 494-495,
    Fig. 11.30)
    Obj. X-C

a. estrogen is secreted, but testosterone is important
   for male development
b. this is sexual identity; usually not related to sexual orientation
c. they considered it typical for men to engage in occasional sexual
   activities with other men
e. this was smaller in homosexual men, but it may not be the cause;
   homosexual life-style may cause brain difference

16. a (pp. 501-502)
    Obj. XII-A

b. people may say yes because it is socially desirable
   to say yes
c. this would mix up ability and the desire to achieve
d. the difficulty should be chosen by the person to see if easy,
   unrealistic, or realistic high goals are set

17. d (p. 502)
    Obj. XII-B-1

a. they put normal or extraordinary effort into easy tasks
b. "do your best" is not an effective goal for anyone
c. they decrease their effort
e. true of people high in need for achievement

18. a (p. 504)
    Obj. XIII-A

b,c. they don't become discouraged if they don't succeed
d. boys are generally encouraged to set higher personal goals

## LECTURE MATERIAL

Don't forget to review your lecture material. Process each topic meaningfully. First, be sure that you understand the material in each lecture--if you don't, ask your instructor or teaching assistant. Associate the material with things that you already know and with your personal experiences. If you can make up mental images of any of the material, do so. Try to think of real-life applications of the concepts. Write notes in the left column on your lecture notes. Then write questions to cover each concept.

----------------------------------------------------------------------------
WAIT AT LEAST 24 HOURS BEFORE PROCEEDING.
LET FORGETTING OCCUR--IT WILL!!
----------------------------------------------------------------------------

## SHORT-ANSWER ESSAY QUESTIONS

Write brief answers to each of the following. The answers are on pp. 230-231, but do try to write the answers yourself before looking at them.

### General Principles of Motivation

1. Explain how motivation involves both physiological drives and incentives.

2. Discuss why Maslow's hierarchy of needs theory cannot explain why a starving person would give food to a needy child.

3. What do motivated behaviors have in common?

**Motivation and Biological States:  The Case of Hunger**

4. Explain how insulin levels are related to hunger.

5. Discuss factors involved in people's food preferences.

6. Discuss two reasons for obesity.

7. Explain how anorexia nervosa and bulimia are similar and how they differ.

**Sexual Motivation**

8. Name and describe Masters and Johnson's four stages of sexual arousal.

9. Discuss evidence that suggests a role for genetics in homosexuality.

10. Describe what seems to have motivated men who have been convicted of rape.

**Achievement Motivation**

11. Explain how goal setting is related to the need for achievement.

12. Discuss sex differences and the need for achievement.

```
*************************************************************************
```
Find the questions that you wrote over lecture material and write answers to them.
```
*************************************************************************
```

## ANSWERS TO SHORT-ANSWER ESSAY QUESTIONS

1. Motivation depends upon a drive to reduce needs; e.g., when a person is hungry she seeks food. Homeostasis is the idea that we are motivated to maintain a state of equilibrium, keeping states fairly constant. But motivation also depends on incentives, or external stimuli; e.g., a person may eat snacks because they are there and look good, not because she is hungry. The overjustification effect occurs because people do some things because of intrinsic motivation and adding an external incentive might actually reduce their tendency to do them. (pp. 462-463)

2. Maslow's theory holds that lower-level needs must be satisfied before higher-level needs can motivate behavior. A starving person has not fulfilled basic physiological needs, so social needs to help others should not be motivating him. (pp. 466-467, Fig. 11.3)

3. Motivated behaviors are directed at reaching a goal. However, they vary from time to time, from situation, and from person to person. Most behavior is motivated by more than one thing. (pp. 467-468)

4. When insulin levels in the bloodstream are low, glucose does not enter the body's cells and people feel hungry. When insulin levels are moderate, glucose enters the body's cells and people are not very hungry. When insulin levels are high, glucose enters the body's cells but a high percentage of it is converted into fat; people feel hungry. This is what occurs when the ventromedial hypothalamus is damaged. (pp. 471-472, Fig. 11.7, p. 473)

5. Bodily needs can affect taste preferences; e.g., if a person has a salt deficiency, salty foods may be preferred. People generally prefer familiar tastes; they tend to like foods that are flavored in ways that they are used to. Associations can affect food preferences; people will avoid foods that are associated with repulsive things, even though the foods are perfectly nutritious. (pp. 475-476)

6. First, there is some evidence for a genetic component to obesity. In mice, there is a specific gene that causes the secretion of excessive amounts of a protein. This protein may alter the activities of the digestive system or it may affect the brain. A similar thing may happen in people, although research hasn't confirmed this yet. Second, overweight people may expend less energy than normal-weight people. People with the lowest energy expenditure were the most likely to gain weight during the next 2 to 4 years. (pp. 477-478)

7. Anorexics and bulimics both starve themselves, but bulimics also have periods of eating binges after which they may force themselves to vomit. Thus, bulimics alternate between starving and eating binges, but anorexics just starve themselves. Both groups have an exaggerated fear of becoming fat, and both are preoccupied with food. Both disorders are more common in women than in men. (pp. 480-483)

8. Excitement: Penis becomes erect, vagina is lubricated, breathing becomes rapid and deep, heart rate, blood pressure increase.
   Plateau: Excitement remains fairly constant.
   Climax or orgasm: Excitement becomes intense followed by relief in the form of orgasm.
   Resolution: Body returns to unaroused state. (p. 492, Fig. 11.28)

9. If one twin is homosexual, then the other twin is more likely to be homosexual if the pair is monozygotic than if the pair is dizygotic. Homosexuality is more common among dizygotic twins than among adopted brothers. However, gay men do not have a higher percentage of lesbian relatives than men who are not gay, and gay women do not have a higher percentage of gay relatives than women who are not lesbians. Thus, if there is a genetic component to homosexuality, it must be different for men and women. (pp. 494-495, Fig. 11.30)

10. Convicted rapists seem to feel anger toward women and they need to dominate and control women. Usually they have a long history of hostility and violence toward both men and women, and many were sexually abused as children. Some rapists actually have weak sex drives or are almost impotent. (pp. 496-497)

11. People who are high in need for achievement tend to set moderately difficult goals that they have some probability of achieving and that they will feel proud to have achieved. They tend to make little effort on easy tasks, and they put forth extra effort when they are being evaluated. When they receive feedback, they tend to increase their effort, no matter what the results were. People who prefer very easy or very difficult tasks may have a high fear of failure. (p. 502)

12. According to some studies, men generally score higher on need for achievement than women. This may be due to social influences later in life. Goals set by high school girls are about as high as those set by boys. Within several years after high-school, girls lower their goals perhaps because they come to believe that men resent and dislike successful women. In 1972, Horner argued that women show a fear of success, but more recent studies have not shown this. (pp. 504-505)

## POSTTEST

Take this test with all of your books and notes out of sight. This should give you a good idea of how well you understand the material.

### Matching

Put the letter of the term on the right in the blank beside the description on the left.

<u>General Principles of Motivation</u>

1. _____ sexual energy postulated by Freud

    A.  extrinsic motivation

2. _____ an external stimulus that "pulls" an animal

    B.  self-actualization

3. _____ based on rewards and punishments separate from the act itself

    C.  overjustification effect

    D.  homeostasis

4. _____ need to achieve one's full potential as a human being

    E.  libido

5. _____ maintenance of equilibrium

    F.  incentive

6. _____ engaging in an act for its own sake

    G.  intrinsic motivation

7. _____ decline in inherent interest in doing an act after rewards are withdrawn

### Multiple-choice

Circle the best alternative.

<u>General Principles of Motivation</u>

1. Drive reduction theory argues that people and animals act:
   a. in order to find an outlet for excessive libido
   b. because they are pulled by incentives
   c. because they develop specific hungers for particular behaviors
   d. because they have a kind of irritation that energizes behaviors
   e. differently depending upon their level in the hierarchy of needs

2. Ravin is having stomach contractions, there is little food in his intestines, and the amount of glucose and fats in his bloodstream is low. He immediately takes off for the nearest fast-food restaurant and orders two jumbo cheese-bacon burgers. He eats until he can eat no more. At this point, his stomach feels full and some food has reached his intestines. This process of bringing the body into equilibrium is:
   a. an overjustification effect
   b. homeostasis
   c. an incentive system
   d. a breakdown in libido
   e. instinctive energy

3. Which of the following best supports an incentive view of motivation?
   a. a hungry rat runs to the end of a maze to get food
   b. a thirsty child turns on the garden hose to get water
   c. a woman eats a piece of birthday cake although she is not hungry
   d. a bear licks its paw to remove a thorn
   e. a diver surfaces as quickly as is safe when he runs out of air

4. A fifth-grader has just learned how to do some simple programming on his dad's computer. Now, his class at school is learning programming and he gets gold stars for doing well. If the overjustification effect occurs, what is likely to happen this summer when he no longer gets stars for programming?
   a. he will work less hard than before the reward
   b. secondary motivation will make him work harder at programming than before his class began programming
   c. he will continue at about the same rate as before he was rewarded
   d. he will work harder than before the reward
   e. both b and d

5. According to Maslow's theory, a person who has fulfilled all basic, social, and esteem needs is motivated by the need for:
   a. libido
   b. sensation seeking
   c. drive reduction
   d. self-actualization
   e. homeostasis

Motivation and Biological States:  The Case of Hunger

6. A rat has a much higher than average weight, it seems to be hungry all the time, and most of what it eats is stored as fat.  This rat probably has damage to the:
   a. set point
   b. lateral hypothalamus
   c. libido
   d. ventromedial hypothalamus
   e. insulin-producing center

7. Which of the following is least likely to cause a person to be overweight?
   a. high levels of insulin
   b. a particular gene that results in excessive secretion of a specific protein
   c. damage to the ventromedial hypothalamus
   d. depression
   e. expending less energy than normal-weight people

8. Injecting insulin in a person whose levels are normal will result in:
   a. a decrease in appetite
   b. a high percentage of each meal being stored as fat
   c. the body's fat supplies being converted to glucose
   d. a low percentage of each meal being stored as fat
   e. both c and d

9. When people are dieting, what happens to their appetite?
   a. it often increases after they have eaten some rich food
   b. it is increased by exercise, showing that dieters should conserve energy and exercise less
   c. it gradually decreases until the drive to eat is gone
   d. it is not influenced by emotional distress
   e. their blood glucose levels are increased which increases appetite

10. Which of the following is true of anorexia nervosa?
   a. it is more common among Asian cultures than among Western cultures
   b. it is related to sexuality in women, but not in men
   c. there is almost always damage to the lateral hypothalamus
   d. it reflects a pathological fear of fatness
   e. it involves frequent binge eating

Sexual Motivation

11. Which of the following is true about sexual behavior?
   a. Kinsey found that most people had similar sexual behaviors
   b. Kinsey found that homosexual experiences were very rare, particularly in men
   c. a higher percentage of women than men report an interest in various sexual activities
   d. the percentage of people having multiple sex partners increases with age
   e. most people think their sexual behavior is normal; anything in excess of it is excessive

12. In today's society in the United States:
   a. about 10% of the people report a predominantly homosexual orientation
   b. about 80% of the heterosexuals having multiple sexual partners use condoms consistently
   c. people in their 50s and 60s report having sex less often than younger people
   d. the threat of AIDS has not really changed sexual behavior
   e. there are more homosexual women than men

13. What is the order of Masters and Johnson's four stages of sexual arousal?
   a. plateau, excitement, climax, resolution
   b. excitement, plateau, orgasm, resolution
   c. plateau, climax, resolution, excitement
   d. resolution, excitement, orgasm, plateau
   e. excitement, orgasm, plateau, resolution

14. Homosexual men:
   a. developed their homosexuality because they were exposed to estrogen as fetuses
   b. have larger clusters of neurons in the anterior hypothalamus than heterosexual men
   c. are less common than homosexual women
   d. are more likely to have male relatives who are gay than heterosexual men
   e. have a mistaken sexual identity

15. Rapists:
    a. often feel anger toward women and have a need to dominate them
    b. have very strong sex drives
    c. are usually not aroused by photos and audiotapes of rape
    d. usually had pleasant childhoods with no evidence of abuse
    e. are more likely to be homosexual rather than heterosexual men

Achievement Motivation

16. How does the Thematic Apperception Test measure the need for achievement?
    a. people look at pictures and tell a story about them; the number of times that a striving for goals is mentioned is counted
    b. people read a story and are asked to complete it; the number of times that people mention quitting or failure is counted
    c. people are asked to toss rings over a peg from different distances; the number of successes is counted
    d. people are asked to toss rings over a peg from different distances; the distance is measured
    e. people are asked whether they are strongly motivated to succeed

17. People who are high in need for achievement:
    a. choose easy tasks to avoid failure
    b. decrease their efforts following positive feedback, but increase them following negative feedback
    c. prefer difficult but not impossible tasks
    d. put forth less effort when they are being evaluated than when they are not
    e. are most highly motivated by "do your best" goals

18. People who have a strong fear of failure are likely to choose which of the following tasks?
    a. an intermediately difficult task that they'll win at half the time
    b. a very difficult task that they'll never accomplish
    c. a difficult task that they have a realistic chance of accomplishing
    d. either a or c
    e. either b or c

19. Which person will probably be most successful in meeting her goal?
    a. Jane, who has an IQ of 90, but who says she will get all A's
    b. Greta, who will do her best
    c. Maria, who says she will try to pass all her courses
    d. Helen, who has an above average IQ and who publicly says she will get all A's
    e. Sally, who says she will get all A's, but who never is in class to find out how she is doing

20. Which of the following is true about women and the need for achievement?
    a. high-school women set much lower goals than high-school men
    b. women today show more fear of success than women in the 1960s
    c. women tend to have a stronger need for achievement than men
    d. women's fear of success probably differs from one historical era and one culture to another
    e. sex differences in need for achievement are clearly biological

## ANSWERS TO POSTTEST

| Correct Answer | Questions Testing a Similar Concept | |
| --- | --- | --- |
| | Comprehension Check | Short-Answer |

**Matching**

| | | |
| --- | --- | --- |
| 1. E (p. 461) | 1a,4d | -- |
| 2. F (p. 463) | 4 | 1 |
| 3. A (p. 463) | 2 | -- |
| 4. B (p. 467) | 3a | 2 |
| 5. D (pp. 462-463) | 4c | -- |
| 6. G (p. 463) | 2b,d | -- |
| 7. C (p. 464) | 2 | -- |

**Multiple-Choice**

| | | |
| --- | --- | --- |
| 1. d (p. 462) | 1 | 1 |
| 2. b (pp. 462-463) | 4c | -- |
| 3. c (p. 463) | 2,4 | 1 |
| 4. a (p. 464) | 2 | -- |
| 5. d (p. 467, Fig. 11.3) | 3 | 2 |
| 6. d (p. 474) | 7d | -- |
| 7. d (pp. 476-477) | 9 | 6 |
| 8. b (pp. 471-472) | -- | 4 |
| 9. a (pp. 479-480) | 10 | 6 |
| 10. d (pp. 481-482) | 11 | 7 |
| 11. e (p. 486) | 13 | -- |
| 12. c (pp. 487-488) | 14 | -- |
| 13. b (p. 492) | -- | 8 |
| 14. d (pp. 494-495) | 15 | 9 |
| 15. a (pp. 496-497) | -- | 10 |
| 16. a (pp. 501-502) | -- | -- |
| 17. c (pp. 502-503) | 17 | 11 |
| 18. b (pp. 502-503) | 17 | 11 |
| 19. d (p. 503) | -- | 11 |
| 20. d (pp. 504-505) | 18d | 12 |

# CHAPTER 11 LANGUAGE ENHANCEMENT GUIDE

## I. VOCABULARY, IDIOMS AND CULTURAL CONCEPTS

**Instructions:**

As you read the text refer to the following list of words and their definitions. The words are listed in the order in which they appear in the chapter. The definitions presented contain the meaning of the word as used by Kalat on the textbook page indicated.

Remember that these words like all words can have different meanings in other sentences. If you do not find a non-technical word on this list it may have been defined on a previous page or chapter of this study guide. The definition of non-technical words may be found in the dictionary at the end of this study guide. Kalat defined each new technical word as it first appears on a page and these may be found in Kalat's summary at the end of the section and in the Glossary at the end the textbook.

### General Principles of Motivation

solo (460) = an activity by a single individual

synthetic = not natural, artificial, made from chemicals

maximize = to increase or make as big as possible

great deal = a large amount, many

self-reports (461) = what people say about themselves

shortcomings = limitations, deficiencies

engage in = participate in

conception (462) = an idea, explanation

obsolete = no longer accepted

optimum = the most favorable condition for health and growth

equilibrium = a condition in which each and all forces are balanced by others resulting in a stable unchanging system

steady = constant with very little change

static = unchanging, no motion, at rest, fixed

anticipation (463) = expectation; to see, do or know in advance

deteriorated (464) = got worse; degenerated

coherent categories (465) = consistent inclusive categories

momentum (466) = speed, pace, force

enthusiastic = a person who shows great excitement or interest in an activity

enormous = very large amounts of something like size, power, motivation, money, etc.

hierarchy = a related set of ideas, motives, people, etc. organized into successive ranks or levels with each level included in or under the influence of the one above or below

apex (467) = the highest point; the top point
priority = the highest level of importance

### Motivation and Biological States:  The Case of Hunger

famine (470) =  a food shortage where many people starve

nutrients (471) = fats, proteins, carbohydrates, vitamins and minerals contained in food

satiated (473) =  to satisfy an appetite, to feel full
monitoring = systematically  paying attention to and controlling a process

satiety (474) = feeling full

triggered by (475) = started by
it turned out = the evidence showed that
enable = allow, permit, empower

gastrointestinal (476) =  stomach and intestines
greasy corn dog = a spicy meat covered with a corn  meal
amusement park = a park with rides like Disneyland
repulsive = unpleasant to see, taste or smell;  disgusting,  nauseating, sickening
go awry = turn away from what is expected
depression =  an emotional  condition characterized by an inability to concentrate, insomnia, and
        feelings of sadness and hopelessness
binge = a period of uncontrolled eating or drinking

consumed (480) = eaten
shaken off = taken off; stopped

preoccupied (482) =  constantly thinking about one thing

persistent (483) = repeating or continuing without stopping
perfectionist = a person who constantly tries to be perfect

### Sexual Motivation

masturbation (486) = sexual self stimulation

homosexual (488) =  sexual desire for others of one's own sex

intravenous (489) = injections of drugs directly into a vein
menstruation = a woman's bloody discharge once a month

condom (491) =  a covering of the male sex organ to prevent infection or pregnancy during sexual
        relations

predisposed (494) =  a behavior tendency
enlightened = to be knowledgeable

humiliate (497) = to lower a persons   pride, dignity, or self-respect

**Achievement Motivation**

straightforward (500) = direct; clear; not ambiguous

extraordinary (502) = more than usual or normal; unusual, exceptional, uncommon

discourage (504) = to make someone less hopeful, confident or enthusiastic

edifice (506) = a large impressive building

## II. VOCABULARY BUILDING

### Word Analysis

As in Chapter 10, the prefixes and suffixes used in each exercise will not be listed along with their meanings. You are being asked to analyze each term from memory. If you have any difficulty in remembering you can look up the terms in Appendix B that alphabetically lists and defines each prefix and suffix.

Instructions:

1. Break each word in the table into its prefixes, roots and suffixes. If you do not remember the meaning of a term look it up in Appendix B.
2. Guess the meaning of the word based on the meaning of its parts.
3. Find the word on the text page indicated in the brackets and redefine the word based on the context of the sentence, paragraph and chapter.
5. Look up the definition of the word in the VOCABULARY, IDIOMS AND CULTURAL CONCEPTS section above, in Appendix A (marked A) or in a college level dictionary. If the word is followed by letter G look it up in the text Glossary.

Exercise 1. Achievement

| Word | Meaning |
|------|---------|
| achievement | |
| anorexia | |
| depression(A) | |
| deteriorated (A) | |
| discouraged (A) | |
| disorientation | |
| disturbance | |
| enable(A) | |
| engage (A) | |
| enlightened (A) | |
| enthusiast (A) | |
| extrinsic | |

## Exercise 2.  Heterosexual

| heterosexual | |
| --- | --- |
| hierarchy (A) | |
| hypothalamus (G ) | |
| incentive (A) | |
| ineffective | |
| intentional | |
| intravenous (A) | |
| intrinsic | |

## Exercise 3.  Lateral

| lateral (G) | |
| --- | --- |
| paraventricular | |
| perfectionist (A) | |
| persist | |
| persistent (A) | |
| predisposed | |
| preference | |
| preoccupied (A) | |
| prevalence (A) | |
| satiation | |
| underachiever | |
| unintentional | |
| ventromedial (G) | |
| homosexual | |

# CHAPTER 12 EMOTIONS, HEALTH PSYCHOLOGY, AND COPING WITH STRESS

## OBJECTIVES

Understand that:

### Emotional Behaviors

I. Emotion is related to physiological arousal. (p. 511)
- A. Emotions may play a role in decision-making. (pp. 511-512)
- B. Autonomic nervous system is involved in emotion. (pp. 512-513, Fig. 12.2)
  - 1. Sympathetic nervous system increases arousal. (pp. 512-514, Fig. 12.4)
  - 2. Parasympathetic nervous system decreases arousal. (pp. 512-514, Fig. 12.4)
- C. Opponent-process principle proposes that emotions swing from one state to the opposite as the original stimulus is removed. (pp. 514-515, Fig. 12.6)
- D. Polygraph measures sympathetic arousal. (p. 516, Fig. 12.7)
  - 1. Polygraph administrators can identify lying more accurately than most people, but they also identify innocent people as lying. (pp. 516-517, Fig. 12.8)
  - 2. Guilty-knowledge test reduces number of innocent people identified as lying. (p. 517)
    - a. Paper and pencil integrity tests can identify dishonest people, but they also misidentify highly honest people. (p. 518)

II. The postulated relationship between physiological arousal and experiencing the emotion differs for different theories. (p.518, Figure 12.9, Table 12.1, p. 522)
- A. James-Lange theory proposes that sympathetic arousal is necessary for emotion. (pp. 518-519)
  - 1. We probably don't determine our emotional state by differences in physiological states. (p. 519)
    - a. We may judge our own facial expressions. (pp. 519-520)
- B. Cannon-Bard theory argues that emotion results from sensory information; autonomic arousal is independent. (p. 520)
- C. Schachter and Singer proposed that emotion is the label given to arousal. (pp. 520-522)
  - 1. A problem with this experiment is that people given placebo injections also felt emotion (pp. 520-522, Fig. 12.11)

III. There may be a limited set of basic emotions. (p. 523)
- A. Basic emotions should emerge early in life, have biological bases, and be the same for people of different cultures. (p. 523)
- B. Facial expressions can communicate emotional states. (pp. 523-525)
- C. People from many cultures show similar expressions. (pp. 525-526, Fig. 12.18)
- D. If basic emotions exist, then different emotions should be affected by different types of brain damage. (pp. 526-527, Fig. 12.19)

IV. Anger and happiness are important emotions. (pp. 528-531)
- A. Anger usually doesn't lead to physical aggression. (p. 528)
- B. Anger occurs when one feels mistreated. (p. 528)
  - 1. The frustration-aggression hypothesis proposes that anger is displayed when an individual is frustrated. (p. 528)
    - a. All unpleasant events may lead to the impulse to fight or flee. (p. 528)
  - 2. Biographical information can predict violence to some extent. (p. 529)
- C. People become happy for different reasons. (p. 530)
  - 1. Most studies show which variables correlate with happiness. (pp. 530-531)

**Health Psychology**

V. Stress results from emotional responses. (p. 533)
   A. Selye's concept of stress is that it is the response of the body to demands. (pp. 533-534)
      1. Responses to stress are alarm, resistance, and exhaustion. (p. 534)
         a. Persistent stress can lead to the general adaptation syndrome. (p. 534)
   B. Posttraumatic stress disorder results from extreme stress. (pp. 534-535)
   C. We must be able to measure stress to look at its effects on health. (p. 535)
      1. Social Readjustment Rating Scale is one measure of stressful events. (pp. 535-536, Table 12.2)
         a. This scale is subject to many criticisms. (pp. 536-537)
   D. Stress depends upon how events are interpreted. (pp. 537-538, Fig. 12.22)
VI. Psychosomatic illnesses are related to stress. (pp. 538-539)
   A. Heart disease may be linked to personality type. (pp. 539-540)
   B. Stress may influence the immune system and be related to cancer. (pp. 540-541)

**Coping with Stress**

VII. One way to cope with stress is to attack the problem. (pp. 543-544)
   A. Predictability and control reduce stress. (p. 544)
      1. We assume that things won't get worse. (p. 544)
      2. We can prepare for predictable events. (p. 544)
   B. If you can't do anything about an event, predicting it may not reduce stress. (pp. 540-541)
VIII. Relaxation can reduce stress. (p. 545)
IX. Exercise can reduce stress. (pp. 545-546)
X. Inoculation involves a small-scale stressful experience. (p. 546)
XI. Social support can be helpful in dealing with stress. (pp. 546-547)
   A. Talking about an experience may to reduce stress. (p. 547)
XII. Distraction can help to reduce pain. (p. 547)
XIII. People often cope by creating false beliefs. (pp. 547-548)
   A. Slightly unrealistic optimism may be the best attitude. (p. 548)

## COMPREHENSION CHECK

Answer these questions soon after reading the chapter. Circle the best alternative. Check your answers on pp. 246-248. If you gave a wrong answer, try to write why it was wrong. Check your reasons on pp. 246-248.

**Emotional Behaviors**

1. The pilot of your airplane just announced that the plane would have to land suddenly and you should tighten your seat belt and put your head between your knees. What will happen to your autonomic nervous system?
   a. the parasympathetic nervous system will become more activated
   b. some parts of the sympathetic nervous system will be activated
   c. some parts of the parasympathetic nervous system will be activated
   d. the sympathetic nervous system will become more activated

Correct _____ If wrong, why? _____

2. The opponent-process principle could best explain which of the following?
   a. one person reacts to a stimulus with anger; another responds with fear
   b. a person who is depressed often feels angry
   c. a person feels very relieved after a terrible event is over
   d. the physiological response to fear is different from the physiological response to anger

Correct _____ If wrong, why? _____

3. The polygraph test:
   a. measures only the electrical conduction of the skin
   b. is close to 90% accurate in detecting lies
   c. is most accurate when the guilty-knowledge test is used
   d. is no more accurate than a person trying to detect lying
   e. is a measure of parasympathetic nervous system activity

Correct _____ If wrong, why? _____

4. When hiking, you suddenly notice a rattlesnake preparing to embed his fangs into you. You promptly beat all known records for the 40-yard dash to get away. According to the James-Lange theory, you:
   a. are afraid because you perceive your heart pounding and you are running away
   b. run away because you are afraid
   c. decide that you are afraid at the same time as your body reacts to the fear
   d. have probably been classically conditioned to fear rattlesnakes

Correct _____ If wrong, why? _____

5. How would the Cannon-Bard theory explain the above situation?
   a. you interpret the sympathetic nervous system arousal as fear because of the situation
   b. you are afraid because you run away
   c. your forebrain triggered the body reaction, which you then interpreted as fear
   d. your fear and the sympathetic arousal happened simultaneously but independently

Correct _____ If wrong, why? _____

6. How does Schachter and Singer's theory of emotions differ from the James-Lange view?
   a. body states are not relevant in the Schachter-Singer theory
   b. body states and the perception of emotion are independent in the Schachter-Singer view
   c. a given body state always leads to the same emotion in the Schachter Singer theory
   d. a given body state may lead to different emotions depending upon interpretation in the Schachter-Singer theory
   e. Schachter and Singer argue that facial expressions can induce emotions; James-Lange theory says they cannot

Correct _____ If wrong, why? _____

7. In different cultures, gestures and facial expressions:
    a. are similar enough that many can be identified cross-culturally
    b. are used in exactly the same situations
    c. are very different; most of the expressions in some cultures are unknown in other cultures
    d. are the same but their interpretation is very different

Correct _____ If wrong, why? _____

8. Which of the following is most consistent with the frustration-aggression hypothesis?
    a. a person who is insulted sometimes attacks the person who insulted him; but at other times, he leaves the room
    b. a foul odor makes someone run from a room
    c. a man who is locked out of his house kicks a passing dog
    d. a rat that can avoid shocks does not attack another rat even though it is frequently shocked
    e. a husband gives his wife the "silent treatment" after she says she doesn't want him to go to the poker party with his friends

Correct _____ If wrong, why? _____

9. Violent behavior:
    a. can be accurately predicted with interviews
    b. can be prevented by severe punishment during childhood
    c. is likely to occur in people who have stronger than normal physiological responses to arousal
    d. is unrelated to the amount of violence watched on television
    e. is associated with not feeling guilty after hurting someone

Correct _____ If wrong, why? _____

10. Which of the following is not true about happiness?
    a. wealthy people in a country are happier than poor people in that country
    b. religious people tend to be happier than people with no religious faith
    c. people who are achieving their goals are happy
    d. people report being less happy as they get older

Correct _____ If wrong, why? _____

## Health Psychology

11. According to Selye, what are the stages that the body goes through in response to stress?
    a. resistance, alarm, general adaptation syndrome
    b. exhaustion, alarm, resistance
    c. general adaptation syndrome, resistance, alarm
    d. alarm, resistance, exhaustion

Correct _____ If wrong, why? _____

12. PTSD:
    a. is a fairly new disorder seen only since the Vietnam War
    b. occurs only in cases involving tough combat
    c. develops anytime someone experiences severe stress
    d. may involve nightmares, constant unhappiness, anger, and guilt
    e. is purely psychological; there are no physiological effects associated with the disorder

Correct _____ If wrong, why? _____

13. The Social Readjustment Rating Scale:
    a. measures the number of unpleasant events in a person's life
    b. measures the stressful events that cause illness
    c. is related to the likelihood of illness
    d. is a very accurate way to measure stress

Correct _____ If wrong, why? _____

14. Psychosomatic illnesses:
    a. are imagined illnesses
    b. are illnesses such as heart disease that are related to stress
    c. occur because emotions lead directly to illness
    d. are not caused by genes and toxic substances

Correct _____ If wrong, why? _____

15. What does the most recent evidence say about people with Type A personalities?
    a. they are more likely to get cancer than Type B people
    b. their impatience and competitiveness leads to heart disease
    c. they usually live in cultures where time isn't very important
    d. they may be more susceptible to heart disease because they show more depression and anger

Correct _____ If wrong, why? _____

**Coping with Stress**

16. Which of the following would be effective in dealing with a stressful situation, such as a loss of a job?
    a. keep the person distracted by constantly thinking about working
    b. convince the person that others were really at fault
    c. have the person join a support group whose members have all lost jobs
    d. make the person understand that he really had no control over the situation
    e. have the person think about other people who are better off

Correct _____ If wrong, why? _____

17. Which of the following is <u>not</u> true about predictability? It:
    a. can make it easier to cope because we can prepare for it at the right time
    b. may not be helpful if you can't do anything about the event
    c. may make an event less stressful if we also perceive that we have control
    d. helps coping only if people actually exert control over the event

Correct _____ If wrong, why? _____

18. Coping by having false beliefs:
    a. only works for minor stresses, and not in life-death situations
    b. only works if people compare themselves with someone else
    c. is basically unhealthy; such beliefs interfere with mental health
    d. can help people to gain a feeling of mastery over their lives

Correct _____ If wrong, why? _____

## ANSWERS AND EXPLANATIONS FOR COMPREHENSION CHECK

<u>Correct Answer</u>                    <u>Other Alternatives Are Wrong Because:</u>

1. d. (pp. 512-514;          a. relaxing situations increase parasympathetic
   Fig. 12.2)                b. sympathetic responds as a unit
   Obj. I-B-1                c. parasympathetic would become less active

2. c. (pp. 514-515,          a. better explained by Schachter-Singer theory
   Fig. 12.4)                b. probably true, but irrelevant to opponent-processes
   Obj. I-C                  d. necessary for James-Lange theory to be correct

3. c. (p. 517)               a. measures heart rate and breathing rate also
   Obj. I-D-2                b. will accurately detect lying about 75% of the time, but will also
                                "detect" innocent people
                             d. it is more accurate then people
                             e. it measures sympathetic activity

4. a. (pp. 518-519,          b. commonsense view; James-Lange is opposite
   Fig. 12.9, Table 12.1,    c. Cannon-Bard view
   p. 522). Obj. II-A        d. may be true, but irrelevant to James-Lange

5. d. (p. 520, Fig. 12.0,    a. this is the Schachter-Singer view
   p. 518, Table 12.1,       b. this is the James-Lange view
   p. 522)                   c. brain sends message to autonomic nervous system and forebrain
   Obj. II-B                    at same time

6. d. (pp. 518-519, 520-522, a. body states are necessary for an emotion
   Table 12.1)               b. perception does depend upon body state
   Obj. II-B, C              c. different emotions can come from same body state, depending
                                upon interpretation
                             e. both theories would agree that expressions might be related to
                                body states, but these theories are aimed at physiological arousal

7. a. (pp. 525-526)
   Obj. III-C
   b. similar expressions are used, but they may be used in somewhat different circumstances
   c. many of the expressions are very similar
   d. people of different cultures can interpret each other's expressions fairly accurately

8. c. (p. 528)
   Obj. IV-B-1
   a. consistent with Berkowitz' theory that unpleasant events lead to either fighting or fleeing
   b. an unpleasant event but no evidence of frustration
   d. even unpleasant stimuli don't always lead to aggression
   e. frustration doesn't lead to calm aggressive behaviors

9. e. (p. 529)
   Obj. IV-B-2
   a. interviews are only a little better than chance
   b. severe punishment may increase future violent behavior
   c. likely to occur in people with weaker than normal responses
   d. watching violence is associated with violent behavior

10. d. (pp. 530-531,
    Fig. 12.20). Obj. IV-C
    a-c. generally true
    d. not true, reported happiness is fairly constant throughout life

11. d. (p. 534)
    Obj. V-A-1
    a, c. alarm is first; general adaptation syndrome is the result of last phase
    b. alarm is first; exhaustion is last

12. d. (pp. 534-535)
    Obj. V-B
    a. it has been recognized following wars throughout history
    b. can occur following extreme stress due to any cause
    c. doesn't develop in everyone having the same stressful experience
    e. Vietnam veterans with PTSD did show elevated endorphin levels after watching dramatized combat

13. c. (pp. 535-537)
    Obj. V-C-1
    a. pleasant events can be stressful, too
    b. events may not cause illness; this is a correlation
    d. it is probably not very accurate

14. b. (pp. 538-539)
    Obj. VI-A
    a. not imagined; they are physiologically very real
    c. emotions don't lead directly to illness; they lead to other behaviors that may increase illness
    d. cancer can be considered a psychosomatic illness, but its primary causes are genetic and toxic substances

15. d. (pp. 539-540)
    Obj. VI-A
    a. more likely to get heart disease than Type B
    b. later research has not shown this
    c. probably more likely in cultures where time is important because they are always in a hurry

16. c. (p. 547)
    Obj. XI

a. distraction is usually used for pain; the person should think about something other than the problem
b. this would make it worse; it would increase perceived loss of control
d. lack of control usually increases, not decreases,. stress
e. needs to think of people who are worse off

17. d. (pp. 544-545)
    Obj. VII-A

a-c. are true
d. they don't actually have to exert control; they just need to perceive that they can exert control

18. d. (pp. 547-548)
    Obj. XIII-A

a. medics in Vietnam used it while risking their lives
b. this was one strategy used by women with breast cancer; they also searched for meaning in the experience, and tried to regain a feeling of mastery
c. such illusions can improve a person's self-image and contribute to mental health

## LECTURE MATERIAL

Don't forget to review your lecture material. Process each topic meaningfully. First, be sure that you understand the material in each lecture--if you don't, ask your instructor or teaching assistant. Associate the material with things that you already know and with your personal experiences. If you can make up mental images of any of the material, do so. Try to think of real-life applications of the concepts. Put your own comments in the left column of your lecture notes. Then write questions to cover each concept.

--------------------------------------------------------------------
WAIT AT LEAST 24 HOURS BEFORE PROCEEDING.
LET FORGETTING OCCUR--IT WILL!!
--------------------------------------------------------------------

## SHORT-ANSWER ESSAY QUESTIONS

Write brief answers to each of the following. The answers are on p. 250-252, but do try to write the answers yourself before looking at them.

### Emotional Behaviors

1. Describe recent research that suggests how emotions might be related to decision making.

2. Explain how a lie-detector test is supposed to work and describe a better way to arrange the test.

3. Schachter and Singer's experiment on cognitive factors in emotion is frequently cited, but what problem is there in the interpretation of that experiment?

4. Describe what happened in the study in which subjects were made to frown smile by holding pens in their lips.

5. What has been found when gestures and facial expressions are studied in different cultures?

6. Describe the original frustration-aggression hypothesis and Berkowitz's modification of it.

7. Describe factors that are related to the accuracy of prediction of violent behavior.

8. Why is happiness difficult to measure in a behavioral way? What problems does this cause for the study of happiness?

**Health Psychology**

9. Describe the effects of prolonged stress on the body.

10. Explain some of the problems that are associated with the conclusion that the Social Readjustment Rating Scale predicts illness.

11. Explain how cancer might be considered a psychosomatic illness.

**Coping with Stress**

12. Describe how predictability and control can help in coping with stress.

13. How can exercise help to reduce stress?

14. Describe how beliefs can serve as coping strategies.

\*\*\*\*\*\*\*\*\*\*\*\*\*\*\*\*\*\*\*\*\*\*\*\*\*\*\*\*\*\*\*\*\*\*\*\*\*\*\*\*\*\*\*\*\*\*\*\*\*\*\*\*\*\*\*\*\*\*\*\*\*\*\*\*\*\*\*\*\*\*\*\*\*\*\*\*\*\*\*\*\*\*\*\*\*\*

Find the questions that you wrote over lecture material and write answers to them.

\*\*\*\*\*\*\*\*\*\*\*\*\*\*\*\*\*\*\*\*\*\*\*\*\*\*\*\*\*\*\*\*\*\*\*\*\*\*\*\*\*\*\*\*\*\*\*\*\*\*\*\*\*\*\*\*\*\*\*\*\*\*\*\*\*\*\*\*\*\*\*\*\*\*\*\*\*\*\*\*\*\*\*\*\*\*

## ANSWERS TO SHORT-ANSWER ESSAY QUESTIONS

1. Damage to the prefrontal cortex seems to result in a loss of emotion. In addition, people who have such damage have trouble making decisions and following plans. One hypothesis is that problems with decision-making occur because of the inability to experience emotions. The patients can't follow through and imagine how they would feel if they made one decision or another, or how they would feel after carrying out a plan. (pp. 511-512)

2. When a person is nervous, the sympathetic nervous system increases breathing rate, heart rate, and sweating. The polygraph measures these variables, which should be higher when a person is lying than when telling the truth. However, polygraph tests result in a number of errors in which innocent people are called guilty. (37% in one study). The "guilty-knowledge" test helps to eliminate these. It asks about specific facts that only the guilty party would know, so an innocent person would not be judged guilty. (pp. 515-518)

3. Participants who were given placebo injections showed about as much emotion as subjects who were given epinephrine. Therefore, an appropriate conclusion may be that people in a euphoria situation act happy and people in an anger situation act angry. (pp. 520-522)

4. Subjects who were made to smile by holding a pen between their teeth rated cartoons as funnier than subjects who were make to frown by holding a pencil in their lips. (pp. 519-520)

5. Facial expressions are pretty much the same, although their frequency and the situations in which they are used differ somewhat. People from one culture are fairly accurate in their interpretations of other cultures' expressions. (pp. 525-526)

6. Whenever individuals experience frustration. (because something prevents them from reaching some goal), they respond with aggression. Berkowitz modified this by saying that all unpleasant events lead to the impulse to fight or flee. Whether one fights or flees depends upon the circumstances. (p. 528)

7. Predictions of the behavior of people in long-term institutions that are based on interviews are not much more accurate than chance. However, predictions based on specific biographical information, such as physical abuse during childhood, history of committing violent acts, having a relative who has been committed to a psychiatric hospital, and watching violence on television, can be more accurate. (pp. 528-529)

8. Although anger is often linked to specific behaviors, happiness is not linked to specific behaviors. This means that the only way to measure happiness is to ask people if they are happy. People have different criteria for happiness, and so one person's low rating may actually mean the same level of happiness as another person's higher rating. (pp. 533-535)

9. According to Selye, reactions to stress go through an alarm, a resistance, and an exhaustion phase. This final phase leads to general adaptation syndrome, which results in weakness, fatigue, loss of appetite, and loss of interest. Continuing stress results in an increase in epinephrine in the body. Posttraumatic stress disorder may result from prolonged exposure to traumatic experiences. (pp. 533-535)

10. People who score higher on this scale are more likely to become ill; but the scale asks about symptoms of illness, so, of course, people with higher scores are more likely to be ill. The scale does not ask about stress from unchanging problems, such as poverty. It also ignores stress from things you worry about, but that do not happen. It may be inappropriate to add together the scores from various events. Having three mildly stressful events is probably not the same as having one very stressful event. In addition, the same event may be stressful for some people but not for others. (pp. 536-537)

11. People's behavior influences the onset and spread of cancer. Lung cancer is related to smoking. Women who examine their breasts can detect breast cancer early to prevent spreading. Severe depression affects the immune system, making depressed people more vulnerable to the spread of tumors. After the onset of cancer, stress weakens the ability of the immune system to attack cancer cells. (pp. 540-541)

12. We assume that a predictable event won't get any worse or, if we have control, that we can control it if it does. We are able to prepare ourselves for predictable events. We need not be constantly aroused if an event is predictable; we can relax during "safe" periods. However, if we can't do anything about a predictable negative event. (such as developing Huntington's disease), we may prefer not to know about it. (p. 544)

13. Exercise can help relaxation. It is particularly helpful to deal with nervousness about an upcoming stressful event. Exercise also helps because people who are in good physical condition react less strongly to stressful events than people who are not in such good condition. (pp. 545-546)

14. Most normal, happy people have a sort of personal fable throughout their lives. They distort bad news to make it seem good, they downplay their weaknesses, and they deny the seriousness of situations. For example, medics in the Vietnam war thought of themselves as invulnerable. Women who had a breast removed looked for meaning in the experience, believed that they knew why they had developed cancer and how they could avoid a recurrence, and compared themselves with others who are worse off. Having slightly unrealistic optimism might be the best attitude for coping with stress. (pp. 547-548)

**POSTTEST**

Take this test with all of your books and notes out of sight. This should give you a good idea of how well you understand the material.

**Matching**

Put the letter of the method of coping with stress beside the description.

Coping With Stress

1. _____ you know a tornado
   is coming, you can prepare for it

    A. inoculation

    B. distorted beliefs

2. _____ being in a quiet place with all
   sources of stimulation removed

    C. predictability

3. _____ a man's wife provides care and
   concern in a stressful situation

    D. distraction

    E. relaxation

4. _____ a person recovering from a heart
   attack thinks that his recovery is
   much faster than average

    F. social support

5. _____ a person who will have surgery sees
   a film of the surgery and imagines what it will be like

6. _____ a patient in a hospital feels little pain because
   he has an interesting view outside the window

**Multiple-choice**

Circle the best alternative.

<u>Emotional Behaviors</u>

1. Your sympathetic nervous system has just been activated. What are you most likely to do?
   a. fall asleep
   b. breath harder and perspire
   c. slow your breathing and heart rate
   d. increase your salivation and digestion rate
   e. feel sorry for something in your environment

2. Why would a scuba diver's first encounter with sharks be more frightening than later encounters, according to the opponent-process theory?
   a. the fear state (A) is stronger initially than the rebound state
   b. the fear state (A) increases with more exposures, but the rebound state gets weaker
   c. there is no rebound state as the person repeats an experience
   d. the rebound state occurs later and later with repeated exposures

3. Which question is a polygraph examiner likely to ask in a guilty-knowledge test?
   a. Have you ever stolen anything?
   b. Did you steal the money from the grocery store on March 21?
   c. Did you rob the gas station as well as the grocery store?
   d. How much money was taken from the store? $50? $100? $200? $1,000?
   e. Are you lying?

4. Godzilla, Frankenstein, a werewolf, King Kong, the creature from the black lagoon, and Dracula all enter your room. How does the James-Lange theory relate your emotions to your behavior?
   a. you perceive the stimuli, are afraid, run away, and then respond physiologically
   b. you feel afraid, and this causes increased sympathetic arousal, which will produce a running response
   c. the stimuli provoke a specific sympathetic nervous system response that you label as "fear"
   d. you aren't really afraid, because epinephrine would be secreted and it produces "cold" emotions
   e. your thalamus simultaneously activates your sympathetic nervous system and sends a message to your cortex that indicates fear

5. Which of the following results from Schachter and Singer's experiment are inconsistent with their theory about cognitive interpretation of emotion?
   a. the groups that were informed about the drug's effects showed little emotion
   b. subjects who were not informed about the drug's effects showed euphoria in that condition and anger in the "angry" condition
   c. the same physiological state was interpreted differently by different subjects
   d. subjects who got a placebo showed almost as much emotion as subjects who got epinephrine

6. Forcing people to make facial expressions by having them move specific facial muscles or holding pencils in their mouths:
    a. does not result in any change in emotions, because there is no sympathetic nervous system arousal
    b. tends to make people feel happier or sadder
    c. makes people sadder, but has no effect on behavior, such as the ratings of cartoons
    d. has some behavioral results, but they are almost entirely due to demand characteristics

7. Across cultures, facial expressions and gestures:
    a. are similar, but people from one culture cannot interpret expressions from another culture
    b. are the same, because they are entirely controlled by genetics
    c. are similar in westernized cultures, but totally different in non-Western cultures, such as Japan
    d. can be identified with perfect accuracy
    e. are similar, but the frequencies with which they are used differ

8. How are anger and aggression related?
    a. people become aggressive far more often than they become angry
    b. when people became angry at family and friends, they usually also display aggression toward them
    c. aggression is more context specific, in that the same level of anger won't always trigger aggression
    d. anger is related to how much violence one watches on television, but actual aggression is not

9. Berkowitz proposed a theory of aggression that is more comprehensive than frustration-aggression theory. Which of the following best describes his theory?
    a. all aggression is caused by frustration, which occurs when a motivated behavior is disrupted
    b. unpleasant stimuli that lead to aggression do so automatically
    c. both frustration and biological factors are important in aggression
    d. all unpleasant events give rise to the impulse to fight or flee; circumstances determine which will happen
    e. aggression will only occur when something goes wrong and there is no one to blame

10. Happiness differs from anger in that:
    a. people who say they are happy all mean about the same thing; people who say they are angry may mean different things
    b. happiness involves sympathetic nervous system arousal; anger does not
    c. anger has more observable behaviors associated with it than happiness
    d. when people become happy, it doesn't always lead to observable behavior; when people become angry it usually leads to observable physical attacks

Health Psychology

11. According to Selye's theory of stress, a person who has had many long-lasting stressful events during the past few months is likely to:
    a. be in the resistance stage
    b. develop the general adaptation syndrome
    c. be in the alarm stage
    d. have reduced epinephrine levels
    e. be less susceptible to disease than someone not so stressed

12. Who is likely to have the highest score on the Social Readjustment Rating Scale?
    a. Oblivia, who just took out a mortgage of $50,000
    b. Dr. Quaalude, who just got married
    c. Erasmus, who just got married and who changed his job
    d. Perplexity, who just graduated from college
    e. Ed Just, who got a speeding ticket and is having trouble with his boss

13. Which of the following conclusions from the Social Readjustment Rating Scale is most appropriate?
    a. high stress scores cause illness
    b. day-to-day problems are more related to illness than major crises
    c. there is a relationship between high stress scores and illness
    d. people of different ages and circumstances respond in a similar manner to the stressful events on the scale
    e. events that people worry about but that don't happen produce the highest scores on the scale

14. People with Type A personality:
    a. are more likely to live in countries in which time is not important and the pace is relaxed than in more time-conscious countries such as the United States
    b. show less increase in heart rate and blood pressure in competitive situations than people with Type B personality
    c. vary in how they handle work assignments, but not in how they behave in leisure activities, such as fishing
    d. develop heart disease because they avoid competitive tasks
    e. often have low scores on the Social Readjustment Rating Scale

15. Which is true about the relationship between emotional states and cancer?
    a. emotional factors are more important in cancer than genes and exposure to toxic substances
    b. severe depression may play a role in cancer by suppressing the immune system
    c. studies consistently show that stress in humans increases the spread of cancer
    d. cancer is most related to anger, rather than to impatience and competitiveness as originally thought
    e. stress influences the onset of cancer more than the course of the cancer following the onset

## Coping with Stress

16. Which is the least likely explanation for why prediction and control can help in coping with stress?
    a. prediction allows an animal or human to prepare for the event
    b. control helps people, but only if they actually exert control, such as turning off an annoying noise
    c. a predictable and controllable event probably will not get any worse; an unpredictable event might
    d. if an event is predictable or controllable, a human or animal does not need to be in a constant state of preparation
    e. if an event is controllable, a human or animal can work harder to control it if it does get worse

17. A person who fears dental work is given a series of mild shocks to the teeth before going to the dentist to help her in coping with the stress associated with dental work. The technique being used here is:
    a. social support
    b. distraction
    c. inoculation
    d. control
    e. exercise

18. A man who has a stroke "knows" that it happened because he had not been exercising enough. He begins exercising to avoid a recurrence. He is coping by:
    a. unrealistic optimism
    b. distraction
    c. inoculation
    d. relaxation
    e. social support

## ANSWERS TO POSTTEST

| Correct Answer | Questions Testing a Similar Concept | |
| --- | --- | --- |
| | Comprehension Check | Short-Answer |

**Matching**

| Correct Answer | Comprehension Check | Short-Answer |
| --- | --- | --- |
| 1. C. (p. 544) | 17 | 12 |
| 2. E. (p. 545) | -- | 13 |
| 3. F. (pp. 546-547) | 16 | -- |
| 4. B. (pp. 547-548) | 18 | 14 |
| 5. A. (p. 546) | -- | -- |
| 6. D. (p. 547) | 16a | -- |

**Multiple-Choice**

| Correct Answer | Comprehension Check | Short-Answer |
| --- | --- | --- |
| 1. b. (pp. 513-514, Fig. 12.2) | 1 | -- |
| 2. a. (pp. 514-515, Fig. 12.6) | 2 | -- |
| 3. d. (p. 517) | 3 | 2 |
| 4. c. (pp. 518-519, Fig. 12.9) | 4,5b,6 | -- |
| 5. d. (pp. 520-522, Fig. 12.11) | 6 | 3 |
| 6. b. (pp. 519-520) | -- | 4 |
| 7. e. (pp. 525-526) | 7 | 5 |
| 8. c. (p. 528) | 8 | 6 |
| 9. d. (p. 528) | 8 | 6 |
| 10. c. (pp. 529-531) | 10 | 8 |
| 11. b. (p. 534) | 11 | 9 |
| 12. c. (pp. 535-537, Table 12.2) | 13 | 10 |
| 13. c. (pp. 535-537) | 13 | 10 |
| 14. e. (pp. 539-540) | 15 | -- |
| 15. b. (pp. 540-541) | 14d | 11 |
| 16. b. (p. 544) | 17 | 12 |
| 17. c. (p. 546) | -- | -- |
| 18. a. (pp. 547-548) | 18 | 14 |

# CHAPTER 12  LANGUAGE ENHANCEMENT GUIDE

## I. VOCABULARY, IDIOMS AND CULTURAL CONCEPTS

**Instructions:**

As you read the text refer to the following list of words and their definitions.  The words are listed in the order in which they appear in the chapter.  The definitions presented contain the meaning of the word as used by Kalat on the textbook page indicated.

Remember that these words like all words can have different meanings in other sentences.  If you do not find a non-technical word on this list it may have been defined on a previous page or chapter of this study guide.  The definition of non-technical words may be found in the dictionary at the end of this study guide.  Kalat defined each new technical word as it first appears on a page and these may be found in Kalat's summary at the end of the section and in the Glossary at the end the textbook..

### Emotional Behaviors

reputed (510) = considered; has a reputation

confession (511) = to tell or admit a failing or guilt to another person
reduced = limited
turbulent =  violently agitated or disturbed; stormy, chaotic
wrecked = damaged or destroyed in an accident
could hardly = had difficulty
suppressed = prevented from happening
personification =  a person who sets an example for a certain characteristic

conscientious (512) = hard working
frustration = feelings that accompany failure or being prevented from reaching an expected goal
revulsion =  a strong feeling of  disgust, displeasure, rejection

charges at you (513) = attacks you
predominately = dominate, control

rebound (514) = to  bounce back,  to recover
subside =    to become less active or intense

prolonged (515) =  requires more time
prospective = likely or expected to be selected or happen

assumption (516) = a claim or idea accepted as true without evidence
bogus =  fake,  false,  counterfeit
convince = to prove, to persuade
suspect = a person who may have committed a crime

convenience store (517) = a small local market that sells food, candy and magazines.
interrogator = a person who asks questions

strangely (518) = unexpectedly
a good percentage = many
transgressions = breaking the law
trivial = not important

respiration (519) = breathing
butterflies in the stomach = an upset stomach.  a nervous stomach

induce (520) = produce
euphoria =  a feeling of great happiness  and well-being

emerge (523) =  to appear or develop, to show up

exaggerate (524) = to make something seem more or bigger than it actually is
spontaneous = happening without a conscious  or external cause

elicit (528) = to produce a reaction, evoke
comprehensive = covering a large part or all of a topic of  study
parole = the release of a prisoner before his/her prison term is completed
parole board = a committee who decides on giving a prisoner parole or release from prison

biographical  (529) =  a  historical summary of the main events in a persons life
counterproductive =  preventing from   reaching a goal or achieving a purpose
impose =  to force or require a behavior
tantrums = an expression of anger with  violent movement and screaming
episode =  an event that is part of  a larger sequence of events
time-out periods = placed in a room alone for a period of time
elusive =  difficult to understand or explain
conglomeration = grouping, collection

**Health Psychology**

multiple sclerosis (533) =
deformities =  refers to a misshapen, twisted or disfigured parts of the body
enhance = improve
provokes = produces, elicits, evokes, triggers

a string of (534) = a series of
is broader than = includes more than
in Selye's sense = in Selye's meaning

endanger (535) =  place in danger
is tough enough = is difficult

ascribes (536) = to assign, to give
laid off from = to lose

exceeding (537) = to be greater than

ridiculous (538) = not believable because it is foolish, stupid and funny
susceptible = easily influenced or infected(to become sick)

toxic substance  (540) = a poisonous chemical that can cause injury, sickness or death

## Coping with Stress

eccentric (543) =  a person who behaves in an unconventional and unusual way; a person who deviates
    from  normally expected behavior
circumstances = the situation accompanying or surrounding an event
a great deal of = a large amount

hard to know  (546) = difficult to know
humiliated = the lowering or lose of pride and self-esteem or self-worth

distraction (547) =   to cause to turn away from or stop paying attention to something

downplay (548) =  to lower the importance of something

## II. VOCABULARY BUILDING

**Word Analysis**

As in the previous two chapters, the prefixes and suffixes used in each exercise will not be
listed along with their meanings.  Again, you are being asked to analyze each term from memory.  If
you have any difficulty in remembering you can look up the terms in Appendix B that alphabetically
lists and defines each prefix and suffix.

Instructions:
1. Break each word in the table into its prefixes, roots and suffixes.  If you do not remember
   the meaning of a term look it up in Appendix B.
2. Guess the meaning of the word based on the meaning of its parts.
3. Find the word on the text page indicated in the brackets and redefine the word based on the
   context of the sentence, paragraph and chapter.
5. Look up the definition of the word in the VOCABULARY, IDIOMS AND CULTURAL
   CONCEPTS  section above, in Appendix A (marked A) or in a college level dictionary.  If
   the word is followed by letter G look it up in the text Glossary.

Exercise 1. Assumptions

| Word | Meaning |
|---|---|
| assumption (A) | |
| biographical (A) | |
| conscientious (A) | |
| counterproductive (A) | |
| deformity (A) | |
| distraction (A) | |
| downplay (A) | |
| endanger (A) | |
| induce (A) | |
| parasympathetic (G) | |
| polygraph (G) | |
| prospective (A) | |
| provokes (A) | |
| rebound (A) | |
| revulsion (A) | |
| suppressed (A) | |
| transgressions(A) | |

## III. STRUCTURAL CLUES:  CAUSE EFFECT

(This section is an adaptation of material developed by Laurie Blass)

In Chapter 8 you saw some common transition expressions, words and phrases that show you the relationship between two ideas in a text.  One of these was  "as a result," which shows a cause and effect relationship.  When you see "as a result, "you know the next sentence or phrase contains the effect (or result) of the previous one.  The following table lists several words and phrases that usually indicate a cause effect claim, relationship or finding.

| Words and Phrases that Imply Cause and Effect |
|---|
| X results from Y |
| X is due to Y |
| X is produced by Y |
| X is caused by Y |
| X is cured Y |
| X is prevented by  Y |
| X is a consequence of  Y |
| X is changed by |
| X comes about as a result of Y |
| X makes Y occur |

Practice identifying the causes and effects in the following sentences . First find and put a bracket around the word or phrase that indicates the cause. Then draw one line under the cause in each sentence and draw two lines under the results or effects. The first item provides and an example.

1. We can conclude that <u>feelings of being hungry</u> or feeling full (result form a combination) of <u>peripheral and central cues, as well as from the influence of learned and social-cultural cues</u>.

2. According to the James-Lange theory, emotions result from specific changes in our bodies, and each emotion has a different physiological basis.

3. Today researchers argue that emotions may result not only from situational or environmental cues but also from our own cognitive processes, such as thoughts, interpretations, and appraisal.

4. In the next section we'll discuss how emotions may result in physical and psychological problems.

5. Researchers now have evidence to support the claim that homosexuality is due to a complex interaction between biological and social-learning factors.

6. According to cognitive appraisal theory, interpreting or appraising a situation as having a positive or negative impact on our lives produces a subjective feeling that we call an emotion.

As you read, look for these cause effect words and phrases as part of your effort to be a active reader who processes the material deeply. As you learned in Chapter 7: Memory, the deeper you process the more you will remember and the greater the accuracy of your recall.

# CHAPTER 13 PERSONALITY

**OBJECTIVES**

Understand that:

**Theories of Personality**

I. Personality consists of stable, consistent ways in which people's behaviors differ  (p. 553)

II. Freud proposed a psychodynamic theory  (p. 553-554)

    A. Psychoanalysis brings unconscious traumatic experiences to consciousness  (p. 555, Fig. 13.5)

        1. This produces cartharsis and relieves the patient of irrational impulses  (p. 555)

    B. Freud proposed five stages of psychosexual development  (pp. 556-558; Table 13.1)

        1. Oral stage--sexual pleasure from stimulation of mouth  (p. 556)

        2. Anal stage--sexual pleasure from bowel movements  (pp. 556-557)

        3. Phallic stage--Oedipus and Electra complexes occur  (p. 557)

        4. Latent period--sexual interest is suppressed  (p. 557)

        5. Genital stage--sexual pleasure from sexual intercourse  (pp. 557)

        6. Freud's stage view is difficult to test empirically  (p. 557-558)

    C. Personality consists of conflicting parts--id, ego, superego  (p. 558, Fig. 13.6)

        1. Defense mechanisms keep some thoughts from consciousness  (p. 558-560, Fig. 13.7, Fig. 559)

            a. Repression--active forgetting  (pp. 558-559)

            b. Denial--refusal to believe facts  (p. 560)

            c. Rationalization--try to prove that actions are rational  (p. 560)

            d. Displacement--diverting behavior to less threatening target  (p. 560)

            e. Regression--a return to more juvenile means of escaping  (p. 560)

            f. Projection--attributing one's own undesirable characteristics to others  (p. 560)

            g. Reaction formation--presenting the self as opposite  (p. 560-561)

            h. Sublimation--transformation of unacceptable urges into acceptable, even admirable, ones  (p. 561)

    D. The unconscious makes itself felt in everyday life  (p. 561)

        1. Slips of the tongue are related to motivations  (pp. 561-562)

    E. Freud's evidence was based on his inferences  (pp. 563-564)

        1. His interpretation with respect to sexual fantasies changed  (p. 563)

    F. Neo-Freudians have remained faithful to some aspect of Freud's theory and changed others  (p. 564)

III. Carl Jung put more emphasis on people's search for meaning in life  (p. 564-565)

    A. Jung added the concept of the collective unconscious  (pp. 565)

IV. Alfred Adler founded individual psychology  (p. 566)

    A. People have a natural striving for superiority  (p. 566)

    B. Mental illnesses stem from faulty life-styles  (p. 567)

        1. People need to develop a social interest  (p. 567)

    C. Concept of inferiority complex has become part of common culture  (p. 567)

V. Humanistic psychologists believe in free will and study of humans as wholes  (p. 568)

    A. Carl Rogers argued that people strive for self-actualization  (p. 568)

        1. All people should be given unconditional positive regard  (p. 569)

    B. Maslow described the self-actualized personality  (p. 569)

**Personality Traits**

VI. Psychologists investigate how people differ (p. 573)
   A. Nomothetic approach seeks general laws about behavior (p. 573)
   B. Idiographic approach concentrates on intensive studies of individuals (p. 573)

VII. Psychologists distinguish between traits and states (pp. 575-576)
   A. A trait is a consistent, long-lasting tendency in behavior (p. 576)
   B. A state is a temporary activation of behavior (p. 576)

VIII. Psychologists try to identify broad personality traits (pp. 573-574)
   A. Many researchers agree on the "big five" personality traits (pp. 574-575)
      1. Neuroticism is the tendency to experience unpleasant emotions easily (p. 575)
      2. Extraversion is the tendency to seek new experiences and enjoy company (p. 575)
      3. Agreeableness is a tendency to be compassionate (p. 575)
      4. Conscientiousness is a tendency to show self-discipline (p. 575)
      5. Openness is the tendency to enjoy being exposed to new ideas (p. 575)
   B. There is both support for and evidence against the "big five" (pp. 575-576)
      1. The five traits are satisfactory in describing men's and women's personalities (pp. 575-576)
         a. Some traits, such as openness, don't vary much in some cultures (p. 576)
         b. People are fairly stable across adulthood (p. 576)
      2. There are also problems with the concept of "big five" (p. 576)
         a. Most data depend on written responses to questionnaires (p. 576)
         b. The five-factor structure is not theoretically satisfying (p. 576)
         c. The selection of five, rather than 7 or 8, traits is arbitrary (p. 576)
   D. Some people are not very consistent across situations (pp. 576-578)

IX. Heredity seems to influence personality more than family environment (p. 578)
   A. Monozygotic twins are more similar than dizygotic twins on some traits (p. 578, Fig. 13.17, p. 579)
   B. Biological parents are more similar to their children than adoptive parents (p. 580, Fig. 13.18, p. 579)

X. There are some sex differences in personality (pp. 578-580)
   A. Masculinity, femininity, and androgyny are basic traits (p. 580)
      1. Androgyny is equal amounts of masculinity and femininity (p. 580)

XI. The problem with the trait approach is that personalities change across situations (p. 580)

**Personality Assessment**

XII. People accept general and vague personality descriptions of themselves (pp. 582-583)

XIII. Standardized personality tests are administered according to specified rules and they are scored in prescribed ways (p. 583)
   A. The MMPI measures tendencies toward psychological disorders (p. 584)
      1. It was constructed by comparing people with mental illness and people who didn't have mental illnesses (p. 584)
      2. The MMPI-2 is a recent revision of the MMPI (pp. 584-585)
      3. The same norms are used for all races, although this may not be appropriate (pp. 585-586)
      4. Test includes a lie scale and measures other types of deception (p. 586)
      5. Test results classify people, but don't tell anything about degree of disorder (pp. 586-587)
   B. 16-PF test results in a personality profile (pp. 587-598)

XIV. Projective tests ask people to respond to ambiguous stimuli (p. 588)
   A. Rorschach invented the inkblot test (pp. 588-589, Fig. 13.22)
      1. Its reliability and validity may depend upon the psychologist (pp. 589-590)
   B. Thematic Apperception Test (TAT) involves telling stories about pictures (pp. 590-591)

XV. Tests continue to be used in spite of problems  (pp. 591-592)
   A. Low baserates of some disorders will result in many people being diagnosed as mentally ill when they are not  (pp. 591-592, Fig. 13.24)

## COMPREHENSION CHECK

Answer these questions soon after reading the chapter.  Circle the best alternative.  Check your answers on pp. 268-270.  If you gave a wrong answer, try to write why it was wrong.  Check your reasons.

**Theories of Personality**

1. Which personality theorist has a view most similar to that of Hobbes, who argued that humans are selfish and must be restrained by government?
   a. Maslow
   b. Rogers
   c. Adler
   d. Freud

Correct _____  If wrong, why? _____

2. According to Freud's psychodynamic theory:
   a. all neurotic behavior can be traced to sexual abuse
   b. libido focuses on different parts of the body
   c. catharsis is what happens if the libido becomes fixated
   d. the unconscious has no thoughts, memories or emotions
   e. the unconscious never manifests itself in everyday life

Correct _____  If wrong, why? _____

3. According to Freud, the Oedipus complex occurs during which stage?
   a. phallic stage
   b. oral stage
   c. anal stage
   d. genital stage
   e. latent stage

Correct _____  If wrong, why? _____

4. Dan is angry with his boss, but he goes home and yells at his wife, who becomes crabby with her daughter, who starts tormenting the dog.  What defense mechanism is being used?
   a. repression
   b. regression
   c. reaction formation
   d. projection
   e. displacement

Correct _____  If wrong, why? _____

5. John sees an attractive young woman. His _____ wants to have sex with her immediately; his _____ says absolutely not, he shouldn't even think such thoughts; his _____ tries to mediate between the other two.
   a. id, superego, ego
   b. superego, ego, id
   c. id, libido, superego
   d. id, ego, superego
   e. ego, id, libido

Correct _____ If wrong, why? _____

6. Karen Horney, an influential neo-Freudian, differed with Freud's views on:
   a. the existence of an ego
   b. the importance of peak experiences
   c. the importance of unconditional positive regard
   d. the importance of sexual motivation
   e. the role of self-actualization

Correct _____ If wrong, why? _____

7. Which of the following is not a correct pairing?
   a. Adler--collective unconscious
   b. Jung--universal symbols in art, religions, and dreams
   c. Adler--individual psychology
   d. Adler--inferiority complex
   e. Horney--importance of cultural influences

Correct _____ If wrong, why? _____

8. Adler believed that:
   a. we inherit archetypes as part of our collective unconscious
   b. each person is aware of his or her own style of life
   c. people with a strong social interest are very outgoing and friendly
   d. everyone has a natural striving for superiority
   e. personality theorists should study the parts of personality

Correct _____ If wrong, why? _____

9. Which of the following is not characteristic of the self-actualized personality?
   a. treat people with unconditional positive regard
   b. a good sense of humor
   c. a self-centered outlook
   d. an accurate perception of reality
   e. follow own impulses

Correct _____ If wrong, why? _____

**Personality Traits**

10. John always seems to be fidgety and anxious.  John's anxiety is probably:
    a. state anxiety
    b. trait anxiety
    c. the result of extraversion
    d. the result of too much openness to experience

Correct _____ If wrong, why? _____

11. The statistical method that identifies basic groups of traits is called:
    a. correlation
    b. trait analysis
    c. idiographic analysis
    d. factor analysis
    e. nomothetic reductionism

Correct _____ If wrong, why? _____

12. Which of the following is <u>not</u> one of the "big five" personality dimensions?
    a. androgyny
    b. extraversion
    c. agreeableness
    d. openness to experience
    e. neuroticism

Correct _____ If wrong, why? _____

13. A valid criticism of the "big five" personality traits is that:
    a. the traits change a great deal with age
    b. the traits do not correlate with each other very well
    c. the trait structure works well for women but not for men
    d. choosing only 5 traits is arbitrary

Correct _____ If wrong, why? _____

14. What is the role of family environment in personality development?
    a. it is strong because adopted children's personalities are much like their adopted parents'
    b. it is strong because adopted children's personalities correlate with their biological parents more than with their adoptive parents
    c. it is strong because unrelated children growing up in the same family are very similar
    d. it is weak because dizygotic twin pairs are more similar than monozygotic pairs
    e. it is weak because parents and their adopted children's personalities don't correlate

Correct _____ If wrong, why? _____

15. A person who is androgynous:
    a. has many masculine and many feminine traits
    b. has more masculine than feminine traits
    c. believes that he or she has control over the outcomes of behavior
    d. changes behavior to fit the situation

Correct _____ If wrong, why? _____

**Personality Assessment**

16. Experiments have been done in which students took tests and were given personality feedback.
    Generally, what was their opinion of the feedback?
    a. they believed it only if it had direct relevance to their answers on the test
    b. they rarely believed the feedback from so-called experts
    c. less than 20% rated a vague and general description as "good to excellent"
    d. about 90% rated a vague and general description as "good to excellent"
    e. about 90% rated a strange, unflattering description as "good to excellent"

Correct _____ If wrong, why? _____

17. The original MMPI:
    a. was developed by asking questions that fitted with the developers' theory of personality
    b. has high validity, so that a clinician can use it alone to evaluate psychological problems
    c. asks questions that are answered differently by people with various psychological disorders and
       other people
    d. asks a series of open-ended questions
    e. is not valid because most people lie

Correct _____ If wrong, why? _____

18. In the Thematic Apperception Test, you would be asked to:
    a. describe what you see in inkblots
    b. tell stories about people in pictures
    c. free-associate in Freud's sense
    d. answer questions that can be used to make a personality profile
    e. describe what people of the opposite sex are doing in pictures

Correct _____ If wrong, why? _____

19. A psychologist administering a Rorschach will:
    a. begin with very clear instructions about what the client should say
    b. only record what you say and not things you do with the cards
    c. almost always administer it using double-blind methodology
    d. show more reliability using objective scoring than using subjective interpretations
    e. be able to identify your specific disorder with about 95% accuracy

Correct _____ If wrong, why? _____

## ANSWERS AND EXPLANATIONS FOR COMPREHENSION CHECK

<u>Correct Answer</u>                     <u>Other Alternatives Are Wrong Because:</u>

1. d  (p. 553, Fig. 13.1)         a. believed in self-actualization, an innate goodness
   Obj. I                         b. argues that people have good, noble goals
                                  c. many people have strong social interest

2. b  (p. 556)                    a. Freud once thought this, but decided it was sexual
   Obj. II                             fantasies, not actual abuse
                                  c. release of tension related to unpleasant experiences
                                  d. unconscious does have these, but it's less logical
                                  e. it does in slips of the tongue; unconscious motivations can influence
                                       such errors

3. a  (p. 557)                    b. sensual pleasure from mouth area
   Obj. II-B-3                    c. pleasure from bowel movements
                                  d. interest in others' and own genitals
                                  e. sexual interest is suppressed

4. e  (p. 560)                    a. Dan would place anger with boss into unconscious
   Obj. II-C-1-d                  b. Dan would behave in a more juvenile way
                                  c. Dan would be very friendly toward his boss to hide the anger
                                  d. Dan would argue that everyone hates his or her boss

5. a  (p. 558, Fig. 13.6)         b. id contains sexual urge; superego is like a conscience;
   Obj. II-C                           ego mediates and deals with reality
                                  c. libido is general sexual energy; superego doesn't mediate, it is
                                       restrictive
                                  d. ego is the mediator; superego is the restrictive part
                                  e. id contains sexual urges; ego mediates and deals with reality; libido is
                                       sexual energy

6. d  (p. 564)                    a. she agreed that ego existed;
   Obj. II-F                      b. in humanistic psychology--moments when people feel
                                       truly fulfilled
                                  c. in humanistic psychology--unqualified acceptance of others
                                  e. fulfillment of potential in humanistic theories

7. a  (pp. 564-566)               a. this was Jung's term for the cumulative experience
   Obj. III                            of previous generations
                                  b-e.  are correct

8. d  (pp. 566-567)               a. this is Jung's idea
   Obj. IV-A                      b. people may not be aware of their style of life
                                  c. refers to striving to benefit the human race
                                  e. people should be viewed as wholes

9. c  (p. 569)                    a,b,d,e.  all are characteristics
   Obj. V-B                       c. they are problem centered

10. b (p. 574)  
   Obj. VII-A

a. seems to be more temporary; a transient condition  
c. directing interest in others; unrelated to anxiety  
d. enjoyment of new experiences; wouldn't cause anxiety

11. d (pp. 574-575)  
   Obj. VIII

a. it uses correlation, but it searches for groups of things  
   that correlate with each other but not with other groups  
b. traits are predispositions to act in certain ways, but many may be  
   related  
c. not a statistical technique, but intensive study of individuals  
e. not a statistical technique, but an approach that seeks general laws  
   about personality

12. a (p. 575)  
   Obj. VIII-A

a. relates to personality differences between men and women, important  
   but not one of the big five; conscientiousness is missing here  
b-e. all are "big five" personality dimensions

13. d (p. 576)  
   Obj. VIII-B-2

a. they change very little with age  
b. they aren't supposed to correlate with each other; that's the point of  
   factor analysis, to find independent factors  
c. the traits work well for both men and women

14. e (p. 578)  
   Obj. IX

a. adopted children and their adoptive parents are not similar  
b. this is evidence for no family environment effect  
c. they are not very similar, arguing against family environment as an  
   important influence  
d. monozygotic twins are more similar, showing a genetic influence

15. a (p. 580)  
   Obj. X-A-1

b. this would be a masculine person  
c. external locus of control, unrelated to androgyny  
d. high self-monitor, unrelated to androgyny

16. d (p. 583)  
   Obj. XII

a. test questions don't have to be related to feedback  
b,c. 90% rated it "good to excellent"  
e. only about 20% rated this description "good to excellent"

17. c (p. 584)  
   Obj. XIII-A-1

a. questions were chosen by trial and error; they just found  
   questions that were answered differently by different groups  
b. validity not that high; should be used with other measures  
d. projective tests do this; MMPI is objective  
e. a lie scale is included, and if the score is too high, test results will not  
   be used

18. b (pp. 592-593)  
   Obj. XIV-B

a. Rorschach  
c. people are given pictures because they often don't talk spontaneously  
d. 16-PF test results in such a profile  
e. people in pictures are mostly of one's own sex

19. d (p. 592)
   Obj. XIV-A

a. the instructions are intentionally vague
b. some psychologists will record all behaviors
c. they should, but most psychologists already know what disorder the person shows
e. can tell whether people have some sort of problem but not specifically which one

## LECTURE MATERIAL

Don't forget to review your lecture material. Process each topic meaningfully. First, be sure that you understand the material in each lecture--if you don't, ask your instructor or teaching assistant. Associate the material with things that you already know and with your personal experiences. If you can make up mental images of any of the material, do so. Try to think of real-life applications of the concepts. Don't forget to put your own notes on each day's lecture notes. Then write questions to cover each concept.

------------------------------------------------------------------------
WAIT AT LEAST 24 HOURS BEFORE PROCEEDING.
LET FORGETTING OCCUR--IT WILL!!
------------------------------------------------------------------------

## SHORT-ANSWER ESSAY QUESTIONS

Write brief answers to each of the following. The answers are on pp. 272-273, but do try to write the answers yourself before looking at them.

**Theories of Personality**

1. Describe Freud's five stages of sexual development.

2. Explain why people use defense mechanisms.

3. Describe how slips of the tongue have been increased so that they could be studied under different motivating conditions.

4. How did Jung and Freud disagree?

5. Describe Adler's individual psychology.

6. Discuss the basic difference between the psychodynamic and humanistic approaches to personality.

**Personality Traits**

7. Discuss the difference between the nomothetic and idiographic approaches to personality.

8. What type of support has been obtained for the "big five" personality traits?

9. Discuss the role of family environment in personality.

10. Describe the two ways in which a person could be androgynous with Bem's original scoring method. How has this been changed?

**Personality Assessment**

11. Describe how the developers of the MMPI guarded against lying. How do employers do a similar thing on job applications?

12. What is the problem with using tests, such as the MMPI-2, that have fairly good reliability and validity as the only means of diagnosing individuals?

\*\*\*\*\*\*\*\*\*\*\*\*\*\*\*\*\*\*\*\*\*\*\*\*\*\*\*\*\*\*\*\*\*\*\*\*\*\*\*\*\*\*\*\*\*\*\*\*\*\*\*\*\*\*\*\*\*\*\*\*\*\*\*\*\*\*\*\*\*\*\*\*\*\*\*\*\*
Find the questions that you wrote over lecture material and write answers to them.
\*\*\*\*\*\*\*\*\*\*\*\*\*\*\*\*\*\*\*\*\*\*\*\*\*\*\*\*\*\*\*\*\*\*\*\*\*\*\*\*\*\*\*\*\*\*\*\*\*\*\*\*\*\*\*\*\*\*\*\*\*\*\*\*\*\*\*\*\*\*\*\*\*\*\*\*\*

## ANSWERS TO SHORT-ANSWER ESSAY QUESTIONS

1. Oral stage: Libido attaches itself to mouth area and infant derives pleasure from sucking.
   Anal stage: Libido attaches itself to anal area and infant derives pleasure from bowel movements.
   Phallic stage: Libido is in genital area and child shows interest in genitals. Oedipus complex occurs because male child wishes to have mother's affection and get rid of father.
   Latent stage: Child is so traumatized by Oedipus complex that libido becomes latent or hidden. Child suppresses sexual interest.
   Genital stage: Libido is in genital area and child takes interest in own and others' genitals. (pp. 556-558, Table 13.1)

2. Personality is made up of the id, which is motivated by biological instincts; the superego, which is highly moral and punishing; and the ego, which mediates between id, superego, and reality. Ego can exclude some of id's impulses from consciousness, and thus avoid some of the guilt caused by superego. Defense mechanisms reduce anxiety by dealing with the conflict between id and superego. (p. 558)

3. Motley and Baars manipulated motivation either by having a sexy female experimenter or by having male subjects hooked up to a shock apparatus. They were asked to read and remember pairs of syllables, some of which would be related to shock or sex if the first letters were interchanged. "Shock" subjects make shock-related errors and "sex" subjects made sex-related errors. (pp. 561-562, Fig. 13.8)

4. Jung put greater emphasis on people's search for meaning in life than Freud did. Jung argued that there was a deeper level of unconscious called the collective unconscious; Freud disagreed. (p. 565)

5. It is the psychology of a person as a whole. Adler argued that people strive for superiority, and if they don't succeed in overcoming helplessness in childhood they may develop an inferiority complex. The plan for achieving superiority determines a person's style of life. If a person contributes to the welfare of the human race, he or she has developed social interest. (pp. 566-567)

6. Psychodynamic theorists agree with Hobbes that basic human instincts are selfish; these instincts are part of the id. Other parts of personality are necessary to keep these instincts from showing up fully. Humanist theorists side with Rousseau and argue that humans are good by nature; a person's full potential emerges in self-actualization. People strive for perfection, and when their true selves emerge, they are basically good, caring people. (pp. 553, 568)

7. The nomothetic approach seeks general laws about how personality influences behavior. Groups of people are compared and statistical analysis is used. The results are meant to be generalized to the population. The idiographic approach focuses on intensive studies of individuals. The results are not meant to be generalized to the population. (p. 573)

8. The five-factor description characterizes personality in both men and women. It works in many languages and cultures, although some cultures may not show enough variation in some of the traits for the description to be meaningful. The "big five" traits seem to be fairly stable across age. (pp. 575-576)

9. Adopted children's personalities generally do not correlate with the personalities of their adoptive parents. Unrelated children growing up in the same home do not develop similar personalities. These findings suggest that personality development is not dependent upon family environment. However, many researchers believe that much of the variation in personality may be due to unshared environment which is the environment that differs from family member to family member. This is difficult to test. Overall, the research suggests a limited role for family environment in personality development. (p. 578-580, Figs. 13.17, 13.18)

10. A person could be androgynous either because he or she checked many feminine traits and many masculine traits or because he or she checked few of either. Today, androgyny is usually defined as being high in both masculine and feminine traits. (p. 580, Table 13.2)

11. Some questions should be answered the same by everyone; if you answer differently, you must be lying. The number of such answers are added up to give a score on the lie scale. Employers sometimes do a similar thing on job applications by asking applicants about experience in doing nonexistent tasks. (p. 586, Table 13.4)

12. Tests should be used as aids and not the sole method of diagnosis. Even if a test correctly identifies 95% of the people with a disorder and incorrectly diagnoses 5% of the normal population, it is misdiagnosing more people than it is correctly diagnosing. This is because the total population of normal people is much greater than the population of people with fairly rare disorders. (pp. 591-592, Fig. 13.24)

**POSTTEST**

Take this test with all of your books and notes out of sight. This should give you a good idea of how well you understand the material.

**Matching**

Put the letter of the approach in the blank beside the description.

Theories of Personality

1. _____ "indivisible" psychology or psychology of person as a whole

2. _____ decreased role for sex; increased role for culture

3. _____ people are basically good and are motivated toward self-actualization

4. _____ approach that includes collective unconscious

5. _____ personality is interplay among forces, many of which are not consciously recognized

6. _____ stable, consistent ways in which one person's behavior differs from others'

A. humanistic

B. psychodynamic

C. Jung's theory

D. personality

E. neo-Freudian approaches

F. individual psychology

**Multiple-choice**

Circle the best alternative.

Theories of Personality

1. Which approach to personality would agree with Rousseau that humans are good by nature?
   a. Freud's approach
   b. psychodynamic
   c. the ancient Greeks' approach
   d. humanistic
   e. neo-Freudian

2. Johnny, who is 8, has absolutely no interest in girls or anything related to sex. According to Freud, Johnny would be in which stage?
   a. latent
   b. anal
   c. oral
   d. genital
   e. phallic

3. Mr. Ku absolutely hates people of other races, yet he sets up free food programs and medical clinics in areas where they live. Which defense mechanism is he using?
   a. denial
   b. reaction formation
   c. displacement
   d. projection
   e. repression

4. If a person has just been sexually aroused, what type of slip of the tongue is most likely?
   a. breast in bed for best in bread
   b. hot shock for shad bock
   c. big pit for pig bit
   d. square meal for mare squeal
   e. all of the above are equally likely

5. In the revision of his theory, what did Freud believe about sexual abuse?
   a. it was responsible for all neurotic behavior
   b. sexual abuse rarely occurs, because patients almost never report it
   c. sexual abuse is the cause of sublimation
   d. sexual abuse is part of the collective unconscious
   e. his patients misled him into believing they had been sexually abused

6. Adler argued that:
   a. people create a master plan for reaching peak experiences
   b. universal symbols occur in art, dreams, and hallucinations
   c. penis envy occurs because of the collective unconscious
   d. everyone has a natural striving for superiority
   e. people become maladjusted if they don't have a peak experience

7. Which of the following is mispaired?
   a. style of life-Adler
   b. inferiority complex-Jung
   c. collective unconscious-Jung
   d. Oedipus complex-Freud
   e. social interest-Adler

8. Behaviorism and psychoanalysis share which assumptions that differ from humanistic psychology?
   a. parsimony and reductionism
   b. determinism and parsimony
   c. "all behavior is learned" and parsimony
   d. determinism and "all behavior is learned"
   e. reductionism and determinism

9. In humanistic psychology, the moment an adolescent clearly decides about a profession is called:
   a. peak experience
   b. self-actualization
   c. growth experience
   d. reaction formation
   e. resolution of the Oedipus complex

10. Unconditional positive regard means:
    a. encouraging a person to act on every impulse
    b. leading a person toward self-actualization
    c. trying to change behavior rather than thoughts
    d. complete, unqualified acceptance of a person
    e. a natural drive to achieve one's own potential

11. Maslow thought that people with self-actualized personalities showed all except:
    a. openness to all kinds of experiences
    b. avoidance of ambiguous perceptions
    c. independence and creativity
    d. good sense of humor
    e. treating people with unconditional positive regard

Personality Traits

12. Factor analysis can be used to:
    a. find traits that will predict behavior perfectly
    b. identify traits that are highly correlated
    c. identify all traits that might be used to describe behavior
    d. determine how often people behave in certain ways
    e. explain a person's behavior

13. Which two traits do most personality theorists agree are the most powerful?
    a. assertiveness and self-discipline
    b. neuroticism and extraversion
    c. conscientiousness and agreeableness
    d. openness to experience and extraversion
    e. conscientiousness and warmth

14. Evidence for a role of genetics in personality includes the finding that:
    a. dizygotic twins are more similar than monozygotic twins
    b. parents' level of extraversion is more similar to their biological children than to their adopted children
    c. unrelated children adopted into the same families don't develop similar personalities
    d. there is little relationship between arousal levels and personality
    e. unshared environments differ from one sibling to another

15. Recent conceptualizations of androgyny:
    a. define it as being equal in male and female traits
    b. define it in terms of biological maleness and femaleness
    c. suggest that one can be high in maleness or femaleness, but not both
    d. put masculine and feminine at opposite poles of a single dimension
    e. define it as being high in both male and female traits

16. Which of the following is not necessary for a standardized test?
    a. it was developed from a specific theoretical viewpoint
    b. items are clear and unambiguous
    c. the mean and range of scores is determined for a large number of people
    d. it is administered according to specific rules
    e. the normal range of scores can be determined

17. The MMPI was devised empirically, which means that:
    a. it was based on a theory about personality disorders
    b. it was revised recently to improve its validity today
    c. items were simply given to groups having different disorders and similar answers given by similar groups were identified
    d. it was normed on many different ethnic groups
    e. it was designed to detect deception

18. Why would a psychologist use a projective test rather than just asking a person to talk about himself or herself?
    a. the projective test will be much higher in validity
    b. the projective test will make it much easier to decide if a person has a severe mental disorder
    c. the projective test should be more effective in getting a person to start talking
    d. different psychologists will come to different conclusions from an interview but not from a projective test

19. Which of the following is the psychologist least likely to do when giving a Rorschach?
    a. notice whether you rotate each card
    b. record how long you study each card
    c. suggest that you should try to see the inkblot as one object
    d. notice whether you say anything about color or movement
    e. count how many responses you give

20. The TAT:
    a. is also called the Taylor Anxiety Test
    b. asks people to describe what they see in 20 blank cards
    c. provides more ambiguous stimuli than the Rorschach
    d. is used only in clinical settings
    e. probably measures current concerns more than fixed personality traits

## ANSWERS TO POSTTEST

| Correct Answer | Questions Testing a Similar Concept | |
| --- | --- | --- |
| | Comprehension Check | Short-Answer |
| **Matching** | | |
| 1. F (p. 568) | 7,8 | 5 |
| 2. E (p. 566) | 6,7e | 4,6 |
| 3. A (p. 570) | 9 | 6 |
| 4. C (pp. 566-568) | 7b,8a | 4 |
| 5. B (p. 556) | 2 | 1,2 |
| 6. D (pp. 555-556) | -- | 7 |

**Multiple-Choice**

| | | |
|---|---|---|
| 1.  d  (p. 555, Fig. 13.1) | 1,9 | 6 |
| 2.  a  (p. 559) | 3e | 1 |
| 3.  b  (p. 562) | 4c | 2 |
| 4.  a  (pp. 563-564) | 2e | 3 |
| 5.  e  (pp. 564-565) | 2a | -- |
| 6.  d  (p. 568) | 7,8 | 5 |
| 7.  b  (pp. 566-568) | 7,8 | 4,5 |
| 8.  e  (p. 570) | 2,8 | 6 |
| 9.  c  (p. 570) | 6b | 6 |
| 10.  d  (p. 571) | 9a | 6 |
| 11.  b  (p. 571) | 9 | -- |
| 12.  b  (pp. 576-577) | 13b | 8 |
| 13.  b  (p. 577) | 12 | 8 |
| 14.  b  (p. 580) | 14 | 9 |
| 15.  e  (p. 582) | 15 | 10 |
| 16.  a  (pp. 585-586) | 17a | -- |
| 17.  c  (p. 586) | 17 | -- |
| 18.  c  (p. 590) | 18,19 | -- |
| 19.  c  (p. 591) | 19 | -- |
| 20.  e  (p. 593) | 18 | -- |

# CHAPTER 13  LANGUAGE ENHANCEMENT GUIDE

## I. VOCABULARY, IDIOMS AND CULTURAL CONCEPTS

**Instructions:**

As you read the text refer to the following list of words and their definitions.  The words are listed in the order in which they appear in the chapter.  The definitions presented contain the meaning of the word as used by Kalat on the textbook page indicated.

Remember that these words like all words can have different meanings in other sentences.  If you do not find a non-technical word on this list it may have been defined on a previous page or chapter of this study guide.  The definition of non-technical words may be found in the dictionary at the end of this study guide.  Kalat defined each new technical word as it first appears on a page and these may be found in Kalat's summary at the end of the section and in the textbook's Glossary.

### Theories of Personality

Houston Astrodome (552) = a covered stadium for sporting events in the city of Houston, Texas
grand theory = a theory that tries to explain all or most of human behavior

selfish (553) =  interested only with oneself
restrained =  limited or restricted; held back
civilized = well behaved; educated
held in check = controlled

stable (554) =  not easily changed
enormous = very large
flimsy = unconvincing; not very strong

traumatic (555) = an emotional shock that produces lasting damage to the psychological development of a person

reconstructed = rebuilt based on inferences

identify with (556) = to become like the person admired

eventually (557) = at a later time

resolve = solve

controversial = disputed, debated, argued

deny = refuse to believe; reject

suppress = to inhibit expression; to hold back;  to prevent thinking about unacceptable desires or thoughts

negotiated (558) = succeed in coping with, solving, accomplishing or managing

derive = get

prohibition =  a refusal to allow; forbidden by law

metaphor = a word or phrase that suggests ways in which two different things may be similar

relegation (559) = removal and sending away

diverting (560) = turning aside; distract

juvenile = child-like, immature, young

attribution = assigning, placing, accusing

transformation = changing

manifestation (561) = showing, displaying, expression, revelation

revelation = manifestation

virtually = practically, actually

backed down (563) = rejected; changed

attributed = assigned a cause

coherent =  to have parts  logically connected

slighted (564) = ignored; not paid attention to

inner circle = a group of people who work together

continuity (565) =  a series of connected events; an uninterrupted flow of events

cumulative = increasing or getting larger by adding new parts

collective = shared

contending  (566) = claiming

reconcile = to reestablish a friendship; settle,  resolve

self-defeating (567) = harming or hurting oneself

compensating = to make up for;  to offset; counterbalance

deliberate (568) = done after careful thought

sacrifice  = to give up something of value

pointless = meaningless

ascribe = assign cause
discrepancy = difference

### Personality Traits

fluctuations (574) = changes

works "well enough" (576) = works effectively
just barely worth = less worth

consistency (578) = stability, behaving in similar ways in the same or different situations

stereotypical (580) = a simplified exaggerated prejudgment about a category of people
wholeheartedly = completely and without any doubts

### Personality Assessment

compensate (581) = to act as an equalizing force; to make up, balance, offset

preposterous (582) = nonsense, foolish, stupid
prescribed = to set down or specify rules or guidelines
out of the air = from imagination

are on the way (584) = are being developed

integral part (585) = an important and necessary part

deception (586) = mislead; misrepresent; lie
exaggerating = claiming that something is more, better or larger than it really is

in the abstract (587) = in generalized terms without any specific examples

occult (589) = dealing with supernatural and metaphysical claims that cannot be scientifically studied

divinity school (590) = a college for religious education that educates and trains ministers

screen job applicants (591) = select job applicants
prone to (592) = having a tendency, likely

## II. VOCABULARY BUILDING

### Word Analysis

Instructions:

1. Break each word in the table into its prefixes, roots and suffixes. If you do not remember the meaning of a term look it up in Appendix B.
2. Guess the meaning of the word based on the meaning of its parts.
3. Find the word on the text page indicated in the brackets and redefine the word based on the context of the sentence, paragraph and chapter.
5. Look up the definition of the word in the VOCABULARY, IDIOMS AND CULTURAL CONCEPTS section above, in Appendix A (marked A) or in a college level dictionary. If the word is followed by letter G look it up in the text Glossary.

## Exercise 1. Agreeableness

| Word | Meaning |
|---|---|
| agreeableness(G) | |
| androgyny | |
| ascribe (A) | |
| attribution (A) | |
| coherent (A) | |
| continuity (A) | |
| deliberate (A) | |
| discrepancy (A) | |
| displacement(G) | |
| enormous (A) | |
| eventually (A) | |
| extroversion (G) | |
| humanistic (G) | |
| idiographic(G) | |
| introversion | |
| misuse | |
| multiphasic (G) | |
| neuroticism (G) | |
| nomothetic (G) | |

## Exercise 2. Objective

| Word | Meaning |
|---|---|
| objective (G) | |
| personality (G) | |
| pointless (A) | |
| prohibition (A) | |
| psychoanalysis (G) | |
| psychodynamic(G) | |
| psychosexual (G) | |
| rationalization(G) | |
| reconstructed (A) | |
| repression(G) | |
| restrained (A) | |
| standardized test  (G) | |
| suppress (A) | |
| thematic (G) | |
| traumatic (A) | |

# CHAPTER 14  ABNORMAL BEHAVIOR

**OBJECTIVES**

Understand that:

**Overview of Abnormal Behavior**

I.  Defining abnormal behavior can be difficult  (pp. 597-598)

    A.  Different disorders occur in different cultures  (pp. 598-600)

    B.  Different views can be used to explain abnormal behavior  (p. 600)

        1.  Psychological disorders may result from biological disorders  (p. 600)

        2.  Psychological disorders may be due to early experiences  (p. 600)

        3.  Psychological disorders may result from stressful environments  (p. 600)

II.  DSM-IV classifies disorders  (pp. 600-601)

    A.  Psychological disorders form a continuum  (p. 601)

        1.  50% of all people endure some diagnosable disorder at some point in their lives  (p. 601, Fig. 14.4)

          a.  Percent of people who "have a problem" is ambiguous  (p. 601)

    B.  DSM-IV has axes of classification  (p. 602)

        1.  Axis I lists disorders that have an onset after infancy and have some likelihood of recovery  (p. 602, Table 14.1, p. 603)

        2.  Axis II lists disorders that persist throughout life  (p. 602, Table 14.2, p. 604)

        3.  Axis III lists physical disorders  (p. 602)

        4.  Axis IV indicates how much stress the person has had to endure  (p. 602)

        5.  Axis V evaluates level of functioning  (p. 602)

    C.  DSM-IV allows clinicians to make differential diagnoses  (pp. 602, 604)

**Anxiety and Avoidance Disorders**

III.  Anxiety is a common reason for psychological disorders  (p. 606)

    A.  Generalized anxiety disorder involves exaggerated worries  (p. 606)

    B.  Panic disorders involve a fairly constant state of anxiety plus occasional panic attacks and overresponse to mild stressors  (pp. 606-607, Fig. 14.5)

        1.  Social phobia involves an avoidance of other people  (p. 606)

        2.  Agoraphobia is an excessive fear of open places  (pp. 606-607)

        3.  People may hyperventilate, causing the symptoms of a panic attack  (p. 607, Fig. 14.6)

IV.  Some disorders involve avoidance  (pp. 607-608)

    A.  Avoidance behaviors are resistant to extinction  (p. 608)

    B.  Some disorders involve exaggerated avoidance behaviors  (pp. 607-608)

        1.  Avoidance behaviors persist long after the response is unnecessary  (p. 608)

    C.  Phobias are strong fears that interfere with everyday living  (pp. 608-609)

        1.  5-13% of the population suffers from phobias  (p. 609)

        2.  Phobias may have developed from classical conditioning  (p. 609)

        3.  Phobias may also develop by observing fearful others  (pp. 610-611)

          a.  Observers need to know what the fearful other is frightened of to develop a fear  (pp. 610-611, Fig. 14.10)

        4.  People may be prepared to develop some phobias  (pp. 611-612)

          a.  People develop phobias most easily to unpredictable and uncontrollable objects  (p. 612)

        5.  Phobias may persist because exposure to the objects doesn't occur  (p. 612)

6. Systematic desensitization and flooding are effective therapies for phobias (pp. 612-614)
E. Obsessive-compulsive disorder involves unwelcome thoughts and repetitive behaviors (p. 614)
1. Obsessions may stem from trying not to think of something (p. 614)
2. One type of compulsion is cleaning excessively (pp. 614-615)
3. Another type of compulsion is checking excessively (p. 615)
4. Drugs that prolong the effects of serotonin seem to help (p. 616)

## Substance-Related Disorders

V. Psychoactive substance dependence occurs when a person cannot quit a destructive habit (pp. 618-619)
A. The more rapidly a substance enters the brain, the more likely it is to be addictive (p. 619)
VI. Some people may be predisposed to become addicted to drugs (p. 620)
A. Genetics plays some role in alcoholism (p. 620)
B. Sons of alcoholics respond differently to alcohol than others (pp. 620-622)
1. Alcohol provides more stress reduction for sons of alcoholics than for others (pp. 620-621)
2. Sons of alcoholics underestimate how much they have drunk (pp. 621-622)
VII. Treatments for addictions are only moderately successful (p. 622)
A. Alcoholics Anonymous uses self-help groups (pp. 622-623)
B. Antabuse makes people ill if they drink (p. 623)
C. It is not clear that substance abuse is a disease (pp. 623-624)
D. Whether alcoholics can learn to drink in moderation is controversial (p. 624)
E. Methadone is the most common treatment for opiate addiction (p. 625)

## Mood Disorders

VIII. Depression can be major, bipolar, reactive, or endogenous (pp. 627-628)
A. Some people may be genetically predisposed to depression (p. 628)
B. Depression is more common in women than in men (pp. 628-629)
1. Postpartum depression occurs after childbirth (p. 629)
2. Women may ruminate more about depression than men (p. 629)
C. Unpleasant events often cause depression (pp. 629-630)
1. Some people are more vulnerable than others (pp. 629-630)
IX. Depressed people may focus on the unpleasant side of life (p. 630)
A. Learned helplessness may be a cause of depression (p. 630)
1. Animals don't learn to escape if they had earlier learned that there was no escape (p. 630)
B. People may become depressed because of their attributions for failure (pp. 630-631)
1. People who make internal attributions for failure have a pessimistic explanatory style (p. 631)
X. People with seasonal affective disorder are depressed in winter (p. 632)
XI. People with bipolar disorder alternate between mania and depression (pp. 632-633)
A. In the depression phase, people may wish they were dead (p. 633)
B. In the manic phase, people follow impulses and are very active (pp. 632-633)
C. Periods in bipolar cycles may run for months or a day (pp. 633-634)
XII. Suicide frequently accompanies depression (p. 634)
A. Women attempt suicide more often than men, but more men die by suicide (p. 634, Fig. 14.24)
B. People who are thinking about suicide need professional help (pp. 634-635)

## Schizophrenia

XIII. In schizophrenia, the emotions and the intellect seem to be separated (p. 637, Fig. 14.25)
A. Schizophrenia afflicts less than 1% of people at some point in their lives (pp. 637-638)
B. Hallucinations occur when sensory experiences don't correspond to the outside world (p. 638)

C. Delusions are unfounded beliefs  (p. 638)

D. People with schizophrenia may show little sign of emotion  (pp. 638-639)

E. People with schizophrenia show loose and idiosyncratic associations  (p. 639)

F. Symptoms of schizophrenia are positive and negative  (p. 639)

    1. Positive symptoms, such as hallucinations, delusions, and thought disorder, are present (p. 639)

        a. Positive psychotic symptoms are hallucinations and delusions  (p. 639)

        b. Positive disorganized symptoms are thought disorder, bizarre behavior, and inappropriate emotions  (p. 639)

    2. Negative symptoms, such as lack of emotional expression, lack of social interaction, are absent  (p. 639)

XIV. There are several types of schizophrenia  (p. 640)

A. Undifferentiated has basic symptoms  (p. 640)

B. Catatonic includes movement disorders  (p. 640, Fig. 14.28)

C. Disorganized is characterized by incoherent speech, lack of social relationships, and odd behavior (p. 640)

D. Paranoid includes hallucinations and delusions  (pp. 640-641)

XV  Schizophrenia has multiple causes  (p. 641)

A. Minor, widespread brain damage accompanies schizophrenia  (pp. 641-642, Fig. 14.29)

B. Dopamine is probably involved, because effective drugs block dopamine synapses  (p. 642)

C. There seems to be a genetic predisposition to schizophrenia  (pp. 642-643, Fig. 14.30)

    1. A marker for schizophrenia is a failure to filter out irrelevant information  (p. 643)

    2. Another marker is an inability to move the eyes smoothly while tracking an object  (p. 643)

D. Stress may trigger schizophrenia  (pp. 643-644)

E. Infants may be infected by a virus or bacterium  (p. 644)


## COMPREHENSION CHECK

Answer these questions soon after reading the chapter.  Circle the *best* alternative.  Check your answers, pp. 288-290.  If you gave a wrong answer, try to write why it was wrong.  Check your reasons, pp. 288-290.

### Overview of Abnormal Behavior

1. The American Psychiatric Association's definition of psychological disorder is:

    a. anything that is different from average

    b. behavior associated with distress, disability, or with increased risk of death, pain, or loss of freedom

    c. patterns of behavior that a particular culture regards as troublesome or unacceptable

    d. any unusual behavior that is caused by a biological disorder

Correct _____ If wrong, why? _____

2. According to DSM-IV, if someone has an Axis I disorder:

    a. the disorder is a part of the person himself or herself and therapy is unlikely to help

    b. the person has a good prospect for effective treatment

    c. there is a physical problem, such as diabetes

    d. he or she would also score high on the Axis V scale of level of functioning

Correct _____ If wrong, why? _____

**Anxiety and Avoidance Disorders**

3. Mary occasionally experiences severe chest pains, sweating, faintness and shaking. At first she thought she was having heart attacks but her doctor says she is fine. From what does Mary suffer?
    a. phobia
    b. obsessive-compulsive disorder
    c. panic disorder
    d. dissociative disorder
    e. a lack of generalized anxiety

Correct _____ If wrong, why? _____

4. Which of the following is a phobia?
    a. Jean looks the other way when the cobra bites the hero in the movie
    b. Mary tries to squash the spiders in her hotel room in a slum area so they don't bite her
    c. Gladys looks around fearfully as she goes to the bank in a "bad" area with a large sum of money
    d. Susan has stopped gardening because there might be a snake outside
    e. all of the above are phobias

Correct _____ If wrong, why? _____

5. Watson and Rayner made a loud sound at the same time that Little Albert saw a white rat. Albert came to fear white rats. Which of the following is true?
    a. the sound is the CS; the rat is the UCS
    b. fear to the sound is the CR; fear to the rat is the UCR
    c. the sound is the UCS; fear to it is the CR
    d. the rat is the CS; fear to it is the CR

Correct _____ If wrong, why? _____

6. Lab monkeys show a fear of snakes:
    a. from birth; apparently the fear is genetic
    b. after watching a wild-born monkey show fear, even though the snake is out of sight
    c. after watching a wild-born monkey show fear, with the snake in sight
    d. only if they have been specifically conditioned to fear snakes with something like a shock as the UCS

Correct _____ If wrong, why? _____

7. The therapist is treating Susan's phobia of snakes by asking her to imagine herself at the bottom of a pit of 1,000 snakes. She cannot escape as they crawl all around on her and some bite her. The type of therapy is:
    a. implosion
    b. systematic desensitization
    c. similar to Skinner's shaping procedure
    d. b and c
    e. gradual exposure to the feared object via virtual reality

Correct _____ If wrong, why? _____

8. A person who constantly thinks about dying has:
   a. a compulsion
   b. an obsession
   c. a preparedness reaction
   d. a checker reaction
   e. a cleaner reaction

Correct _____ If wrong, why? _____

**Substance-Related Disorders**

9. Addictive substances:
   a. usually stimulate dopamine synapses in the brain
   b. enter the brain more slowly than non-addictive substances
   c. are addictive because of their characteristics, not because of the user
   d. are more likely to cause addiction if they are eaten than if they are smoked

Correct _____ If wrong, why? _____

10. Sons of alcoholics:
    a. show less of a decline in stress when they drink alcohol than sons of nonalcoholics
    b. show the effects of alcohol on motor and cognitive performance more than sons of nonalcoholics
    c. underestimate the amount of alcohol they have drunk
    d. show the effects of alcohol on motor and cognitive performance less than sons of nonalcoholics

Correct _____ If wrong, why? _____

11. Alcoholism:
    a. must be treated with total abstinence to prevent relapse
    b. may be treated with disulfiram, which produces a threat of sickness
    c. is clearly a progressive disease, because alcoholics always grow worse with time if they do not abstain
    d. is little affected by environmental factors, giving good evidence for the disease concept
    e. is best treated by controlled drinking

Correct _____ If wrong, why? _____

**Mood Disorders**

12. Joe suffers from major depression; it is severe and has lasted for several months. The depression developed gradually and cannot be traced to any specific event. His depression is:
    a. reactive
    b. bipolar
    c. due to learned helplessness
    d. endogenous

Correct _____ If wrong, why? _____

13. A type of evidence that there is a genetic predisposition to depression is that:
    a. some women show postpartum depression following childbirth
    b. some types of depression respond better to drugs than to psychotherapy
    c. adopted children usually have more adoptive than biological relatives who are depressed
    d. relatives of depressed people often show sleep abnormalities or develop anxiety disorders

Correct _____ If wrong, why? _____

14. Dogs are held in place in a shuttle box while a tone precedes a shock. Later, the dogs can jump to escape the shock. What happens?
    a. the dogs learn the escape response faster than animals who aren't shocked first, because they learn that a tone predicts shock
    b. the dogs show many symptoms of schizophrenia
    c. the dogs develop learned helplessness
    d. the dogs show seasonal affective disorder

Correct _____ If wrong, why? _____

15. Each of the people below has just failed two tests. Given the explanatory styles below, which person is most likely to become depressed?
    a. Greg, who thinks he failed because the tests were bad
    b. Sally, who thinks she failed because she is stupid
    c. Mary, who thinks she failed because she didn't study hard
    d. John, who thinks he failed because he partied all night

Correct _____ If wrong, why? _____

16. Rob recently quit his job and sold his house, and is building a sports shop that will specialize in snow skiing. This is a great idea because there are no such shops in his city in Florida. Rob probably has:
    a. severe unipolar depression
    b. schizophrenia
    c. reactive depression
    d. mania

Correct _____ If wrong, why? _____

## Schizophrenia

17. The term schizophrenia refers to:
    a. bipolar as compared with unipolar disorder
    b. split personality--a person who alternates between two or more personalities
    c. a split between emotional and intellectual aspects of personality
    d. a person who alternates between extreme happiness and extreme sadness

Correct _____ If wrong, why? _____

18. A patient who has been diagnosed as schizophrenic thinks that "they" are trying to control his mind. This person has what type of schizophrenia?
    a. undifferentiated
    b. paranoid
    c. catatonic
    d. disorganized
    e. delusion of grandeur

Correct _____ If wrong, why? _____

19. Schizophrenia is:
    a. more likely to be diagnosed in younger than older adults
    b. more common in women than men
    c. usually characterized by sudden onset
    d. develops in adults who had many friends as children
    e. probably caused by a bad mother

Correct _____ If wrong, why? _____

20. According to the dopamine theory of schizophrenia, drugs that are effective for schizophrenia:
    a. work by killing the bacteria or viruses that might have caused the disorder
    b. reduce symptoms by blocking dopamine synapses
    c. reduce symptoms by increasing activity at dopamine synapses
    d. work by shrinking the ventricles in the brain
    e. work by modifying the pursuit eye movement patterns

Correct _____ If wrong, why? _____

## ANSWERS AND EXPLANATIONS FOR COMPREHENSION CHECK

| Correct Answer | Other Alternatives Are Wrong Because: |
|---|---|
| 1. b (p. 597)<br>Obj. I | a. this would include unusually happy or successful people too<br>c. some societies may be intolerant of behaviors that are quite normal in other societies<br>d. biological causes are only one point of view |
| 2. b (p. 602)<br>Obj. II-B-1 | a. this describes Axis II, things like mental retardation and personality disorders<br>c. physical problems are on Axis III<br>d. a person with an Axis I disorder would be unlikely to score highly on the level of functioning scale |
| 3. c (pp. 606-607, Fig. 14.5)<br>Obj. III-B | a. her anxiety is not attached to a specific object<br>b. doesn't have repetitive thoughts or actions<br>d. hasn't separated one set of memories from others<br>e. too much anxiety; persists when there is nothing to be anxious about |

4. d (pp. 608-609)  
   Obj. VI-B

a. normal; doesn't interfere with her life  
b. her fear is not irrational; she's doing something about it  
c. her fear is rational and limited to one situation  
e. see a, b, and c

5. d (pp. 609-610)  
   Obj. IV-C-2

a. children naturally fear loud sounds, so that is the  
   UCS; the rat is the CS  
b. Albert showed no natural fear of the rat, so fear to it is the CR; fear  
   to sound is UCR  
c. fear to sound is UCR

6. c (pp. 610-611)  
   Obj. IV-C-3-a

a. lab-reared monkeys show no fear of snakes  
b. lab-reared monkey has to see the snake also to develop the fear  
d. can be learned via observational learning; direct conditioning is not  
   necessary

7. a (pp. 613-614)  
   Obj. IV-C-6

b. the feared stimulus would be exposed gradually  
   and the person would remain relaxed while imagining  
c. b is similar to shaping, which involves gradual increases in mastery  
   of the response  
d. see b  
e. exposure here isn't gradual; it's sudden

8. b (p. 614)  
   Obj. IV-D-1

a. not unless repetitive behavior also occurs  
c. means that some things are easily learned because of evolutionary  
   influences; not relevant  
d. not unless he constantly checks his body for physical symptoms  
e. not unless he constantly washes and bathes

9. a (p. 619)  
   Obj. V-A

b. addictive substances enter it faster  
c. depending upon how a substance is used, it may or may not be  
   addictive; addiction is in the user  
d. smoking is more likely to be addictive because the substance enters  
   the brain faster

10. c (pp. 620-622)  
   Obj. VI-B-2

a. they showed more decline in stress after alcohol  
b,d. no difference in performance for sons of alcoholics and  
   nonalcoholics

11. b (p. 623)  
   Obj. VII-B

a. alcoholics treated with abstinence also relapse  
c. some don't grow worse  
d. environmental factors, such as reinforcers for things other than  
   drinking, can help  
e. controversial; most relapse after such treatment

12. d (p. 628)  
   Obj. VIII

a. develops suddenly following a great loss  
b. must have manic phases also  
c. maybe, but no specific evidence that he has learned to fail

13. d (p. 628)
Obj. VIII-A

   a. may show a relation between depression and hormones, not genetics
   b. true, but not evidence for a genetic component
   c. it's the opposite; more depression among biological relatives

14. c (p. 630)
Obj. IX-A-1

   a. instead, they learn that they are helpless and don't try to escape later
   b. show signs of depression
   d. occurs in humans, not dogs; becoming depressed during a specific season, usually winter

15. b (pp. 630-631)
Obj. IX-B-1

   a. external; his attribution is outside of himself
   c. internal, but unstable; she can study more next time
   d. he can attribute failure to partying

16. d (p. 632)
Obj. XI-B

   a. is showing mania, so can't have unipolar depression
   b. no evidence that social relations and self-care have deteriorated
   c. he isn't depressed, he's manic

17. c (p. 637, Fig. 14.25)
Obj. XIII

   a. bipolar alternates between mania and depression; unipolar is depression only; neither is schizophrenia
   b. multiple personality, a different disorder
   d. manic-depressive disorder

18. b (pp. 640-641)
Obj. XIV-D

   a. basic symptoms, but not delusion of persecution
   c. no movement disorders here
   d. no evidence for incoherent speech or silly behavior
   e. the patient may have delusions of grandeur, but that is not a type of schizophrenia

19. a (p. 638)
Obj. XIII

   b. equally common in men and women
   c. usually gradual onset
   d. opposite; schizophrenics had few friends as children
   e. probably not; it develops after child is independent of mother and occurs even if child is adopted and raised by normal mother

20. b (p. 642)
Obj. XV-B

   a. infection in infancy is a theory of schizophrenia; effective drugs work on brain synapses
   c. drugs for depression may do this
   d. ventricles are enlarged, but drugs don't do anything to this condition
   e. patterns may differ, but drugs work on brain to produce improvements

## LECTURE MATERIAL

Don't forget to review your lecture material. Process each topic meaningfully. First, be sure that you understand the material in each lecture--if you don't, ask your instructor or teaching assistant. Associate the material with things that you already know and with your personal experiences. If you can make up mental images of any of the material, do so. Try to think of real-life applications of the concepts. Write comments on each day's lecture notes. Then write questions to cover each concept.

## SHORT-ANSWER ESSAY QUESTIONS

Write brief answers to each of the following. The answers are on pp. 293-296, but do try to write the answers yourself before looking at them.

### Overview of Abnormal Behavior

1. Discuss the three competing views of abnormal behavior.

2. Describe how DSM IV categorizes psychological disorders.

### Anxiety and Avoidance Disorders

3. Explain how superstitions are related to phobias.

4. Describe the experiment with monkeys in which they learned fear by watching other monkeys who were afraid.

5. Describe how systematic desensitization might be used to treat someone who fears elevators. How might this be modified to use virtual reality technology?

6. Describe how obsessive-compulsive disorder might begin.

7. Describe an experiment that shows how memory in obsessive-compulsive "checkers" may differ from that of normal people.

**Substance-Related Disorders**

8. Discuss the things that make a substance addictive.

9. What are two ways in which the sons of alcoholic parents differ from the sons of non-alcoholic parents?

10. Describe the view of alcoholism taken by Alcoholics Anonymous. What is the alternative view?

11. Describe how methadone has been used to help people who are addicted to opiates.

**Mood Disorders**

12. Discuss the risk factors involved in depression.

13. Describe the learned-helplessness theory. How has it been modified to help to explain depression?

14. Describe seasonal affective disorder.

15. Describe the bipolar cycles in people with bipolar disorder.

**Schizophrenia**

16. What symptoms must a person show to be diagnosed as schizophrenic?

17. Discuss three characteristics of disordered thought in schizophrenia.

18. Discuss the evidence for a genetic predisposition to schizophrenia.

\*\*\*\*\*\*\*\*\*\*\*\*\*\*\*\*\*\*\*\*\*\*\*\*\*\*\*\*\*\*\*\*\*\*\*\*\*\*\*\*\*\*\*\*\*\*\*\*\*\*\*\*\*\*\*\*\*\*\*\*\*\*\*\*\*\*\*\*\*\*\*\*\*\*\*\*\*\*\*\*\*

Find the questions that you wrote over lecture material and write answers to them.

\*\*\*\*\*\*\*\*\*\*\*\*\*\*\*\*\*\*\*\*\*\*\*\*\*\*\*\*\*\*\*\*\*\*\*\*\*\*\*\*\*\*\*\*\*\*\*\*\*\*\*\*\*\*\*\*\*\*\*\*\*\*\*\*\*\*\*\*\*\*\*\*\*\*\*\*\*\*\*\*\*

## ANSWERS TO SHORT-ANSWER ESSAY QUESTIONS

1. One point of view is that psychological disorders result from biological disorders, including things like genetics, brain damage, hormonal abnormalities, disease, and the effects of drugs. A second point of view is that disorders result from disordered thinking caused by early experiences. That is, traumatic experiences early in life may interfere with later thinking. The third point of view is that psychological disorders are learned reactions to a stressful or unsupportive environment. (p. 600)

2. Clients are classified along five axes. Axis 1 lists disorders that have a particular time of onset and a realistic probability of recovery. Axis 2 lists disorders that persist throughout life, such as personality disorders and mental retardation. Axis 3 lists physical disorders, such as diabetes or cirrhosis of the liver. Axis 4 involves an evaluation of stress. Axis 5 is an overall evaluation of the person's level of functioning. (p. 602)

3. Superstitions are behaviors that cannot be expected to be effective. People persist in them because nothing goes wrong if they do them and, if something does go wrong, they assume that they did not try hard enough. Phobias are similar in that if people avoid the feared object, they never get hurt by it. Because they don't get close to it, they never learn that it really is harmless. (pp. 608-609)

4. Lab-reared monkeys have no fear of snakes, but wild-reared monkeys show a strong fear of snakes. A lab-reared and a wild-reared monkey both saw a snake. Later, when the lab-reared monkey saw a snake, it showed fear. The lab-reared monkey had to see that it was a snake that the wild-reared monkey was afraid of; simply seeing the wild-reared monkey show fear was    not enough for the lab-reared monkey to develop a fear. (pp. 610-611)

5. The person would first be taught to relax. Then, while in a relaxed state, she would be asked to imagine something that is not very frightening, such as looking at an elevator across the room. Then she would be asked to imagine gradually more frightening things until she is finally able to imagine being in an elevator that is stuck between floors. If the distress becomes too severe at some point, she would go back to imagining an easier scene. In the high-tech version, the client is given a helmet that displays a virtual-reality scene, so that the client can feel as if he or she is actually present in the scene. The therapist can change the scene to gradually expose the client to progressively more frightening situations, and the display can be turned off if the client becomes too fearful. (pp. 612-613)

6. Obsessive-compulsive disorder usually begins with a distasteful thought that may be hostile, sexual, or anything else. People try to suppress the thought, but trying not to think about something only increases the thought. The thought also becomes associated with lots of things in the environment which trigger it. Thus, trying to suppress an anxiety-causing thought may only serve to make that thought more probable. (pp. 615-616)

7. Subjects read a word and thought of an associated word. Later, they were asked to identify which words they had read and which words they had only thought. The two groups were equally accurate in their identifications, but the obsessive-compulsive group was less confident in their answers. They may not trust their memories as much. (p. 615)

8. Drugs that enter the bloodstream quickly are more likely to be addictive than drugs that enter more slowly. A given drug is more addictive if it is taken in a way that makes it enter the bloodstream more quickly; e.g., injected cocaine is more addictive than sniffed cocaine. One theory is that addictive substances all activate the dopamine synapses that are responsible for locomotion. Actually, almost any substance can become addictive, but the addiction is in the user and not in the substance itself. (pp. 618-619)

9. Young men whose fathers were and were not alcoholics were placed in stressful situations. Half of the men were given alcohol to drink before the stressful situation. Drinking alcohol reduced heart rate and resulted in less reported anxiety. However, these effects were larger in the sons of alcoholics than in the other men. In a second study, sons of alcoholics and nonalcoholics drank varying amounts of vodka. They then estimated how much they had drunk and how intoxicated they were. The sons of alcoholics underestimated how much they had drunk and how intoxicated they were. (pp. 620-622)

10. AA believes that alcoholism is a disease that will grow worse with time and that can only be helped by total abstinence. A single drink can cause a complete collapse in control. The disease view downplays the importance of environmental factors. An alternative view is that drinking is a habit that can be controlled. Whether or not controlled drinking works is still controversial. (pp. 622-624)

11. Many addicts continue to have recurring urges to take opiates even after the withdrawal symptoms have subsided. Methadone can be taken in pill form, which does not produce the "rush" associated with opiates, but it does satisfy the craving. People using methadone are still addicted to opiates; but many can hold a job, and they commit fewer crimes than when they were using heroin or morphine. (p. 625)

12. There is a genetic component, in that depressed people are more likely to have biological relatives who are depressed than are nondepressed people. Depression is more common in women than men. Hormones may influence the timing of depression in women, because postpartum depression sometimes occurs after the birth of a child when hormonal changes are great. However, the hormonal changes may not cause depression but they may trigger an episode. Severe losses early in life may make people more vulnerable to depression and people with little social support may be more vulnerable. (pp. 628-630)

13. Animals who have learned that they cannot escape some bad event, such as shock, do not learn later that shocks are escapable. They learn that they are helpless. In humans, it isn't failing itself that results in depression, but why people think they've failed. People who make internal (the cause is within me), stable (it's a permanent characteristic), and global (it applies to many situations) attributions have a pessimistic explanatory style that is related to depression. (pp. 630-631)

14. Most people with this disorder become depressed in the winter and are normal or slightly manic in the summer. They seem to respond to the amount of sunlight they see each day. The disorder can be helped by having people sit in front of lights to artificially lengthen the day. Annual summer depressions also occur in some people. (p. 632)

15. Mood alternates between mania, being constantly active and uninhibited, and depression, feeling helpless, guilt ridden, and sad. In the depressive phase, people have trouble sleeping and often contemplate suicide. In the manic phase, people may either be angry or happy. They have trouble inhibiting their impulses. They may show rambling speech, jumping from one topic to another. Each mood may last for months or just a few days. (pp. 633-634)

16. The person must show a deterioration in daily activities for at least 6 months. This includes work activities, social relations, and self-care. In addition, a person must show at least two of the following: hallucinations, delusions, incoherent speech, grossly disorganized behavior, thought disorders, or a loss of normal emotional responses and social behaviors. However, if a person shows severe hallucinations or delusions, no other symptoms are necessary. (p. 637)

17. <u>Use of loose associations and idiosyncratic associations</u>: Illogical leaps and misuse of words.
    <u>Difficulties in using abstract concepts</u>: Tendency to interpret everything literally.
    <u>Vague, roundabout ways of saying things</u>: Saying things in complex rather than simple ways.
    (p. 639)

18. Adopted children who develop schizophrenia often have biological relatives who are schizophrenic. If one identical twin has schizophrenia, there is a 50% chance that the other one will, and both have an equal probability of having schizophrenic children whether or not both are schizophrenic. Environmental factors determine if the genes will show up, so the term genetic predisposition is used. Markers for whether or not schizophrenia will develop include a failure to filter out irrelevant information and rapid jerky eye movements instead of smooth movements when following a target. (pp. 642-643)

## POSTTEST

Take this test with all of your books and notes out of sight. This should give you a good idea of how well you understand the material.

### Matching

Put the letter of the disorder in the blank beside the description.

Mood Disorders and Schizophrenia

1. _____ includes silly behavior and incoherent speech

2. _____ reaction to great loss, such as death of loved one

3. _____ deterioration of daily activities plus hallucinations, delusions, or thought disorder

4. _____ constantly suspicious in addition to basic symptoms

5. _____ alternate between being slow, inactive, and inhibited and very active and uninhibited

6. _____ includes movement disorders

7. _____ great sadness that develops gradually and not linked to any event

A. undifferentiated schizophrenia

B. endogenous depression

C. paranoid schizophrenia

D. bipolar disorder

E. reactive depression

F. catatonic schizophrenia

G. disorganized schizophrenia

### Multiple-choice

Circle the best alternative.

Overview of Abnormal Behavior

1. Multiple personality:
   a. is another term for schizophrenia
   b. means that the person has a single, seriously disordered personality
   c. is one of the most common mental disorders
   d. is diagnosed less often now than in the past
   e. means that one has several distinct personalities

2. What is the problem with statistics about the frequencies of mental disorders?
    a. they may be misleading because psychological disorders are a matter of degree
    b. it is impossible to give differential diagnoses to psychological disorders
    c. too many people show no symptoms at all
    d. there are no accepted guidelines for diagnosis
    e. both b and d

3. Which of the following is not an axis of DSM-IV?
    a. list of disorders that involve use of addictive substances
    b. list of disorders that last throughout life
    c. list of physical disorders
    d. evaluation of how much stress a person must endure
    e. evaluation of person's overall level of functioning

Anxiety and Avoidance Disorders

4. In panic disorder:
    a. people feel a strong state of anxiety in response to mild stress or exercise
    b. generalized anxiety attaches itself to a specific object
    c. people don't breath deeply enough
    d. people don't show a physiological response to stressful situations
    e. the panic attack usually lasts several hours

5. Which of the following is true about phobias?
    a. systematic desensitization is an effective therapy
    b. they are easily treated by explaining that there is no reason to be afraid
    c. "irrational fears" is the best definition
    d. people rarely show any physical symptoms when they confront the object
    e. they are more common for objects that are part of technological societies (guns, cars) than for natural objects (animals, lightning)

6. Watson and Rayner's study with Little Albert showed that phobias:
    a. represent unconscious desires
    b. are only developed to objects that have caused injury
    c. develop any time one animal observes another animal showing fear
    d. are genetic in that people are born with a few intense fears
    e. can develop through learning

7. What was the conditioned stimulus in the Little Albert study?
    a. the loud sound
    b. the white rat
    c. trembling to the loud sound
    d. trembling to the white rat
    e. the sight of Watson

8. What would a therapist using implosion do to treat a phobia of snakes?
   a. first try to discover the origin of the phobia
   b. have the client imagine being in a place with many snakes
   c. attempt to identify which type of snake was the UCS
   d. have the client begin by imaging a small picture of a snake and gradually work up to a large realistic image or to an actual snake
   e. have the client try to understand what snakes represent so that the real problem can be discussed

9. Which of the following is <u>not</u> characteristic of both obsessive-compulsive checkers and cleaners?
   a. drugs that inhibit the reuptake of serotonin usually help
   b. realize that their rituals are inappropriate
   c. are usually average or above average in intelligence
   d. feel better after their rituals
   e. tend to be hard-working, perfectionist people

10. How do the memories of obsessive-compulsive people differ from those of normal people?
   a. Obsessive-compulsive people are less able to remember what they did and what they thought
   b. Obsessive-compulsive people are much slower to learn in avoidance learning
   c. Obsessive-compulsive people are less confident in their judgments of what they did and what they thought
   d. Obsessive-compulsive people show very fast extinction in avoidance learning
   e. Obsessive-compulsive people are overconfident in the accuracy of their memories

<u>Substance-Related Disorders</u>

11. Alcohol addiction:
   a. may be more likely for sons of alcoholics because alcohol reduces stress more for them than for sons of nonalcoholics
   b. always gets worse and worse
   c. is best treated using the AA approach according to the research
   d. can easily be turned into controlled social drinking
   e. is independent of culture

12. Which of the following is true about the statement "alcoholism is a disease"?
   a. it is true because it fits all of the medical criteria for the term disease
   b. it is a bad definition because if makes alcoholics feel too guilty about their own role in their disorder
   c. it is true because alcoholism always gets progressively worse
   d. it is misleading because it downplays the role of environmental factors
   e. it is true because "controlled drinking" programs are unsuccessful

13. Why is methadone better as a morphine substitute than heroin?
   a. methadone does not produce the rush that heroin does and it does not produce rapid withdrawal symptoms
   b. methadone, when taken as a pill, is so fast-acting that it doesn't produce any rush, so addicts quickly stop using it
   c. methadone enters the brain faster than heroin
   d. methadone actually cures the addiction, heroin doesn't
   e. heroin is addictive, methadone is not

## Mood Disorders

14. Jane's husband has died and she's been very depressed for several months: Her depression would best be described as:
    a. endogenous depression
    b. bipolar depression
    c. reactive depression
    d. pessimistic depression
    e. manic-depressive disorder

15. Why do women develop depression more often than men?
    a. hormonal changes in the menstrual cycle cause depression
    b. they have lower status and power
    c. women are likely to be diagnosed as depressed but men are likely to be diagnosed as alcoholic
    d. women ruminate more about depression whereas men distract themselves
    e. all of the above may contribute to depression, but none of the alternatives explain why there is a sex difference

16. A hospital removes all of the fire alarms from a floor because the patients continually pull them. The patients on this floor probably have:
    a. mania
    b. major depression
    c. learned helplessness
    d. an internal, stable, and global explanatory style
    e. seasonal affective disorder

17. John seems like two different people. One week he is extremely happy and uninhibited. The next week he is very depressed and can only think of suicide. John's disorder is:
    a. endogenous depression
    b. learned helplessness
    c. suicidal tendencies
    d. multiple personality
    e. manic-depressive disorder

18. Suicide:
    a. is the most common cause of death among people over age 50
    b. attempts are more common among men than among women
    c. is not usually committed by people who talk about it
    d. is often committed by people who are depressed
    e. will not be committed by someone who has tried and failed

## Schizophrenia

19. The term schizophrenia:
    a. means split personality, another name for multiple personality
    b. is Latin for premature senility
    c. comes from the Greek terms meaning disordered thought
    d. refers to a split between emotional and intellectual parts of personality
    e. refers to a split between the situation and a person's reactions to it

20. A person who believes that she has been selected to receive messages from outer space that will ultimately save the world has:
    a. delusions of persecution
    b. catatonic schizophrenia
    c. manic-depressive disorder
    d. undifferentiated schizophrenia
    e. delusions of grandeur

21. Which of the following is not a characteristic of the thought disorder of schizophrenia?
    a. highly limited vocabularies
    b. roundabout ways of saying simple things
    c. difficulty with abstract concepts
    d. use of loose and idiosyncratic associations
    e. literal interpretations of words

22. Schizophrenia:
    a. is more common in rural areas than in cities
    b. afflicts approximately 8% of the population
    c. is usually diagnosed in the teens or 20s
    d. is more common in women than men
    e. is easiest to treat if the patient has mostly negative symptoms and few positive symptoms

23. Which of the following is true about the cause of schizophrenia?
    a. there is some brain damage in that cerebral ventricles are too small
    b. since effective drugs work by blocking dopamine receptors, schizophrenics may have too little dopamine in their brain
    c. confusing signals from the mother may cause schizophrenia
    d. schizophrenia has no genetic component
    e. prenatal infections may result in brain damage that leads to schizophrenia

## ANSWERS TO POSTTEST

| Correct Answer | Questions Testing a Similar Concept | |
| --- | --- | --- |
| | Comprehension Check | Short-Answer |

**Matching**

| | Comprehension Check | Short-Answer |
| --- | --- | --- |
| 1. G (p. 640) | 18d | 17 |
| 2. E (p. 628) | 12a | -- |
| 3. A (p. 640) | 18a | 17 |
| 4. C (pp. 640-641) | 18 | 17 |
| 5. D (p. 627) | 12b,17d | 15 |
| 6. F (p. 640) | 18c | 17 |
| 7. B (p. 628) | 12 | -- |

**Multiple-Choice**

| | | |
|---|---|---|
| 1.  e  (p. 637) | 17b | -- |
| 2.  a  (p. 601) | 1 | 2 |
| 3.  a  (p. 602) | 2 | -- |
| 4.  a  (pp. 606-607) | 3 | -- |
| 5.  a  (pp. 608-610) | 4 | 3 |
| 6.  e  (pp. 609-610) | 5 | -- |
| 7.  b  (pp. 609-610) | 5 | -- |
| 8.  b  (pp. 613-614) | 7 | -- |
| 9.  d  (pp. 614-616; Table 14.3) | 8 | 7 |
| 10.  c  (p. 615) | -- | 7 |
| 11.  a  (pp. 620-621) | 11 | 9,10 |
| 12.  d  (pp. 623-624) | 11 | 10 |
| 13.  a  (p. 625, Table 14.5) | -- | 11 |
| 14.  c  (p. 628) | 12a | -- |
| 15.  e  (pp. 628-629) | 13a | -- |
| 16.  a  (p. 632) | 16 | 15 |
| 17.  e  (p. 632) | 16 | 15 |
| 18.  d  (pp. 634-635) | -- | -- |
| 19.  d  (p. 637) | 17 | 16,17 |
| 20.  e  (p. 638) | 18e | 17 |
| 21.  a  (p. 639) | -- | 17 |
| 22.  c  (p. 638) | 19 | -- |
| 23.  e  (p. 644) | 20 | 18 |

## CHAPTER 14  LANGUAGE ENHANCEMENT GUIDE

### I. VOCABULARY, IDIOMS AND CULTURAL CONCEPTS

**Instructions:**

As you read the text refer to the following list of words and their definitions. The words are listed in the order in which they appear in the chapter. The definitions presented contain the meaning of the word as used by Kalat on the textbook page indicated.

Remember that these words like all words can have different meanings in other sentences. If you do not find a non-technical word on this list it may have been defined on a previous page or chapter of this study guide. The definition of non-technical words may be found in the dictionary at the end of this study guide. Kalat defined each new technical word as it first appears on a page and these may be found in Kalat's summary at the end of the section and in the Glossary at the end the textbook.

### An Overview of Abnormal Behavior

hardly knew (596) = did not know well
commit = send

dreaded (597) = feared
exaggeration = to make something seem bigger than it actually is, overstating
disordered = confused, disturbed
prevalence = frequency of occurrence, percentage of cases

entailed (598) = involves, has

babbles incoherently = a meaningless confusion of words or sounds

dreadful mistake = a very serious mistake

bizarre = very unusual, odd, grotesque, or distorted

possessed by a demon = a belief that an evil supernatural being controls behavior

exorcised = removed or chased out

indiscriminate (599) = not making careful distinctions; unselective; confused

extraordinarily = beyond what is ordinary or usual

unintentionally (601) = without plan or intent

induced = produced, made happen

imbalance = not balanced

inadequate = not enough

approximately = almost, very similar, close to

continuum (601) = a continual sequence

bouts = times when we face an illness or a problem

frankly = spoken freely and sincerely

fundamentally = basically; of great significance; importance

maladaptive (602) = does not fit or adjust to the situation

inflexible = not changing, rigid

integral part of = a basic or natural part of

malfunctioning (604) = non-working; diseased; broken

## Anxiety and Avoidance Disorders

plagued (606) = disturbed by repeated attacks

predisposition = tendency, susceptibility, weakness

incapacitated = deprived of strength or ability; disabled

disconnects (608) = turns off

superstition = a belief or behavior based on ignorance of the laws of nature or by faith in magic or chance

interferes with (609) = prevents

demonstrate = to show

whimper (610) = to cry

virtual-reality scene (613) = computer generated pictures that look real

gruesome (614) = horrible, frightful, shocking

persistence = continuing

impulse = a sudden wish, thought or behavior

suppress = stop, inhibit, hold back

elaborate = to tell with care and detail; develop thoroughly

abandoned (615) = left alone, given up, deserted

perfectionist = a person who is unhappy with anything that is not perfect or does not meet extremely
   high standards

inappropriate (616) = not acceptable

run in families = be inherited

substantial = strong, real; not imaginary

## Substance Related Disorders

incidence (620) = frequency of occurrence

tolerant = accepting

feasible (621) = able to be done; possible

anonymous (622) = nameless, no one know the names of the group members

connotations (623) = implied meanings

inevitable (624) = certain to happen; impossible to avoid or prevent

deteriorate = to grow worse, to weaken

controversy = a dispute or disagreement between sides holding opposing views

## Mood Disorders

persist (627) = continue

bipolar = having two opposite or contradictory ideas or behaviors

endogenous (628) = originating or growing from within, internal biological influences

distinction = characteristic

difficult to draw = difficult to say in words

postpartum (629) = occurring in the period shortly after childbirth

ruminate = to think about something over and over again

silver lining (630) = something good

wrap it in a cloud = make it sound bad

## Schizophrenia

incoherent (637) = unable to think or express one's thoughts in a clear or orderly manner

persecution (638) = punishment

idiosyncratic (639) = behavioral characteristic unique to an individual or a group

roundabout = indirect; confusing

fluctuate = change

impairment (643) = to decrease or loose ability or strength

longitudinal studies (644) = research that covers many years in the lives of the subjects

epidemic = a rapid spreading of a disease to many people in an area or a population

## II. VOCABULARY BUILDING

**Word Analysis**

Instructions:

1. Break each word in the table into its prefixes, roots and suffixes.  If you do not remember the meaning of a term look it up in Appendix B.
2. Guess the meaning of the word based on the meaning of its parts.
3. Find the word on the text page indicated in the brackets and redefine the word based on the context of the sentence, paragraph and chapter.
5. Look up the definition of the word in the VOCABULARY, IDIOMS AND CULTURAL CONCEPTS  section above, in Appendix A, or in a college level dictionary.  If the word is followed by letter G look it up in the text Glossary.

Exercise 1.  Agoraphobia

| Word | Meaning |
|---|---|
| agoraphobia (G) | |
| alcoholism (G) | |
| bipolar (A) | |
| desensitization (G) | |
| deteriorate (A) | |
| detoxification (G) | |
| disconnects (A) | |
| disordered (A) | |
| dissociative (G) | |
| exorcised (A) | |
| extraordinarily (A) | |

Exercise 2.  Inappropriate

| Word | Meaning |
|---|---|
| inappropriate (A) | |
| incoherent (A) | |
| inflexible (A) | |
| maladaptive (A) | |
| malfunctioning (A) | |
| postpartum (A) | |
| predisposition (A) | |
| psychogenic (G) | |
| somatoform (G) | |
| underestimate | |
| unintentionally (A) | |

# CHAPTER 15 TREATMENT OF PSYCHOLOGICALLY TROUBLED PEOPLE

## OBJECTIVES

Understand that:

**Psychotherapy**

I. Freud founded psychoanalysis to bring out unconscious material (p. 650, Table 15.1, p. 657)
    A. Free association--patient says whatever comes to mind (p. 650)
    B. Dreams represent wish fulfillment (p. 651)
        1. Manifest content of dreams is the surface content (p. 651)
        2. Latent content of dreams is the hidden, symbolic content (p. 651)
    C. Transference--patient reacts to therapist as someone else (pp. 651-652)

II. Behavior therapists assume that behavior is learned and can be unlearned (p. 652, Table 15.1, p. 657)
    A. Behavior modification is an effective way to treat anorexia nervosa (p. 652)
    B. Bed-wetting can be helped through classical conditioning (pp. 652-653, Fig. 15.2)
    C. Aversion therapy involves punishment for inappropriate behavior (pp. 653-654)

III. Some therapies focus on thoughts and beliefs (p. 654)
    A. Rational-emotive therapy assumes that abnormal behavior is due to irrational thoughts (p. 654)
    B. Cognitive therapy strives to have people discover their inappropriate beliefs and change them (p. 655, Table 15.1, p. 657)
    C. Cognitive-behavior therapy attempts to change behavior but puts emphasis on people's interpretations of situations (pp. 655-656)

IV. Person-centered therapy is the best-known humanistic therapy (p. 656, Table 15.1, p. 657)
    A. The therapist provides an atmosphere in which the client can freely explore feelings (p. 656)

V. Family systems therapy involves working with the entire family (pp. 656-657, Table 5.1)
    A. Many therapists combine approaches and use eclectic therapy (pp. 657-658)

VI. Therapists today have modified and combined approaches (pp. 657-658)
    A. Brief therapies usually have time limits (pp. 658-659)
        1. HMOs sometimes force therapy to be too brief (p. 659)
    B. Group therapy sessions are less expensive and they allow individuals to relate to others with similar problems (pp. 659-660)
    C. Self-help groups do not include a therapist (p. 660)

VII. Paradoxical intervention involves telling a person to do something but giving them an undesirable reason for doing it (p. 660)

VIII. The effectiveness of therapy can be determined by comparing treated and non-treated people (pp. 661-662)
    A. Psychotherapy patients do show more improvement than nontreated people (p. 662, Fig. 15.4)
    B. All kinds of therapies are helpful, although cognitive and cognitive-behavioral produce slightly more benefit (p. 662)
        1. Experienced therapists are not necessarily better than non-professionals (pp. 663-664)
            a. However, therapists are always willing to listen and they keep conversations confidential (p. 664)
    C. Therapies help because they rely on a therapeutic alliance between therapist and client (p. 664)
        1. Commitment to change by the client is necessary (pp. 664-665)

IX. Guidelines for choosing a psychotherapist (p. 665)

**Medical Therapies**

X. Medical therapies attempt to change brain functioning directly  (pp. 668-669)

XI. Anxiety and avoidance disorders are treated with drugs  (p. 669)

    A. Benzodiazepines relieve anxiety, relax muscles, and induce sleep  (pp. 669-670)

    B. Clomipramine helps with obsessive-compulsive disorder  (p. 670)

XII. Depression can be treated with drugs or ECT  (pp. 670-672)

    A. There are three main classes of drugs  (p. 670, Fig.  15.8, p. 671)

        1. Tricyclics block reabsorption of neurotransmitters  (p. 670)

        2. Monoamine oxidase inhibitors (MAOIs) block metabolic breakdown of released neurotransmitters  (p. 670)

        3. Second-generation antidepressants block serotonin reabsorption  (p. 670)

    B. Drugs work better than placebos, are faster and cheaper than therapy, but they have side effects  (p. 671)

    C. Electroconvulsive therapy (ECT) produces a brain seizure, which alleviates depression (p. 672)

        1. Why this works is unclear  (p. 672)

        2. It is controversial because there may be long-term side effects  (p. 672)

XIII. Lithium is an effective treatment for bipolar disorder  (p. 673)

    A. It isn't a cure because symptoms return after the drug is stopped  (p. 673)

XIV. Neuroleptic drugs are effective in treating schizophrenia  (p. 673)

    A. They work by blocking dopamine receptors  (p. 673)

    B. Tardive dyskinesia (a movement disorder) is a side effect  (pp. 673-674)

    C. Psychotherapy can be a valuable adjunct to drug therapy  (pp. 674-675)

XV. Drugs and therapy may be differentially effective for different people  (p. 675)

**Social and Legal Issues in the Treatment of Troubled People**

XVI. Older mental hospitals were much like prisons  (pp. 677-678)

    A. Drugs and advances in psychotherapy allow hospitals to offer short-term care  (p. 678)

    B. Deinstitutionalization refers to moving people from hospitals to community-based treatment centers  (p. 678)

XVII. There are a number of legal issues related to treatment  (p. 679)

    A. Psychologically disturbed people can refuse treatment  (p. 679)

        1. Preventive detention can be used to involuntarily commit someone to a mental institution who is dangerous to society  (pp. 679-680)

            a. Deciding who is dangerous is difficult  (p. 680)

XVIII. Most mental patients are not dangerous  (pp. 681-682)

    A. An illusory correlation may make us think they are dangerous  (p. 681)

XIX. People are not responsible for their behavior if they are "insane"  (p. 682)

    A. Under the M'Naghten rule, people must not realize that they are committing a crime  (pp. 682-683)

    B. Under the Durham rule, a defendant is not responsible if suffering from a mental disease or defect  (p. 683)

    C. The Model Penal Code says that the person must suffer from a mental disease and not realize that he or she has committed a crime  (p. 683)

XX. Community psychologists attempt to prevent disorders from occurring or from becoming worse  (p. 683)

    A. Society can take some actions to prevent disorders  (pp. 683-684)

## COMPREHENSION CHECK

Answer these questions soon after reading the chapter. Circle the best alternative. Check your answers, pp. 310-312. If you gave a wrong answer, try to write why it was wrong. Check your reasons.

### Psychotherapy

1. In psychoanalysis:
   - a. the therapist uses hypnosis to gain access to the patient's unconscious
   - b. the therapist explains the universal meaning of symbols in a dream
   - c. the therapist uses free association to censor embarrassing thoughts
   - d. the patient may begin to treat the therapist as someone else when transference occurs

Correct _____ If wrong, why? _____

2. How do behavior therapies differ from psychoanalysis and humanistic therapies?
   - a. behavior therapists attack the behavior, not the thoughts
   - b. behavior therapies dwell more on the discovering hidden meanings than the other two
   - c. behavior therapists tend to stick with the same procedure longer (even its not working) than the other two
   - d. the goals of behavior therapy are broader and more vague than the goals of the other two

Correct _____ If wrong, why? _____

3. Bed-wetting has been treated most effectively with:
   - a. classical conditioning
   - b. behavior modification
   - c. aversion therapy
   - d. Gestalt therapy

Correct _____ If wrong, why? _____

4. How does rational-emotive therapy differ from cognitive therapy?
   - a. cognitive therapy deals with changing cognitions; rational-emotive therapy deals mainly with changing emotions, with the idea that changes in thoughts will follow
   - b. cognitive therapists usually use Freud's methods; rational-emotive therapies don't
   - c. rational-emotive believes emotions lead to thoughts; cognitive believes thoughts lead to emotions
   - d. rational-emotive therapists often tell their patients what to think; cognitive therapists have patients discover this

Correct _____ If wrong, why? _____

5. Person-centered therapy:
   - a. tries to increase the incongruence between a person's self-concept and his or her ideal self
   - b. tries to direct a person toward worthy goals
   - c. directs the client away from inappropriate thoughts toward more appropriate ones
   - d. includes unconditional positive regard
   - e. was pioneered by Aaron Beck

Correct _____ If wrong, why? _____

6. A therapist helps his clients to set specific goals for changing behavior, and then he works with them to change their interpretation of problems. What type of therapy is this?
   a. rational-emotive therapy
   b. family systems therapy
   c. cognitive-behavior therapy
   d. person-centered therapy
   e. behavior modification

Correct _____ If wrong, why? _____

7. Dr. Therup often interprets his clients' dreams; sometimes tries to get them to understand whether they are playing the role of child, adult, or parent; uses reinforcement for appropriate behavior; and tries to get them to change their irrational thoughts. Dr. Therup is a(n):
   a. psychoanalyst
   b. eclectic therapist
   c. multiple personality
   d. family therapist
   e. brief therapist

Correct _____ If wrong, why? _____

8. What is the advantage of family systems therapy?
   a. it is cheaper because the whole family shares the expense
   b. a deadline is used so both therapist and the family are motivated to bring therapy to a successful conclusion
   c. communication and unreasonable demands within a family can be dealt with
   d. a therapist is not needed; people "treat" each other

Correct _____ If wrong, why? _____

9. Which of the following is true about the effectiveness of psychotherapy?
   a. people who receive no therapy improve at about the same rate as people who are treated
   b. people who receive psychotherapy show greater improvement than about 80% of untreated people
   c. therapy works best with patients who have vague, general complaints
   d. success depends a lot on the therapy; some are much better than others
   e. trained therapists produce much more improvement than "caring" individuals

Correct _____ If wrong, why? _____

10. In all psychotherapies:
    a. the therapist does most of the talking
    b. clients must make some commitment to change
    c. therapists use reverse psychology and ask the client to do the opposite of what's desired
    d. the therapist and client concentrate on the reasons behind behaviors

Correct _____ If wrong, why? _____

**Medical Therapies**

11. Which of the following is <u>not</u> true about medical therapies and talk therapies?
    a. the client must agree to receive talk therapy treatment but not medical therapy
    b. talk therapists require that clients be committed to change; medical therapies can work without such commitment
    c. meetings between physician and client are not integral parts of medical therapies
    d. medical therapies try to change brain functioning directly; talk therapies try to change experiences

Correct _____ If wrong, why? _____

12. The class of drugs called benzodiazepines:
    a. work by prolonging the effects of serotonin
    b. block the reabsorption of serotonin, norepinephrine, and dopamine
    c. are made from natural substances that can't be patented
    d. cause tardive dyskinesia as a side effect
    e. allow GABA molecules to attach more easily to membrane receptors

Correct _____ If wrong, why? _____

13. Why would ECT be used rather than antidepressant drugs?
    a. antidepressant drugs decrease certain neurotransmitter molecules, but ECT increases them; an increase is helpful to some patients
    b. drugs do not help to adjust sleep patterns; ECT does
    c. drugs only help 20-30% of all depressed people
    d. ECT takes effect faster than drugs
    e. drugs produce side effects, such as nausea and blurred vision, even if the dose is only slightly greater than the recommended level

Correct _____ If wrong, why? _____

14. According to the dopamine theory of schizophrenia, drugs such as chlorpromazine and haloperidol:
    a. work by producing tardive dyskinesia in the brain
    b. reduce symptoms by blocking dopamine synapses
    c. work faster if the onset of schizophrenia was gradual
    d. continue to improve behavior for a year or more
    e. cure schizophrenia

Correct _____ If wrong, why? _____

**Social and Legal Issues in the Treatment of Troubled People**

15. State mental hospitals:
    a. have changed today so that they can provide quality short-term care
    b. have had a steady increase in patients since 1950
    c. are more costly than alternative care
    d. promote psychological adjustment better than alternative care

Correct _____ If wrong, why? _____

16. Patients with mental disorders:
    a. are likely to commit violent crimes whether they have a past history of doing so or not
    b. can be institutionalized against their will using preventive detention laws if they lack capacity to make informed decisions concerning treatment
    c. can refuse the right to treatment even if they have been involuntarily committed to a hospital
    d. are less likely to commit acts of violence than the general public

Correct _____ If wrong, why? _____

17. In which case should a person be called insane according to the original M'Naghten rule?
    a. Fred understood that he was committing a crime, but he couldn't stop himself
    b. John, who has brain damage, did not know that what he was doing was wrong
    c. Michael, who is schizophrenic, says that he knew what he was doing was wrong, but he could not control his impulses
    d. Brian committed a bizarre crime that he agreed was wrong, but that is the only evidence for insanity

Correct _____ If wrong, why? _____

18. Which of the following is not a primary prevention strategy?
    a. a program is set up in a popular bar and people who drink nightly are identified; these people are then treated for early signs of alcoholism
    b. funding of child-care programs is instituted
    c. people who lose their jobs are given counseling and education to help them get back into the work force
    d. classes for disadvantaged pregnant women are begun; those programs teach about the dangers of using drugs while pregnant and also about how certain viruses and infections can affect fetuses

Correct _____ If wrong, why? _____

**Answers and Explanations for Comprehension Check**

| Correct Answer | Other Alternatives Are Wrong Because: |
|---|---|
| 1. d (pp. 651-652)<br>Obj. I-C | a. Freud used hypnosis at first, but then he decided it didn't work<br>b. what each symbol means to the individual is important<br>c. thoughts are totally uncensored; person says whatever comes to mind |
| 2. a (p. 657, Table 15.1)<br>Obj. I, II, IV | b. psychoanalysis searches for hidden meanings, and behavior therapy doesn't at all<br>c. behavior therapists often change after a few sessions if something isn't working; psychoanalysts and humanists change much less<br>d. goals are more specific |
| 3. a (pp. 652-653)<br>Obj. II-B | b. uses reinforcements; although some reinforcement occurs here, therapy is mainly based on classical conditioning<br>c. punishments for bedwetting aren't very effective<br>d. a "talk" therapy; usually used with adults |

4. d (pp. 654-655)
   Obj. III-A,B

   a. both deal with changing thoughts or beliefs
   b. neither use Freud's methods
   c. both believe that cognitions must be changed

5. d (p. 656)
   Obj. IV

   a. tries to increase <u>congruence</u>--a match between
      self-concept and ideal self
   b. it is nondirective--therapist encourages client to seek own goals
   c. nondirective; all the person's thoughts are appropriate in the therapy
      setting
   e. Carl Rogers; Beck pioneered cognitive therapy

6. c (pp. 655-656)
   Obj. III-C

   a. would try to change irrational beliefs, but not necessarily
      set goals for changing behavior
   b. would work with several family members
   d. wouldn't set behavioral goals; wouldn't try to change interpretations
   e. emphasis here more on changing thoughts than on changing specific
      behaviors

7. b (pp. 657-658)
   Obj. V-A

   a. he may be, but he uses more types of therapy
   c. unlikely, unless a distinct personality goes with each of his therapies
   d. not necessarily; unless he treats families rather than individuals
   e. not necessarily; his therapy may go on for a long period with no
      deadline

8. c (pp. 656-657)
   Obj. V

   a. reason why group therapy developed; family would
      probably pay costs for individual therapy anyway
   b. maybe, but only if brief therapy is used
   d. true with a self-help group; therapist involved in family therapy

9. b (pp. 661-662, Fig. 15.4)
   Obj. VIII

   a. recent studies show that treated people do better
   c. works best with specific, clear-cut problems
   d. studies show that various forms of therapy produce similar results
   e. they produced about equal benefits

10. b (pp. 664-665)
    Obj. VIII-C-1

   a. true for some therapies, not for others
   c. this is paradoxical therapy, not the norm
   d. not true for all therapies, especially not behavior therapy

11. a (pp. 668-669)
    Obj. X

   a. clients must agree to any type of treatment
   b-d. these are differences

12. e (pp. 669-670)
    Obj. XI-A

   a. clomipramine for obsessive-compulsive disorder does this
   b. tricyclics for depression do this
   c. lithium for bipolar disorder is a natural substance
   d. side effect of neuroleptic drugs, used for schizophrenia

13. d (pp. 670-672)
    Obj. XII-A,C

    a. drugs increase these neurotransmitters; ECT may do the same
    b. drugs do help adjust sleep patterns
    c. drugs help 50-70%; placebos help 20-30%
    e. side effects of lithium, used for bipolar disorder

14. b (p. 673)
    Obj. XIV-A

    a. movement disorder that is side effect of drugs
    c. work faster if onset was rapid
    d. most recovery takes place during the first month
    e. doesn't necessarily cure; symptoms often return if the person stops taking drug

15. c (p. 678)
    Obj. XVI

    a. although this is their goal today, few have changed so they can accomplish this
    b. the number has dropped because of drugs
    d. other forms of care are often more effective

16. c (pp. 679-681)
    Obj. VII, VIII

    a. past history of violence is the best predictor of future violence
    b. preventive detention can only be used when a person is dangerous to society
    d. people with some types of disorders are more likely to commit violent acts

17. b (pp. 682-683)
    Obj. XIX-A

    a. not according to original rule; he had to be unaware that what he had done was wrong
    c. insane according to Durham rule, but knew he had done wrong
    d. knew he was wrong; not insane according to Model Penal Code-- need more than bizarre crime

18. a (p. 683-684)
    Obj. XX

    a. a secondary prevention program because alcoholism caught in early stages
    b-d. all primary prevention programs; changing the environment before the mental disorders occur

## LECTURE MATERIAL

Don't forget to review your lecture material. Process each topic meaningfully. First, be sure that you understand the material in each lecture--if you don't, ask your instructor or teaching assistant. Associate the material with things that you already know and with your personal experiences. If you can make up mental images of any of the material, do so. Try to think of real-life applications of the concepts. Write comments on each day's lecture notes. Then write questions to cover each concept.

---

WAIT AT LEAST 24 HOURS BEFORE PROCEEDING.
LET FORGETTING OCCUR--IT WILL!!

---

## SHORT-ANSWER ESSAY QUESTIONS

Write brief answers to each of the following. The answers are on pp. 314-316, but do try to write the answers yourself before looking at them.

### Psychotherapy

1. If you go to a therapist who uses psychoanalysis, what would you expect?

2. How does person-centered therapy differ from the psychoanalytic therapy that you described above?

3. Describe a behavioral therapy for anorexia nervosa.

4. Treating people in groups has become increasingly common. Describe three types of such treatment.

5. Evaluate the effectiveness of psychotherapy.

6. Discuss the things that all forms of psychotherapy have in common.

### Medical Therapies

7. Explain how antidepressant drugs work.

8.  Describe ECT and the conditions under which it is used today.

9.  Discuss an effective therapy for manic-depressive disorder.

**Social and Legal Issues in the Treatment of Troubled People**
10. How have mental hospitals changed since the 1950s?

11. Discuss the issues related to whether a psychologically disturbed person can refuse treatment.

12. Discuss whether or not mental patients are dangerous.

\*\*\*\*\*\*\*\*\*\*\*\*\*\*\*\*\*\*\*\*\*\*\*\*\*\*\*\*\*\*\*\*\*\*\*\*\*\*\*\*\*\*\*\*\*\*\*\*\*\*\*\*\*\*\*\*\*\*\*\*\*\*\*\*\*\*\*\*\*\*\*\*\*\*\*\*\*\*\*
Find the questions that you wrote over lecture material and write answers to them.
\*\*\*\*\*\*\*\*\*\*\*\*\*\*\*\*\*\*\*\*\*\*\*\*\*\*\*\*\*\*\*\*\*\*\*\*\*\*\*\*\*\*\*\*\*\*\*\*\*\*\*\*\*\*\*\*\*\*\*\*\*\*\*\*\*\*\*\*\*\*\*\*\*\*\*\*\*\*\*

## ANSWERS TO SHORT-ANSWER ESSAY QUESTIONS

1.  The therapist would ask me to lie down on a couch and say anything that comes to mind.  I would be asked to free associate and not censor or omit anything.  The therapist would interpret what I say.  I might also be asked to describe my dreams, and the therapist would find meaning in them.  He would try to look beyond the manifest content and find the latent content of my dreams.  He would also expect me to show transference.  (pp. 650-652)

2. The humanistic therapist would not try to interpret or direct the therapy as the psychoanalytic therapist would. The humanistic therapist would not look for unconscious motives, but rather she would allow the client to explore his own feelings. The humanistic therapist would show unconditional positive regard and be totally accepting of everything the client says. In person-centered therapy, the "cure" comes from the client himself; in psychoanalytic therapy, the "cure" comes from the interpretation and direction of the therapist. (pp. 650-652, 656, Table 15.1, p. 657)

3. Reinforcement is given whenever the client exhibits a target behavior, in this case whenever weight is gained. In one successful case, a woman was confined to a hospital room and was not allowed to leave. She was reinforced for weight gain with radio or television, reading material, the opportunity to leave the room, or the right to have visitors. (p. 652)

4. In group therapy, a group of 7-8 people with similar problems are treated at once. They can spread the cost of the therapy among group members and they also can work on interpersonal relationships. Self-help groups are similar to group therapy, except there is no therapist. People talk with each other and try to help each other. Family systems therapy is a special type of group therapy in which entire families are treated to improve communication and interaction among family members. Each family member often has problems, and all must be resolved for an individual to be helped .(pp. 656-657, 659-660)

5. An early assessment of therapy suggested that treated people were no better off than people who were not treated. However, more recent studies have shown that the average psychotherapy patient improves more than 80% of all untreated people. People who have specific complaints are more likely to improve than people who have more general complaints. Certain therapies may be better for some disorders than for others, but so far there has not been much research support for this. There is some evidence that an inexperienced lay person can be as helpful as a licensed therapist. (pp. 661-662)

6. Psychotherapy requires a commitment to change one's life. A therapeutic alliance is formed between the therapist and the client that is characterized by acceptance, caring, respect, and attention. Clients talk about beliefs, emotions, and actions and gain self-understanding. The therapist conveys an expectation that the client will improve. Actual improvement, however, may depend largely on the client's commitment to work on problems outside the therapy sessions. (pp. 664-665)

7. Tricyclic drugs block the reabsorption of dopamine, norepinephrine, and serotonin by the axon's terminal button. MAOIs block the conversion of these neurotransmitters into nonactive molecules. Second-generation antidepressants are also known as serotonin reuptake blockers. They block the reuptake of serotonin. Thus, each type of drug increases the time period in which these neurotransmitters can activate surrounding neurons. (pp. 670-671, Fig. 15.8)

8. Electroconvulsive therapy consists of a brief electric shock across the head. People are usually given muscle relaxants and anesthetics. It is used when antidepressant drugs have been ineffective, for people with serious thinking disorders, and for people who are suicidal. It works faster than drugs, so it is effective in suicidal patients. (p. 672)

9. Lithium salts reduce both the mania and the depression. They do not cure the disorder, but control the symptoms. Side effects include nausea and blurred vision. How lithium works is unknown. Its primary effects appear to be on chemical pathways within neurons and not on transmission at synapses. (p. 673)

10. Older mental hospitals were large hospitals built by states to house severely disturbed people who would probably never return to society. These hospitals often resembled prisons. The advent of antidepressant and anti-schizophrenic drugs have reduced the number of long-term residents so that the mental hospital population declined. The goal now is to supply short-term care until the patient can return home. Community mental health centers and halfway houses have become alternatives to large state hospitals. These types of care are effective, but many people who would have been in large hospitals are now in nursing homes, prisons, or they are homeless. (pp. 677-679)

11. Some people with psychological disturbances fail to recognize that there is anything wrong with them. One argument is that such people should be treated. The arguments against such treatment are that families often put unwanted relatives in institutions and psychiatrists may overuse ECT and drugs. With "preventive detention," psychologically disturbed people who are considered dangerous to society can be put in mental hospitals against their will. This raises the question of how responsible a therapist is for a client who warned her or him about intended violence. (pp. 679-681)

12. Most mental patients are harmless. We hear about the few who commit crimes and we remember them creating an illusory correlation (a relationship where one really doesn't exist). People who are arrested for committing crimes and sent to mental institutions will probably commit more crimes when released, but people who were not arrested don't commit crimes upon release. The probability of committing a violent act is highest among people alcohol and drug abuse. (pp. 381-382)

## POSTTEST

Take this test with all of your books and notes out of sight. This should give you a good idea of how well you understand the material.

### Matching

Put the letter of the psychotherapy in the blank beside the description.

Psychotherapy

1. _____ sets explicit goals for changing behavior and emphasizes people's interpretations of situations

2. _____ attempts to change people's inappropriate beliefs

3. _____ free association and dream analysis

4. _____ doesn't rely on talking as main method

5. _____ frees client from inhibiting social influences so client can solve own problems

6. _____ may use any type of therapy, but treats several family members

7. _____ involves no therapist

A. person-centered therapy

B. self-help group

C. cognitive-behavior therapy

D. family systems therapy

E. psychoanalysis

F. rational-emotive therapy

G. behavior therapy

**Multiple-choice**

Circle the best alternative

<u>Psychotherapy</u>

1. A therapist asks you to describe your dream and he then interprets it for you. The therapist is probably using which therapy?
   a. humanistic
   b. person-centered
   c. psychoanalysis
   d. nondirective
   e. behavioral

2. A client is angry that the therapy doesn't seem to be helping and he tells the therapist, "I'm going to stop coming if things don't get better soon". A therapist using person-centered therapy is likely to respond:
   a. you are angry with me because you are treating me like your father
   b. thinking that everything must work quickly is irrational
   c. you must not let such thoughts enter your mind or the therapy will never work
   d. think about what you can do to make <u>me</u> happy
   e. so you don't think this is helping; tell me more

3. How does aversion therapy differ from most behavior therapy programs?
   a. it is based on operant conditioning; most behavior therapy programs are based on classical conditioning
   b. aversion therapy deals more with thoughts; behavior therapy programs deal with specific behaviors
   c. aversion therapy is very similar to systematic desensitization; behavior therapy is similar to implosive therapy
   d. aversion therapy relies on punishment; behavior therapy usually relies on positive reinforcement

4. Which type of therapy focuses more on changing what people do than what they think?
   a. behavior therapy
   b. rational-emotive therapy
   c. cognitive therapy
   d. psychoanalysis
   e. person-centered therapy

5. Cognitive therapists differ from rational-emotive therapists in that they:
   a. try to help people substitute more favorable beliefs; rational emotive therapists don't
   b. focus more on past experiences than rational-emotive therapists
   c. focus on behavior much more than rational-emotive therapists
   d. try to get clients to make their own discoveries; rational emotive therapists often tell clients what to think
   e. cognitive therapists treat the family as a unit; rational emotive therapists treat individuals

6. Why might self-help groups be preferred over other types of group therapy?
    a. the treatment takes place over a strictly limited period of time
    b. people can work on how they relate to others
    c. all members are available to one another at any time, without charge
    d. self-help group leaders have greater education and experience
    e. self-help groups treat the entire family and not an individual alone

7. Brief therapy:
    a. is less effective than long-term therapy, although it is cheaper
    b. is ineffective, but so are most therapies
    c. usually lasts less than 1 month
    d. usually makes a client begin dealing with main problems promptly
    e. involves a time limit set by the therapist, but that is unknown to the client

8. All psychotherapists:
    a. only treat people with identifiable psychological disorders
    b. try to get clients to commit to making changes
    c. concentrate on getting clients to understand the reasons behind their behaviors
    d. try to change clients' irrational thoughts
    e. allow therapy to go on as long as is necessary

Medical Therapies

9. Most antidepressant drugs work by:
    a. altering the pattern of blood flow in the brain
    b. making people forget that they are depressed
    c. affecting the chemical pathways within neurons
    d. prolonging the stimulation of dopamine, norepinephrine, or serotonin synapses in the brain
    e. increasing the body's ability to use vitamins, such as B-1

10. ECT probably works by:
    a. making the depressed person forget why he or she was depressed
    b. increasing stimulation of dopamine and norepinephrine synapses
    c. causing the patient to become ecstatic just before the seizure
    d. threatening the patient; he or she had better stop being depressed or more shocks will be given
    e. blocking dopamine receptors

11. Lithium salts:
    a. are used to cure manic-depressive disorder
    b. produce side effects including nausea and blurred vision
    c. have been aggressively marketed by drug companies in the U.S.
    d. are especially effective for undifferentiated schizophrenia
    e. decrease the amount of dopamine in the brain

12. A person whose schizophrenia had a gradual onset has been "normal" for the year that he has been taking haloperidol, so he decided to stop taking the drug. What is most likely to happen?
    a. schizophrenic symptoms will return briefly but then go away
    b. schizophrenic symptoms will return and grow worse
    c. he will be normal because the drug has permanently altered the synapses of the brain
    d. he will be normal at first but will become susceptible to major depression
    e. he will be normal because the drug revives dead brain cells

13. Antipsychotic drugs, such as haloperidol and chlorpromazine:
    a. increase the neurotransmitter, tardive dyskinesia, in the brain
    b. cure schizophrenia if used over a period of months
    c. block dopamine synapses in the brain
    d. increase activity at dopamine and norepinephrine synapses
    e. increase the sex drive in men

Social and Legal Issues in the Treatment of Troubled People

14. State mental hospitals:
    a. have shifted from having a goal of short-term care to long-term custody
    b. usually provide therapy by psychologists and psychiatrists
    c. provide much better care than community health centers
    d. are often prisonlike even today
    e. have received large increases in funding  as their goals have changed

15. Deinstitutionalization has:
    a. successfully moved most patients from mental institutions to community-based care
    b. probably helped to increase the number of homeless people
    c. forced states to plan adequate alternatives for care and housing
    d. resulted in more cost to states because alternative care is more expensive than hospitals

16. Under preventive detention:
    a. anyone who lacks capacity to make an informed decision and who has a severe, treatable mental disorder can be institutionalized
    b. a person can be institutionalized if they have a defect of reason from a disease of the mind
    c. people are moved from state hospitals to alternative care in the community
    d. intervention is done to prevent disorders from starting
    e. psychologically disturbed people who are dangerous to society can be institutionalized

17. Which of the following is true?
    a. people who refuse treatment show hostility, emotional withdrawal, and disordered thinking
    b. more people would be judged insane by the M'Naghten Rule than by the Model Penal Code
    c. most people who say they feel like killing someone do end up killing someone
    d. the laws concerning involuntary commitment are the same from state to state
    e. psychiatrists usually agree on whether a defendant is sane or insane

18. A community psychologist practicing secondary prevention might do which of the following?
    a. start an afternoon recreation program for teenagers
    b. conduct an education program for older women returning to the workforce
    c. open a halfway house for homeless people with mental disorders
    d. work to ban toxins that can cause brain damage
    e. open high quality day care centers

## ANSWERS TO POSTTEST

| Correct Answer | Questions Testing a Similar Concept | |
| --- | --- | --- |
| | Comprehension Check | Short-Answer |

**Matching**

| | | |
| --- | --- | --- |
| 1. C (pp. 655-656) | 6 | -- |
| 2. F (p. 654) | 4,6a | -- |
| 3. E (pp. 650-651) | 1,2b | 1,2 |
| 4. G (p. 652) | 2,3 | 3 |
| 5. A (p. 656) | 5,6d | 2 |
| 6. D (pp. 656-657) | 8 | 4 |
| 7. B (p. 660) | -- | 4 |

**Multiple-Choice**

| | | |
| --- | --- | --- |
| 1. c (pp. 650-651) | 1 | 1,2 |
| 2. e (p. 656) | 5,6d | 2 |
| 3. d (pp. 653-654) | 3c | -- |
| 4. a (p. 652) | 2,3 | 3 |
| 5. d (pp. 654-655) | 4 | -- |
| 6. c (p. 660) | -- | 4 |
| 7. d (pp. 658-659) | 7e | -- |
| 8. b (pp. 664-665) | 10 | 6 |
| 9. d (pp. 670-671, Fig. 15.8) | 12 | 7 |
| 10. b (p. 672) | 13 | 8 |
| 11. b (p. 673) | 13e | 9 |
| 12. b (p.673) | 14 | -- |
| 13. c (p. 673) | 14 | -- |
| 14. d (pp. 677-678) | 15 | 10 |
| 15. b (pp. 678-679) | -- | -- |
| 16. e (pp. 679-680) | 16 | -- |
| 17. a (pp. 680-681) | 16,17 | 11,12 |
| 18. c (pp. 683-684) | 18 | -- |

## CHAPTER 15: LANGUAGE ENHANCEMENT GUIDE

## I. VOCABULARY, IDIOMS AND CULTURAL CONCEPTS

**Instructions:**

As you read the text refer to the following list of words and their definitions. The words are listed in the order in which they appear in the chapter. The definitions presented contain the meaning of the word as used by Kalat on the textbook page indicated.

Remember that these words like all words can have different meanings in other sentences. If you do not find a non-technical word on this list it may have been defined on a previous page or chapter of this study guide. The definition of non-technical words may be found in the dictionary at the end of this study guide. Kalat defined each new technical word as it first appears on a page and these may be found in Kalat's summary at the end of the section and in the Glossary at the end the textbook.

**Psychotherapy**

intimidating (648) =  threatening; fear producing
shackles =   limitations, restrictions; a metal chain used around the ankle or wrist of a prisoner

ignore (649) =  refusing to pay attention to; disregard
concentrate = focus effort or attention

simpleton (651) = a person who is  deficient in judgment, ability or intelligence; a fool
fulfillment =  accomplish,  to make into a  really

metal foil (653) = thin sheets of metal

scrupulously (clean) (654) =  very very clean; conscientious and exact
intervene =  take direct action to change things

deliberately (656) =   carefully thinking about a choice to be made
incongruence = mismatch, difference

practitioners (658) =  people who practice something like an occupation,  a profession,  or a
    technique

paradox (660) = a statement that contradicts itself

mainstream (661) =  main attitudes, behaviors or values of a society or group

preliminary (662) =  something that precedes, prepares for, or introduces an activity

**Medical Therapies**

harmonious (668) =  pleasing
ultimate = final
glimpse =  a brief, incomplete look at something
supreme =   greatest, perfect,  ideal

not altogether glorious (669) = embarrassing

adjunct (674) = supplement; along with

barely begun (675) = just started

**Social and Legal Issues in the Treatment of Troubled People**

nearsighted (677) = people who cannot see distant objects
ridiculous =   nor reasonable,  outrageous
merciless = unkind,  not forgiving
ridicule =  make fun of, to cause others laugh at a person or thing
confine =   to shut or keep in, to imprison

custodial (678) =   taking care and supervising a person
integrate = to include into a larger group

detention (679) = keeping a person in a hospital or prison by law

felony (682) = a very serious crime, such as murder, rape, or burglary

ghastly = very unpleasant, disagreeable

## II. VOCABULARY BUILDING

**Word Analysis**

Instructions:

1. Break each word in the table into its prefixes, roots and suffixes. If you do not remember the meaning of a term look it up in Appendix B.
2. Guess the meaning of the word based on the meaning of its parts.
3. Find the word on the text page indicated in the brackets and redefine the word based on the context of the sentence, paragraph and chapter.
5. Look up the definition of the word in the VOCABULARY, IDIOMS AND CULTURAL CONCEPTS section above, in Appendix A, or in a college level dictionary. If the word is followed by letter G look it up in the text Glossary.

Exercise 1. Combination

| Word | Meaning |
|---|---|
| combination | |
| deinstitutionalization (G) | |
| depression (G) | |
| disadvantaged | |
| incongruence (A) | |
| intervention | |
| involuntary | |
| nearsighted (A) | |
| practitioners (A) | |
| psychoanalysis (G) | |
| remission (G) | |
| resistance (G) | |

Exercise 2. Symbolically

| | |
|---|---|
| symbolically | |
| transactional (G) | |
| transference (G) | |
| unanswered | |
| unconditional | |
| unconscious | |
| undesirable | |
| unravel | |

# CHAPTER 16  SOCIAL PSYCHOLOGY

## OBJECTIVES

Understand that:

### Attitudes and Attitude Change

I.  An attitude is a learned like or dislike of something or somebody  (p. 689)
- A.  Attitudes are usually measured with rating scales  (p. 689)
    - 1.  These are imperfect because people use the scale differently  (pp. 689-690)
    - 2.  People are often unaware of their attitudes  (p. 690)
- B.  Often attitudes are only weakly related to behavior  (p. 690)
    - 1.  High self-monitors change their behavior to make the right impression  (p. 690)

II.  Attitudes are often difficult to change  (pp. 690-691)
- A.  Attitudes can be changed by central and peripheral routes  (p. 691)
- B.  Messages sometimes have a delayed effect on attitudes  (p. 691)
    - 1.  The sleeper effect is a delayed attitude change after an initial rejection  (p. 691)
    - 2.  Minorities can change attitudes in the long run if they are outvoted at first  (p. 692)
- C.  The way a message is presented can affect its effectiveness  (pp. 692-693)
- D.  Some people are more easily persuaded than others  (p. 693)
- E.  Intelligent people are persuaded by complex messages, but less intelligent people are more easily persuaded by poorly supported ideas  (p. 693)
- F.  The forewarning and inoculation effects reduce persuasion  (p. 694)

III.  Cognitive dissonance theory suggests that changes in behavior precede changes in attitude  (p. 695)
- A.  People who lie for little money are more likely to change their attitudes than people who lie for more money  (pp. 695-696)

### Social Perception and Cognition

IV.  First impressions influence perceptions of individuals  (p. 698)
- A.  What we learn first about a person is weighted heavily in our impressions  (p. 698)
- B.  Physical characteristics affect how people are perceived  (p. 699)
    - 1.  Nonverbal behavior can be influential in impressions of people  (p. 699)

V.  Social cognition involves combining and remembering information about others  (p. 700)
- A.  People's judgments of others are often unreliable and inaccurate  (p. 700)
- B.  Stereotypes are overgeneralizations about groups of people  (pp. 700-701)
    - 1.  Prejudice is a negative attitude about a group  (p. 700)
        - a.  Some people show ambivalence toward racial groups  (pp. 701-702)
- C.  Prejudice may be overcome by having people work toward common goals  (pp. 702-703)

VI.  Attribution is the process of assigning causes to behavior  (p. 703)
- A.  Behavior is attributed to internal or external causes  (pp. 703-704)
    - 1.  Consensus information involves comparing behavior to that of others  (p. 704)
    - 2.  Consistency information involves comparing behavior across time  (p. 704)
    - 3.  Distinctiveness involves comparing behavior toward different objects or people  (p. 704)
- B.  We often assume that behavior results from internal causes  (pp. 704-705)
    - 1.  The fundamental attribution error is an overemphasis on internal causes for other people  (p. 704)
    - 2.  The actor-observer effect makes people more likely to attribute internal causes to other's behavior than to their own  (p. 704)

C. Attributions for our own behavior may produce a self-serving bias  (p. 706)
    1. We may adopt self-handicapping strategies as excuses for failures  (p. 706)

## Interpersonal Attraction

VII. People have a need to have relationships with other people  (p. 709)
    A. People crave long-term relationships  (p. 709)
    B. Temporary relationships are cultivated for limited purposes  (p. 710)
        1. People who face a future difficulty like to be with others facing the same difficulty  (p. 710)
VIII. Long-lasting relationships are developed with relatively few others  (p. 711)
    A. People choose friends who live close to them; this is called proximity  (p. 711)
    B. The more exposure to something, the more it is liked; this is familiarity  (p. 711)
    C. People choose friends who are similar to themselves; this is similarity  (pp. 711-712)
    D. Each party should get the best deal possible in the relationship  (pp. 713-714)
        1. This idea comes from exchange or equity theory  (p. 713)
IX. Selection of a marriage partner is different because it may include raising children  (p. 713)
    A. Sociobiology can explain differences between men and women  (p. 713-714, Table 16.3)
        1. Women need mates who are fertile, healthy, and who have substantial resources  (p. 714)
            a. Once a mate is found, nothing is gained by having additional sex partners  (p. 714)
        2. Men are motivated to spread their genes  (p. 714)
            a. Multiple sex partners and younger women increase this  (p. 714)
    B. Physical attractiveness is important in dating, especially at first  (pp. 714-715)
X. Romantic love may occur as relationships develop  (p. 716)
    A. Liking and love are different  (p. 716)
        1. Sternberg argues that love has three dimensions (pp. 716-717)
        2. Hendrick and Hendrick claim that there are three styles of love  (p. 717)
    B. Romantic relationships have beginnings, middles, and sometimes ends  (pp. 717-718, Fig. 16.16)

## Interpersonal Influence

XI. Conformity is the tendency to do what others are doing  (p. 720)
    A. People will conform to a group of 3-4 as much as to a group of more  (p. 721-722)
    B. Having an ally reduces conformity  (p. 722)
XII. People sometimes accept responsibility toward others and sometimes not  (p. 722)
    A. Bystanders often will not help if others are present because of diffusion of responsibility  (pp. 722-723)
    B. Social loafing means working less hard when sharing work with others  (p. 723)
    C. Many people volunteer, resisting bystander apathy and social loafing  (p. 724)
XIII. Decisions of groups may differ from decisions of individuals  (pp. 724-725)
    A. Groups usually come to more extreme decisions than individuals; this is called the group polarization effect  (p. 725)
    B. Groupthink occurs when group members do not question others' ideas and don't ask probing questions  (pp. 725-726)
    C. Juries are groups who don't know each other and who have no special competence (p. 726)
        1. Lawyers may try to eliminate some jurors with peremptory challenges  (pp. 726-727)
        2. Judges' instructions can affect the outcome of trials  (p. 728)

## The Power of the Social Situation

XIV. Much behavior is controlled by social situations  (p. 730)
    A. Behavior traps force people into self-defeating behaviors  (pp. 730-731)
        1. Escalation of conflict occurs when people continue a behavior to avoid defeat  (pp. 731-732)

2. Situations like the prisoner's dilemma result in uncooperative behavior (pp. 732-733, Fig. 16.23)
    3. The commons dilemma involves overuse of limited resources (p. 733)
XV. Several strategies can be used to elicit compliance (pp. 734-735)
    A. Compliance is the tendency to do what someone asks us to do (p. 734)
        1. The foot-in-the-door technique involves increasing a modest request to a large one (p. 735)
        2. The door-in-the-face technique begins with a large request and then scales it down to a smaller, more reasonable one (p. 734)
        3. The that's-not-all technique begins with an offer that is quickly improved (p. 735)
    B. Milgram found that many people showed obedience to authority and would "punish" another person (pp. 735-737)
        1. The ethical issues raised by his study resulted in clearer rules for treating research subjects (p. 738)

## COMPREHENSION CHECK

Answer these questions soon after reading the chapter. Circle the best alternative. Check your answers on pp. 330-332. If you gave a wrong answer, try to write why it was wrong. Check your reasons.

### Attitudes and Attitude Change

1. Measurement of attitudes is:
    a. often done on a Likert scale
    b. very accurate because people are aware of their attitudes
    c. similar across cultures in that people tend to use rating scales in the same way
    d. more accurate for implicit attitudes than for explicit ones
    e. useful because they accurately predict behavior

Correct _____ If wrong, why? _____

2. The central route to persuasion:
    a. is more likely to be followed for decisions that are unimportant
    b. involves paying attention to a speaker's appearance and reputation
    c. involves paying attention to the evidence and logic behind a message
    d. involves paying attention to the sheer number of arguments and not to their quality

Correct _____ If wrong, why? _____

3. How can a minority group best influence public opinion?
    a. by making themselves seem as different as possible from the public
    b. by presenting very frightening messages telling people that disaster is imminent and there is nothing they can do about it
    c. by forewarning people that they will hear a persuasive message
    d. by beginning with a weak message and then strengthening it
    e. by repeating a single, simple message over and over

Correct _____ If wrong, why? _____

4. According to cognitive dissonance theory, what is the relationship between attitude change and behavior change?
    a. attitudes must be changed before behavior can be
    b. attitude change and behavior change are unrelated
    c. behavior only changes if people are forewarned about attempts to change attitudes
    d. if behavior is changed, then attitude change will follow

Correct _____ If wrong, why? _____

5. According to cognitive dissonance theory, which of the following should be true?
    a. students should be happier at a very expensive college than at a cheaper one
    b. people should like an organization that is easy to join better than one that is difficult to join
    c. larger amounts of foreign aid should make one country like another one better than smaller amounts
    d. strong threats should make people obey the law better than milder ones

Correct _____ If wrong, why? _____

**Social Perception and Cognition**

6. Which of the following is <u>not</u> true about forming impressions of new acquaintances?
    a. physically attractive people are likely to be judged more favorably
    b. facial expressions and body movements are more likely to be used than conflicting verbal information
    c. information that is learned first is more influential than information that is learned later
    d. information that is learned last is more influential than information that is learned earlier

Correct _____ If wrong, why? _____

7. Stereotypes probably get started because people:
    a. discount internal causes if there is an external cause as stated in the discounting principle
    b. do not remember the behavior of minority groups
    c. rely on consistency information more than distinctiveness information
    d. remember unusual behaviors of minority groups

Correct _____ If wrong, why? _____

8. Which of the following shows ambivalence toward African Americans?
    a. a European-American student praises the African-American lawyer who fights for people's rights, but condemns the African-American gang member who can't find a job
    b. a European-American student interprets a certain behavior as more violent when it is performed by a African-American person than by a European-American person
    c. a European-American student says that another European-American student did what he did because he is basically honest, but he says that a African-American student did the same thing because he would have gotten arrested otherwise
    d. if the first information gained about a African-American person is that he is very successful, later information that he is dishonest has less impact than if it came before the successful information

Correct _____ If wrong, why? _____

9. The fundamental attribution error involves overemphasizing:
   a. external as opposed to internal causes of behavior
   b. distinctiveness rather than consensus information
   c. internal as opposed to external causes of behavior
   d. consensus rather than distinctiveness information

Correct _____ If wrong, why? _____

10. Self-handicapping refers to:
   a. creating external causes for our failures
   b. a tendency to attribute internal causes to others people's behavior but external causes to one's own behavior
   c. attributing emotional arousal to external stimuli
   d. creating internal causes for our successes

Correct _____ If wrong, why? _____

**Interpersonal Attraction**

11. If people are led to expect severe shocks, with whom would they prefer to wait?
   a. other people, whether or not those people expect shock
   b. alone; people know that misery increases misery
   c. other people who are also expecting shock
   d. most people say they don't care

Correct _____ If wrong, why? _____

12. The likelihood of developing a friendship is increased by:
   a. proximity; people who live close together are more likely to become friends
   b. familiarity; people who are very familiar as children are likely to develop romantic relationships
   c. dissimilarity because opposites attract
   d. having a dominant person who gets a better deal from the relationship than the other person

Correct _____ If wrong, why? _____

13. With respect to romantic partners, women are more likely than men to prefer:
   a. someone younger than themselves
   b. casual sex partners
   c. prefer multiple partners
   d. partners who have wealth

Correct _____ If wrong, why? _____

14. What is the relationship between physical attractiveness and attraction?
   a. opposites attract; generally people who are very different in attractiveness have the strongest relationships
   b. attitudes and personality are much more important than attractiveness in determining how much people like dating partners
   c. while personality and attitudes may draw two people together initially, physical attractiveness is what determines whether they stay together
   d. people like physically attractive dating partners better than unattractive ones

Correct _____ If wrong, why? _____

15. According to Sternberg's view of love:
   a. men are more ludic and women are more storgic
   b. men are more storgic and women are more ludic
   c. love consists of both liking and loving
   d. relationships go through five stages: initial attraction, buildup, continuation and consolidation, deterioration, ending
   e. love has three dimensions: intimacy, passion, and commitment

Correct _____ If wrong, why? _____

**Interpersonal Influence**

16. In which situation would you expect a true subject to conform the most?
   a. two people give a wrong answer
   b. seven people give a wrong answer
   c. five people give a wrong answer, and one person gives the correct one
   d. four people give a wrong answer
   e. b and d would be about equal

Correct _____ If wrong, why? _____

17. Would you expect to get help faster if your car broke down on a highway that has relatively few travelers or on a busy highway?
   a. on the busy one, because of bystander intervention
   b. on the lightly traveled highway, because of the ambiguity on the busy one
   c. on the busy one, because of diffusion of responsibility
   d. on the busy one, because of social loafing
   e. on the lightly traveled one, because of diffusion of responsibility

Correct _____ If wrong, why? _____

18. A group of professors is trying to decide what to do about academically deficient students. Each writes down what he or she thinks is appropriate, but in the end the group decides on more severe action than the average recommendation of the individuals. What has happened?
    a. the group polarization effect
    b. social loafing
    c. bystander intervention
    d. a peremptory challenge
    e. volunteerism

Correct _____ If wrong, why? _____

19. Which of the following is an example of groupthink?
    a. cooperating with a group to help in a major disaster
    b. competing with a group that has different goals from yours
    c. failing to challenge the assumptions of group members
    d. gathering information before making a group decision

Correct _____ If wrong, why? _____

**The Power of the Social Situation**

20. If nations act as people do in the prisoner's dilemma, what will happen in a nuclear arms race?
    a. each nation will build more weapons, because that is the best for the individual nation
    b. all nations will stop building such weapons, because this is best for each individual nation
    c. all nations will continue to build weapons, because that is best for the nations as a group
    d. communication among nations will probably increase the nuclear buildup

Correct _____ If wrong, why? _____

21. What happened in the experiment in which students could take nuts out of a bowl in which the nuts would double every 10 sec.?
    a. they competed and grabbed nuts for themselves immediately
    b. they cooperated and waited until there were many nuts and then divided them
    c. they took more nuts sooner when working as individuals than when working in a group
    d. they cooperated, just as they do in the prisoner's dilemma
    e. both b and d

Correct _____ If wrong, why? _____

22. An example of the foot-in-the-door technique is:
    a. a volunteer worker first asked me to give $100, and when I said no, she asked for $10
    b. a salesman places his briefcase in the door so that I can't close it until I have heard his spiel
    c. a beggar follows a pedestrian up the street constantly asking him for money
    d. a survey worker asks if I will answer a simple question, and after I do that, she asks if I will fill out a long questionnaire
    e. a salesman tells me the price of an item, and then immediately adds that another item will also be included in the price

Correct _____ If wrong, why? _____

23. In Milgram's experiment in which "teachers" shocked "learners":
    a. subjects did not obey unless they were sadists
    b. many normal people continued to give shocks, although they had misgivings about it
    c. whether or not the experimenter was in the room was irrelevant for obedience
    d. more people quit the experiment when a confederate followed orders than when they worked alone

Correct _____ If wrong, why? _____

## ANSWERS AND EXPLANATIONS FOR COMPREHENSION CHECK

| Correct Answer | Other Alternatives Are Wrong Because: |
|---|---|

1. a (p. 689)
   Obj. I-A

   b. people are often unaware of attitudes
   c. cultures differ in how they use rating scales
   d. people are unaware of implicit attitudes, so they are difficult to measure
   e. attitudes often do not predict behavior

2. c (p. 691)
   Obj. II-A

   a. peripheral is followed for unimportant decisions
   b. this is the peripheral route
   d. this is the peripheral route

3. e (p. 692)
   Obj. II-B-2

   a. attitudes are changed more by people who are similar
   b. frightening messages are usually effective only if people can do something about the disaster

   c. forewarning effect reduces persuasion
   d. inoculation effect reduces persuasion

4. d (p. 695)
   Obj. III

   a. theory says the opposite
   b. attitudes do change if behavior does
   c. forewarning effect; decreases attitude change

5. a (pp. 695-696)
   Obj. III-A

   b. if it's difficult, they think that they've done all this to join it, so they must really like it
   c. with large amounts, they may decide they're just being friendly because of the money
   d. people will assume that they're avoiding doing illegal things because of the law, not because they don't like to do those things

6. d (p. 698)
   Obj. IV-A

   a-c. these are true
   d. information learned first is more influential

7. d (p. 700)
   Obj. V -B

   a. true, but such external attributions should not lead to stereotypes
   b. they remember unusual behaviors
   c. information used to decide about internal and external attributions; not necessarily relevant to stereotypes

8. a (pp. 701-702)
   Obj. V-B-1-a

    b. shows how stereotypes can distort perceptions
    c. fundamental attribution error; not necessarily related to stereotypes and prejudice
    d. primacy effect; happens in impression formation

9. c (p. 704)
   Obj. VI-B-1

    a. overemphasis of internal causes
    b,d. information used in making attributions; neither distinctiveness nor consensus necessarily overemphasized

10. a (p. 706)
    Obj. VI-C-1

    b. this is the actor-observer effect
    c. may be an example of misattribution if cause is wrong
    d. refers to explanations for failure, not success

11. c (p. 710)
    Obj. VII-B-1

    a. they want to be with others undergoing same experience
    b,d. prefer to wait together

12. a (p. 709)
    Obj. VIII-A

    b. this is an exception to the familiarity rule; people are very familiar as children don't develop romantic relationships
    c. similar people are usually attracted to each other
    d. equity theory argues that both people should get a fair deal

13. d (p. 714, Table 16.3 )
    Obj. IX-A-1

    a. men prefer younger partners who will be fertile for more years
    b. men are more likely to have casual sex partners
    c. men spread their genes more with multiple partners

14. d (pp. 714-715)
    Obj. IX-B

    a. similarity is the rule; according to the equity principle, both parties should be about equally attractive
    b. physical attractiveness is most important
    c. it's just the opposite; attractiveness is more important initially

15. e (pp. 716-717)
    Obj. X-A-1

    a. correct, but the Hendricks' view
    b. reversed version of the Hendricks' view
    c. Rubin's view
    d. Levinger's view

16. e (pp. 720-722)
    Obj. XI

    a. at least three are needed for maximum conformity effect
    b. conformity will occur but no more than with four people
    c. having an "ally" reduces conformity
    d. about the same amount of conformity occurs with four and seven people

17. e (pp. 722-723)
    Obj. XII-A

    a. refers to whether people will help; not an explanation of why they help
    b. a car breakdown should be equally ambiguous on both types of highway
    c. diffusion should lead to less help; people assume others will help
    d. refers to tendency to work less hard in a group, not to whether bystanders will help

18. a (p. 725)
Obj. XIII-A

   b. not a matter of how much effort an individual puts forth, but of a group's influence on decisions

   c. refers to whether people will help; both may be due to diffusion of responsibility

   d. refers to lawyers' rights to reject potential jurors; not relevant to group decision making

   e. people's tendency to help others; not relevant to group decision making

19. c (pp. 725-726)
Obj. XIII-B

   a,b. groupthink involves decision making

   d. information, especially dissenting opinions, is not gathered when groupthink occurs

20. a (pp. 732-733, Fig. 16.23)
Obj. XIV-A-2

   b. best for group, not individuals; if one country has weapons and others don't, that country can dominate

   c. not best for group; possibility of nuclear war

   d. communication should foster cooperation

21. a (p. 733)
Obj. XIV-A-3

   b. cooperative response, but not what people do

   c. groups are usually more greedy than individuals

   d. in this commons dilemma and the prisoners dilemma, people behave competitively

   e. b and d are wrong

22. d (p. 734)
Obj. XV-A-1

   a. this also works, but is opposite of foot-in-door

   b. foot-in-door doesn't refer to forceful entry

   c. foot-in-door doesn't refer to persistent asking

   e. this is the that's-not-all technique

23. b (pp. 735-737, Fig. 16.29)
Obj. XV-B

   a. over half obeyed; they were "normal"

   c. obedience increased when the experimenter was in the room

   d. obedience increased when a confederate obeyed

## LECTURE MATERIAL

Don't forget to review your lecture material. Process each topic meaningfully. First, be sure that you understand the material in each lecture--if you don't, ask your instructor or teaching assistant. Associate the material with things that you already know and with your personal experiences. If you can make up mental images of any of the material, do so. Try to think of real-life applications of the concepts. Write your own notes on each day's lecture notes. Then write questions to cover each concept.

---
### WAIT AT LEAST 24 HOURS BEFORE PROCEEDING.
### LET FORGETTING OCCUR--IT WILL!!
---

# SHORT-ANSWER ESSAY QUESTIONS

Write brief answers to each of the following. The answers are on pp. 335-336, but do try to write the answers yourself before looking at them.

## Attitudes and Attitude Change

1. Describe the two routes to persuasion and discuss the conditions under which each might be used.

2. You are trying to convince people to give money to public television. Discuss the techniques that you might use.

3. Describe cognitive dissonance theory.

## Social Perception and Cognition

4. Discuss the factors that are important in first impressions.

5. What is an attribution, and what types of information are important in making internal and external attributions?

6. Give some reasons for why people tend to make external attributions for their own behavior and internal attributions for the behavior of others.

**Interpersonal Attraction**

7. Describe three things that are important in who dates whom.

8. Describe how equity theory applies to romantic relationships and friendships.

9. Different theorists have proposed different dimensions of love. Describe two of these systems.

**Interpersonal Influence**

10. How is social loafing related to bystander apathy?

11. Explain why the group polarization effect occurs.

**The Power of the Social Situation**

12. Contrast the foot-in-the-door, door-in-the-face, and that's-not-all techniques for gaining compliance.

13. Describe Milgram's experiment on obedience and discuss what we can learn from such an experiment.

*********************************************************************
Find the questions that you wrote over lecture material and write answers to them.
*********************************************************************

## ANSWERS TO SHORT-ANSWER ESSAY QUESTIONS

1. When people hear persuasive arguments, they sometimes evaluate the evidence and logic behind the message. This is called the central route to persuasion, and it occurs for serious decisions. An alternative route that is used for less serious decisions is the peripheral route to persuasion. People pay more attention to the speaker's appearance and reputation, and to the sheer number of arguments regardless of their quality. (p. 691)

2. Have someone who is similar to the potential supporters give the message. If supporters of public television are in the minority, continuing to repeat a simple message about the benefits of public television might eventually persuade the majority. Frightening people by saying how bad television might become without the public television option might help if the fear message is believable, not too frightening, and if people believe they can prevent the decline in quality by donating money. (pp. 692-693)

3. The idea is that if people behave in ways that are inconsistent with their beliefs, they will change their beliefs. The original theory argued that tension builds up if people's behavior and attitudes do not match. They reduce this tension by adopting a new attitude that justifies their behavior. (p. 695)

4. First impressions are based on physical attractiveness, people's nonverbal behaviors, and information that is learned first. In addition, expectations that are derived from stereotypes about groups of people influence first impressions. (p. 698)

5. Attribution is the process of assigning causes to someone's behavior. *Consistency information* (how much a person's behavior varies), *consensus information* (how similar a person's behavior is to that of other people), and *distinctiveness information* (how much a person's behavior depends upon the situation) are important. Behaviors that are high in consistency, dissimilar to those of other people, and not distinctive to a situation are attributed to internal causes. (pp. 703-705)

6. This actor-observer effect may occur because people who are watching someone assume that behavior results from characteristics within that person. It might occur because we know that our own behavior is not consistent across situations, but we know less about others' behavior. Another possibility is that we attribute unexpected behaviors to external events and our own behavior is not unexpected. A third explanation is that we do not see ourselves as objects, so we tend to focus on the environment, or external stimuli. (p. 704)

7. Similarity is important. Couples tend to resemble each other in age, social class, religion, intelligence, etc. Proximity is important. People tend to date people who live close to them. For first dates, physical attractiveness is important; people like physically attractive dates better than less attractive dates. (pp. 711-712)

8. Equity theory assumes that social relationships are transactions in which partners exchange "goods." Each partner wants to get the best deal possible. Partners look at the pluses and minuses of relationships and decide whether the exchange seems fair. (p. 713)

9.  Sternberg suggests that there are three dimensions: intimacy--how well partners can talk and confide in each other; passion--erotic attraction; and commitment--intention to continue in the relationship. The Hendricks propose three primary styles of love: eros--passionate love; ludos-- uncommitted, game-playing love; and storge--friendship love.  In addition they postulate three secondary styles: mania--possessive love; pragma--  practical love; and agape--selfless love.  (pp. 716-717)

10. Both may occur because of diffusion of responsibility because people in groups do less than individuals.  Bystanders are less likely to help strangers in trouble when there are more, rather than fewer, people around.  They assume either that others will help or that it may not really be an emergency situation.  In social loafing, people do less work in a group than alone, perhaps because their own efforts won't be evaluated.  (p. 723)

11. If the members of a group generally agree on a position at the beginning, they often move toward the extreme because of diffusion of responsibility (the group is responsible, not me), because individuals hear many reasons for their position, and because they receive reinforcement from the group for agreeing.  (p. 725)

12. The foot-in-the-door technique involves getting agreement for a small request first and then making a much larger request.  The door-in-the- face technique is the opposite; begin with the large request and then scale down to the smaller one.  The that's-not-all technique makes a better offer before the person has responded to the first one.  With each technique, the second request is more likely to be agreed to than if the first was not made.  (p. 734)

13. Students served as teachers in what they thought was an experiment on  obedience.  They presented word pairs to a "learner" who made many  mistakes in his recall of the pairs.  Students were to administer a  higher shock level following each mistake.  Over half of the students  continued and administered the highest shock level.  This shows that people have such great respect for authority that they may carry out  unreasonable and dangerous instructions.  (pp. 735-737)

## POSTTEST

Take this test with all of your books and notes out of sight. This should give you a good idea of how well you understand the material.

### Matching

Put the letter of the term in the blank beside the description.

Interpersonal Influence; The Power of the Social Situation

1. _____ results in decisions that are more extreme than the average of the individuals' decisions

2. _____ overuse of resources that have a fixed rate of replacement

3. _____ beginning with a small request and escalating to a much larger one

4. _____ failure to challenge assumptions and ask probing questions

5. _____ beginning with a large request and scaling it down

6. _____ situation in which competition is pitted against cooperation

7. _____ assuming that someone else will do what's needed

8. _____ changing behavior to be consistent with a group's standards

A. prisoner's dilemma

B. foot-in-the-door

C. groupthink

D. door-in-the-face

E. group polarization effect

F. commons dilemma

G. conformity

H. diffusion of responsibility

### Multiple-choice

Circle the *best* alternative.

Attitudes and Attitude Change

1. The measurement of attitudes:
   a. is very accurate and reliable
   b. is rarely done with subjective rating scales
   c. results in good prediction of behavior for high self-monitors
   d. may be inaccurate because people may not be aware of their attitudes
   e. is fairly constant across cultures so that a rating scale in one culture is interpreted similarly in other cultures

2. The sleeper effect refers to:
   a. persuasion via a superficial approach
   b. persuasion via careful evaluation of evidence
   c. a change in attitude by a high self-monitor
   d. changing attitudes after noticing that behaviors and attitudes don't match
   e. changing attitudes after initial rejection of a message

3. A message is most likely to be persuasive if it:
   a. comes from a minority as opposed to a majority group member
   b. is logical and scientific and presented to a person who is very low in intelligence
   c. is a fear message, but there is nothing that people can do to prevent the disaster
   d. is preceded by a weaker version arguing the same position
   e. is simple and repeated, even if it comes from a minority

4. According to the cognitive dissonance theory, people:
   a. will change their behavior only after their attitudes have changed
   b. try to understand and explain their behavior
   c. change their attitudes to reduce the tension that results from inconsistent attitudes and behaviors
   d. will like an activity if they receive a large payoff for doing it
   e. will dislike an activity if they avoid it because of a severe threat

Social Perception and Cognition

5. According to the primacy effect in impression formation, you will be more influenced by:
   a. physical characteristics than by nonverbal behaviors
   b. ordinary information than by unusual information
   c. information received first, rather than that received later
   d. peripheral rather than central traits
   e. nonverbal behaviors than by physical characteristics

6. 75% of the people you meet belong to group X and 25% belong to group Y. Members of both groups perform an equal number of unusual acts. When asked to decide which group does more unusual things, you will say:
   a. Group Y, because unusual acts committed by a minority group stand out
   b. Group X, because unusual acts committed by a majority group stand out
   c. Group Y, because unusual acts committed by a majority group stand out
   d. they are equivalent, because they actually are
   e. Group X, because unusual acts committed by a minority group stand out

7. Which of the following is an internal attribution?
   a. John failed the test because he had to work last night
   b. Mary forgot the party because she was so busy at work
   c. Sally invited me over for dinner because she owed me a favor
   d. Fred hung up on me because he has a short temper
   e. both a and b

8. The actor-observer effect is shown in which of the following?
   a. Jane left the party because she is not very friendly; I left it because people were using drugs
   b. Mike failed the test because it was too difficult; I failed it because I am basically stupid
   c. John dropped the tray because he is a klutz; I dropped the tray because I am clumsy
   d. Sally fell because it was slippery; I fell because my boots don't have good tread
   e. all of the above

9. People sometimes intentionally put themselves at a disadvantage on tasks so they can attribute their:
    a. successes to external factors
    b. failures to internal factors
    c. failures to external factors
    d. successes to internal factors
    e. outcomes to the fundamental attribution error

## Interpersonal Attraction

10. In the experiment in which subjects were either made afraid of the upcoming shock or not made afraid:
    a. the subjects chose to wait alone in both conditions
    b. the subjects chose to wait together in both conditions
    c. the highly anxious subjects were more likely to choose together, but only with other anxious subjects
    d. the highly anxious subjects wanted to wait with other people whether or not the other people were in the same experiment
    e. both b and d

11. People's friends in a graduate housing project were mostly people:
    a. who lived near them
    b. who looked like them
    c. who lived in other buildings
    d. of the same sex
    e. who had the same occupational goals

12. Rubin found that:
    a. people like almost everyone they love, but don't love everyone they like
    b. love consists of intimacy and passion; liking consists of commitment
    c. liking and loving were perfectly correlated
    d. women are more likely to see love as friendship, but men are more likely to be uncommitted and game-playing
    e. people are satisfied with their relationship if they are in love, even though the costs of the relationship are high

## Interpersonal Influence

13. In Asch's experiment, subjects were to judge the length of bars after hearing other people give a wrong answer. What happened?
    a. people rarely conformed, because the situation was not ambiguous
    b. people conformed much more if there were seven other people than if there were only three
    c. people conformed even if there was only one other person
    d. everyone conformed if there were seven other people
    e. most people did not conform if they had an "ally" who gave the correct answer

14. Under which situation would you most expect social loafing to occur?
    a. an individual shooting while playing on a basketball team
    b. a person who has a unique specialty doing something in a group
    c. people thinking up unusual uses for a brick when they know that others will know how many uses they gave
    d. people clapping as part of a group

15. The city council is discussing whether a license to operate a new bar should be approved. Each
    member is slightly against approval. What is the group decision likely to be and why?
    a. in favor of the license because of groupthink
    b. a split vote because of social loafing
    c. against the license because of the group polarization effect
    d. a split vote because of the group polarization effect
    e. in favor of the license because of social loafing

16. Military strategists all agreed on a plan to attack an island. No one questioned whether it was
    reasonable and whether they would succeed. What happened during that meeting?
    a. peremptory challenges
    b. diffusion of responsibility
    c. social loafing
    d. groupthink
    e. fundamental attribution error

## The Power of the Social Situation

17. Situations like gas wars in which one gas station lowers prices and then other nearby stations must
    do the same or lose customers are similar to the:
    a. dollar auction
    b. prisoner's dilemma
    c. commons dilemma
    d. door-in-the-face technique
    e. that's-not-all technique

18. The foot-in-the-door technique is one trick to facilitate persuasion. What is another way that
    involves doing just the opposite?
    a. have an expert give the message
    b. start with a small request and then make a large one
    c. begin by arguing the opposite and gradually make arguments that support the desired view
    d. begin with a very large request and then scale it back
    e. make the arguments in a way that people don't know that they are being persuaded

19. Today, a Human Subjects Committee may still approve Milgram's procedures. Why?
    a. few psychologists and psychiatrists predicted that subjects would actually "shock" others
    b. there was no possibility of physical harm to any participants, and that is all that concerns Human
       Subjects Committees
    c. researchers abide by less-strict human subjects regulations than when Milgram did his study
    d. none of Milgram's subjects were upset by the procedures, so there is no reason for concern

**ANSWERS TO POSTTEST**

| Correct Answer | Questions Testing a Similar Concept | |
|---|---|---|
| | Comprehension Check | Short-Answer |

**Matching**

| Correct Answer | Comprehension Check | Short-Answer |
|---|---|---|
| 1. E (p. 725) | 18 | 11 |
| 2. F (p. 720) | 21 | -- |
| 3. B (p. 734) | 22 | 12 |
| 4. C (pp. 725-726) | 19 | -- |
| 5. D (p. 734) | 22a | 12 |
| 6. A (pp. 732-733) | 20 | -- |
| 7. H (pp. 722-723) | 17 | 10 |
| 8. G (p. 720) | 16 | -- |

**Multiple-Choice**

| Correct Answer | Comprehension Check | Short-Answer |
|---|---|---|
| 1. d (p. 689) | 1 | -- |
| 2. e (p. 691) | -- | -- |
| 3. e (pp. 692-693) | 3 | 2 |
| 4. c (p. 695) | 4,5 | 3 |
| 5. c (p. 698) | 6c | 4 |
| 6. a (p. 700) | 7 | -- |
| 7. d (pp. 704-705) | 9 | 5,6 |
| 8. a (p. 704) | 10d | 6 |
| 9. c (p. 706) | 10 | -- |
| 10. c (p. 710) | 11 | 7 |
| 11. a (p. 711) | 12a | 7 |
| 12. a (p. 716) | 15c | 9 |
| 13. e (pp. 721-722) | 16 | -- |
| 14. d (p. 723) | 18b | 10 |
| 15. c (p. 725) | 18 | 11 |
| 16. d (pp. 725-726) | 19 | -- |
| 17. a (p. 731) | -- | -- |
| 18. d (p. 734) | 22 | 12 |
| 19. a (p. 738) | 23 | 13 |

# CHAPTER 16 LANGUAGE ENHANCEMENT GUIDE

## I. VOCABULARY, IDIOMS AND CULTURAL CONCEPTS

### Instructions:

As you read the text refer to the following list of words and their definitions. The words are listed in the order in which they appear in the chapter. The definitions presented contain the meaning of the word as used by Kalat on the textbook page indicated.

Remember that these words like all words can have different meanings in other sentences. If you do not find a non-technical word on this list it may have been defined on a previous page or chapter of this study guide. The definition of non-technical words may be found in the dictionary at the end of this study guide. Kalat defined each new technical word as it first appears on a page and these may be found in Kalat's summary at the end of the section and in the Glossary at the end the textbook.

### Attitudes and Changing Attitudes

abolishing (688) = removing, destroying, canceling

usurpation = seizing and holding by force and without legal authority

invariably = not changing or subject to change; constant

evinces = shows, demonstrates

despotism = governing or ruling a county with absolute power

characterization = description

nevertheless = nonetheless, however

uncompromising = not willing to settle differences or come to an agreement

inoculation (694) = introducing an idea or attitude into the mind; introducing a serum, a vaccine, or some substance into the body to produce or increase immunity to a specific disease

forewarning = advanced warning of an event

### Social Perception and Cognition

inevitably (698) = predictably, impossible to avoid or prevent

Ku Klux Klan or other white -supremacist group = groups of people who believe that white people are superior to all other racial groups

attribute (703) = assign

### Interpersonal Attraction

pointless (709) = meaningless; senseless

cultivate (temporary friends)

casual affiliations (710) = not close or intimate; passing; superficial

most stable (712) = lasting

simultaneously (713) = at the same time

great deal = a large amount

does not necessarily follow exactly the same strategy = follow a different strategy

high-tech (714) = new developments is medical science
Scandinavian cultures = the cultures of Norway and Sweden

irregularities (716) =   not straight, uniform, uneven, jagged, crooked
asymmetries =  out of balance;  non symmetrical

passionate (717) =  strong powerful emotions; strong sexual desire
commitment =  dedication, devotion
intimacy = a close sharing friendship

**Interpersonal Influence**

awkward (720) = uncomfortable.  not at ease, nervous

confederates (721) =  people who assist the researcher in an experiment

consensus (725) = agreement
NASA = The National Science and Space Administration.  A government organization assigned to
    explore space, the moon and the planets

**The Power of the Social Situation**

Martin Luther King Jr.  (730) = a civil rights leader who during the 1950's and the 1960's led the
    civil rights movement for African Americans
Mother Teresa = a Catholic nun who works to aid the poor in India
virtually compels us = forces us

conviction (731) = beliefs
progressively escalates = increasingly increases

fruitlessly (732) = unsuccessfully, without success

replenishment (733) = replacement

## II.  VOCABULARY BUILDING

### Word Analysis

Instructions:
1. Break each word in the table into its prefixes, roots and suffixes.  If you do not remember the meaning
    of a term look it up in Appendix B.
2. Guess the meaning of the word based on the meaning of its parts.
3. Find the word on the text page indicated in the brackets and redefine the word based on the context of
    the sentence, paragraph and chapter.
5. Look up the definition of the word in the VOCABULARY, IDIOMS AND CULTURAL CONCEPTS
    section above, in Appendix A (marked A), or in a college level dictionary.  If the word is followed by
    letter G look it up in the text Glossary.

## Exercise 1.  Abolishing

| Word | Meaning |
|------|---------|
| abolishing (A) | |
| ambivalence (G) | |
| compliance | |
| conformity (G) | |
| consensus (G) | |
| diffusion (G) | |
| discounting (G) | |
| dissonance (G) | |
| forewarning (G) | |
| fruitlessly (A) | |
| groupthink (G) | |

## Exercise 2.  Impression

| Word | Meaning |
|------|---------|
| impression | |
| invariably (A) | |
| irregularities (A) | |
| meaningless | |
| overcome | |
| pointless (A) | |
| polarization | |
| prejudice (G) | |
| primacy (G) | |
| responsibility | |
| superficial | |
| uncompromising | |
| unsuccessfully | |

# APPLIED PSYCHOLOGY

## OBJECTIVES

Understand that:

### Industrial and Organizational Psychology

I. Selection and training involves choosing applicants and training them for a job  (p. 743)
   - A. Interviews are not very valid predictors of job performance  (p. 744)
   - B. Cognitive tests are good predictors of job success  (pp. 744-745)
     1. African-American and Latino applicants score lower on these and this may make them less likely to be hired  (pp. 744-745)
   - C. Personality tests are only slightly useful for job selection  (p. 745)
   - D. Physical standards may be set if they are related to job performance  (p. 745)
   - E. Biographical data can be useful in selecting for some jobs  (p. 746)
   - F. Self-selection can be useful if only the highly qualified would apply  (p. 746)
   - G. Women still face barriers in advancing in business  (pp. 746-748)

II. Employees may fail because of job design  (pp. 748-749)
   - A. The scientific-management approach (Theory X) assumes that employees are lazy, uncreative, and indifferent  (p. 748)
   - B. The human-relations approach (Theory Y) holds that jobs should be challenging and interesting  (p. 749)
     1. Job enrichment gives employees responsibility for specific tasks  (p. 749)

III. Pay is only one motivator  (pp. 749-751)
   - A. Workers want to believe that they are earning their pay  (p. 750)

IV. The relationship between job satisfaction and productivity is low  (p. 751)

V. Industrial-organizational psychology is related to motivation, learning and memory, standardized testing, and social psychology  (p. 751)

### Ergonomics, or Human Factors

VI. Machinery should be designed so that person-machine systems operate efficiently  (p. 753)
   - A. The principle of compatibility uses people's existing expectations  (p. 754)

VII. Controls should be standardized so people can transfer without mistakes  (p. 755)

VIII. Information displays should be arranged so that people can read them easily and accurately  (pp. 755-757 )

IX. Ergonomists can help make everyday warning signs more effective  (p. 757)

### School Psychology

X. School psychologists identify the needs of children and make plan to treat the needs  (p. 759)
   - A. School psychologists help schools provide appropriate education for all children  (p. 759)

XI. School psychologists deal with a wide range of problems  (pp. 760-763)
   - A. School phobia involves apprehension, and maybe panic, about school  (pp. 760-761)
   - B. Attention-deficit disorder is common among school children  (p. 761)
   - C. Learning disability means that a child has failed in some area and we have no explanation  (pp. 761-762 )
     1. School psychologists identify problem areas and make plans to overcome weakness  (p. 762)
   - D. Gifted children need to be challenged  (p. 762)
   - E. School psychologists encounter other types of psychological problems also  (p. 762)

XII. Mainstreaming disabled children is still controversial  (p. 763)

**Epilogue**

XIII. Psychological conclusions are tentative, but psychologists have discovered many things about human behavior (p. 765)

## COMPREHENSION CHECK

Answer these questions soon after reading the chapter. Circle the best alternative. Check your answers on pp. 348-349. If you gave a wrong answer, try to write why it was wrong. Check your reasons.

### Industrial and Organizational Psychology

1. Dr. Arbiter is an I-O psychologist. This means that he is an:
   a. input-output psychologist
   b. industrial-organizational psychologist
   c. international-organizational psychologist
   d. integrated-optimistic psychologist

Correct _____ If wrong, why? _____

2. The least valid method of job selection is:
   a. cognitive tests
   b. letting people self-select after being honest about job requirements
   c. biographical data
   d. the interview

Correct _____ If wrong, why? _____

3. The use of a quota system to hire minority applicants:
   a. is always forbidden by law
   b. can be required if a disproportionately small number of minorities is hired
   c. can be avoided by using different norms for different groups
   d. is unnecessary when cognitive tests are used because minority groups score equally on valid tests

Correct _____ If wrong, why? _____

4. What is the situation today with respect to women and promotions in the workplace?
   a. they are promoted as often and to as high a level as men
   b. they don't get promoted as often as men and those who are promoted are less successful than men
   c. they get promoted less often than men, but those who get promoted have salaries equal to men's
   d. they are frequently promoted to middle management levels, but not to top levels

Correct _____ If wrong, why? _____

5. Proponents of Theory X would try to:
   a. use a scientific management approach in arranging jobs
   b. take a human-relations approach in arranging jobs
   c. use job enrichment to make work more meaningful to employees
   d. give workers more responsibility and let them see the results of their work
   e. give employees flexibility in how and when they do parts of their jobs

Correct _____ If wrong, why? _____

6. A worker who is paid fairly high wages by the hour believes that she is overpaid. How will her performance compare with that of a person who believes that her pay is about right?
    a. she will put out more work per hour
    b. she will cut back on the amount of work, but she will increase the quality
    c. she would neglect important chores not directly related to her pay
    d. she would complain about the constant pressure to work harder

Correct _____ If wrong, why? _____

**Ergonomics, or Human Factors**

7. Ergonomics is:
    a. related to economics; it's how people respond to economic changes
    b. the study of people at work
    c. the study of people using machines
    d. the study of students in school

Correct _____ If wrong, why? _____

8. Which of the following shows the principle of compatibility as used in ergonomics?
    a. designing a boat so that turning the wheel clockwise moves the boat to the right
    b. putting the height of a control halfway between the right height for men and women
    c. finding personality types who get along well together
    d. making sure that gauges and control knobs are in the same place

Correct _____ If wrong, why? _____

9. Warning signs are:
    a. most effective if they are short
    b. most effective if they explain the nature of the danger
    c. most effective if they are non-verbal
    d. out of the domain of ergonomics

Correct _____ If wrong, why? _____

**School Psychology**

10. School psychologists:
    a. only deal with children who have difficulty succeeding in school
    b. are trained in psychology departments
    c. use IQ tests exclusively to place students
    d. both identify problems and devise plans for dealing with problems

Correct _____ If wrong, why? _____

11. Attention-deficit disorder:
    a. occurs more often in boys than in girls
    b. is usually diagnosed after a child has been in school three to four years
    c. means that the child fails in some task and there is no good explanation for failure
    d. involves repetitive tics and odd movements

Correct _____ If wrong, why? _____

12. Mainstreaming:
    a. involves creating challenging activities for gifted children
    b. is usually unsuccessful because other children are exposed to diversity
    c. may be more or less successful depending upon the skill of the teacher
    d. requires that special classrooms be created for children with disabilities

Correct _____ If wrong, why? _____

## ANSWERS AND EXPLANATIONS FOR COMPREHENSION CHECK

| Correct Answer | Other Alternatives Are Wrong Because: |
|---|---|

1. b (p. 743)
   Obj. I

a. computer terms
c. not international but <u>industrial</u>
d. nonsense, but I suppose all psychologists should be like this

2. d (p. 744)
   Obj. I-A

a. often the only valid predictors
b. can be a good predictor for some types of jobs
c. good predictor for some jobs

3. b (p. 745)
   Obj. I-B, 1

a. if a disproportionately small number of minorities is hired,
   a quota system may be required by the courts
c. the government considers this to be a quota system in disguise
d. African-American and Latino applicants receive lower scores than
   European-American applicants

4. d (p. 747)
   Obj. I-G

a. promotions to top levels are less frequent for women
b. those who are promoted to top levels are successful
c. salaries for women at the same level as men are lower

5. a (p. 748)
   Obj. II-A

b-e. Theory Y does these things to increase motivation
   and morale

6. a (pp. 749-751)
   Obj. III

b. if she were paid by the piece
c. true for individuals paid on commission or by the piece
d. true for people paid by the piece or given bonuses for high
   productivity

7. c (p. 753)
   Obj. VI

a. not related to economics
b. this is industrial-organizational psychology
d. this is school psychology

8. a (p. 754)
   Obj. VI-A
   b. may be useful, but not compatibility which refers to allowing people to use learned expectations
   c. not part of ergonomics which matches people and machines
   d. important, but not a good illustration of principle of compatibility

9. b (p. 757)
   Obj. IX
   a. not necessarily; they're more effective if they explain the danger
   c. true for road signs because they break the language barrier and they can be seen from a distance
   d. signs are a topic of interest to ergonomists

10. d (p. 759)
    Obj. X
    a. deal with gifted children also
    b. may be trained in education departments
    c. shouldn't use IQ tests alone, but use them as one piece of evidence

11. a (p. 761)
    Obj. XI-B
    b. usually diagnosed within the first two years
    c. this is learning disability
    d. this is Tourette's disorder

12. c (p. 763)
    Obj. XII
    a. mainstreaming refers to placing disabled children in regular classrooms
    b. exposure to diversity is a plus; children should learn to respect diversity
    d. just the opposite; involves placing children in regular classrooms

## LECTURE MATERIAL

Don't forget to review your lecture material. Process each topic meaningfully. First, be sure that you understand the material in each lecture--if you don't, ASK your instructor or teaching assistant. Associate the material with things that you already know and with your personal experiences. If you can make up mental images of any of the material, do so. Try to think of real-life applications of the concepts. Write your own notes on each day's lecture notes. Then write questions to cover each concept.

--------------------------------------------------------------------------------
WAIT AT LEAST 24 HOURS BEFORE PROCEEDING--
LET FORGETTING OCCUR--IT WILL!!
--------------------------------------------------------------------------------

## SHORT-ANSWER ESSAY QUESTIONS

Write brief answers to each of the following. The answers are on pp. 350-351, but do try to write the answers yourself before looking at them.

### Industrial and Organizational Psychology

1. Interviews are not very valid ways of selecting employees. Why not?

2. The scores of minorities on cognitive tests are a major impediment to using such tests for hiring decisions.  Why is this?

3. Describe Theory X and Theory Y as they contribute to job design.

4. Discuss the relationship between pay, job satisfaction, and productivity.

**Ergonomics or Human Factors**

5. Describe how ergonomists have set up information display gauges and their controls so that they are easy to read and to use.

**School Psychology**

6. How has the Education for All Handicapped Children Act influenced the practice of school psychology?

7. What does the term *learning-disabled child* mean?

\*\*\*\*\*\*\*\*\*\*\*\*\*\*\*\*\*\*\*\*\*\*\*\*\*\*\*\*\*\*\*\*\*\*\*\*\*\*\*\*\*\*\*\*\*\*\*\*\*\*\*\*\*\*\*\*\*\*\*\*\*\*\*\*\*\*\*\*\*\*\*\*\*\*\*\*
Find the questions that you wrote over lecture material and <u>write</u> answers to them.
\*\*\*\*\*\*\*\*\*\*\*\*\*\*\*\*\*\*\*\*\*\*\*\*\*\*\*\*\*\*\*\*\*\*\*\*\*\*\*\*\*\*\*\*\*\*\*\*\*\*\*\*\*\*\*\*\*\*\*\*\*\*\*\*\*\*\*\*\*\*\*\*\*\*\*\*

## ANSWERS TO SHORT-ANSWER ESSAY QUESTIONS

1. The interviewer often asks irrelevant questions, asks different questions of different applicants, takes few notes, and makes a subjective judgment.  Interviewers may favor physically attractive candidates, and they may use other irrelevant criteria in their decisions.  (p. 744)

2. African-American and Latino applicants receive lower scores on the average than European-American applicants on cognitive tests. This means that they are less likely to get jobs if the results of such tests are used in job selection. One solution to this is to use different norms for different ethnic groups and to hire some top percentage (e.g., 20%) in each group. However, the government considers this to be a quota system in disguise, and use of a quota system is forbidden (unless a disproportionate number of minorities has been hired and the courts require the use of a quota system). (pp. 744-745)

3. Theory X is the scientific-management approach. The job is broken down so that it is simple and efficient. Workers should make few errors. Theory Y is the human-relations approach. It argues that job enrichment should be used to make work meaningful. Employees should do more complex jobs and be able to see the completed results of their work. In some cases this may lead to more errors. (pp. 748-749)

4. Pay is one factor in selecting a job, although prestige, friendly coworkers, and an opportunity to accomplish something are also important. Workers don't want to feel cheated in their pay. If workers are paid high wages that are higher than they think they earn, they may produce more work if paid by the hour or a higher quality of work if paid by the piece. Generally, workers whose pay is based on productivity produce more than workers paid on salary, but they complain about constant pressure to produce. They may also neglect other aspects of the job that aren't specifically related to their pay. (pp. 749-751)

5. The controls should operate as expected, e.g., up for on or more, down for off or less. A series of gauges can be arranged so that the position of the normal reading is the same on each gauge (e.g., at the top for all gauges). Control knobs and gauges can be located side-by-side so that reading and control can be done at the same time. (pp. 755-757)

6. PL94-142, as the Education for All Handicapped Children Act is called, specified that the public schools must provide a free and appropriate education for all children. Children should be educated in the least restrictive way. This means that disabled children must be served by the public schools and that they should be integrated into regular classrooms to the extent possible. School psychologists were called upon to identify special difficulties and needs and to devise plans for dealing with the special needs. (p. 760)

7. The term *learning-disabled child* is a loose term that refers to a child who performs normally in most regards but who has difficulty in one or more specific academic activities. Such children usually have normal hearing and vision and normal IQs. They fail in some area and there is no explanation for the failure. School psychologists try to identify the nature of the child's disability and to create an academic program that minimizes the weaknesses. (pp. 761-762)

## POSTTEST

Take this test with all of your books and notes out of sight. This should give you a good idea for how well you understand the material.

### Matching

Put the letter of the term in the blank beside the description.

School Psychology

1. _____ Attention-deficit disorder      A. apprehension or panic associated with school

2. _____ Tourette's disorder            B. restlessness and distractibility in school

3. _____ School phobia                  C. repetitive tics and odd movements

4. _____ Mainstreaming                  D. educating disabled children in least restrictive environments

5. _____ Learning disability
                                        E. especially talented children

6. _____ Gifted
                                        F. failure at specific task with no apparent reason

### Multiple-choice

Circle the best alternative.

Industrial and Organizational Psychology

1. Which of the following is not a problem with the interview?
   a. interviewers tend to put the same questions to all applicants
   b. interviewers use irrelevant criteria
   c. first impressions are often used to make hiring decisions
   d. interviewers usually take few notes during the interview
   e. decisions are often made following a rating of just one person

2. A problem with using cognitive tests to make hiring decisions is that:
   a. women will be underrepresented among the successful candidates
   b. the tests don't predict performance on the job
   c. it is illegal to use such tests for hiring decisions
   d. African Americans and Latinos will be underrepresented among successful candidates
   e. abilities tapped by the tests are irrelevant to most jobs

3. Women in the workforce:
   a. have about equal responsibility for their children as do men
   b. miss work less to care for sick children if they have a good day care available
   c. have more difficulty finding low-level management jobs than men
   d. are generally rated as effective as men at the same level
   e. make salaries that are equivalent to men's if they did not interrupt their career for family reasons and if they are willing to move to a new city

4. Which approach to job design is most consistent with Theory X?
   a. make the task foolproof, so that there are set rules to be followed that will always result in success
   b. give the worker flexibility so that he or she can do different parts of the job in different ways
   c. make the job as challenging and interesting as possible
   d. have the employees take responsibility for their work
   e. have each employee be in charge of all of the services for specific clients so that he or she keeps a number of different types of records

5. An I-O psychologist takes a human-relations approach. Which of the following would she be most likely to recommend?
   a. supervise the workers closely
   b. make up a manual with specific procedures and rules in it
   c. set up the job carefully so that it will be almost impossible to make errors
   d. have each employee do one specific task
   e. send information about job performance directly to the employee

6. Increased pay would most likely lead to increased productivity when workers:
   a. feel that they are underqualified but the pay is low even with the increase
   b. earn bonuses for productivity levels that are achievable
   c. must achieve an impossibly high level of performance for a bonus
   d. feel they are being cheated in their pay
   e. are paid on an hourly basis that is unrelated to productivity

7. Harry makes a high hourly salary and he is being paid more than other people who have similar qualifications and do the same job. Indeed, he often thinks he is overpaid. Relative to the work of lower-paid employees, Harry will:
   a. do more work per hour
   b. produce more per hour, but it will be of poorer quality
   c. do less work per hour
   d. do less work per hour, but it will be of higher quality
   e. do the same amount of work, because pay and performance are unrelated

Ergonomics, or Human Factors

8. Which of the following does not illustrate the principle of compatibility?
   a. people expect knobs on a stove to map to burners in a clockwise fashion
   b. switches are easier to use if up is on and down is off
   c. the numbers of a gauge are easier to understand if they go up from left to right
   d. correct answers are found faster if they're highlighted than if incorrect answers are highlighted
   e. knobs are the same shape on all aircraft

9. What is the advantage to using non-verbal road signs?
   a. they can be read easily at a distance
   b. they easily show information about why something is hazardous
   c. different ones can be created for different languages
   d. they adhere to the principle of compatibility
   e. they adhere to Theory Y

10. What type of psychologist would try to create a challenging program for a gifted child?
    a. ergonomist
    b. human factors specialist
    c. I-O psychologist
    d. scientific-management specialist
    e. school psychologist

11. Which of the following is the most traditional role for a school psychologist?
    a. administer IQ tests
    b. create programs for mainstreaming disabled children
    c. help teachers create special classes for gifted children
    d. work with children in a class to accept and respect a child with a disability
    e. help teachers deal with disabled children in their classes

12. A child who is diagnosed as learning disabled is one who:
    a. repeats words and parts of words
    b. is restless and cannot sit still in class
    c. fails at some specific tasks for no apparent reason
    d. finishes regular tasks quickly and becomes bored
    e. has repetitive tics and odd movements

## ANSWERS TO POSTTEST

| Correct Answer | Questions Testing a Similar Concept | |
| --- | --- | --- |
| | Comprehension Check | Short-Answer |
| **Matching** | | |
| 1. B  (p. 761) | 11 | -- |
| 2. C  (p. 762) | 11d | -- |
| 3. A  (p. 760) | -- | -- |
| 4. D  (p. 763) | 12 | 6 |
| 5. F  (pp. 761-762) | 11c | 7 |
| 6. E  (p.762) | 10a | -- |
| | | |
| **Multiple-Choice** | | |
| 1. a  (p. 744) | 2 | 1 |
| 2. d  (pp. 744-745) | 2a | 2 |
| 3. d  (pp. 746-748) | 4 | -- |
| 4. a  (p. 748) | 5 | 3 |
| 5. e  (p. 749) | 5c,d,e | 3 |
| 6. b  (pp. 749-751) | 6 | 4 |
| 7. a  (pp. 749-751) | 6 | 4 |
| 8. e  (p. 754) | 8 | 5 |
| 9. a  (p. 757) | 9c | -- |
| 10. e  (p. 759) | 10 | -- |
| 11. a  (p. 759) | 10c | -- |
| 12. c  (pp. 761-762) | 11c | 7 |

# APPENDIX A: TEXTBOOK DICTIONARY

The textbook makes use of many Standard Dictionary English Level words. If you do not have a vocabulary at the 12th grade level, you may not be able to understand much of the text, tests and lecture. Fortunately, the Kalat text and your instructor use many of these college level vocabulary words over and over in the book and in the lectures. The following alphabetically listed words are defined in ways that are used in the text book. Based on these definitions you will be able to determine the meaning of the words presented and related words from the context of the sentence. Remember that many of these words have other meanings in other contexts.

The following dictionary does not include the technical vocabulary words used in your textbook. For technical words consult your Text Glossary/Subject Index.

## A

a bit more = slightly more

a fair amount = a large amount

a good percentage = many

a great deal = much; a large amount

a little sooner = earlier in time

a string of = a series of

abandon = to give up; stop accepting, leave alone

abduction = to carry away by force

abolishing = removing, destroying, canceling

absolutely = exactly

absolute distance = exact distance

abstention = to stop using or doing something

abstinence = the act of permanently stopping from doing something

abstract = refers to a concept, symbol, picture or phrase that represents a large group of different items, behaviors or organisms that, though different, have one or more features in common. For example, the concept animal is more abstract than the concept mammals, and mammals is more abstract than dogs.

abuse = to misuse and cause illness or injury to one's self or others

acceleration = speeding up or slowing down

accommodate = to do a favor or service; to admit, hire, accept

accomplish = to succeed in doing, to complete; achieve

acquire = to get

act strange = behave in an unusual way

acting in parallel = acting together at the same time

addressed the right questions = asked the right questions

adjacent = close to; lying near.

adjunct = supplement; along with

administered = given

adolescents = people between the ages of 13 to 18

adores = loves or likes

ads = advertisements

advocate = to speak, plead, or argue in favor of a cause; a person who argues for a cause; a supporter or defender of a cause

affinity = an attraction to or for something; a feeling of kinship

aggressive streak = behaving aggressively from time to time

aggressive = to behave in a hostile threatening way

agreeableness = pleasing, acceptable

akin to = similar to

alerts us to = signals us to

alien = from another planet

aligned = arranged in a line

alleged = to say something is true without providing evidence

allegedly = to make a claim or prediction without any evidence

alluded = to refer to; to point to

alter behavior = change behavior

altered = changed or made different; modify

ambiguous = open to more than one interpretation; words, sounds or events; a word or phrase that has two or more meanings and the meaning is not clear

amnesia = partial or total loss of memory due to shock, emotional upset, brain injury or illness

amputation = the cutting off of an arm or a leg due to accident or by surgery

an era of = a period of time characterized by particular events, or a famous person

analogous = similar or alike in some way

analogy = a form of logical inference, based on the assumption that if two things are known to be alike in some ways, then they must be alike in other ways

analyze = to break down something into its parts

ancient = hundreds to millions of years old

and so forth = this expression indicates that other examples can be listed

anesthesia = loss of sensation or pain

anesthetic = a drug that stops pain

anesthetized = loss of sensation due to disease, injury or an anesthetic, such as chloroform

anonymous = nameless, no one know the names of the group members

anticipate = expect

anticipation = expectation; to see, do or know in advance; to wait for

apex = the highest point; the top point

apparatus = equipment; machines; tools

apparently = easy to understand, clearly or obviously

appealed to = attracted; was of interest

appears promising = looks like it would work

applicants = people who apply for a job or admission to college

appropriate = suitable; acceptable

approximate = almost correct; closely resembling

approximately = almost, very similar, close to, almost exact or correct

arbitrary = determined by chance, or impulse, and not by reason, or principle; based on personal judgment or preference

ardent practitioner = showing strong enthusiasm for doing something

are on the way = are being developed

are packed with = many things grouped together

aroused = excited, awake from sleep

arousing = emotionally exciting, stimulating

artificial = made by human beings rather than being natural

as an outsider = a person who is not a member of the group

as it may sound = appears to be

ascribe = assign cause, to assign

aspects = characteristics; features; properties

assertion = to make a claim; to express with a strong feeling

assertive = outgoing, demanding

asses = to evaluate, to judge

assessment = test

assume = to accept an explanation or idea without evidence

assumption = a claim, belief or idea accepted as true without supporting evidence

astounding = surprising and hard to believe

asymmetries = out of balance; non symmetrical

atmosphere = the social environment; the air in our physical environment

attribute = assign; characteristic

attribution = assigning, placing, accusing

autonomy = independence

aversion = a very strong feeling of not liking along with avoidance or rejection of something

awkward = uncomfortable. not at ease, nervous

axis = a straight line about which the body turns

## B

babbling = sounds made by a baby

backed down = rejected; changed

barely begun = just started

bear in mind = remember

bewildering = To confuse with many different parts

bind to = hold on to

binge = a period of uncontrolled eating or drinking

biography = a historical summary of the main events in a person's life

bipolar = having two opposite or contradictory ideas or behaviors

bit far fetched = not likely to be true

bizarre = very unusual, odd, grotesque, or distorted

blink on and off = turn on and off

blot out = to hide

blurry = unclear; difficult to see

blurting out = to suddenly say something without thinking

bogged down = to focus too much time or effort on something

bogus = fake, false, counterfeit

bombarded = received many stimuli at one time

bound to succeed = are likely to succeed

bouts = times when we face an illness or a problem

brainwashing = the process of changing a person's beliefs by torture and sleep deprivation combined with teaching methods

branch of medicine = a sub field or area of specialization in medicine

breaks out = occurs suddenly

broaden their horizons or scope = to look for new experiences and challenges; enlarged to include more topics to study

broader term = a more general or abstract word

built -in predisposition = an unlearned tendency or inclination

butterflies in the stomach = an upset stomach. a nervous stomach

by the same token = in the same way

## C

can hardly see = can not see clearly

can still make = can make

capacity = the total amount that can be stored; ability to perform, produce or carry

captivated = to be attracted by skill, excellence, charm or beauty

casino = a public room or building used for gambling and entertainment

casual = not serious; not careful; superficial;

census = a count of all the people who live in an area

channels = directs

characteristics = a feature that helps to identify or describe something

characterization = description

charges at you = attacks you

charlatan = a person who makes fraudulent claims such as having supernatural powers or skill; a quack or fraud.

check = inspect or test for accuracy or quality; examine

checking = evaluating, examining, inspecting, testing

chronic = lasting for a long period of time

circumstances = the situation accompanying or surrounding an event

civilized = well behaved; educated

claim = to state as true; to state as a fact

clearly articulated = clearly understandable words

client = a person who seeks the help of or uses the professional services of a doctor, clinical psychologist, or lawyer, etc.

cling to = hold on to

coherent = to have parts logically connected

coincidence = an accidental sequence of events that seems to have been planned or arranged

cold turkey withdrawal effect = the painful physical symptoms that occur when a person suddenly stops using a drug

collective = shared

commit = send

commitment = dedication, devotion

compare(comparative) = to study and show differences and similarities between things

compensate = to act as an equalizing force; to make up for, balance, offset ; to replace

component = a part of something

compound = to produce or create by combining two or more ingredients or parts, something that is made of two or more parts

comprehend = understand

comprehensive = covering a large part or all of a topic of study

compromise = a settlement of differences through mutual concession .

concede = to accept a claim as true; acknowledge; to yield; admit

conceive (conceivable) = to form an idea in the mind; imaginable; thinkable

concentrate = focus effort or attention

concept = an idea formed in the mind that can represent an object or event

conception = an idea, explanation

concert = a musical performance in a large room or theater

conditioning = learning; training

condom = a covering of the male sex organ to prevent infection or pregnancy during sexual relations

confederates = people who assist the researcher in an experiment

confession = admitting to or revealing secrets, sins or criminal behavior

configuration = arrangement of parts or elements

confine = to shut or keep in, to imprison, isolate

confirmed = to support a claim; verify

confounded = distorted, biased, confused, made complex

conglomeration = grouping, collection

connotations = implied meanings

conscientious = hard working

consecutive = following one after another without interruption

consensus = agreement

consequences = the results or effects of a behavior

consider = think about

consider alternatives = look at two or more different way to act

considerable = a large amount; many

consistency = stability, behaving in similar ways in the same or different situations

consistent = unchanging

consistently replicable = to get the same results over and over again

constitute = to be part of; compose

constitutes one way of = is one of many methods

constrain = to limit; to hold back ; to confined within required limits or rules

construct = concepts are called constructs when they are used to label and or explain cause effect relationships; to build, to make

consumed = eaten or drank; used up

contagious = easily spread from one person to another; infectious

contemplate = think about, consider

contending = claiming

contestant = a person taking part in a contest

context = the part of a text or statement that surrounds a particular word or passage and determines its meaning; the circumstances in which an event occurs; a setting.

continuity = a series of connected events; an uninterrupted flow of events

continuum = a continual sequence; a range of values

contradict = to state or express the opposite of (a statement).

contradictory evidence = opposite evidence

contrary = unfavorable; opposite in direction

contributes = gives or supplies

controversy = a dispute between two or more individuals or groups holding opposing views, disagreement

conversion = to change; sorting one form to another form

converted = changed from one thing to another

conviction = belief

convince = to prove, to persuade

coordination = a balanced combining of muscles to carry out movements

cope = to solve a problem; to manage

could hardly = had difficulty

counterproductive = preventing from reaching a goal or achieving a purpose

cramming = only studying the night before a test

criteria = a standard or rule used to make a judgment or decision

cue = a signal, such as a word or an action used to prompt another event

culminating = reaching the highest or final level of development

culprit = a person charged with or is guilty of crime

cult = a religious group considered to be extremist or false, with its followers often living in an unconventional way under the control of an authoritarian, charismatic leader

cultivate = develop

cumulative = increasing, growing or getting bigger by getting new parts added

curiously = interesting to know

curriculum = material and procedures for teaching

custodial = taking care and supervising a person

customs = patterns of behavior and rules of living followed by people of a particular group or region

## D

deals with = covers; presents

dealing with = interacting with

deals with different aspects = to focus on different parts of a process

decade = a period of ten years

deceleration = a decrease in speed

deception = mislead; misrepresent; lie; to trick or to fool

declined = decreased; reduced in amount

deduce = to reach a conclusion by reasoning; to infer from a general principle; to infer a general principle based on many examples

defendant = the accused person or criminal in a court of law

deficiencies = not having required skills or abilities

deficient = missing an essential quality or element

deficit = a weakening or loss in mental or physical functioning; an unfavorable condition or position; a disadvantage

deformities = misshapen, twisted or disfigured parts of the body

degrading = reducing in worth, moral, dignity or value

deliberate = done after careful thought

delinquency = breaking the law or not doing what the law requires

delusion = false and improbable beliefs

demonstrate = to show

densely packed = many things grouped together

deny = refuse to believe; reject

depression = an emotional condition characterized by an inability to concentrate, insomnia, and feelings of extreme sadness and hopelessness

deprivation = the process of taking something away from someone

derive = get

derives its roots = beginning, origin

designated = indicated, labeled, named, characterized by

despair = to lose all hope

despotism = governing or ruling with absolute power

destination = the place to which you are going

detention = keeping a person in a hospital or prison by law

deter = stop

deteriorate = to diminish or lessen in quality, value or amount; to grow worse; degenerate

devised = invented; developed

devote = to give or apply time and effort to a specific activity

difficult to draw = difficult to say in words

diffuses = to spread out or scatter; disseminate; to make less bright; soften

dignitary = a person of high rank or position like a mayor or president

dilemma = a situation that requires a choice between two or more equally unfavorable or favorable alternatives

disadvantageous = not beneficial; not favorable

disassociate = to stop an association

disconnects = turns off

discounted them = disregarded them as untrustworthy

discourage = to make someone less hopeful, confident or enthusiastic; to persuade (a person) not to do something

discrepancy = distance or differences between objects; differences or deviations between claims, ideas theories, etc.

discriminate against = to act or state unreasonable judgments against a group of people

disordered = confused, disturbed

dispense = stop using; get rid of

displace = move from side to side

disproportionate = very large

dispute = argue, debate, question the truth of a claim

dispute = to question; to argue about

disregard = to ignore; to stop looking at something

disrupt = disturb; change

disruptive = to throw into confusion or disorder, to upset; to stop progress

distinct = easily seen as different from other things; distinguishable from all others; discrete

distinction = characteristic; difference

distinguish = to pay attention to differences between things; to show how things are different

distinguishing between = recognizing the difference between

distraction = to cause to turn away from or stop paying attention to something; diversion

distress = to cause or experience anxiety or suffering

diverting = turning aside; distracting

dominance = having the most influence or control

downplay = to lower the importance of something

drawing up a plan = to make a plan

dreaded = feared

dreadful mistake = a very serious mistake

drifted downward = decreased

driving off = chase away

drops sharply = rapidly decrease

duration of time = a period of time

## E

earlier intervention = to take action at an earlier time

eccentric = a person who behaves in an unconventional and unusual way; a person who deviates from normally expected behavior

edifice = a large impressive building

elaborate = to tell with care and detail; develop thoroughly

elaborate equipment = special tools used to carry out a research study

eleemosynary = relating to or dependent on charity; contributed to charity

elicit = to produce a reaction, evoke

eliminate = to remove

elusive = difficult to understand or explain

emanating from = coming or sending out from

embryo = an organism at any time before it is born or hatched

emerge = show up; to come out

eminent = outstanding; famous; distinguished

empirical = relying on or based on observation or experiment

enable = allow, permit, empower

encounter = a meeting that is unexpected or brief.

endanger = place in danger

endogenous = originating or growing from within, internal biological influences

enduring = long lasting

engage in = participate in

engaged = to be occupied; to participate in an activity

enhance = improve

enlightened = to be knowledgeable

enormous = very large amounts of something like size, power, motivation, money, importance

entailed = involved, had

enthusiastic = showing a lot of excitement or interest in a subject or cause

entity = something that exists, such as an object or person

epidemic = a rapid spreading of a disease to many people in an area or a population

episode = an event that is part of a larger sequence of events

equilibrium = a situation in which all influences are canceled by others, resulting in a stable, balanced, or unchanging system

era = a period of time characterized by a major event or person

erase = to remove; to destroy

err = to make a error, to make an mistake

estimate = to guess or calculate the approximate amount, extent, magnitude, position, or value of something

ethical = guidelines for right and wrong behavior

ethicist = a people who study the rules of morality - the goodness or badness of human behavior

euphoria = a feeling of great happiness and well-being

eventually = occurring at an unspecified time in the future

everyday object = a common object or thing

evidently = the evidence shows

evinces = shows, demonstrates

exaggerate = to make something seem greater or bigger than it actually is; overstate

exasperated = to become very angry, impatient and annoyed

exceeds = to be greater or better than; transcends, outdoes, surpasses, excels

excel = to do better than others

excitation = activation; elicit; arouse; stir to action

exorcised = removed or chased out

expectation = to look forward to something; anticipate

explicit = fully and clearly expressed; specific ; leaving nothing implied

extract = material taken out of something; to take out or remove

extraordinary = more than ordinary; exceptional; remarkable

extremely weak = very weak

## F

face certain obvious problems = has easy to identify problems

facilitates = to make an activity easy or easier

facilitating = making something easier or less difficult

fall into the trap = accept

famine = a food shortage where many people starve

fantasize = imagine

fascinated = showed great interest in something

fatal disease = an illness that lead to death

fatalities = deaths resulting from an accident

fatigue = physical or mental tiredness resulting from exertion.

feasible = able to be done; possible

feedback loop = the return of information about the result of a process or activity

felony = a very serious crime, such as murder, rape, or burglary

ferocious = murderous; wanting to kill; violent; destructive ;extremely savage; fierce; vicious or merciless; brutal

fetus = an unborn child from the end of the eighth week after conception to the moment of birth

filters out = removes

find out what = to learn or discover

fixation = to focus one's eyes or attention on something;( to attach oneself to a person or thing in an immature or neurotic fashion)

fixation point = point of focus

flanking = to the right or left side of

flashback = suddenly remembering a painful past experience

flimsy = unconvincing; not very strong

fluctuate = change

fluctuations = irregular variations in the value or amounts of something; rising and falling in value, changes

follow-up question = the next related question

for instance = for example

foretold = to predict an event before it occurs

forewarning = advanced warning of an event

frankly = openly, directly, honestly

fruitful = very productive

fruitlessly = unsuccessfully, without success

frustration = feelings that accompany failure or being prevented from reaching an expected goal

fulfillment = accomplish, to make into a reality

fundamental tenets of physics = basic principles or laws

fundamentally = basically; very important ;of great significance

funneling = to direct or guide; to move through or as if through a funnel

furthermore = in addition

## G

gastrointestinal = stomach and intestines

gaze back = look back

generalizing = to apply a finding from a few people to many or all people

generally = usually, typically, often

generating = producing, thinking of, creating

genes = thousands of hereditary units located in every cell of the body that determines each characteristic in an organism.

genetic differences = difference due to heredity

get along without it = do without it

get by with = to recover; to adjust

ghastly = very unpleasant, disagreeable

gibberish = nonsensical or meaningless talk or writing

giggles = repeated short laughs

give-and-take process = sharing, each person makes a contribution

gives rise to = produces

glimpse = a brief, incomplete look at something

go awry = turn away from what is expected, go wrong

going around in circles = going from one definition to another definition without being specific

good deal of = many; much; a lot of

grand theory = a theory that tries to explain all or most of human behavior

granted = accepted the idea that; acknowledged that

great deal = a large amount, many

great strides = much progress

groping = to search blindly or uncertainly; feel one's way

gruesome = horrible, frightful, shocking

grunt = a low pitch sound or words that can't be understood

## H

habituate = to become familiar with something through constant practice, use, frequent repetition or prolonged exposure

had the technology to = had the research equipment

hail a cab = call a taxi cab

haphazard = having a random pattern without organization or structure or purpose; occurring by chance

harass = to annoy; tease; torment; embarrass; bother

hard to know = difficult to know

hard to shake the idea = difficult to change

hardly ever = seldom; not very often; rarely

hardly knew = did not know well

harmonious = pleasing; in balance

has solid evidence = evidence supported by scientific research

have been so wild = uncontrolled

hazardous = dangerous to life or health

health provider settings = places like hospitals and medical clinics

hearing-impaired = unable to hear sound

held in check = controlled

hesitation = delay, slowness to respond

hibernate = to sleep through winter

hidden flaw = an error or mistake that was not seen

hierarchy = a related set of ideas, motives, people, etc. organized into successive ranks or levels with each level included in or under the influence of the one above or below

high-tech = new development technology

highlights = the main ideas; the most important facts

homosexual = sexual desire for others of one's own sex

honeymoon period = a harmonious period in a relationship; a holiday or trip taken by a newly married couple

humanely = acting with kindness, mercy or compassion.

humidity = refers to air with a high amount water vapor

humiliate = to lower a person's pride, dignity, or self-respect or self-esteem or self-worth

hunch = An intuitive feeling or idea

hyperactivity = behavior characterized by constant overactivity and sometimes difficulty paying attention or concentrating

## I

identify with = to become like the person admired

idiosyncratic = behavioral characteristic unique to an individual or a group

ignore = refuse to pay attention to; disregard

illuminated = to brightened with light

illusion = a mistaken perception or belief

imaginary = existing only in the mind; not real

imbalance = not balanced

imitated = copied

immensely = very

impaired = lost ability, strength, value, or quality; damaged

impair = to make worse; to decrease worth, value or strength; reduction; lessening

implant = to establish, to put in

implausible = not likely to be true; not credible

implication = interpretation, suggestion, effects, consequences; meanings; outcomes; applications

implicit = indirect

impose = require

impose = to force or require; to establish, apply

impoverished = very poor; made poor

impulse = a sudden wish, thought or behavior

impulsive = to act quickly without thinking about the effects of the act

in one way or another = in some way, by some means

in other words = another way to summarize this study

in practical consequences = useful in daily life

in principle = possible; in fact

in short = in summary; briefly, in conclusion

in the abstract = in generalized terms without any specific examples

in the course of = during

inability = not being able to do something

inadequate = not enough

inanimate objects = non-moving or non-living things

inappropriate = not acceptable

incapacitated = deprived of strength or ability; disabled

incentive = Something, like fear of punishment or the expectation of reward, that stimulates or motivates behavior

incidence = frequency of occurrence

incoherent = unable to think or express one's thoughts in a clear or orderly manner

incompatible = two or more things(habits, behaviors) that cannot occur at the same time

incomprehensible = difficult or impossible to understand

inconclusive = no conclusion can be made ( conclusive = to put an end to doubt or uncertainty) incongruous = does not fit, inconsistent, clashing, conflicting, discrepant

inconsistent = not regular or predictable

indecisively = without an ending or conclusion; uncertain, tentative

independent = not influenced or controlled by others; self-reliant (See G for independent variable)

independent practice = psychologists who are self-employed

indiscriminate = not making careful distinctions; unselective; confused

indistinct = not clear

induce = to cause, influence, persuade

induced = produced, made happen

inducing = starting

ineffective = not effective

inevitable = certain to happen; impossible to avoid or prevent

inevitably = predictably, impossible to avoid or prevent

infallible = without error, sure, certain, reliable, unfailing

inference = an inference is a conclusion about an event or condition that we did not directly see based on what we did or can see; inferences are claims that must be supported by observations.

inflexible = not changing, rigid

inhibited = to suppress or hold back a behavior, feeling, an impulse consciously or unconsciously

inhibitory = decrease

inner circle = a group of people who work together

inoculation = introducing an idea or attitude into the mind; introducing a serum, a vaccine, or some substance into the body to produce or increase immunity to a specific disease

insensitive = not responding to; not aware of

inseparable = cannot be separated

instantaneously = quickly; without any delay

insulation = preventing the passage of heat, electricity, or sound into or out of something, especially by surrounding it with a nonconducting material

insurmountable = impossible to overcome or solve

integral part = an important and necessary part

integrate = to include into a larger group

intellectual powers = ability to think, plan and solve problems

intention = plan, purpose, goal, objective, intent, motive

interaction = two or more events effecting each other

interacts = two events effecting each other

interferes with = prevents

intermediate = occurring between two extremes or in a middle position

internal states = physical conditions inside of the body

interpretation = to determine meaning; to think of different applications or uses

interrogated = questioned

interstellar = between the stars in the sky

intervene = take direct action to change things

intervention = an action or influence on another event

intimacy = a close sharing friendship

intimidated = threatened, inhibited

intimidating = threatening; fear producing

intravenous = injections of drugs directly into a vein

introspective = thinking about and reporting one's own experience

intrusion = to force in without an invitation or permission

invariably = not changing or not subject to change; constant

investigator = a person who carries out a research study

involuntary = acting against one's will or without self control

irregularities = not straight, uniform, uneven, jagged, crooked

irrelevant = not related to

irresistible = not able to resist or stop

irritating = mild pain

is a product = is the result of

is broader than = includes more than

is governed by = is controlled or influenced by

is not fixed throughout life = not remaining the same; not constant

is tough enough = is difficult

is well suited to = appropriate; all right; OK

isolate = to set apart or cut off from others; detach, remove

it first arose = it got started

it might seem = it looks. appears

it turned out = the evidence showed that

it will fade = disappear, vanish

# J

jiggling = shaking; rapid movement

job discrimination = not being given a job because of one's gender, age, race or ethnic identity

just barely worth = less worth

juvenile = child-like, immature, young

juvenile delinquents = young people who break the law

## K

keep track of = keep written records
keep-up-to-date = keep current

## L

laid off from = to lose
lateral = at or on the side
less prevalent = not accepted or widely practiced by many people a job
let us deal with = consider
like begets like = children are similar to their parents
limitation = a use beyond which a study does not apply or is not effective
loading = including more; packing, filling
localized = confine or restrict to a specific location
lock into = pay attention to
long-shot = an event with a very low probability of occurring
longitudinal studies = research that covers many years in the lives of the subjects
loosely defined = vaguely defined
loses track = forgets
lucrative = profitable; money making

## M

maintained = to claim something as true
mainstream = main attitudes, behaviors or values of a society or group
make little use = seldom used
makes a big mess = gets dirty
maladaptive = does not fit or adjust to the situation
malfunctioning = non-working; diseased; broken
mammal = warm-blooded animals with hair and the females nurse their young with milk.
manifestation = showing, displaying, expression, revelation
manipulate = to manage; to control to one's own advantage; to exploit, maneuver or trick.
manuscript = a document, a book
masturbation = sexual self-stimulation
maturation = the physical growth of the body and nervous system
maximize = to increase or make as big as possible
may check = may look at
menstrual cycle = taking place on a monthly basis
menstruation = a woman's bloody discharge once a month
mention = to refer to
merciless = unkind, not forgiving
merely = only

merely(mere) = nothing more than
metaphor = a word or phrase that suggests ways in which two different things may be similar
might have some bearing on = can effect
might not want to mention = does not want to say
migrate = to move from one country or region and settle in another
military junta = a group of military officers ruling a country after overthrowing the government and taking power
mimicking = to copy or imitate behavior, speech, expression, etc.
miscellaneous = made of many different characteristics or parts
mischievously = causing trouble
misconception = incorrect interpretation; misunderstanding
misestimate = to guess with an error
misinterpret = to interpret or explain with errors , explain incorrectly
mobilizing = activating, put into use
modify = to change
modifications = changes or alterations
momentum = speed, pace, force
monitor = to keep track of something systematically; to collect information about an event; control a process
monotonous = spoken in an unchanging tone; boring
morality(moral) = social rules that are used to guide and judge behavior
moratorium = a temporary delay in an activity or process
more likely = probable; more frequently occurring
moreover = in addition
most convincing = easiest to believe
most prone to = likely to
most stable = lasting
much is at stake = there are serious consequences
multitude = many
musing = thinking

## N

natural phenomena = events in nature
natural sciences = science like physics, biology, psychology
navigability = deep or wide enough to provide passage
nearsighted = inability see distant objects
needless to say = it is obvious that
neglect = to fail to do or carry out a task; to fail to pay attention to something
negotiated = succeeded in coping with, solving, accomplishing or managing

neuroscience = branch of biology that studies the brain and the nervous system

never mind = disregard; do not pay attention to

nevertheless = however; in spite of that; nonetheless

norms = descriptions of the frequencies at which scores on a test occur

not altogether glorious = embarrassing

not coincidentally = not accidentally

not insurmountable = not impossible to overcome

not merely = not just

not refute = not reject; not disprove; not prove false

note that = remember that

novel situations = unusual, unconventional, not typical, not ordinary

novelist = a person who writes books with long fictional imagined stories

nutrients = fats, proteins, carbohydrates, vitamins and minerals contained in food

nutritional deficiencies = not enough food or vitamins

## O

objectionable = undesirable; not wanted

objective = impersonal, unbiased

observation = seeing, hearing, touching, measuring the object or event so you can make a description of it.

obsolete = no longer accepted

obvious = easily perceived or understood; apparent ; clear, plain, unmistakable

occasional = periodic, occurring from time to time, intermittent

occult = dealing with supernatural and metaphysical claims that cannot be scientifically studied

ominous = indicating or warning of danger or misfortune; threatening

omission = to not do something; to leave out; to neglect

omit = to take or leave out; drop, remove, eliminate, delete

open-minded = willing to listen to or accept new ideas

operational definitions = a definition that specifies the process used to measure a variable or produce an event

optimistic = expecting and focusing on the most hopeful aspects of a situation.

optimum = the most favorable condition for health and growth

options = things that are chosen or available as a choice

ordinary = of no special quality, common, average, plain, commonplace, unexceptional.

orienting response = looking at or listening to changes in the environment

other things being equal = other conditions are the same

out of synchrony = not occurring at the same time

out of the air = from imagination

overall = total

overall pattern = total pattern

overcomes all odds = a successful outcome that is not expected; the occurrence of a low probability event

overdoes = to use or do something when it is not needed

overlooked = to fail to notice, see, or consider; miss ; disregard

overmedicated = the use of drugs even when not needed

overriding concern = a major problem, a major cause for anxiety or worry

oversimplified = made too easy

overstated = to claim more than the evidence justifies; exaggerated

overwhelmingly = mostly

## P

pairing = two stimuli that occur at the same time

paradox = two claims with opposite predictions; a statement that contradicts itself

paradoxically = a statement or claim that sounds contradictory or false but may be true

paralyzed = made unable to move or act

parole = the release of a prisoner before his/her prison term is completed

parsimony = adoption of the simplest assumption in the formulation of a theory or in the interpretation of data

passionate = strong powerful emotions; strong sexual desire

peculiarity = an unusual or unexpected characteristic

penalized = punished; lowered your test scores

people went crazy = people acted foolishly or out of control

perceive = to see

perfectionist = a person who is unhappy with anything that is not perfect or does not meet extremely high standards

periodic = an event that is repeated over time

periodically = every few minutes; at regular intervals; recurring or reappearing, intermittent

peripheral = seeing near the outer edges of the retina; located in, or forming an outer boundary persecution = punishment

persist = continue

persistent = repeating or continuing without stopping

personification = a person who sets an example for a certain characteristic

perspective = point of view

pertinent = related to; relevant; can be applied to

pessimistic = expecting and focusing on the worst aspects of a situation

pharmacological effects = the effects of drugs on the body

phase = a specific stage or step in a sequence;

phenomena = an event; something that happens; observable events

philosophy = love and pursuit of wisdom by intellectual means and moral self discipline; a system of inquiry; inquiry into the nature of things based on logical reasoning rather than empirical methods.

physical = refers to the body as distinguished from the mind or spirit.

physically merged = combined

pick up a few tricks = learn new symptoms or skills

plagued = disturbed by repeated attacks; upset

plainly visible = can be easily seen

plausible = probably true, likely to be valid; acceptable; credible; believable

plenty of time = enough time, lots of time

pointless = meaningless; senseless

polishing the ideas = improving or perfecting the ideas


throws himself/herself = dedicates, devotes time

ponder = to think about; to consider with great care

pool their resources = combining their ability or powers

poorly articulated = poorly pronounced, speech that is difficult to understand

poses = presents

poses some thorny problems = presents a difficult problem

possessed by a demon = a belief that an evil supernatural being controls behavior

postbehaviorist = the period of time after behaviorism when it was no longer a ruling point of view

postpartum = occurring in the period shortly after childbirth

pouting = sticking the lips out to express unhappiness

practical concerns = a focus on useful activity or things

practical difficulties = problems that occur when something is used

practitioners = people who practice something like an occupation, a profession, or a technique

practitioners of hocus-pocus = people who claim to have magical powers

precursors = anything that precedes and indicates someone or something to come; a forerunner or predecessor

predict = to state, tell about, or make known in advance, especially on the basis of special knowledge; to foretell something; prophesy

predisposed = a behavior tendency

predisposition = likely to be influenced; habit, tendency, inclination, or susceptibility

predisposition = tendency, inclination, or susceptibility.

predominantly = most common or important; dominate, control

preliminary = something that precedes, prepares for, or introduces an activity

premature = too soon; too early

prenatal = existing or occurring before birth

preoccupied = constantly thinking about one thing

preposterous = nonsense, foolish, stupid, can't be believed; not true; not reasonable; absurd

prescribed = to set down or specify rules or guidelines

presumably = assume; taken for granted; a reasonable guess; to accept as true without evidence

presuming = assuming; accepting

presuppose = to believe a claim is true before evidence in available; to accept something as fact without proof

pretend = make believe; play-act

prevail upon = persuade; force

prevalence = widely or commonly occurring, existing, frequency of occurrence

previous = existing or occurring before something else in time or order; prior

priority = the highest level of importance

prodding = to jab or poke with a pointed object

profound = thoughtful and wise; with many implications; very serious;

progression = a movement from one step to the next on a continuous series or sequence

progressive = doing something in a steady step-by-step manner

progressively escalates = increasingly increases

prohibition = a refusal to allow; forbidden by law

prolific = very productive; doing a lot of work

prolonged = to lengthen or require more time

prolonged malnutrition = lack of enough food for many days or weeks

prompted = stimulated; signaled; motivated

prone to = having a tendency, likely

prospective = likely or expected to be selected or happen

prospects = opportunities

provoke = produce, elicit, evoke, trigger

Psychics = people who claim special abilities such as extrasensory perception and mental telepathy

purely theoretical concerns = focus on theory

put the brakes on = to stop

# Q

qualified conclusions = limited, restricted, or modified

quality(qualitative ) = a characteristic of an object event or person. For example, gender(male, female), marital status(married, single, divorced), etc.

quantity (quantitative) = refers to the numerical amounts of something on a scale of measurement or a frequency count. For example weight, age, IQ score, number of dreams per night, number of miles per gallon, etc.

quit your job = leave a job; stop working

quite a range of = many different

# R

radically new = very new and different

rare = very few; uncommon

rates of decay = speed of fading away

rear children = bring up; raise

reasonably good = adequate

reborn hopes = renewed hopes

rebound = to bounce back, to recover

recollection = recalled memories

reconcile = to bring oneself to accept; to reestablish a friendship; settle, resolve

reconstruct = restore, recover, rebuild

recruit = to supply or find new members or employees

reduced = limited

redundancy = repetition of message or idea

refined the ability = improved

refinements = improvements

reflex = an unlearned, automatic response to a stimulus

regardless = disregarding, in spite of everything; anyway

reinforce = give a reward that strengthens a habit or a behavior

relative distance = approximate or almost exact distance

relative rate = speed or amount

relatively insensitive = does not respond to

relegation = removal and sending away

religious devoutness = devoted to religion or to religious duties

reluctant = not willing

remarkable = worthy of notice

repentant = apologetic, sorry, contrite, regretful

replenishment = replacement

replicable = able to be copied, reproduced, or repeated

representative = one that serves as an example or a type for others of the same classification

repulsive = unpleasant to see, taste or smell; disgusting, nauseating, sickening

repulsive-looking = ugly

reputable institutions = having a good reputation; honorable

reputed = considered; has a reputation

resemble = look like; similar to

resolve = solve

resorted to = started to

respiration = breathing

respondent = the person who answers questions

restoration = an act of repairing or recovering

restrained = limited or restricted; held back

resume = to start over again

retain = keep, store

retarded children = children with very low intelligence who cannot care for them selves or learn in school

retrospect = reviewing the past; looking backward

reveal = to show

revelation = disclosing something not previously known

reverts to = goes back to

revolutionary reorganization = a major change in organization

revulsion = a strong feeling of disgust, displeasure, rejection

ridicule = make fun of, to cause others to laugh at a person or thing

ridiculous = not believable because it is foolish, nor reasonable; stupid and funny

rigid = not flexible; difficult to bend or change

ritual = the required order of a religious ceremony

rough gauge = an approximation, almost exact or correct

roughly = approximately

roughly speaking = commonly speaking

roundabout = indirect; confusing

rousing = something that produces enthusiasm or excitement

ruminate = to think about something over and over again

run in families = be inherited

runner-up = the person who finishes in second place in a contest

ruptured = broken or opened

## S

saccharin = a white powder that tastes about 500 times sweeter than cane sugar, used as a calorie-free sweetener

sacrifice = to give up something of value

sarcastic = humorous, insulting statements that make its victim suffer emotional pain

satanic = refers to Satan, the devil or evil

satanic cult = a cult that worships the devil

satanic message = messages from the devil

satiated = to satisfy an appetite, to feel full

satiety = feeling full

scattered more widely = spread over a wide area

schizophrenia = a group of psychological disorders usually characterized by withdrawal from reality, illogical thinking, delusions, and hallucinations.

scowl = to twist or move the eyebrow to show anger or disapproval

screen job applicants = interview people seeking a job

scrupulously (clean) = very very clean; conscientious and exact

seduction = behaving to get sexual favors

seemed inclined = wanted to

seizures = sudden attacks, spasms, or convulsions

self-defeating = harming or hurting oneself

self-reports = what people say about themselves

selfish = interested only with oneself

seriously entertain = think about

severed = cut

shackles = limitations, restrictions; a metal chain used around the ankle or wrist of a prisoner

shaken off = taken off; stopped

short-lived = lasting a few minutes

shortcomings = weaknesses, flaws, deficiencies, limitations

should not fault = should not blame or criticize

shrug = to raise the shoulders as a gesture of doubt

silver lining = something good

simpleton = a person who is deficient in judgment, ability or intelligence; a fool

simultaneously = at the same time

skeptical = doubtful; questionable; not to be believed

skepticism = a doubting or questioning attitude

sketchpad = a piece of drawing paper

slap = to hit with the open hand or with a flat object

slighted = ignored; not paid attention to

small fraction = small part of

so "right" = almost perfect

so far as we can = with great effort

social lubricant = an act that reduce social problems or conflict

soft -drink = bottles or cans filled with flavored water; a non-alcoholic beverage

solar-powered = powered by the sun's heat energy

solo = an activity by a single individual

some aspect = characteristic

sophisticated abilities = complex and more adult-like abilities

spank = to hit on the buttocks with a flat object or with the open hand,

specialization = focus on a particular activity or product, to develop a specific skill or function

specificity = to state exactly with accuracy and precision

spectacular = impressive or sensational.

spectacular = impressive, amazing, sensational, a big display

speculation = an opinion based on guessing with limited information

speculative = guessing or making a risky claim without much evidence; uncertain; open to question

spend a lifetime = take many years of study

spends time = to do things that take time

sphere of attention = focus of attention

split second = less than a second of time

sponsoring = taking responsibility for another person or activity

spontaneous = happening without apparent external cause; self-generated

sporadically = occurring at irregular intervals; having no time pattern or order

spot the vertical = see the vertical

stable = not changing over time; strong

stare = to look at

states = conditions of conscious awareness, health or functioning

static = unchanging, no motion, at rest, fixed

stationary = not moving

steady = constant with very little change

stereotypical = a simplified exaggerated prejudgment about a category of people

stick close = be similar to; not very different

sticks together = stay together; to form a group

straightforward = direct; clear; not ambiguous

strangely = unexpectedly

stratagem = method

strategy = a plan of action

subjective = based on individual judgment or thought; the term subjective has the connotation that the evidence may be distorted by personal experiences, attitudes, opinions, values, motives or preconceived ideas.

subsequently = following in time or order; succeeding

subside = to become less active or intense

substantial = strong, real; not imaginary ; large

substantial period = a long time

subtly = to be difficult to see, not immediately obvious

successive = following in uninterrupted order

suffer exposure = be exposed to

suits our purpose = is helpful

superficial = not carefully analyzed or thought about; trivial; insignificant

superstition = a belief or behavior based on ignorance of the laws of nature or by faith in magic or chance

suppose = to accept something as true or real for a short period of time; to assume something is true for the sake of argument or explanation

suppress = to inhibit expression; to hold back; to prevent thinking about unacceptable desires or thoughts; stop, inhibit, hold back , prevent from happening

suppresses = puts an end to; stops

supreme = greatest, perfect, ideal

surmised = to infer something without much evidence

susceptible = easily influenced or persuaded; easily infected (to become sick)

suspect = a person who is believed to have committed a crime

symmetrical = a figure where the left and right sides of a dividing line are the same

synchronized = occurred together

synchrony = together; occurring at the same time

synonymous = having the same or a similar meaning

synthesis = combining of separate elements to form a new whole

synthesize a color = to combine to form a new color

synthetic = not natural, artificial, made from chemicals

systematically = carried on using step-by-step procedures; purposefully regular; methodical

## T

taboo = not allowed, banned, forbidden, prohibited

take our (categories) for granted = accept without question

tantrums = an expression of anger with violent movement and screaming

taste preferences = a persons choice

techniques = methods

telepathic powers = the ability to communicate through means other than the senses

temporal = relating to or limited by time

temporal contiguity = being close together in time

tempted = invited; to be invited to do or believe something that is wrong, not correct

tendency = a likelihood, a predisposition to think, feel, or behave in a specific way.

tentative and subject to revision = temporary; to accept a claim only until more evidence is available

tentatively = not fully worked out, not final

terminology = the technical words used in a subject, science, sport or art; nomenclature

theme = a topic or idea that is studied or discussed

the point of = the main goal or idea

the relative contribution of heredity = the amount given by heredity

the whole enterprise of psychology = all of psychology

they would flock = gather together in a group

they would submit = they would suggest

time-out periods = placed in a room alone for a period of time

tips (had any tips) = suggestions

to be fair = to be without bias

to be taken literally = exactly as stated

to condition = to teach or train a response

to cope with = to manage; to live with

to distinguish between = to see the difference between

to drop out = to stop participating; to stop coming

to engage in = to do the act, behave

to get away from = escape

to lack = to have something missing

to make matters worse = to produce more problems

to make sense = to understand; to make meaningful

to recap = to review

to reveal themselves = to tell others about personal feelings and experiences

to the contrary = opposite or opposing

to wind up in = to be sent to

toddler = a young child just learning to walk

tolerant = accepting

tomography  see the surrounding text

totalitarian = a form of government in which the leaders have complete control over all aspects of life  and opposing political points of view are suppressed; dictatorial, tyrannical, despotic

toxic = poison that can cause injury sickness or death

transfer = to carry from one place to another

transform = to change the appearance or form of something

transformation = changing

transgressions = breaking the law

transition is not sharp = the change is gradual

transmission = sending; passing on

transparent = material, like glass, that you can see through

traumatic = an emotional shock that produces lasting damage to the psychological development of a person

tremor = shaking or vibrating movement

trend = a general direction in which something tends to move; a current popular custom

triggered by = started by

trivial event = not important; ordinary

trivially easy = very easy

tryout = athletes show their skills and the best performers are selected for the team

turbulent = violently agitated or disturbed; stormy, chaotic

## U

ultimate = the last in a series or process; the final point, a fundamental fact, solution or principle

ultimately = the end result; finally

unable to inhibit = cannot prevent

unambiguous = a word or idea with a very clear meaning

unanesthesized = not given drugs for pain

uncompromising = not willing to settle differences or come to an agreement

underestimate = to make too low an estimate of the quantity, degree, or worth of something

underscores = emphasizes

undesirable = not wanted; not pleasing; objectionable.

unintentionally = without plan or intent

unique = being the only one of its kind; the only one in a particular category

until you hit on = find

upheaval = a sudden, violent change, disruption or upset

usurpation = seizing and holding by force and without legal authority

utterances = spoken words

## V

vague = unclear; a word or statement with several meanings and the intended meaning is unknown

vanish = disappear, fade away

verify = to determine or test the truth or accuracy of a claim; to prove the truth of by presenting evidence

vast terrain = a large land area

vertebrate = animal with a back bone like dogs, cats and monkeys

vertebrate species = animals with a back bone

via = by

vicarious = another person's experience or emotions is felt as one's own

violent = acting with great force that injures, hurts or causes pain to others

virtual-reality scene = computer generated pictures that look real

virtually = almost ; nearly; practically

virtually compels us = forces us

virtually forever = a very long time

## W

was soundly defeated = completely defeated

way beyond reach = cannot be studied

we are far from understanding = we are just beginning to understand

we soon encounter = we soon have

whimper = to cry

wholeheartedly = enthusiastically, with great energy ;completely and without any doubts

will engage in = will do

will react pretty much the same way = act the same way

will you address = will you study or consider

willing to admit to themselves = to tell themselves, to acknowledge

withdrawn = quiet, shy

witness = a person who sees something happen; a person who gives evidence, testifies in a court of law

woefully inadequate = very inadequate

works "well enough" = works effectively

would seem to be = is likely to be

would support = provide evidence for

wrap it in a cloud = make it sound bad

wrecked = damaged or destroyed in an accident

## Y

yell at = give commands or criticize in a loud voice

you are facing = you have

# APPENDIX B:  PREFIX AND SUFFIX DICTIONARY

The following tables contain alphabetically arranged prefixes, suffixes and roots and their definitions and examples. These tables contain word parts that cover a large majority of terms used in the textbook.  You will find that memorizing these roots, prefixes and suffixes and using them to determine the meaning of words will help you increase your reading vocabulary,  speed up your reading rate and improve your understanding of the text book.

However, you must remember that many words in the English language are made up of separate word parts that have been borrowed from many other languages such as Latin, Greek, Spanish, German, etc.   This can create a problem for word analysis when the same prefix or suffix is borrowed from different languages and has different meanings. Word analysis therefore requires you to examine the context of the sentence for clues for the meaning intended. You must be cautious in your word analysis because as helpful as it is most of the time there will be times when you can and will make errors.  With practice and by checking a dictionary when you are in doubt your word analysis skill will improve.

## Word Families

Knowledge of prefixes, suffixes, and roots can help you guess the meanings of new words in context. An additional related technique is to know word families.  Word families are groups of words that come from the same root, but are different parts of speech.  Examine the text glossary and you will find many word families.  Studying word families will help you analyze and remember the word parts.  In the following example taken form your text glossary notice how three roots and four suffixes can be used to figure out the meaning of over a dozen words.

| Root | Meaning |
|---|---|
| path | disease/disorder/feeling/suffering |
| psyche | soul /mind. |
| therap/therapy | treatment/ cure |

| Suffix | Meaning |
|---|---|
| ology | the study of |
| al/ological | like/being/belonging/ characterized by/ process/conditions |
| ist | a person who practices and studies /a believer |
| ic | characteristic/ having to do with/having the power to/belonging to |

| Word Family | Meaning |
|---|---|
| psychology | the scientific study of behavior and mental processes |
| psychologist | a person who practices and studies psychology |
| psychological | belonging to or having to do with psychology |
| psychopathology | the study of emotional and behavioral disorders |
| psychopathological | a person who has the symptoms of a behavioral or emotional disorder |
| psychotherapy | the treatment of behavioral and emotional disorders by methods that rely on the relationship between a trained therapist and a client. |
| psychotherapist | a person who practices psychotherapy on people who have emotional and behavioral problems |
| psychic | a person who claims special abilities such as extrasensory perception and mental telepathy |
| psychiatry | a branch of medicine that specializes in diagnosing and treating disorders of behavior and mental process |
| psychiatrist | a medical doctor who treats disorders of behavior and mental process |
| psychiatric | belonging to or having to do with psychiatry |
| psychoanalysis | Sigmund Freud's method and theory of analyzing personality |
| psychoanalyst | A psychotherapist who relies on Freudian theory |

**Word Family Exercise**

Try to figure out the definition of each of the following terms with the help of the prefix, suffix and root tables and then check your answer with the text glossary.

  psychoanalytic theory, psychodynamic therapy, psychogenic fugue, psychosomatic illness, psychometric, psychosexual development, psychosexual pleasure

**PREFIX TABLE**

| Prefix | Definition | Examples |
|---|---|---|
| a | in/on | asleep/aboard |
| a/an | not/without/lacking/from | anorexia, analgesia, anesthesia, apathy, amoral |
| ab/abs | away from | abnormal, abstract, abstinence |
| anti | against | antibiotic, anti-abortion |
| auto | self | automobile, automatic, |
| bene | good/well | benefit, beneficial |
| bi | two | biracial, biweekly, bilateral |
| clu/clud/clus | close/shut | conclude, exclude, exclude, include |
| co | together/with | co-therapist, co-author, coexist, codetermine |
| con | with/together | consecutive, configure |
| contra/contro | against/opposite | contradict, contradiction, controversy |
| de/dis/ab | down/off/away from/ out of/reversal | decelerate, depress, depart |
| dis/ab/de | away from/apart/not/without | discomfort, disadvantageous, disbelief |
| dys | bad | dysfunctional, |

| | | |
|---|---|---|
| e/ex | out/from/former | exclaim, ex-president, emit, erect, evict, |
| equ/equi | equal | equate, inequality, inadequate, equitable |
| extra/extro | outside | extrovert, extraordinary |
| hetero | different/opposite | heterosexual, heterochromic |
| homo | same/ same kind | homosexual, homogeneous |
| hyper | over/too much | hyperactivity, hypersensitive |
| im | without | impotent, imperfect |
| in, ill, ir | in/into/within | illuminated, illustrated, incision, |
| in/im | not/without | inactive, immature, inadequate, insensitivity |
| inter | among, between | interaction, international, intercede |
| intro | into/inside | introspect, introvert, introduce, introduction |
| ity | being | activity, sincerity, reality, hostility |
| mal | evil/bad/badly/poor/poorly | malfunction, malformed, maladjusted |
| metri | measure | metric system, symmetrical |
| mis(1) | bad/wrong | mistake, misconception, misunderstand, misbehave, miscalculation, mislabel |
| mis(2) | to hate | misogamy, misanthrope |
| mono | one/single | monotone, monogamy |
| multi | many/much | multicultural, multipurpose, multiracial |
| neur/neura/neuro | nerve/nervous system | neurology, neurotic, neurosurgery |
| non | not | nonsense, noncognitive, nonexistence |
| b | against/to/toward | object, objectionable, objector |
| per | through/throughout | perception |
| poly | many | polychrome, polytheism |
| post | after | postsynaptic, postgraduate |
| pre | before | prehistoric, premature, precognition |
| pro/proto | forward/ahead/before/ first/original | propose, proactive, proposal prototype |
| re | back/again | recall, reheat, replace, resell |
| retro | back/backward/behind | retroactive, retrospect, retrograde |
| sequ/secu | follow | consecutive, |
| sub | under/below/nearly | subgroup, subcommittee, substandard |
| syn/sym | with/together | synthesize, symmetrical, sympathy, synchronize, synonym, synonymous |
| trans | to send/carry across/beyond | transmit |
| tri | three | triangle, triweekly, trichromatic |
| un/under | not/opposite | undo, unnatural, uneven, unloved, unfair |
| uni | one/single | uniform, unify, unity |

| Suffix | Definition | Examples |
|---|---|---|
| able/ible | able to/ able to make | sensible, visible, readable, curable |
| al | like/being/belonging/ characterized by/ process/conditions | musical, comical, seasonal, racial, arrival. approval, international, temperamental |
| alg/algia | pain/ache | algesia, neuralgia |
| ance/ancy/ence/ency | being/ing | pregnancy, compliance, maintenance, importance, resistance |
| ant/net | person who is/ device for | hesitant, assistant, lubricant |
| ate | having/resembling/holding office/ specializing in | moderate, concentrate, graduate doctorate |
| ced/cede/ceed | go/move/surrender (cedė = yield, surrender) | precede, intercede, succeed, exceed concede |
| en | made of/ to make | woolen, silken, soften, harden, ripen |
| ence | quality/state/condition/act/means/results | sequence |
| ent/ant | being/having/doing/ performing/showing/device for | inconsistent, intermittent |
| er | one who | plumber |
| fer | bring/carry | transfer, conger, refer, defer, prefer, infer, reference, conference, suffer |
| ful | full of | truthful, harmful, thoughtful |
| gam | marriage | monogamy, polygamy |
| graph | writing/recording | biography, autograph, demography |
| gress | go/move/come | progress, regress, transgress, regression |
| ia | quality/condition/act/state/ result of/result of/process of | amnesia, anorexia, analgesia, anesthesia |
| ian | a person who is/does/ or is a specialist | librarian, electrician, dietitian, musician |
| ian/an | native of | American, Mexican, Indian, African |
| ic | characteristic/ having to do with/having the power to/belonging to | behavioristic, domestic, optimistic, psychiatric |
| ify | to make/ to become | modify, electrify, codify |
| ion/tion | act/process/means/results of | celebration, conversation, explanation, deceleration |
| ion/tion | the process/ the act of | motion, transportation, repression |
| ish | acting like/native of | childish, Spanish |
| ism | belief/practice/ doctrine /theory/\ system | behaviorism, alcoholism, racism, |
| ist | a person who practices or studies/ a believer | therapist, psychologist, typist, artist psychiatrist |
| ity | being | activity, sincerity, hostility, legality |

| ive | tending to (be)/ having to (be) | effective, retrospective, proactive secretive |
|---|---|---|
| ize | to make/to use/to become | memorize, mechanize, reorganize |
| ject | throw | reject, eject, project, projection |
| logy | study/science | psychology, zoology, anthropology |
| ly(1) | in the manner of/ to the degree/ in the direction of | generally, gladly, badly, northwardly, carefully, conceptually, normally |
| ly(2) | having the characteristics of/happening at a specific time period | seasonally, totally, daily, yearly |
| ment | act/means/result of/ process of | improvement, government, management |
| mit | send | transmit, emit, commit, admit |
| ness | having the characteristics of/being | goodness, messiness |
| or/tor/er | person who/something that | doctor, conductor, member, motor, engineer |
| ous/ious | full of/having to do with | religious, mountainous, famous, envious |
| pel/pul | drive/push | compel, compulsive |
| phil | love | philosophy, philanthropy |
| phobe | excessive fear | homophobic, |
| plete/pleta | fill/full | complete, deplete, completion |
| pos/pose/posi | put/place | compose, propose, impose, expose, suppose, transpose, depose |
| tech | skill | technique |
| tri | three | triangle, triweekly, trichromatic |
| ure | being/ ___ing | exposure, mixture, rupture, procedure, conjecture |
| vers | turn | reverse |
| vert | turn | introvert, convert, invert, revert, subvert, convertible |

## ROOT TABLE

| Root | Meaning | Examples |
|---|---|---|
| alg | pain/suffering | analgesia, neuralgia |
| analyze | to break something into its parts, stages or categories | analysis, psychoanalysis, |
| andro/andr | man/human | anthropology, polyandry, androphobic |
| cede | yield/give/assign/transfer | |
| ceptive | aware/see | perceptive, perception |
| chrom/chroma/chromato | color | chromatology, trichromatic, monochrome |
| chrono | time/ in order | chronic, chronology, chronometer |
| clu/clud/clus | close/shut | conclude, exclude, include |
| code | arbitrary symbols used to represent words or ideas | encode, decode, codify |

| | | |
|---|---|---|
| cognn/cogni/cogno | to think/to be aware/to know | cognition, cognitive, recognize, cognizant |
| duc/duct/duce | lead/take/bend | deduct. conduct, transducer, induce, reduce, deduction, ductility |
| dynamic | movement/interaction/ conflict | psychodynamic |
| ego | I/self | egocentric. egomaniac, egotism, egoist |
| esthe | sensation/feeling | anesthesia |
| ethn/ethno | nation/tribe/same culture | ethnic, ethnocentric |
| fin | end/limit | infinite, finite, finish, final, finalist, define |
| flex/flect | bend/curve | flexible, reflex, reflect, reflection |
| flux/flu | flow | fluent, fluency, fluid, influence, influx |
| gen/gene/genea | race/kind/produce | genetic, genetics, geneology, genocide |
| gyne/gyn/gyneco | women | gynecology |
| hes/her | stick | cohesive, adhesive, coherent, adherence |
| mand | order | command, demand, mandate, commander |
| mani/mania/maniac | crazy/insanity | manic depressive, |
| mediate | middle | intermediate |
| mene | to recall/ to remember | amnesia |
| ment | mind | mental, mentality, demented, |
| metr/meter | measure/measuring equipment | speedometer |
| mo | move | motion, movement, mobile, motive |
| mobile | move/change position/ to affect emotions | mobility, automobile, autonomous |
| orex | desire/appetite | anorexic |
| path | disease/feeling/suffering | pathology, psychopath, pathologists |
| sci | knowledge/know/aware | science, conscious, conscience, |
| soma | body | psychosomatic |
| soph/sophy | wisdom/knowledge | philosophy |
| spect | to look | introspection |
| stabl/stabil | able to stand firm | stable, stability, stabilize, establishment |
| therap/therapy | treatment/ cure | psychotherapy, drug therapy, therapist |
| vis/visi/visual | see | visible, invisible, visualization, visualize |
| voc/vok | call/voice | invoke, revoke, evoke, provoke, revocable vocalize, vocalist, vocation, convocation |